WHERE THE EVIDENCE LEADS

Where the Evidence Leads

AN AUTOBIOGRAPHY

Dick Thornburgh

UNIVERSITY OF
PITTSBURGH PRESS

Published by the University of Pittsburgh Press,
Pittsburgh, Pa., 15260

10 9 8 7 6 5 4 3 2 1

Library of Congress Cataloging-in-Publication Data

Thornburgh, Dick.
    Where the evidence leads : an autobiography / Dick Thornburgh.
        p.   cm.
Includes index.
    ISBN 0-8229-4220-8 (cloth : alk. paper)
    1. Thornburgh, Dick. 2. Attorneys general—United States
—Biography.
I. Title.
    KF373.T56A3 2003
    353.4'092—dc2   2003007696

To my friend, colleague and mentor,
Judge Jay C. Waldman
of the United States District Court
for the Eastern District
of Pennsylvania
(1944–2003)

CONTENTS

List of Illustrations   ix

Preface   xi

1. Beginnings   1

2. Tragedy and Recovery   13

3. Running for Office   25

4. Federal Prosecutor   37

5. Serving in Washington, D.C.   62

6. Running for Governor: The Primary   74

7. The Victory!   86

8. A Rough Start: Three Mile Island   105

9. Reshaping Pennsylvania's Economy   125

10. A Governor's Agenda   147

11. The Politics of the Governorship   175

12. Harvard and a Return to Washington   196

13. Battling White-Collar Crime   208

14. Crime-Fighting in the Department of Justice   227

15. A Global Effort   248

16. The ADA and Other Domestic Endeavors   261

17. Criticisms: Fair and Unfair   277

18. Running for the Senate   300

19. A Sojourn at the United Nations   316

20. Return to the Law and Other Pursuits   334

Afterword   363

Index   *367*

ILLUSTRATIONS

Following Page 146

With mom and dad

A longtime Pittsburgh Pirates fan

Ginny Hooton Thornburgh with sons

Ginny Judson, October 12, 1963

Billboard from 1966 campaign

With Pennsylvania Governor Bill Scranton

Western Pennsylvania's racket-busting United States attorney

Caricature of a vigorous prosecutor

Farewell tribute from *Pittsburgh Post-Gazette* cartoonist

Second inauguration as governor, 1983

Budget address to the Pennsylvania General Assembly

Visit to the control room, Three Mile Island nuclear reactor

Press conference on Three Mile Island nuclear accident

$1 billion clean-up plan for Three Mile Island

Greeting Pope John Paul in Philadelphia, 1979

Jimmy Stewart receiving the first Distinguished Pennsylvania Artist award, 1980

With Penn State's legendary football coach Joe Paterno

At the Great Wall of China, 1980

"You've got a friend in Pennsylvania" travel and tourism promotion campaign, 1980

With family, celebrating 1982 reelection

U.S. attorney general swearing-in, 1988

President-elect George H. W. Bush and AG Dick Thornburgh, 1988

Cover of the *New York Times Magazine*, May 21, 1989

Testifying at the Americans with Disabilities Act hearings

Outside the Supreme Court, 1988

With Soviet Justice Minister Yakovlev, 1989

Addressing guests after the signing of the ADA

Former U.S. attorneys general celebrate the 200th anniversary of the office

At the Department of Justice

With President and Mrs. Ronald Reagan

With President Bush in the Oval Office

With General Colin Powell, chairman of the Joint Chiefs of Staff

An audience with Pope John Paul

With Somali child, as undersecretary-general of the United Nations

The Larry King Live team

With Yale roommates and President George W. Bush, 2001

Vacationing in Maine

Family reunion in Pennsylvania, 2001

Unless otherwise indicated in the captions, all illustrations are from the Dick Thornburgh Archival Collection at the University of Pittsburgh.

PREFACE

The title of this book reflects my oft-repeated admonition that investigators and prosecutors should "follow the evidence wherever it leads," refusing to be influenced by private prejudices or predeterminations. In writing this book, I have tried my utmost to apply similar standards. This is, of course, a challenge when writing about one's own life. In only a few instances, however, and then only to prevent hurt to innocent individuals, have I omitted any facts or circumstances I consider relevant. It is my hope that the reader can "follow the evidence" set forth herein and draw his or her own conclusions about all the matters discussed.

Errors and omissions have no doubt crept in due to the vagaries of recollection. Times, dates and conversations are given as accurately as I can recall them, and the dramatis personae are portrayed as I best remember them. For any inaccuracy that survives, I express my regret and take full responsibility.

Many people have made contributions to this work. Four, however, were essential to my efforts. My beloved wife, Ginny, read and reread with care and compassion every single word set forth. To her I extend my heartfelt gratitude for her tenacity and insight. No better partner could ever have been enlisted on my behalf. And to our friend Nancy Watson, faithful keeper of my papers and files, without whose heroic efforts many a detail would have been undiscovered or misstated, I offer thanks for her persistence and patience in dealing with my demands.

My thanks also go to my editor, Lynn Stewart, who carried out with great skill and sensitivity the task of reducing my original manuscript to a more "user friendly" length and format, and to Cynthia Miller, director of the University of Pittsburgh Press for her support and guidance throughout this project.

Special thanks are due as well to Professor Ted Muller of the University of Pittsburgh and the late Michael Weber, provost of Duquesne University, for their review and comment on an earlier draft of this effort; to Pennsylvania political historian Paul Beers for his critique of material relating to my tenure as Pennsylvania governor; and to Dr. Walter Plosila for his observations on the text concerning our economic development policy. I am, of course, greatly indebted to my friend, colleague and mentor, the late Judge Jay C. Waldman of the United States District Court for the Eastern District of Pennsylvania, for his sound advice and wise counsel throughout most of my public life.

Finally, to my family—my four sons, two daughters-in-law and six grandchildren—I tender the hope that their reading of this work will give them some insight into the many remarkable opportunities I have been granted during my lifetime. I pray that my efforts toward fulfillment prove worthy of their respect and esteem.

WHERE THE EVIDENCE LEADS

1

Beginnings

My EARLIEST MEMORIES are of warmth—the warmth of family, the warmth of friends, the warmth of community.

The community was Rosslyn Farms, established in the early 1900s about seven miles west of Pittsburgh, Pennsylvania. On July 16, 1932, the date of my birth, it was still almost "country," a comfortable upper-middle-class community of a hundred or so households where my family had settled during the 1920s. Rosslyn Farms was racially, ethnically and religiously homogeneous, and virtually untouched by the Great Depression. Any issues that surfaced were generally mundane and noncontentious. It was the kind of community where doors were often left unlocked at night and mothers looked after their neighbors' children as well as their own. Well-tended lawns, open fields and woods abounded, available for exploration and enjoyment by children and adults alike. The annual Fourth of July observance, featuring firecrackers, a community parade, picnicking and games, exemplified a now bygone era in its patriotic celebration of a singular way of life.

Both my parents' families had been in this country since colonial times. My mother, Alice Sanborn Thornburgh, was a direct descendant on her mother's side of William Bradford, who came to these shores on the *May-flower* in 1620 and later served as governor of the Plymouth colony. My father, Charles Garland Thornburgh, was descended from Thomas Thornburgh, who arrived in Virginia from England in 1616 and later served as a legislator in both Maryland and Virginia.

My mother was deeply involved in community activities—the Girl Scouts, the Garden Club, the Foreign Policy Association, the Gray Ladies (during the war), the Altar Guild at Trinity Episcopal Church in Pittsburgh and many others. My father was a reserved, to some austere, man to whom his family and his work as a civil engineer were all-encompassing concerns. Although not given to public expressions of affection, my parents obviously felt a deep and abiding love and respect for one another, undimmed by the passage of time.

I was born at home around six o'clock in the evening on a summer Saturday. My sister Virginia was already fourteen, my sister Ann thirteen, and my brother, Charles, eleven. Being the youngest by far, I was treated more as an only child than as one of four. Indeed, while I was young, my older siblings were generally away at boarding school or college, and I was at the center of my parents' attention. We spent many an evening together reading, talking and listening to the radio in those pretelevision days.

I remember the four-room Rosslyn Farms Elementary School, which I attended from kindergarten through eighth grade, with great fondness. Class sizes rarely exceeded eight or ten, and the schooling was first-rate. Our teachers sought to guide, rather than direct, our intellectual curiosity, and they had a willing audience. Report cards were taken seriously, and despite an occasional trip to the cloakroom, behavioral problems were virtually nonexistent. I did once encounter retribution at home for an act of petty larceny resulting from temptation being placed in my way. Sallie McWilliams, one of my mother's Girl Scouts, made the mistake of giving me her fifty cents dues to deliver to my mom. I diverted it to a grand treat of my classmates at Buchner's candy shop, maintained at a home nearby. All was well until the next Girl Scout meeting, when my mother inquired about Sallie's dues. "Oh," she said, "I gave them to Dickie." Upon my evasive response to my mother's inquiry, my father administered my one and only paddling with a ruler.

Several of my schoolmates became lifelong friends. We engaged in games and sports of all kinds, but our principal activity reflected the outbreak of World War II in 1939, as we were entering the second grade. On afternoons and weekends, we engaged in elaborate "maneuvers," attired in such military garb as we could cobble together and equipped with a variety of handcrafted (and, occasionally, store-bought) toy weaponry. Roaming the countryside and operating out of war rooms and "forts" in or near our homes and outbuildings, we subdued imaginary Axis enemies with only occasional (but generally highly dramatic) casualties.

Our "war effort" had other aspects as well. Like many Americans, I learned of the bombing of Pearl Harbor from a bulletin interrupting the New York Philharmonic radio concert on Sunday, December 7, 1941. Thereafter, my schoolmates and I participated in scrap drives, took first-aid courses, gathered old newspapers and took up collections for various worthy causes. The last enterprise was particularly attractive when it involved soliciting in movie theaters, because it meant a free viewing of the evening's offering. A friend and I also constructed an elaborate tabletop re-creation of the Battle of Guadalcanal, using our growing armies of miniature lead soldiers. And in eighth grade, our class sidestepped a great deal of our prescribed curriculum in favor of a massive "war map" project tracing the Allied efforts to bring hostilities to a close. Of great interest to all the boys, this project was greeted with somewhat less enthusiasm by our teacher and the girls.

From time to time during these years, my mother and I accompanied my father on business trips. I remember, in particular, trips to New York. I would position myself on a bench in Grand Central Station by the hour to watch people from around the world moving through the terminal—Sikhs in turbans, Arabs in flowing robes, soldiers and sailors from many countries, people of all races and nationalities—gaining for the first time some notion of how truly large and diverse the world was.

The 1941 baseball season was the catalyst for my lifelong interest in sports. I attended my first Pittsburgh Pirates game at Forbes Field that summer—a devastating doubleheader loss to the Chicago Cubs. Thereafter, baseball became a consuming passion that continues to this day. For Christmas that year my folks gave me my first Ethan Allen's All-Star Baseball game, an early tabletop effort in which player discs placed upon a spinner reproduced the on-field action. This game turned into a mania for me over the next five years; I constructed discs out of shirt cardboard to reproduce all sixteen major league teams and recorded each priceless statistic gleaned from nearly daylong sessions of the game in hand-printed versions of *The Sporting News* and other archives. In later years I came to recognize the wisdom of Professor Jacques Barzun's observation, "Whoever wants to know the heart and mind of America had better learn baseball."

My entrepreneurial instincts began to develop during this period as well. I accumulated a list of customers for grass cutting as well as other odd jobs—shoveling coal, and washing and painting walls. My bedrock income producer, however, was my paper route.

My other major interest was reading. Newspapers were daily fare; I turned to the sports page first, of course, but kept abreast of world affairs as well. Books were pretty well restricted to classic boys' reading, including the Hardy Boys series, which I devoured on publication, and Richard Haliburton's adventure tales. I was even more interested, however, in *Life* magazine, then the leading source of information on domestic and world affairs for many American families. I not only consumed each weekly issue but periodically carted piles of back editions up from their basement storage closet to our living room for refreshers on recent history. To this day, I can't pass by a vintage *Life* without remembering those days when my education in politics and public affairs began.

Later in my life, I was to devote almost every spare moment to reading. While I occasionally delve into the fiction of my friend Jim Michener and that of John Updike (my favorite), F. Scott Fitzgerald, John O'Hara and other chroniclers of twentieth-century American social mores, my principal interests have always been biography, history and political punditry. Among my all-time favorites are Carl Sandburg's *Lincoln*; Robert Caro's *The Power Broker* (a study of Robert Moses) and his biographies of Lyndon Johnson; Edmund Morris's *The Rise of Theodore Roosevelt* and *Theodore Rex*; James T. Patterson's *Mr. Republican: A Biography of Robert A. Taft*; David McCullough's *Truman* and *John Adams*; Doris Kearns Goodwin's *The Fitzgeralds and the Kennedys*; William H. McNeill's *The Rise of the West*; Barbara Tuchman's *The Proud Tower* and *The Guns of August*; and Professor Barzun's *From Dawn to Decadence*. I also read in fascination countless accounts of the years between the two world wars, described elsewhere as "a dark time of global depression that displaced millions, paralyzed the liberal democracies, gave rise to totalitarian regimes, and, ultimately, led to the second world war." Of course, there was always room for the occasional baseball book and, in later years, more reading about other countries and cultures. My time spent with books was a constant joy, and I learned much from the trials and tribulations of other public figures, past and present.

Political participation, of a sort, came early for me. My dad was an unreconstructed Jeffersonian Democrat whose views reflected his conservative southern roots. He also shared the 1930s businessman's attitude about "that man in the White House," meaning President Franklin D. Roosevelt. So in 1940, at age eight, I took to the stump—or rather, to the back of my friend Tucker Gordon's rubber-tired wagon—to deliver my first political speech in support of Wendell Lewis Willkie, the Republican presidential candidate. No text survives, but I well remember its somewhat hysterical tone, warning that "in Germany, it was the Third Reich; in Russia, it was the Third International; don't let it be a Third Term in America!" Needless to say, my glib screed did not prevent President Roosevelt from steamrollering Mr. Willkie.

Notwithstanding my early partisanship, I shared the sense of loss we all felt when President Roosevelt died on April 12, 1945. My schoolmates and I received the news as we returned from our annual school picnic. He was the only president we had ever known, and his death marked the end of an era for us.

With graduation from elementary school in 1945 came, as well, an end to my childhood. Already, one of the more "advanced" girls in the neighborhood had shared the message about the "facts of life" with an awed audience; few of us had been instructed about these mysteries by our parents. High school loomed on the horizon, and for most of us that meant leaving the comfortable confines of "the Farms" for the nearby town of Carnegie.

CARNEGIE, PENNSYLVANIA, in the 1940s had a population of about 10,000, some light industry, various commercial establishments and, like many Western Pennsylvania communities in those days, its own brewery. The town was heavily ethnic, with strong Irish, Italian and Eastern European strains as well as occasional black and Jewish families. While Rosslyn Farms families did their shopping in Carnegie stores, hired their domestic help from among its citizens, went to one of its four movie theaters and even, in some cases, went to church there, they in general held the neighboring community at arm's length.

Carnegie High School was about two and a half miles from Rosslyn Farms, a forty-five-minute walk (though I often picked up lifts from sympathetic motorists). But it was an alien world in which a single classroom contained as many students as the entire school I had attended for eight years. High school introduced me to a mixed ethnic, religious and racial milieu with which I was almost totally unfamiliar and to an emphasis on competition—for girls, athletic prowess, and macho preeminence—for which I was ill prepared by both inclination and experience.

I became a straight-A student in short order. Unfortunately, I also developed a talent for making smart remarks and passing notes in study hall. My new instructors' frequent inquiry was, "Don't you have enough to do,

Thornburgh?" While a truthful answer would clearly have been "No," I usually affected a look of contrition and stuck my nose into the nearest book, awaiting an opportunity for the next salvo. Some of my group's activities were not so frivolous, as we became intrigued by the amount of merchandise we could "hook," i.e., steal, from local stores. None of these larcenies were significant, but they did leave tinges of guilt that prevented me from attempting larger criminal enterprises.

Friends came quickly, and I learned to disregard the visible, often stereotypical, characteristics of individuals and look to their real worth. For this I will be forever grateful to Carnegie High School, for my somewhat insular existence both before and after my time there might otherwise have delayed my full appreciation of the exciting diversity of humankind. Our class produced a host of distinguished citizens—doctors, nurses, lawyers, architects, accountants, teachers, public officials and successful business-people. Of course, there were a few racketeers and common crooks as well, but they only enrich my memories of that brief first year's experience in "the real world."

My parents were more aware than I that the challenges of Carnegie High School had been much too easy for me to master. After some discussion, it was decided that I would go away to school the next year. I was ashamed to tell my school friends of the move for fear they would think I had gone "high hat" on them, so I spent the summer in hibernation and just faded away in the fall. My destination was Mercersburg Academy, a boarding school in south central Pennsylvania. With my departure, I ended my sojourn in the warm and comfortable cocoon of Rosslyn Farms, never really to return.

THE ALL-MALE, all-white Mercersburg student body practiced most of the tribal customs chronicled in the prep-school genre of American fiction. Unfortunately, as I could once again get by with a minimum amount of effort in the classroom, my time there was a significant wasted opportunity. It was only years later that I acknowledged this to have been my fault rather than the school's. My most fulfilling activity was sports writing for the school newspaper, to which I turned after several fruitless athletic endeavors of my own. A finely developed capacity for wisecracks led me to be voted the "wittiest" member of the graduating class of 1950. It also established me as a class leader in the ultimate sanction for miscreant students: "guard duty," a combination of forced study hall and trudges around a well-worn "guard" path on a hillside. Ironically, in 1993, I received the coveted Class of 1932 award, given to Mercersburg graduates who distinguish themselves during their careers. In my mind's eye I conjured up a phalanx of former faculty members and administrators rolling their eyes in disbelief.

The saving grace for me during this somewhat static interval was Virginia Kendall Hooton. We met at a New Year's Eve party on December 31, 1948, when I was sixteen and she nearly fifteen. It was magic from almost the start. Ginny had a constantly sunny disposition and a marvelous sense of humor. She also displayed an exceptional talent for the piano and provided all who knew her, then or thereafter, with hours of entertainment from the keyboard. I was her biggest fan, and she catered to my love of jazz, in particular, by copying the styles of such masters as Erroll Garner, George Shearing, Fats Waller and Ralph Sutton. We were the proverbial perfect match, and we spent the next two years engaging in the usual moonstruck activities of teenagers in innocent love.

Though I remember those times with great fondness, I quake at some of the risks we ran. By this time, all of us had been introduced, with much bravado, to intoxicating beverages—first beer, then a variety of spirits, my first mixed drink being a concoction of gin and Squirt. It will ever be so, but I hope future parents will somehow be able to inoculate their children with a dose of good sense when it comes to alcohol abuse, especially mixed with unsafe driving. I am most thankful that none of my teenage excesses in this regard ended in tragedy, and that today's young people have adopted practices such as the designated driver.

In the spring of 1950, with graduation impending, I began to think about colleges. I fastened on two choices—Lehigh, where my grandfather, a distinguished mathematician, had taught and my father and several relatives, all engineers, had matriculated, and Yale, a somewhat mystical-sounding place with an aura of elitism. My grades were only so-so, but I did well enough on the college boards to gain entry to both and chose Yale. After graduation, a friend and I went off on a "toot" to New York, seeing a number of Broadway shows, visiting some well-known jazz spots and enduring a hilarious encounter with some low-rent hookers at a dime-a-dance joint off Times Square. The negotiations went nowhere. So much for our sophistication!

My choice of engineering as a college major is one of the great mysteries of my life. My aptitude for things mathematical and mechanical had never been high, and my principal interest in secondary school had been writing. Perhaps I was acting out of a misguided sense of loyalty to my heritage.

From the outset I was on the wrong track. I had the choice of long hours of study or poor performance, and I chose the latter. Calculus remains an absolute mystery to me, the subject of recurring nightmares to this day. In science, I was equally at sea. I was simply not cut out for engineering, but a combination of pride and stubbornness kept me at it, even though I found my courses in the liberal arts and humanities far more fulfilling. These courses also produced the As and Bs necessary to balance my near-failing grades in science and math. Clearly, I could have used some judicious counseling. But none was forthcoming, and I certainly did not seek it. In later years, I was to lament that I had not taken full advantage of the rich intellectual environment at Yale, but I was consoled by the insights I did pick up through keeping my engineering curriculum to a bare minimum.

In 1950, the fall of my freshman year, I joined the Yale Freshman Dramat and sought to master the campus social scene. Like many of my day, I determined that consuming vast quantities of alcohol was a sure way to do this. I also taught myself to smoke cigarettes. And for some time, I tried to transform myself into a "Yale man" right out of F. Scott Fitzgerald and John O'Hara. Expecting all my classmates to be preppies, I tried to portray myself accordingly. That my freshman roommates put up with me for a year is to their eternal credit, for I must have seemed an insufferable snob, intent upon conforming in dress and affectation to the stereotype I had fashioned. In time, I came to appreciate that my Yale experience had to encompass more than "wine, women and song" with a narrow group of conformists. I developed lifelong friendships with a diverse group of individuals far beyond the confines of the Fence Club, the "social" or "white shoe" fraternity I joined my sophomore year. I was never at ease with the club's ambience and made decreasing use of its dining and bar facilities after being rebuffed in an early attempt to involve it in some worthwhile community efforts.

In December of my sophomore year, I received the sudden and terrible word that my father had died of a cerebral hemorrhage. I was wholly unprepared to deal with such a catastrophe. My academic problems increased the following spring and by the end of the year, I had been "grounded" from participation in any extracurricular activities until my academic situation improved.

This was 1952, a presidential election year, and for the first time in many years, Republicans were actually excited about their prospects. I had been a close observer of the 1944 and 1948 campaigns, following the conventions carefully by radio as our party twice sent New York governor Thomas E. Dewey to the well. In 1948 I had "admitted myself" to the Mercersburg infirmary on election eve to hear the radio reports; when I heard the news of Harry Truman's upset win, I emerged truly ill.

My early Republicanism was mostly a product of inheritance and environment, to be sure, but also reflected preferences for a limited role for government, fiscal responsibility and probusiness policies to encourage economic growth and job creation. None of these were evident in FDR's New Deal, which, prior to World War II, had made very little impact on the ravages of the depression. Over time my political beliefs were to become less one-dimensional, but my allegiance to the GOP continued through thick and thin.

The contenders for the 1952 GOP nomination were General Dwight D. Eisenhower and Senator Robert A. Taft of Ohio. I favored Taft at the outset as the more fiscally conservative candidate but became an enthusiastic "Ike" supporter after the Chicago convention. That fall, for the first time, I had the opportunity to vote and to celebrate a Republican victory, as Eisenhower swept to an easy win over Governor Adlai Stevenson of Illinois.

At this time the influence of Senator Joseph McCarthy, whose shrill and demagogic efforts to root out Communists from government produced more unjustifiably ruined careers than real subversives, was at its height. After a period of expressing some support for McCarthyism, I came to reject it completely, recognizing that the frequent argument "I may not approve of his methods, but he's on the right track" begged the essential issue: the methods were unfair and, in many cases, un-American. Later in my Yale days, the televised Army-McCarthy hearings, which we watched faithfully every day, eventually brought an end to the flamboyant Wisconsin senator's career.

I had spent the previous two summers working on construction jobs, but before my senior year, I enjoyed a watershed experience: my first trip abroad. My friend Will Watson and I embarked for Europe on a converted Liberty ship crammed with students engaged in one continuous party. Arriving in Le Havre with little idea what our itinerary was to be, we spent a packed six weeks enjoying France, Germany, Italy, Switzerland, England and Scotland. We went to Italy with some misgiving, due to the false stereotypes that existed in the United States at the time about the country and its people. It proved to be a highlight of the trip. It was also the only place where we exceeded our strict dollar-a-night limitation on lodging expenses, spending all of $2.50 a night in Florence.

I came back from my trip a changed person with a vastly expanded worldview. While my outlook remained all too carefree, exposure to a whole new world of people, places, culture and history had enriched my views and stretched my understanding in ways that I would never have imagined possible. I owe my mother thanks and credit for it was her insight that urged and underwrote this experience.

After a period at Connecticut College for Women (now Connecticut College) in New London, the closest women's college to New Haven, Ginny Hooton had transferred to the Eliot-Pearson School of Tufts University near Boston, where she would spend the next two years preparing to be a nursery school teacher. In the fall of my senior year, I formally proposed marriage. Parental approval was forthcoming at Thanksgiving, though her father, Don, wanted to be sure that I "wouldn't be off to graduate school." I gave this assurance in good faith but subsequently reneged upon it, to the advantage of all.

My academic fortunes picked up somewhat during my senior year, as I squeezed in an art course and a superior experimental course critiquing Marxism from economic, political, philosophic and sociological points of view. My term paper in the latter was adjudged so superior that it was "cribbed" by one of the big men on campus the next semester and, I assume, produced a similar result for him. My most significant academic encounter that year, however, was a course in business law offered by the engineering school to help prepare us for the outside world. This survey course was not too demanding, but it captured my interest and produced one of my highest grades.

In 1954, there was a strong market for engineering graduates, even those with my undistinguished credentials. I received some substantial job offers, but I had finally realized that an engineering career was not for me. As luck would have it, during a trip to Boston that winter, I visited a Saturday class at Harvard Law School and was immediately enchanted by the Socratic method and by a vision of my interests in government, politics, history and the English language converging to some useful end. After considerable pondering, I made a major change in course and applied to law school. Given my lackluster Yale record, I was very grateful to be accepted at the University of Pittsburgh School of Law.

My final memorable activity at Yale was service on the Senior Prom

Committee, helping plan the last major social event of our years there. Alas, my work as the committee's treasurer resulted in the first deficit anyone could recall. The following day I received my diploma and ended my long twilight struggle with the engineering profession.

Our class graduated in May 1954, the same month in which the United States Supreme Court decided the landmark case of *Brown v. Board of Education*, holding unconstitutional the "separate but equal" doctrine that had excluded African Americans from so many opportunities in our society. It is not without significance that ours was the last Yale class to include no black students. Thereafter, we would all be compelled to face up to the inequities of our segregated nation and participate in the redress of grievances long festering.

LAW SCHOOL PROVIDED me, for the first time, with a real sense of purpose and accomplishment. I also—finally—began working up to my academic potential, ranking second in my class at the end of our first year and earning a place on the law review. All of that year, however, was but a lead-in to the big event in my life—Ginny's and my wedding. It was held on June 25, 1955, and followed with a gala wedding reception and a honeymoon in Bermuda.

We returned to a one-bedroom apartment, furnished with what we could scrape together from our families and wedding gifts. That fall Ginny began teaching at the nursery school of the Shadyside Presbyterian Church; later she added a job teaching dependent and neglected children at the Allegheny County Juvenile Court Nursery School. Her work was our sole means of support, other than my mother's gracious payment of my tuition. We sometimes borrowed my mother's television set for a big evening, and we developed a taste for corned beef sandwiches and cheesecake at a local delicatessen. Meals at our parents' homes also relieved the pressure on Ginny, who did not count cooking among her major interests. In fact, my principal domestic assignment was to plan the week's meals. These often included a questionable concoction we, for some reason, called "chestnut burrs," stuffing encapsulated in a hamburger casing.

In my second year in law school, I was selected for our moot court team, which argued a mock appellate case in competition with teams from other law schools. Our team won only the first round at the regional competition, but I was able to use my research for a law review case note involving merger issues under the Clayton Act. The next year I published a rather substantial article on the availability of federal income tax returns in civil litigation; this was reprinted, to my great satisfaction, in the *Journal of Taxation*, a nationwide publication for tax practitioners.

After graduation, I accepted a position as staff counsel for the Aluminum Company of America, headquartered in downtown Pittsburgh. Though the work proved interesting, I took the position largely because ALCOA offered to pay me more than anyone else—an important consideration at the time, as I was about to become a father.

In fact, my new job had to take an immediate backseat to our first baby, John Kendall Thornburgh, who arrived on September 15, 1957. He was joined by David Bradford Thornburgh on October 6, 1958. Vigorous diaper washing became my particular domestic expertise. Our third "unplanned" baby boy, Peter Lewis Thornburgh, arrived on February 28, 1960.

By this time I was coming to realize that opportunities for the future were more important than today's paycheck. On March 1, 1959, I left ALCOA to become the nineteenth lawyer at the firm of Kirkpatrick, Pomeroy, Lockhart & Johnson. I hoped to be a litigator, but soon found that most of the firm's trial practice involved either lengthy corporate matters, carried on through extensive discovery, or personal injury claims, usually settled on the courthouse steps. Thus, while I tackled my assignments with zeal, they did not involve the courtroom practice I had naively envisioned. In time, I became more involved in corporate mergers and acquisitions and securities offerings.

As Ginny and I celebrated our fifth wedding anniversary, we were about as content as a young couple could be at ages twenty-eight and twenty-six, with three fine little boys and a promising employment situation. Our next goal was to secure a larger house where we could relax and enjoy our blessings for a spell.

2

Tragedy and Recovery

Some days you notice more than others. Some days you remember better than others. Some days you never forget. Such a day for me was Friday, July 1, 1960.

Ginny offered to drive me to the office that morning, as she did from time to time, partly to keep the boys entertained. I waved good-bye as they set off to return home and settled into my routine. About 10:25, the telephone rang. The caller identified himself as a police officer. "Mr. Thornburgh," he said, "there has been an accident." My mind raced during the fifteen-minute cab ride to South Side Hospital, where my wife and sons had been taken. I prayed for their safety and for strength to deal with whatever awaited me. I did not anticipate, however, the terrible news I was to receive. As soon as I reached the hospital, a doctor appeared and told me, "Mr. Thornburgh, your wife is dead. She was killed instantly."

Blessedly, the boys had survived. Soon I was able to visit with John and David, who had escaped without serious injury. I then somehow got to Mercy Hospital, where Peter, only four months old, had been taken under circumstances that I was to learn only later. He had been virtually catapulted out of his infant seat, his head had smashed into the dashboard, and he had suffered multiple skull fractures. Tubes were attached to his little body at every imaginable point, and there was little sign of movement.

The cause of the accident remained a mystery. Apparently, Ginny had somehow lost control of the car and crossed the center line to collide head-on with a truck coming in the opposite direction. Those at the site who had helped the boys were heroes to me. Immediately following the impact, an elderly couple named Mr. and Mrs. Profit had gathered up John and David and sped them to the nearest hospital, which was South Side. The right front seat of our Volkswagen had sprung forward, obscuring Peter's tiny form on the floor. When firefighters or police pulled back the seat, they discovered Peter and thrust him into the arms of John Smith, a black man, who drove him to Mercy, which was the closest hospital to his own home.

Funeral services for Ginny were held on July 4. John and David were released from the hospital the next day, and we began the long task of healing and rebuilding our family, supported by an extraordinary outpouring of care and assistance from family and friends. These included the Kirkpatrick law firm "family," whose love and support during this dark time I will never forget.

I also had a most unexpected distraction: the Pittsburgh Pirates were leading the National League. After struggling through the 1940s and 1950s (their all-time nadir was 1952, when they compiled a 42–112 record), the Buccos looked capable of winning their first pennant since 1927. They clinched it on September 25 and went on to win the World Series in the last half of the ninth inning of the seventh game on Bill Mazaroski's home run, defeating the mighty New York Yankees of Mickey Mantle, Roger Maris, Yogi Berra, and Whitey Ford. Ginny would have been the first to approve of my taking solace in our national pastime at this agonizing time.

Peter had suffered severe brain injury. Part of his skull had been removed, and he was on life support. His doctors, Richard Hershey and George Gray, and the Sisters of Mercy who attended him were as devoted as I to the survival of this plucky infant. The sisters were especially attentive and provided the only sustained nurturing contact he had during his nearly six months in the hospital. I often observed them going about their duties with Peter in their arms. For the first three months, I visited him every lunch hour, until the sisters gently reminded me of my responsibilities to the other boys as well.

Well-meaning family and friends asked me whether what they called heroic efforts were truly justified on Peter's behalf, or whether it might be "God's will" that "nature run its course." As gently as I could, I turned aside such questions. Peter was my son, and I had vowed to do all I could to ensure his survival.

A week before Christmas, Peter was finally discharged from the hospital. He rewarded our delight at having him home with the smiles and the warm disposition that have characterized him ever since.

FOR SEVERAL YEARS after Ginny's death, my social life was quite limited. Friends went out of their way to include me in their activities, but it was obviously not the same without Ginny. Gradually, I became accustomed to the idea of "dating" again, but it was not easy.

As 1963 began, I was practicing law, serving on the boards of the boys' nursery school and the Pittsburgh School Volunteers Association, and maintaining a somewhat desultory social life. My family had settled into a comfortable routine, aided by a loving housekeeper. Little did I know that I was soon to meet the woman who was to restore real meaning to my life and to provide our family once again with the love and care that only a mother can give.

Chuck Grimstad, a fellow associate at Kirkpatrick, asked me to be an "extra man" during the prenuptial events leading up to his marriage to Julie Howard in April 1963. It was at the rehearsal dinner that I first met Ginny Judson, one of Julie's bridesmaids. She was a vivacious, buxom, self-possessed young woman who immediately stole my heart.

Born in 1940, Ginny had had an upbringing very similar to mine in a community much like Rosslyn Farms: the Westchester County suburb of Hastings-on-Hudson, about twenty miles north of New York City. Her father, Cyrus Field Judson Jr., was the grandson of Cyrus West Field, the man renowned for laying the Atlantic cable, which opened a new era in communications. Cyrus's brother Stephen Field served as a justice of the United States Supreme Court, while his brother David Dudley Field wrote the first American code of civil procedure. Ginny's mother, Virginia Walton Needham, had a family history of Republican activism. Ginny herself had graduated from Wheaton College in Norton, Massachusetts, and earned her master's degree from the Harvard Graduate School of Education. She was a third-grade teacher in Lincoln, Massachusetts, and had made plans to spend the summer in Ghana teaching English with Operation Crossroads Africa, a forerunner of the Peace Corps.

Ginny and I spent much of the wedding weekend together, and after she returned home to Boston, we continued to meet as often as possible. It was readily apparent to both of us how special our relationship was. Ginny and my first wife shared not only a name but many characteristics that would no doubt have made them fast friends. By Memorial Day, just a few weeks after we had met, I had told Ginny, "I don't want you to go to Africa this summer . . . or to teach in Massachusetts next year." That was as close to a formal proposal as I offered. We were married, six months after we met, on October 12, 1963.

Joining our family was a considerable challenge for Ginny. Peter, now nearly four years old, was not toilet trained, was unable to speak and had little mobility, and of course the older boys had needs of their own. However, Ginny later described adapting to life with me as the biggest challenge of all. I tried to answer her questions about our "first mom" but volunteered very little, knowing that comparisons were not constructive and that my lives with each were separate and distinct. There were a few tears, but she quickly took command of the situation. She was also able to continue her work with Operation Crossroads Africa, helping with fund-raising and promotion in the Pittsburgh area, and she became involved with the Pittsburgh Council on International Visitors, an organization providing home experiences for travelers from abroad.

In January 1964, Peter was enrolled as the first day student with a brain injury at the nearby Home for Crippled Children (now the Children's Institute), originally established to serve children with polio. A more caring environment could not have been imagined. The Home set to work devising programs to help us help Peter on his long road to greater self-sufficiency. Such achievements as toilet training and elementary language skills were difficult, but with Ginny's determination and the support of the Home, we began to observe the first signs of real progress. A major step was Peter's being fitted out with a helmet to protect the soft spot in his head, so that he could play with other children and fall just as safely as any other child learning to walk. Several years later, a plate was inserted in the soft spot to replace the helmet.

I was later to chair a $3 million fund-raising effort for the Home at the request of two of its most influential board members, community activists prominent in Pittsburgh social circles. Though I was frankly uneasy with the notion of soliciting funds for any cause, I tackled the job with zeal. The successful campaign not only was personally satisfying but taught me important new skills and brought me into contact with a number of Pittsburgh leaders upon whom I would rely in future endeavors.

The final entry in Ginny's diary for 1964, her first full year of motherhood, was, "A perfect year!" With all of its ups and downs, I don't think any of our family would have disagreed. One year later, Ginny formally adopted John, David and Peter, a very important day for all of us.

MY RETURN TO more or less full-time law practice after the accident had been marked by a shift in priorities. Deeply impressed with just how finite our lives are, I had begun to realize the importance of using every available opportunity to try to make a difference for the better. Financial rewards receded as ultimate goals; dreams of the "good life" took second place to concerns for society as a whole. Gradually I devoted less and less time to the practice of law, and by the end of the decade I had moved to public service as a full-time career. None of this might have happened had it not been for that tragic accident. It not only made me a far stronger person but kept every professional setback I ever experienced firmly in perspective.

My first steps toward public service were tentative. In 1960 I was elected to office in what was then known as the Junior Bar Section of the Pennsylvania Bar Association. I also continued my affiliation with the *University of Pittsburgh Law Review*, contributing for five years to an annual survey of developments in Pennsylvania law. In November 1962, when Republican congressman William Scranton was elected governor of Pennsylvania, I made my first timid inquiry about public service in a visit to John Tabor, a Kirkpatrick partner serving as Governor Scranton's secretary of commerce. Nothing came of it, however, and that dream was deferred.

Through the Junior Bar, I became involved in organizing a January 1964 conference in Philadelphia on modernizing the Pennsylvania judicial system. This marked the beginning of a lifelong commitment to judicial reform and introduced me to many leaders who shared this concern.

Pennsylvania is one of the minority of states that still elects all of its judges on a partisan basis. One of the most contentious items at the conference was a proposal that the governor appoint all judges from a pool of nominees identified by a nonpartisan citizens' commission. After considerable discussion, the conference endorsed this merit selection proposal. The other major reform proposed addressed the minor judiciary, the state's thousands of magistrates and justices of the peace. All of these officials were elected (save in Philadelphia and Pittsburgh, where the positions were patronage plums), and none had any training in the law, except coincidentally. Many were corrupt and others developed into minor tyrants, exercising political, as well as judicial, authority in their neighborhoods. The conference recommended replacing them with community courts, staffed by lawyers appointed by merit selection and subject to strict supervision. On the whole, the conference was a success, highlighting many shortcomings of the state judicial system and broadening the constituency for reform.

At this time I also began working to improve the quality of legal services available to the poor. Most legal rights can mean very little to persons denied the services of lawyers. In the 1963 case of *Gideon v. Wainwright*, the Supreme Court of the United States had found that criminal defendants had a constitutional right to counsel and required that lawyers be furnished to defendants who could not afford them. As a basis for the ensuing revamping of criminal procedures in Pennsylvania, I compiled an assessment of the legal services available before *Gideon*. This survey, published in the *Pennsylvania Bar Association Quarterly* in October 1964, provided a firm foundation for later legislation creating the office of public defender.

This work led naturally to a concern for meeting the legal needs of poor people in civil matters as well. In due course, I became an incorporator and original board member of the Neighborhood Legal Services Association of Pittsburgh. This organization was later to become extremely controversial, but it was designed simply to level the playing field in everyday disputes between those with competent legal advice, generally the powerful, and those without, generally the powerless.

SIX WEEKS AFTER Ginny and I married, all of America was shocked and saddened by the assassination of President John F. Kennedy. This event ushered in a period of anxiety and concern about our nation that continues to this day. We were glued to our television set for the funeral observances and the ghastly on-screen assassination of Lee Harvey Oswald.

The 1964 presidential campaign, which pitted Lyndon Johnson against Barry Goldwater, was supposed to be the long-predicted showdown—"a choice, not an echo"—between liberals and conservatives in our nation. President Johnson was an unabashed New Deal populist with an ambitious liberal agenda and political skills finely tuned by years of wheeling and dealing on Capitol Hill. Goldwater's nomination had been shrewdly orchestrated by a well-organized group of conservative activists who had begun their effort in the wake of Richard Nixon's defeat in 1960.

The campaign was not much of a contest, as sentimental support for Johnson as Kennedy's successor and his own consummate campaigning skills overpowered Goldwater's oversimplified conservative tenets. Moreover, strains of racism, McCarthyism and jingoism characterized all too many of the GOP candidate's most rabid supporters. Although I took no part in the campaign that year, I was concerned about this latter development and the attempted takeover of the Republican Party in certain areas by those preaching a political philosophy alien to mine. I began to read extensively about the radical right and organizations such as the John Birch Society.

The conspiracy theories spun by these groups found putative Communists everywhere and ascribed to these subversive elements of our society many postwar advances in human rights and civil liberties. Most were racist in tone and isolationist in the extreme, characterizing anyone with an internationalist leaning as bent upon destruction of our freedoms. They exhibited all the characteristics described in Richard Hofstadter's famous work, "The Paranoid Style in American Politics." All of this seemed to me to be designed to divert the Republican Party and its candidates from the central messages that had attracted many of us to the party in the first place. It was a troubling time, so troubling that I even attended the opening of a downtown Pittsburgh headquarters for "Republicans for Johnson" in an attempt to puzzle through my concerns about where my party was being led.

I did play a small role in a senatorial campaign that year. United States Senator Hugh Scott, a Republican moderate, faced an uphill battle to retain his seat as two popular Democrats, Michael Musmanno and Genevieve Blatt, vied for the nomination to oppose him. At the request of the Scott campaign, I did some background research on Musmanno, turning up a number of intriguing inconsistencies in his record. Blatt won the primary by 491 votes out of over a million cast, and Scott went on to defeat her in the fall. Presumably the Scott forces had used my research to aid Blatt in the primary, since she was perceived to be the weaker of the two candidates.

On election night, as it became apparent that the Democratic ticket had virtually swept from coast to coast, my frustration boiled over. After pacing most of the evening, I composed a letter to the *Pittsburgh Post-Gazette* venting that frustration and expressing my concern that moderates had stood by and let the radical right take over our party. The letter, published on November 6, 1964, occasioned a good deal of positive reaction and raised my political profile for the first time. The Republican defeat had also given me a sense of mission to participate in a rebuilding of the Grand Old Party.

Given my specific policy views, some have suggested that I might just as easily have jumped ship at this time, changing from a moderate Republican to a moderate Democrat. This, then, is perhaps a good place to articulate the underpinnings of my unwavering lifelong loyalty to the Republican Party. I did this most clearly, I think, over twenty years later, at an appearance at Yale in November 1985. By then, of course, the party had recovered from the Goldwater debacle and from that of President Nixon's impeachment and resignation, and had triumphed with the coming to office of President Reagan and his resounding reelection in 1984.

The thrust of my speech was that the party's ascendancy at that time had little to do with "headline-grabbing debates over the so-called social issues of abortion, school prayer or changing American values" or with "'supply-side' economic theory or neo-isolationism or protectionism." Rather, the fundamental differences in principle that distinguished the two parties went back to the GOP's deep beliefs in "the individual, the free-enterprise system, fiscal responsibility, strong state and local governments, and a combination of toughness and compassion at home and abroad."

Our belief in the individual, I noted, went back to Abraham Lincoln. Creating more individual opportunity, not more government, should be our aim, because "society is best served by limiting government interference in the day-to-day affairs of individual men and women who are trying to make a living, raise their families, worship their God and improve their quality of life." Though it may on occasion be necessary to enlist the power of government to serve individuals, big government itself, like big business and big labor, can be an enemy of individual freedom. "In confronting the 'bigs' on behalf of the individual," I pointed out, "Republicans have vastly expanded their agenda for freedom in general." Sometimes, I acknowledged, this change had "diluted the party's historic identification with minority rights." However, rather than "pandering to every special interest group or each new trend or cause," we should work to bring minorities home to the party "as fully participating Americans whose needs basically are the same as those of other Americans."

The free-enterprise system, I continued, was the key to the economic growth that would produce individual opportunity. This belief dated to the party's roots as "the party of the small independent entrepreneur." With America "being challenged anew by the rise of foreign competition, the aging of its resources and the march of advanced technology," private enterprise represented our best hope for real jobs and real growth. While the GOP was frequently disparaged as the "party of business," I noted, "If we are to have sustained growth and high employment, if we are to compete effectively in international markets, and, perhaps most importantly, if we are to provide for the individual needs of individual citizens, then someone had better be 'the party of business,' the party that recognizes, in the words of John Gardner, that 'the best social program is a good economy'."

My call for fiscal responsibility encompassed a commitment to "smaller and more efficient government . . . fewer and lower taxes and a more disciplined and effective budget process" founded on a balanced-budget amendment to the federal Constitution.

Stronger state and local governments were important because Republicans do not believe that "all the wisdom of America resides in Washington, D.C." Indeed, states, the "laboratories of democracy," were more often in a position to respond to the real needs of the people. President Reagan's reversal of a fifty-year trend of centralizing decision-making authority in Washington was a "true milestone of achievement for traditional Republican principles."

Finally, I defined toughness abroad as "standing up to aggression, terrorism and totalitarianism, whether in Afghanistan, Central America, Africa or the Middle East, and whether from the left or the right." Compassion abroad means "extending a hand to the world's needy—without regard to politics or belief." Toughness at home requires cracking down on violent criminals while vigorously pursuing fraud, waste and corruption within government itself. Compassion at home means "helping those trapped by social, personal or economic circumstances beyond their control, but in ways designed to break, rather than perpetuate, the tragic cycle of welfare dependency."

Though some of the specific issues I discussed in that speech had not appeared on the political radar screen in 1964, my core views on the principles of my party were already formed. They were to govern my entire public career.

IN DECEMBER 1964 I unsuccessfully sought a place on the board of governors of the Allegheny County Bar Association. I made no effort to organize any support and paid the price, just as I had years before in law school, when I had sought the presidency of the student bar association. These failures taught me that electoral success requires all-out commitment and absolute concentration—and that seeking and considering the views of others is almost always a good way to strengthen one's own case.

My restiveness continued. I applied unsuccessfully for a White House fellowship and considered several other possibilities: the U.S. and Pennsylvania Departments of Justice, the Allegheny County public defender's office, various law school faculties and the office of Congressman John Lindsay, then a rising symbol of moderate Republicanism. I did chair the Public Service Committee of the Allegheny County Bar Association from

1966 through 1969, using this position to advance the wide availability of legal representation.

Ever since my postelection letter of lament, I had sought out friends and acquaintances like the Ancient Mariner, eager to share my views on repairing the party's fortunes. That this was becoming tedious was brought home to me late one evening, at a boozy post–dinner party political talk marathon, when our hostess interrupted my latest diatribe with the question, "Why don't you do something about it?" With all the bravado I could muster, I responded, "I will!"

In the cold light of dawn, I realized just how ill equipped I was to make good on that commitment. At age thirty-two, I didn't know what voting district of which ward I lived in, didn't know the political leadership of my community and, aside from a few fellow Yale graduates, had not even a nodding acquaintance with anyone holding public office.

Over the next six weeks, I undertook a crash course in Practical Politics 101. Studying census tracts and election results, I constructed a fairly reliable political profile of Pittsburgh and Allegheny County, the extent of my immediate horizons. At breakfast, lunch and dinner, I met with leaders in housing and urban development, the social services, the African American communities, business, labor and the academic world, learning about the problems our communities faced and keeping copious notes against the day I might use them in some yet-to-be-defined quest. One of my first and most crucial contacts was with Elsie Hillman, the doyenne of Pittsburgh's moderate Republicans. An original "Eisenhower Girl" in the 1952 campaign, she had since labored tirelessly on behalf of the party and its candidates.

The major local office on the ballot in 1965 was that of mayor of Pittsburgh. Then held by Joseph Barr, a protégé of longtime political boss and former governor David L. Lawrence, the post was looked upon as a Democratic fiefdom. No Republican had come close to claiming it since 1949, and no challenger was in sight as this election year began. Shortly after our conversation, Elsie Hillman called to ask if I would meet with a group of county Republican leaders to discuss my interest in the race. I was dumbfounded, to say the least. In retrospect, their interest reflected more the sad state of the party than any appeal I might have had as a candidate. Our meeting was cordial, but short. We did, however, touch on some of the issues that a candidate might have to deal with, and the insights of these veteran pols provided some focus for my own thinking and research.

The result was a paper, "The Republican Party in the City of Pittsburgh." Circulated privately among local and state party leaders, it set forth the history of the decline of the party, a political analysis of the relationship between the city and its suburbs, an issue-by-issue treatment of the political agenda, and a diagnosis of the ills of the present leadership. It concluded to the effect that Republican failures "had already cost the party a city. Now they could cost the city a party." As a result of the paper, the question of my candidacy was revisited. Some state party leaders seemed genuinely to want me to run, but as they could guarantee little specific support from the local leadership, I declined. The party's eventual nominee, local contractor Vince Rovitto, went down to a predictable defeat in November.

My appetite whetted, I began to meet regularly with a group plotting the strengthening of the local Republican Party. It included Elsie, state representative Sheldon Parker, and three Pittsburgh attorneys: Al Capozzi, a former candidate for Congress; Wendell Freeland, a leader in the African American community; and Harold Blaxter, my contact in the 1964 Scott campaign. This group, dubbed by Elsie the "007s," was a considerable source of political lore and intelligence. While I was able to contribute little, I learned a great deal. For instance, it eventually became apparent to me that one of the party's troubles was the ill feeling left over from the 1964 presidential campaign. Some party leaders, such as Elsie, had supported Governor Scranton's brief candidacy; others, such as Robert W. Duggan, had committed to Goldwater. Duggan had been elected district attorney of Allegheny County in 1963 at age thirty-seven with substantial help from Scranton, but had since been building his own power base on the right.

Meanwhile, George Pott, the county party chairman, appointed me to the GOP platform committee, where I renewed, with little effect, many of the proposals contained in my paper. I also continued my round-robin of meetings with community leaders and for the first time met H. John Heinz III, then twenty-six, who had served as an aide to Senator Scott. Extremely bright, energetic, and genuinely committed to public service, Heinz obviously had big plans.

All this political interest coalesced in the fall of 1965 in an obscure race for judge of the Juvenile Court of Allegheny County. The interim holder of the position, my friend and Kirkpatrick colleague Maurice "Pinky" Cohill, faced a strong challenge from Democrat Pat Tamilia; the Democratic voter registration edge in Allegheny County was overwhelming. John Heinz was enlisted as a citizen campaign chairman, and Ginny and I pitched in to help with volunteers. I also sent the judge a five-page letter outlining my strategy for victory. Most of my recommendations were self-evident, but nearly all were followed to the letter. Ginny's and my finest hour was organizing an all-day mailing exercise, using hundreds of volunteers, to deliver a highly effective direct-mail piece to every Democratic voter's home just before election day. To the surprise of many, Judge Cohill was solidly elected. The whole process was a most valuable learning experience for the Thornburghs, and we enjoyed every minute of it.

So much so that I finally decided to take the plunge myself, entering the 1966 race for the U.S. congressional seat in Pittsburgh's Fourteenth District.

3

Running for Office

THE FOURTEENTH CONGRESSIONAL District basically encompassed inner-city Pittsburgh: downtown, several comfortable residential
neighborhoods, and some of our most segregated and poverty-ridden sectors. It was multiethnic, with Irish, Italian, Polish and other Eastern European strains predominating, and vital black and Jewish communities.
Democrats outnumbered Republicans by over three to one, and the area
had long been represented by a Democratic congressman.

The four-term incumbent was William S. Moorhead Jr., a wealthy lawyer from a prominent Pittsburgh family, who had been handpicked by the
Lawrence machine in 1958. He was a good congressman and his campaigns
had been easy ones, as the organization was able to turn out a strong vote
every two years. In fact, Bill Moorhead was to prove unbeatable, retiring
after twenty years of service in 1978.

Ginny and I had no particular issues on which to challenge Moorhead
and no illusions about our ability to win the seat. We knew, however, that we
had to test our interest in running for public office. Besides, we expected
minimal competition for the nomination, and the opportunity to be nominated for an office of such prominence might not recur.

Al Capozzi acted as campaign manager, and Elsie Hillman offered her
friendship, enthusiasm and financial backing. We eventually recruited a

larger group of able campaigners, but Ginny and I did most of the heavy lifting at the outset. On February 11, we drove to all the local newspapers and radio and television stations to hand-deliver my announcement and a campaign biography. Saturday's *Pittsburgh Post-Gazette* carried a small story headlined "Seeking Congress Seat, Thornburgh Declares," while the afternoon *Pittsburgh Press* followed with an even smaller entry, buried in the back pages and more realistically entitled "Lawyer Seeking Moorhead Seat."

Ginny took charge of an ambitious effort to accumulate signatures on nominating petitions and recruited a hundred or so of our friends and acquaintances to circulate these papers door to door across the district. They were to congregate at our house on February 18 to pick up their petitions and get instructions and a pep talk. Early that morning, we received the saddest news possible. My mother, weakened by a stroke, had died peacefully in her sleep the night before. Ginny and I decided to go ahead with our event nonetheless, as we hoped my mom would have wished. (When she had seen the newspaper articles about my candidacy, she had called me, weeping with pride.) We somehow mustered the strength to distribute petitions to the enthusiastic crowd of volunteers, whose efforts produced some 7,500 signatures. We told only a few close friends of our loss so as not to take the edge off this generous outpouring of friendship and support. But it was a very long and taxing day.

We spent most of the primary campaign at Republican ward meetings, soliciting the endorsement of the organization, for what it was worth. A similarly inexperienced primary opponent named Tom Raith had emerged, so the exercise was not academic. Our one significant rally—at the North Side Carnegie Hall, a traditional Democratic site—was a huge success, attended by 500 or so loudly cheering Republicans. In retrospect, the campaign probably peaked on that April evening, as we were unable thereafter to duplicate similar crowds or enthusiasm. However, in the primary on May 17, we corralled 78 percent of the meager Republican turnout.

Bigger news for us was Ginny's pregnancy. Although again "unplanned," it was most welcome, particularly in view of the loss of my mother, our beloved "Nana." As so often happens, the Lord seemed to couple the tragedy of death with the joy of birth to remind us of the fine balance He seeks to maintain in our lives.

The campaign, now chaired by John Heinz, had come together quite well on the substantive side, aided by superb research done by our volunteers. Most of the positions we articulated were to recur in my later career—most notably, a hard line against organized crime and official corruption; a concern for the elderly; a focus on urban problems; a strong civil rights position; support for an effective United Nations; conservative fiscal policies supplemented by support for federal revenue sharing; and attention to transportation problems, job training and public education. Notably missing were such later hot-button issues as abortion, gun control and homosexual rights, which were not even on anyone's agenda in 1966.

Financing was also smoothly handled. I was determined not to put any of my own funds into the effort or expose my family to any financial liability. We raised $75,000 to support the campaign, an amount that was then above the average for Pennsylvania congressional campaigns.

Ginny took charge of getting our literature into the hands of every possible voter through door-to-door distribution. She attacked her task with astonishing vigor and recruited a huge corps of volunteers. Our advertising and public relations featured a handsome brochure depicting me in a variety of settings. (The family picture portrayed a very pregnant Ginny and three sons looking not at all enthusiastic about the entire venture.)

We produced a billboard that showed me, with my crew cut and horn-rimmed glasses, holding an enormous wooden spoon; the accompanying message was "Dick Thornburgh will stir things up in Congress." This "stirred" considerable comment. We also ran a series of hilarious radio ads featuring local humorists. We generated a potpourri of campaign trinkets, such as emery boards, calorie counters, and baseball and football schedules with a somber Dick Thornburgh glaring out at the voter. I had somehow fastened on the idea of using Pittsburgh's official colors of gold and black on all our campaign materials, a combination mocked by most until years later, when a national survey concluded that these were the most effective colors that could be used! I also identified myself to voters as "Thornburgh as in Pittsburgh." (Different generations and individuals have spelled the Thornburgh name differently; some thirty variations included "burg," "borough," "brough," "borrow," "barrow," "burrow," "brugh," "bury," "berry," "boro" and "ber.") Voters may have learned from my quip how to spell my name, but they did not yet equate that with a desire to elect me.

We trekked endlessly through the district for old-fashioned door-to-door solicitations, stops at shopping centers and plant gates, and innumerable coffee sessions, for which hostesses had to be solicited and literature provided. The coffees all got the same pitch—an explanation of the need for new leadership to replace the "rubber-stamp" incumbent and a description of how Pittsburgh would prosper from having me in Congress. I must often have sounded as if I were running for mayor, but I tackled these sessions with relish. Sometimes as many as fifty neighbors would respond to an invitation, but in one case, when a solitary soul showed up, she got the full treatment anyway.

One rarely publicized gastronomic challenge of retail politics was illustrated on the evening when, after a busy campaign day, I grabbed a quick supper of baked beans and hot dog chunks at home with the boys before heading out again. After my first speech, I was offered a large plate of baked beans and hot dogs, which I had to wolf down, lest I be perceived as ungrateful. I then went on to a public housing project in a staunchly Democratic area, where my area chairman (later convicted on homicide charges) had attracted only the local clergyman to hear my pitch. After an abbreviated speech, I was ushered into the chairman's kitchen to savor his wife's specialty—hot dogs and baked beans—which she had prepared in copious quantities in anticipation of a large turnout. Needless to say, when I arrived home that night, I felt as if I had a medicine ball in my stomach.

My transportation through all this was the Star Car, a clunker of a Rambler station wagon, painted white and festooned with red and blue stars and an enormous "Thornburgh for Congress." The hit songs of 1966 (such as "Cherish," "Downtown," "Monday, Monday," and "Summer in the City") played over and over on the radio as I drove through Pittsburgh in search of votes and are indelibly implanted in my memory.

In the fall, Moorhead and I had three debates, the upshot of which was an accurate press verdict that we differed little on the issues. I nettled him somewhat by beginning a practice, followed in all my subsequent elections, of making a full financial disclosure. Moorhead, a millionaire, resisted this and, in those pre-Watergate days, got away with a "no comment." My own disclosure did not go down particularly well with Ginny, who valued our privacy and felt these matters were nobody else's business. She also felt compelled to explain to friends why we were worth so little!

Despite all our efforts, getting attention was difficult. We shot a television commercial but scrapped it, both because we lacked the funds for sufficient airtime and because I was blissfully unaware of the incredible effect this medium was to have on the political process. I was still a devotee of the print media and a more personal approach to politics. Our only big media plays came from piggybacking on the appearances of visiting dignitaries, including gubernatorial candidate Ray Shafer, Senator Scott, and Philadelphia district attorney Arlen Specter.

Just before election day, one issue, then just beginning to attract public notice, commanded some attention. My uneasiness about the war in Vietnam prompted me to undertake some lengthy discussions with a developing group of antiwar activists in the academic community. Although I did not agree with many of their views, I found it most useful to hear them out and to obtain their input. My own position was that a negotiated settlement should be sought in discussions that included the Viet Cong and that a suspension of offensive military operations might be in order to help turn the tide. I stated my views in a carefully crafted paper and a well-received speech to some 1,500 attendees at a local speak-out on the war. That very night, however, Democratic boss David L. Lawrence was fatally stricken at a final rally for party candidates not two blocks away, and that, of course, was the big story.

Late in the campaign, the *Wall Street Journal* ran a front-page article about the illegal Pittsburgh-area gambling operation of one Anthony Michael Grosso and the "protection" he was allegedly paying to local law enforcement officials. I issued a strident call for an investigation. While little response was forthcoming, both the corruption charges and Tony Grosso were to play major roles in my later career.

I believe to this day that we ran an excellent campaign, but there was no way that anyone, particularly an unknown, was going to beat Bill Moorhead. On election day, the margin was 82,732 to 38,528—slightly better than two to one. I took some minor solace in having cut into the Democrats' three-to-one registration edge.

At 2:30 the next morning, Ginny and I were awakened by a frantic call informing us that the building next to our campaign headquarters had blown up and the headquarters was on fire. I rolled over and prepared to go back to sleep. I had not counted on Ginny, whose response was, "We have to rescue the volunteer cards! Let's go!"

So off we went, in pouring rain, amid hoses, police, firefighters and knots of spectators, no doubt wondering what we were up to. Grabbing files by the armful, we ran toward our car. Ginny, eight months pregnant and exhausted, stumbled and dropped a file box into the gutter, which was awash with rainwater and the output of the fire hoses. Our three-by-five cards with all their valuable intelligence began to float away, the ink already running. In one last, superhuman effort, Ginny scooped up most of the spilled cards, and we returned home to bed. Later, we realized how fortunate it was that when the explosion occurred, the building was not full of celebrating campaign workers, as it would have been if we had won.

Three days after the election, on November 11, William Field Thornburgh surprised us by entering the world three weeks before we expected him. Bill Moorhead sent us a dozen roses in his honor.

ALL OUR EFFORT, of course, was not for naught. Ginny and I discovered how much we enjoyed the campaign process—meeting voters, puzzling through our positions on difficult issues, feeling that we could make a difference for the better in people's lives. Many friends and supporters from this campaign stayed with us throughout my public career. The reviews of our effort were generally favorable. Finally, the campaign solidified my relationship with Senator Scott's office and got us off on a good footing with soon-to-be Senator Richard Schweiker. These relationships were to prove advantageous later, when the powers that be were deciding who should become U.S. attorney western Pennsylvania.

Meanwhile, another Thornburgh campaign was soon under way. Ray Shafer, who had won the gubernatorial race, had made constitutional reform a priority for his administration, and in the spring of 1967 the voters approved the assembling of a limited constitutional convention. Three delegates were to be elected from each state senatorial district, and in each district, no more than two could be from the same party. I sought and obtained my party's designation as one of its two candidates from my heavily Democratic Forty-third District. The other was Robert Doyle, an attorney and former FBI agent.

My two primary emphases in the campaign were reform of the minor judiciary and reorganization of local government, particularly its consolidation into "efficient and responsive governing units," as I stated to the *Pittsburgh Press*. This bordered on the radical for Pittsburgh and Allegheny County, where "metropolitanism" had been a fighting word throughout the twentieth century. The city of Pittsburgh was, and remains to this day, the hole in the doughnut of greater Pittsburgh. The city had a population then of about half a million, while the surrounding 129 municipalities ranged from fifty to fifty thousand, totaling close to another million and a half. Attempts to create a governmental unit encompassing the city and the county had failed, with smaller communities' fears of being "swallowed up" being most vocally expressed by those local officials concerned for their sinecures or satrapies.

Bob Doyle and I garnered the endorsements of the two major newspapers, and I got the blessing of the Americans for Democratic Action, the only Republican to be favored by this liberal activist group. But citizen interest in the race was not particularly great. On election day, I won the minority delegate spot in our district by a minuscule 215 votes.

THE CONSTITUTIONAL Convention opened in December 1967 in Harrisburg. My first contribution was a critique of the draft rules of procedure for the convention; the final rules took most of my suggestions into account. The degree to which such "technicalities" can affect substantive outcomes often goes unrecognized. In this case, alphabetical seating intermixing Republican and Democratic delegates, rather than the usual caucus format, was crucial to the convention's ultimate success.

I also introduced the first proposed amendment to the constitution: the Pennsylvania Bar Association's judicial reform plan, upon which I had worked for the last five years. The amendment provided for merit selection of judges and for replacement of the minor judiciary with community courts presided over by professional judges.

Attacks on the proposal focused primarily on the merit selection provisions. After considerable debate, the forty-two-member Judiciary Committee reported out an amended version by a 22–16 vote, the bare minimum required. This version applied merit selection to the appellate courts and established a local option for all others. Unfortunately, the convention decided to require a citizen referendum in 1969 on even this watered-down proposal. In the absence of voter approval, the worst result imaginable would be forthcoming as "reform"—continued partisan election of all judges followed by "yes-no" retention elections at regular intervals.

The minor judiciary was a tougher nut to crack. The committee's eventual proposal, adopted again by the bare minimum of votes, was to retain the existing system, except in Philadelphia, but to allow local voters to replace it with community courts. As reported in the *Post-Gazette*, my response was emphatic: "We're not giving up. We'll fight on the convention floor to get rid of the justices of the peace. This is not the end." Ginny reported to me that, when she read that account to the boys at breakfast, they responded, "Way to go, Dad!" However, the convention ultimately approved the committee's watered-down proposal.

Before final action was taken on the judiciary article, the Philadelphia Republican delegation hosted a dinner at which I first met the fabled Billy Meehan, one of the last of the big-city Republican bosses. The dinner was clearly meant to build support for an amendment that would add ten judges to the Philadelphia Court of Common Pleas, all to be appointed by the governor, presumably from a list presented by Meehan. During floor debate, however, I characterized the amendment as "a gross usurpation of the legislative process," and it was voted down. This did not endear me to the Philadelphia Republican organization, as I was to be reminded years later.

The convention passed a strong local-government proposal providing for home rule, merger and consolidation and more efficient procedures. And fellow delegate K. Leroy Irvis and I cosponsored a constitutional provision mandating the establishment of a public defender's office in every county.

The convention closed on schedule on February 28, 1968, and I embarked on a vigorous speaking tour to solicit voter support for our proposals. Strong and articulate opposition developed, but the electorate approved all of the amendments that May. (I was chosen the Republican committeeman for the first district of the fourteenth ward in the same election.) Unfortunately, the next year the watered-down judicial merit selection plan was defeated in its separate referendum, and judicial selection in Pennsylvania remained in the Dark Ages.

In my view, Ray Shafer has never received enough credit for making constitutional reform a priority, postponing budgetary and tax measures for later consideration. The resolution of these questions eventually cost him dearly in public support.

SHORTLY AFTER the convention, H. J. (Jack) Heinz II and Joseph Hughes of the Mellon interests asked me to participate in New York governor Nelson Rockefeller's campaign for the 1968 Republican presidential nomination. Almost immediately, however, Rockefeller announced that he was not going to run. Within ten days, after a sound showing by maverick antiwar senator Eugene McCarthy in the New Hampshire primary, President Johnson made the dramatic announcement that he would not run either. And Senator Robert Kennedy entered the race.

Within less than a week, on April 4, came the devastating news of the assassination of the Reverend Martin Luther King Jr., the nation's most prominent black civil rights leader. The assassination set off civil disturbances around the country, and soon we could see palls of smoke rising from the Hill District, Pittsburgh's largest African American community. The National Guard was dispatched. The year before, because of my activities in support of providing legal counsel for indigent persons, I had accepted an invitation to join the board of directors of the local American Civil Liberties Union chapter. Thus, I received a call to join other ACLU lawyers at the downtown police station to assist those being arrested. Outraged myself at the King assassination, I spent the night providing basic legal advice to a stream of black arrestees, principally very frightened and very agitated young men.

Later my civil rights activities brought me another unconventional "client." A sizable demonstration was mounted to protest the lack of jobs for black construction workers. Among those arrested was Nate "Available" Smith (so named during his previous prizefighting career), head of Operation DIG, a group working to increase minority employment. His lawyer, Dan Berger, a prominent liberal Democrat and fellow ACLU board member, recommended that he have a Republican counsel as well and suggested me. I appeared with Dan, the charges against Nate were dismissed (they no doubt lacked any substance anyway) and I had a friend for life in Nate, a charming rogue with an infinite capacity for hustle. By year-end, my representation of Nate and my work with the ACLU, the Neighborhood Legal Services Association and the bar association's Public Service Committee had often put me at odds with District Attorney Duggan's hard-line "law and order" office.

One more horrendous event was yet to chill our nation. Ginny and I awoke the morning of June 5 to learn, via our bedside radio, that Robert Kennedy had been assassinated. I literally buried my head in my pillow in disbelief and horror. Our nation seemed to be losing its bearings, careening from one violent act to another. What could we do to restore its center of gravity?

The opportunity to throw myself into a frenzy of activity was at hand. Early in May, Governor Rockefeller had reentered the presidential race. His team had recruited me as their western Pennsylvania chairman, and we began immediately to gear up. Money, for once, was literally no object, and all of the state Republican leaders were in the governor's camp. Locally, the Hillman forces leaned toward Rockefeller, but those headed by Duggan were committed to former vice president Richard Nixon.

The Rockefeller candidacy foundered when the last-minute entry of California governor Ronald Reagan split the anti-Nixon vote. In the fall, I joined the Nixon effort. A highlight for me was being joined by John Thornburgh, now eleven, at 4:30 A.M. on election day to put a door hanger upon every doorknob in our neighborhood.

Nixon had learned important lessons from Goldwater's disastrous 1964 campaign. No longer were shrill and simplistic attacks on the "radical" opposition the centerpiece of the Republican message. Racist and jingoistic appeals, not being part of the candidate's makeup, were shelved, fortunately seldom to reappear in GOP campaigns. The Democrats proved to be their own worst enemy; the turmoil within the party reached a crescendo during its convention in Chicago, which President Johnson could not even attend. Nonetheless, with Alabama governor George Wallace siphoning off some of the far right votes, Nixon's victory over Hubert Humphrey, LBJ's vice president, was a narrow one. We celebrated it with somewhat muted enthusiasm. The cataclysmic events of 1968 were ominous harbingers of ongoing racial, ideological and generational conflicts.

DURING ALL THIS political activity, our family reached a number of important milestones as well. Peter's regimen changed dramatically when the staff at the Home for Crippled Children told us they had done all they could for him and it was time for him to move on. They were absolutely correct, but Ginny and I had come to depend so much on them that the news came as quite a shock. We had always kept in mind the possibility that Peter might someday have to be institutionalized, but as time went on, we became more and more determined to keep him within the family that he had enriched beyond description and to which he meant so much.

His traumatic entry into the public school system helped to galvanize Ginny into a lifetime of advocacy for persons with disabilities. When she went to visit Peter's proposed new surroundings at Larimer School in East Liberty, she was ushered into a dark, dank basement classroom near the furnace. A group of students, aged six to twelve, were occupied in making pot holders. When Ginny confronted the principal, she was coolly told, "These kids don't care." Furious, she immediately set about to remedy the burden of second-class citizenship imposed on children and adults with mental retardation in our community. Her involvement with the Allegheny County Chapter of the Pennsylvania Association for Retarded Citizens (now ACHIEVA) eventually led her to its presidency and to leadership in statewide and national efforts to improve care for these and other persons with disabilities.

Ginny and I, Presbyterian and Episcopalian, respectively, had searched for a site to worship where we were both comfortable and finally settled on a local Presbyterian church. Ginny became active in an attempt, opposed by conservative elements, to make our church more relevant to the community and more socially responsible. One of her efforts was to include Peter in our family's worship. As she noted, upon Bill's arrival, many in the congregation asked us, "When are we going to see that beautiful new baby of yours in the nursery?" But no one asked about Peter, generally at home on Sunday mornings with a sitter.

Ginny secured the blessing of the church to open a Sunday school class for mentally retarded children, found the space and a volunteer teacher with a special education background, and advertised the availability of the class. But on opening day, Peter was the only one who showed up. This was a heartbreaker for Ginny. Did families with children with mental retardation not believe that the church cared about them? Were they so accustomed to being excluded that they couldn't even imagine a welcoming church? These questions and the general absence of people with disabilities from worship services were to haunt her for years and foreshadowed her very important work to make all houses of worship more welcoming.

NOT SURPRISINGLY, my political preoccupations had not advanced my law firm career. The firm had continued to pay me an associate's salary during my congressional campaign and my stint at the Constitutional Convention, although I was devoting 100 percent of my time to non-firm matters. Of course, I was immensely grateful for their support. Even when I was in the office, however, my productivity was low, and my ability to carry my share of the load seemed actually to be declining. While several of my contemporaries and, by this time, my juniors, had become partners, my own efforts did not warrant such recognition, and I knew it. This situation clearly could not continue indefinitely. By 1968, I had resumed a rather full schedule at the firm, but as the year drew to a close, I was obliged to take stock of my prospects.

I was seriously considering running for mayor of Pittsburgh in 1969—perhaps even on a "fusion" ticket—and felt much more secure than I had four years earlier about challenging Mayor Barr. I had already begun a round of radio and television appearances to discuss the city's problems. As luck would have it, I was presented with a major issue at year-end, when the mayor attempted to secure a $2,500 pay raise from the City Council. My examination of the law indicated that such a raise was clearly illegal. The legislature in 1965 had stipulated that the mayor's salary "shall not be increased or diminished during the term for which he shall have been elected." I held a widely covered press conference to attack the raise; the mayor and his lawyer, the city solicitor, were obliged to agree with me and to back down.

This episode projected me into the public view, but I needed a broader theme upon which to build a true reform campaign. This I found in the issue of home rule. The new constitutional amendments authorized all local government units to adopt home rule charters, which would enable the people to govern themselves free of interference from Harrisburg. Home rule also offered the opportunity to streamline government, reducing the number of local government units and rationalizing the often duplicative and overlapping provision of municipal services. Entrenched political interests, predictably, were not at all enthusiastic about such changes.

Over the 1968 Christmas holidays, I drafted a paper entitled "Blue Print for Modern Government: A Home Rule Charter for Pittsburgh." This package of recommendations—some of which, years later, were actually included in the Pittsburgh charter—received a good deal of publicity and editorial approval. By this time media commentary regularly referred to me as "a potential Republican candidate for mayor," and I began a series of discussions with party leaders and participants in our 1966 congressional effort to sketch some plans for the race.

But my potential candidacy was derailed by an unexpected February phone call from Elsie Hillman, by then the Republican county chairwoman. Speaking for Senators Scott and Schweiker, she inquired about my interest in being appointed by President Nixon as United States attorney for western Pennsylvania.

4

Federal Prosecutor

MY INITIAL RESPONSE to Elsie's question was, "What does a U.S. attorney do?" Nonetheless, I set about to explore the ramifications of the offer. Elsie and Bob Duggan were engaged in a struggle over the position, which Duggan sought for his cousin, First Assistant District Attorney James Dunn. I found the intensity of Duggan's opposition to me somewhat surprising, as we had had a cordial enough relationship, and he had even campaigned for me in 1966. Only in years to come did the probable reasons for his concern over the appointment of someone not under his control become apparent.

After educating myself on the nature of the job, I agreed to become a candidate for U.S. attorney, abandoning the mayoral race. This was the first of a number of occasions on which my career was to take a totally unexpected turn. I never devised a game plan for my political life, and I have counseled younger aspirants that attempting to do so is folly. It is simply impossible to chart a clear course to a particular office; huge elements of uncertainty and chance come into play, as they do in all careers. The course of my public life has therefore been a function of the opportunities with which I have been blessed.

Nixon diehards promptly suggested that my work for Rockefeller disqualified me from the position. They even claimed that I had been a member of "Republicans for Johnson," an allegation quickly refuted by the former chair of that effort. A further complication was resentment over a supposed Kirkpatrick "monopoly" on high-level appointments. Governor Shafer had appointed Kirkpatrick partner Tom Pomeroy to the Pennsylvania Supreme Court. Other Kirkpatrick "alumni" in office included Judge Cohill and John Tabor, who had served, successively, as Pennsylvania's secretary of commerce, secretary of internal affairs and secretary of labor and industry.

After a lengthy FBI background check (my first experience with having my friends and neighbors questioned about me and my lifestyle) and a visit to the Department of Justice in Washington for a once-over, I was officially nominated and unanimously confirmed. My swearing-in ceremony on June 4, 1969, marked my first ascendance to full-time public office. I felt a special sense of awe in swearing to "uphold the Constitution of the United States against all enemies, foreign and domestic," a challenge that was to prove worthy of my every effort.

Coincident with my nomination as U.S. attorney, I had been named the nonsalaried chairman of the Allegheny County Regional Planning Council for the Pennsylvania Crime Commission (later the Governor's Justice Commission). This agency was charged with devising plans for the expenditure of federal funds under the Omnibus Crime Control and Safe Streets Act of 1968 to improve police, prosecution, courts and correctional institutions. There was later some question as to whether, as a federal official, I should have held this post; I rationalized the seeming conflict by reminding myself that I had accepted it before assuming federal office. By holding both positions, I became somewhat of a czar on criminal justice in the county—a position I put to good use. Needless to say, this did not endear me further to Bob Duggan.

During my tenure, the council took the first systematic look ever at the criminal justice system in Allegheny County. Our recommendations included 100 percent state funding of the courts and correctional systems; better training and compensation for probation and correctional personnel; more halfway-house and work-release programs; a countywide police force to handle major investigations; community-based centers for alcohol and drug abusers; and more full-time, amply compensated prosecutors and public defenders. Central to all of our proposals was a reduction in the number of police forces in the county. There were 115 such forces, ranging from the city of Pittsburgh's sizable and professional department to one that depended on part-time officers who passed a single revolver from hand to hand with every shift change. Our proposal for regional police forces, however, not only threatened 115 chiefs but raised the same specter of metropolitan government that had caused home rule efforts to founder.

My service on the council ended rather abruptly. I had been advised to talk to Sam Begler, Governor Shapp's patronage boss, if I wanted to keep my position. Begler had numerous affiliations with organized crime figures, and I was not about to seek his support. Upon my return from a trip to Japan for supposedly up-and-coming leaders in our country in December 1972, I discovered that the council had undergone a "purge" clearly designed to strengthen the interests of Sheriff Eugene Coon, the county Democratic Party chairman. That was the last straw, and I resigned with a strong blast at the politicizing of the council's mission. A couple of other members followed suit, and most of the staff soon resigned as well. The council was never again to play a vital role.

I was obliged to give up several other fulfilling activities because of the press of time or potential conflicts of interest. The ACLU was bound to be a constant litigant in the federal courts. Moreover, I was increasingly uneasy with its shift toward more purely political involvement in areas such as antiwar activity, draft resistance and the protection of pornography. Later it would move on to the death penalty, homosexual rights and abortion. Since all of these matters far transcended my original reasons for involvement with the ACLU—the right to counsel for indigent persons and the rights of persons with disabilities—I was, in years to come, to be completely at ease with my resignation.

More regrettable was the need to resign from the board of the Neighborhood Legal Services Association because of its potential involvement in federal litigation. I was sorry that I could not remain active in the effort to secure counsel for indigent persons. I did remain a board member of the Urban League of Pittsburgh, then the most effective civil rights group in the community.

MY FIRST OFFICIAL encounter with Chief Judge Wallace Gourley of the U.S. District Court for the Western District of Pennsylvania set a tone for my conduct as U.S. attorney that was to serve me well. At the time, however, it was far from felicitous.

A juror in a Federal Employers Liability Act suit had reported to District Judge Edward Dumbauld that a priest had approached her on behalf of the plaintiff, and a mistrial was declared. Subsequently Robert and Constance Torquato were indicted for instigating the attempted "fix."

Robert Torquato had previously served as chief deputy clerk of the district court. Federal investigators suspected that the real moving party had been the firm of Evans, Ivory & Evans, which had represented the plaintiff and now represented Constance Torquato. To develop the connection between the Torquatos and the firm, telephone records were lawfully obtained from the phone company. The firm predictably objected to their use in the trial. Shortly after I took office, this matter came on for argument before Judge Gourley. Although a Department of Justice attorney from Washington was trying the case, the office was shorthanded, so it fell to me to argue this motion.

At attorney Robert Ivory's suggestion that the judge resolve the matter by examining the government's file in the case, Judge Gourley asked for the file. I responded by requesting an open hearing instead. The judge erupted, "This is the first time I ever have had a United States attorney deny me the right to look at government files. I have been insulted before, but this is the first time by a United States attorney!" Whereupon he stormed off the bench, leaving Ivory and me in an empty courtroom. Needless to say, I did not relish being told that I had insulted a veteran jurist in my maiden courtroom appearance as U.S. attorney. It did not help that the newspapers gave the story wide play.

A strange sequence of events then unfolded. Judge Gourley first signed, then vacated an order barring the phone records. Next he removed himself from the case altogether and shortly thereafter resigned as chief judge, assuming senior status. To this day, I don't know exactly what prompted this precipitous series of actions, but we had clearly touched a sensitive nerve. Ultimately, the Torquatos were convicted—and I ended up with a useful reputation as a forceful advocate for the government, not to be intimidated by judicial bluster.

ON THE VERY DAY that my appointment was announced, the Pennsylvania Crime Commission released its first report on organized crime in the state. Its conclusions were startling. The report outlined a network of activities in illegal gambling, narcotics, extortion, labor racketeering and public corruption. Among its more sensational disclosures was an estimate that law enforcement officials in Allegheny County were paid $4–6 million a year to protect illegal activities. The report also concluded that even the best state and local law enforcement agencies were ill equipped to deal with sophisticated organized crime operations.

Thus, from the very outset of my tenure, the battle against organized crime became a top priority. Never before had a concerted effort been mounted to deal with mob operations in western Pennsylvania. Such an effort could make a real contribution to the quality of life in communities where racketeers had gained a foothold.

Not long after I took office, the FBI arrested five key members of the Sebastian John La Rocca family for misuse of labor union welfare and pension funds. This was headline news in Pittsburgh, as La Rocca was the acknowledged boss of organized crime in western Pennsylvania. Shortly thereafter, I held my first press conference on the issue. I set forth plans for stepped-up antiracketeering efforts, including better coordination and cooperation among federal, state and local agencies, as well as use of a special strike force to concentrate federal efforts. Before year-end, I assigned two assistant U.S. attorneys to concentrate on battling organized crime.

One of the more curious writings I encountered during my "crash course" on organized crime was the so-called Susce Report, prepared in 1943 by Andrew Susce, a rookie revenue agent in the Pittsburgh office of the then Bureau of Internal Revenue. Susce became fascinated by local organized-crime figures and compiled a sizable file on their activities and related political corruption. His superiors discouraged him—partly, I suspect, because they felt they lacked jurisdiction over this type of crime, but doubtless partly out of fear of powerful political figures in the Lawrence machine. Pulitzer Prize-winning *Post-Gazette* reporter Ray Sprigle described the situation in Pittsburgh as follows: "Racket bosses elect and finance aldermen and constables. The ward chairmen then maintain and protect the operation of the racket bosses in their wards through control of the police department and police inspectors."

Given the later disclosure of high-level corruption within the Bureau of Internal Revenue, it is not inconceivable that an effort was mounted to cover up Susce's information. Susce himself believed this had happened, particularly since his investigation eventually resulted in his termination. He was still seeking vindication when I took office. Susce was no Eliot Ness, but I am convinced that, if qualified investigators had followed up on his findings in a timely manner, organized crime and public corruption in Pittsburgh could well have been dealt an early deathblow.

As it was, new laws and additional resources would be necessary to pursue the mob effectively. The Omnibus Crime Control and Safe Streets Act of 1968 had set forth a procedure for court-authorized wiretapping—a kind of "electronic search warrant"—that would permit federal agents to burrow inside illegal operations to collect evidence. The year after I took office, the Organized Crime Control Act of 1970 vastly increased federal jurisdiction over racketeering. It defined new federal offenses in the areas of illegal gambling (which I called the "cash register" of organized crime) and public corruption; provided for witness immunity to compel underlings to testify against bosses; created the Racketeer-Influenced and Corrupt Organizations (RICO) Act to reach mob fronts posing as legitimate businesses; lengthened prison sentences for racketeering; and authorized special investigative grand juries to concentrate on organized crime. These tools were to transform the role of the U.S. attorneys.

In June 1970, I secured a commitment from the Justice Department to establish a special strike force in Pittsburgh, the fourteenth such antimob field office in the nation. By year-end, we had eighteen prosecutors on board, twice the number in place when I took office. Two of these—Jim Seif, who, while a Yale student, had put in long hours on my congressional campaign, and Jay Waldman, who had served as a judicial law clerk to an old family friend from Rosslyn Farms—were to play major roles in my career.

It was no coincidence that the first case I tried in my life involved a mob figure, albeit a minor one. To learn the litigation ropes, I had haunted the federal courtrooms for months. This made my assistants very nervous, as they thought I was monitoring their trial performance. In reality, I was learning where to stand in the courtroom and how to enter documents into evidence. My unwitting assistants did a good job teaching me the basics. In early 1970, I assigned myself the case of Augustine Ferrone, charged with assaulting three IRS agents who had raided his home with a warrant in search of sports-gambling paraphernalia. At one point, remembering what my coaches had taught me (examine your own witnesses from the back of the jury box, so that they are eyeballing the jurors; examine the defense witnesses up close, to deny them eye contact with the jury), I edged close to a defense witness, only to have the judge bark at me, "Go back to where you were for the other witnesses! What have you been doing? Reading books on how to try a case?" I retreated in some embarrassment, cognizant of how close to the truth he had come.

With Ferrone's conviction, I began a winning streak that was to continue for five exciting years. I had finally become a true litigator. One of my family's enduring memories from this period is of me sitting in my library chair, almost oblivious to them, meticulously mapping out trial strategies on a yellow legal pad. My corporate training was not wasted, however. In one complicated fraud case, an assistant asked me for help in drafting an indictment that coherently connected the parties and the offenses. My days of working with complicated indentures and underwriting agreements led me to suggest that he add a definitions section, which would allow him to abbreviate later references to the defined terms. Our litigators had not been in the habit of using definitions sections, but the practice proved very useful.

Court-authorized wiretapping offered us an unprecedented opportunity to gather evidence, especially against major gambling and narcotics operations. We were required to show the court that we had probable cause to believe that identified telephones were being used in illegal activities; work with the phone company to make the proper connections; and then monitor and record relevant conversations for use in court. Our local FBI office tackled this assignment with zeal.

The effort almost died aborning, however, because of sloppy practices at the Department of Justice in Washington. We were flabbergasted to learn that a number of wiretap authorizations required to be signed by the attorney general, then John Mitchell, were instead signed by one of his assistants. The Supreme Court ultimately threw out a whole group of cases based on this faulty procedure. There had been a furor about court-authorized wiretapping when the legislation was passed, with some viewing it as a threat to civil liberties. As a result, the U.S. attorneys had considered it particularly important to comply strictly with the prerequisites of the law, and it was a shock to discover that some of our colleagues in Washington thought differently. Fortunately, only a couple of our minor wiretaps were thrown out.

The first successful wiretaps in western Pennsylvania helped bring down the massive sports-gambling operation of Robert "Bobby I" Iannelli. After accumulating sufficient wiretap evidence, over 100 FBI agents staged a series of raids on twenty-two suspected gambling locations on November 21, 1970, seizing gambling records and paraphernalia. This action sent shock waves through the illegal-gambling community, which had thought only interstate activities were within the reach of federal investigators. It also produced some personal satisfaction in the form of a message on my desk the following Monday morning: "A lady from McKees Rocks called to say 'Thank you.' Her husband could not place a bet. She said 'We had a nice day at home Sunday.'"

In early 1971, we impaneled the first special grand jury in the nation under the 1970 Organized Crime Control Act. The evidence gathered in the raids was presented, and an indictment was returned against Iannelli and twenty-five others on federal gambling charges. All were subsequently convicted. We had struck our first effective blow at the rackets.

We obtained a number of other gambling convictions, but our primary target was the biggest operator of them all—Tony Grosso. My file review when I assumed office had moved Grosso's numbers operation and alleged protection payoffs to the top of our priority list. During more than twenty years in the illegal numbers business, Grosso had spent only six months in jail, a condition we were determined to remedy.

By June 1971, we had enough probable cause to begin two weeks of wiretapping of Grosso's far-flung empire, followed by raids on thirty separate locations. On March 29, 1972, the special grand jury returned indictments against forty executive-level members of this notorious crime cartel, later joined by fifteen more. The evidence established a $50,000-a-day volume for the business and detailed an intricate network of telephone relay stations through which the business was handled.

After considerable pretrial skirmishing, the first case, involving Tony, his brother Sam and two other top executives of the organization, came to trial in late April 1973. The strike force's Ken Bravo and I painstakingly led the jury through eighty-seven wiretapped conversations and through explanations of the seized records by witnesses compelled to testify under grants of immunity. Grosso offered no defense.

The jury found the four defendants guilty on all counts, and all the remaining defendants were convicted or pleaded guilty thereafter. We had finally broken the back of one of the country's biggest illegal numbers operations. Tony himself received the maximum sentence of ten years in prison, and the organization, for the time being, was left in shambles. Furthermore, alert FBI work turned up an attempt to "fix" the jury. Tony was indicted on that charge as well, and his bond, pending appeal, was revoked. Tony Grosso was finally on his way to a federal prison.

Later, a special grand jury impaneled in Erie probed gambling operations in northwestern Pennsylvania. It returned three indictments against twenty-two individuals involved in illegal sports and numbers wagers estimated at $15 million a year.

Our battle with organized crime led to a battle with the Pennsylvania Crime Commission, later joined by the ACLU. The commission had compiled, but never released to the public, a list of over 375 legitimate businesses involved in varying ways with criminal syndicates. I suggested to the commission that Pennsylvania citizens might find this "shoppers' guide" useful. My request went unheeded. In July 1972, it was discovered that the

Allegheny County mass transit agency had entered into a contract to have all its vehicles washed at a car wash owned and operated by Sebastian John La Rocca. The following year, a state police retirement fund was disclosed to have accepted contributions from a firm associated with Russell Bufalino, the mob's northeastern Pennsylvania boss. Still the list went unpublished. I asked, "If the state police and governmental authorities don't know who they are dealing with, how can the ordinary businessman be expected to refrain from patronizing mob-controlled enterprises?" A year and a half later, Attorney General Israel Packel, chairman of the commission, responded that release of the list would be "inappropriate." The ACLU agreed that "innocent persons" might be identified, and my quest was stymied.

A strike force crackdown on labor racketeering had mixed results. Longtime mob associate Tom Pecora, head of Local 1058 of the Laborers Union, was convicted of receiving $25,000 in "gifts" solicited from employers, and United Mine Workers (UMW) District 5 president Michael Budzanoski and an associate were convicted of filing false expense accounts. Embezzlement convictions were obtained against Kenneth D. Albertson of an Erie local of the International Brotherhood of Painters and Allied Trades; three officials of the Westinghouse Electric Corporation Salaried Employees Union; Paul Hilbert, former District 15 director of the United Steel Workers; and Carl Carnish, former secretary-treasurer of Local 3 of the International Association of Bridge, Structural and Ornamental Iron Workers. However, efforts to prosecute Teamsters boss Henry Trotto and Boilermakers head Fred Gualtieri were unsuccessful. The strike force also did some innovative work in applying the mail fraud statutes to arson cases. Proof of falsified insurance claims sent through the mail resulted in several mob figures being convicted of arson.

In my first experience with the tenacity and resourcefulness of the FBI, our office had been peripherally involved in a far more somber union-related case directed out of Washington. On December 31, 1969, UMW official Joseph "Jock" Yablonski, his wife, Margaret, and his daughter, Charlotte, had been murdered in their bedrooms. Yablonski, although reputed to have his own blemishes, was then engaged in a "reform" effort to turn out of office longtime UMW boss, W. A. "Tony" Boyle.

Investigators rapidly identified the triggermen, Aubran "Buddy" Martin, Paul Gilly and Claude Vealey, and they, along with Gilly's wife, Annette, and her father, Silous Huddleston, were convicted or pleaded guilty. Mrs. Gilly told prosecutors that Huddleston, who was also a UMW official, and William Prater, a UMW organizer, had funneled cash from union higher-ups to the killers, and that the slayings had had Tony Boyle's approval. Huddleston implicated Prater and Albert E. Pass, a member of the UMW international executive board.

Prater was indicted on federal conspiracy charges stating that Yablonski had been murdered to prevent him from presenting evidence of criminal conduct to a federal grand jury looking into UMW matters. Pass was indicted as well. Shortly thereafter, Boyle himself was called before the grand jury, together with three top aides. By that time, Boyle's election had been set aside.

Prater and Pass were convicted in state court. In September 1973, a federal indictment charged Boyle with directing Pass and William J. Turnblazer, another UMW official, to arrange for Yablonski's murder and authorizing the transfer of nearly $20,000 from union headquarters in Washington to pay the killers. Boyle was eventually convicted in state court and sentenced to life in prison.

This ghastly case made me a firm believer in a limited death penalty in certain cases of willful premeditated murder. I had been somewhat ambivalent on the subject up to then and had actually favored dismantling the state's electric chair to frustrate the application of its then overbroad death penalty statute. But cases like this were different. The killers had systematically stalked the Yablonski family, awaiting their chance. Though it could not be proven empirically, common sense told me that murderers who stalked their quarry over an extended period, rather than acting in the heat of the moment, might rethink their intentions if they risked forfeiting their own lives. The United States Supreme Court would ultimately uphold the death penalty and set down limits forestalling, to the maximum extent possible, any injustice in its application. Of course, this problem has been further neutralized of late by developments in the use of DNA evidence.

OF OUR VARIOUS political corruption cases, that of the talking telephone pole was one of the more amusing. It resulted in the first conviction under the 1968 federal statute barring illegal interception of phone conversations.

Michael Newman, an up-and-coming thirty-year-old Democratic city councilman in McKeesport, had been accused of improprieties in the use of city-owned equipment to remove rubbish from a car wash in which he had a financial interest. School Director Eugene T. O'Neill made these "free work" charges at an open City Council meeting. Shortly thereafter,

Mrs. O'Neill, on the way to a neighbor's home, heard her daughter's voice coming from a telephone pole outside.

When O'Neill came home that evening, his wife told him the phone was tapped. He told her, "You wouldn't know a wiretap if you saw one," but went outside to check out the system. When his wife picked up the phone, he heard from the pole a dial tone and then her voice. Meanwhile, a large crowd had gathered, including the police, alerted by a Bell employee to whom O'Neill had passed on his wife's concern. They lowered from the pole a large plastic-wrapped box in which they found a tape recorder.

A Bell employee, Thomas Nee, was swiftly identified as the wiretapper. He had twice been seen near the pole, and the FBI identified his voice on one of the tapes recovered with the recorder. On the day in question, he had inadvertently pushed the "broadcast" button rather than the "record" button. Nee pleaded guilty and proceeded to implicate Newman, who was promptly indicted. At the trial, Nee recounted that Newman had approached him for help in learning how much O'Neill actually knew about the alleged free work at Newman's car wash. Newman was convicted—and defeated in his bid for reelection.

Other public officials successfully prosecuted on corruption charges included former state representative Leonard Sweeney; Sheriff John Heinman of Beaver County; Mayor John Matz and other public officials in the Borough of Clairton; three North Braddock borough councilmen; and Police Chief Donald Crandall of North Versailles Township.

Republican congressman Irving Whalley pleaded guilty to payroll padding, and our investigation of Democratic congressman Frank Clark resulted in his conviction on similar charges after I left the office. Howard Coe, U.S. Customs Service port director, was given a five-year prison sentence for embezzling over $9,000 in customs duties. Investigations undertaken after my departure uncovered widespread corruption in the Pennsylvania Department of Transportation's county operations.

State Representative Max Homer had shaken down my boyhood friend Tucker Gordon's family petroleum business in connection with the issuance of building permits. His conviction was one of two cases that gave me particular satisfaction because they involved friends victimized by criminal conduct. I was proud of their coming forward to blow the whistle on powerful figures in their community. The other case involved mob figures who had attempted to extort $10,000 from the gardeners who helped to tend the landscaping at our home.

My interest in bringing to heel people of power and substance who abused the process was to continue throughout my career. I was proud that Democrats and Republicans alike were, if corrupt, pursued with equal vigor, as I felt that betrayal of the public trust was subversive of our democratic processes.

Public interest in the corruption and racketeering cases was high, and I spoke to an increasing number of groups about our efforts. In an address to Private Jacob Greenfield Post 181, Jewish War Veterans, on February 28, 1971, I coined a phrase that was to characterize the principal focus of our office during the balance of my tenure.

Many in this country see a threat in what they term the "military-industrial complex." In western Pennsylvania, I say they should direct their attention to the "politico-racket complex" which has a near stranglehold on a number of communities in our area.

To my mind, there is no more subversive element in this land than the corrupting influence of organized crime syndicates which seek to control whole sections of our government, economy and community life. [It] can happen anywhere—in any community where the criminal conglomerates dealing in illegal gambling, narcotics, loan-sharking, labor-racketeering and the like are successful in efforts to "buy off" legitimate government.

[I]f the "politico-racket complex" is not headed off, a whole generation of American youth may come to maturity accepting the "fix" and the payoff as a way of life and our system of justice will be dealt a mortal blow.

The pursuit of the "politico-racket complex" and, eventually, all forms of public corruption was to dominate the efforts of federal law enforcement in western Pennsylvania during the 1970s. By the time I left office in mid-1975, we had mounted an unprecedented effort against corruption at the federal, state and local levels.

This effort began on a small scale. An IRS gambling investigation coordinated with the state police and the Westmoreland County district attorney disclosed that local numbers boss James Chick had paid protection money to Mayor Michael Reihl and Police Chief Arthur Rinaldi of the Borough of Jeannette. The three were indicted in July 1971 and ultimately convicted. Both the indictments and the convictions were the first in the nation under the anticorruption provisions of the 1970 Organized Crime Control Act.

Much more spectacular results were to come. IRS agents had long been looking into allegations of corruption within the Detective Bureau of District Attorney Duggan's office. Most of these allegations centered on payoffs to the chief of the Racket Squad, Samuel G. Ferraro, to protect illegal gambling operations.

When I assumed office, IRS agents informed me that eleven detectives sought to be interviewed in connection with the corruption allegations had refused to testify on the ground that their testimony might incriminate them. All were represented by Samuel Reich, counsel for Sam Ferraro. We asked a federal grand jury to investigate this potential obstruction of the IRS inquiry, not the Ferraro allegations themselves. Subpoenas were issued to the detectives in the summer of 1970, and most once again asserted their Fifth Amendment rights. I advised Duggan of this development to give him the chance to clean up his own office. No response was forthcoming.

Faced with what the *Pittsburgh Post-Gazette* later called a "conspiracy of silence," we began to bring the detectives before a federal judge. Pursuant to our request under the 1970 act, he compelled them to testify, on condition that truthful testimony could not be used against them in a criminal proceeding. Several of the detectives then testified falsely that they were ignorant of any payoffs, and we were able to get them convicted of perjury. Despite criticism concerning his detectives' activities, the well-financed Duggan was elected to a third term in November 1972 over a weak Democratic candidate who ran a lackluster campaign.

The allegations against Ferraro, however, were too much for officials in Hampton Township, where he had been hired as public safety director in 1970. He was fired soon after being "fingered" by a numbers writer at one of the detectives' trials. In February 1973, Ferraro was indicted for income tax fraud growing out of a failure to report over $20,000 in illegal payoffs from racketeers from 1966 through 1968.

The news of Ferraro's indictment broke shortly after Tony Grosso began his ten-year prison sentence. Soon Grosso contacted FBI Special Agent Ron Wetherington and began unfolding an extraordinary tale of a string of payoffs made to Allegheny County law enforcement officials to protect his operations. The only quid pro quo for his cooperation was that our office would, as in any other case, bring it to the attention of the judge at any hearing on a request for a reduced sentence.

Grosso's testimony led to a superseding indictment alleging that Ferraro had received over $289,000 in unreported income, including payoffs of $4,950 per month from Grosso from July 1966 to July 1971. An additional count under the anticorruption provisions of the 1970 act charged a conspiracy to obstruct law enforcement.

Meanwhile, the IRS, suspecting that the payoff trail had not stopped with Ferraro, had begun investigating Duggan's own finances. This was an extremely delicate matter, because Duggan not only was a prominent elected official but also had strong connections with the Nixon administration. Indeed, Deputy Attorney General Dick Kleindienst had come to Pittsburgh for a Duggan fund-raiser just two days before the perjury indictment of the first detective, Jim Hockenberry. The Department of Justice in Washington generally gave the U.S. attorneys' offices a reasonably free hand, but both the IRS and I were careful to keep our Washington counterparts closely apprised of our actions in this case.

The IRS came to focus upon a business called Abstracts, Incorporated, ostensibly set up to handle the searching of real estate titles as an adjunct to Duggan's private law practice. Duggan's grand jury testimony shed little light on this "inactive" corporation, but its bank accounts evidenced substantial financial activity. When the grand jury subpoenaed his personal financial records, Duggan stated that he intended to assert his Fifth Amendment privilege.

Media attention now turned, however, to the trial of Sam Ferraro. The FBI and the IRS, in a rare spirit of cooperation, were fully geared up for Pittsburgh's most sensational criminal trial in years.

My first surprise witness was Jim Hockenberry. Deciding to "clear his conscience," Hockenberry testified that he had received payoffs from a numbers writer and delivered them to Sam Ferraro. The next witnesses, a numbers writer and his lady friend, testified that he had paid Ferraro up to $500 a month for "protection."

All of this was but a prelude to the main attraction—Tony Grosso. Tony testified that for five years he had paid Sam Ferraro $4,950 a month, and that during this period, none of the three to five thousand numbers writers in his business were arrested except, occasionally, "by mistake." He also testified that Ferraro had given him advance notice of raids. Samuel Grosso, the organization's bookkeeper and Tony's younger brother, confirmed that Tony had told him to enter the monthly payments on the books with the notation "Sam F."

Ferraro did not take the stand. The defense, consisting of fellow detectives seeking to establish that he had conducted an active antiracket operation, lasted only four hours. The jury took less than a day to return a verdict of guilty on all seven counts. Sam Ferraro was sentenced to a $30,000 fine and six years in prison.

A recurring problem in trials like this was the character of the government's witnesses, who could often have been defendants themselves. A local newspaper took us to task on this score, and I responded: "Admittedly, 'it would be nice,' in your terms, to obtain convictions of corrupt public officials solely on the testimony of pillars of the community who possess impeccable credentials and unblemished character. Unfortunately, however, these are not the type of persons who engage in making payoffs to corrupt public officials to protect illegal activities." I was obliged to repeat this argument many times during my service as a federal prosecutor.

Our attention now returned to District Attorney Duggan, who had characterized himself as "surprised" by the verdict against his former Racket Squad chief. Unable to ascertain where Ferraro kept his payoff money or how he had spent it, IRS agents surmised that he might have passed much of it on to someone else. They had also assembled considerable evidence to establish a "net worth" tax case against Duggan, showing expenditures that far outpaced his known income. He had, in fact, cultivated what one reporter called a "life of luxury" since becoming district attorney. He traveled so frequently that he became known as an absentee prosecutor. He maintained a 240-acre estate in fashionable Ligonier and a luxury apartment in Pittsburgh. In Florida he owned a Spanish-style condominium, other real estate investments and a thirty-one-foot cabin cruiser. He belonged to ten different clubs, owned three cars and maintained a private chauffeur, maids and groundskeepers.

Harder evidence was needed, however, and an alert IRS agent found it. In purchasing his Florida condominium in January 1968, Duggan had made the colossal mistake of writing a check for $37,000 on a previously unknown Abstracts, Incorporated, bank account. The agent spotted the check and ascertained that the records previously furnished to the grand jury had excluded this account. Between 1967 and 1970, some $250,000 in cash had been deposited there. The deposits stopped abruptly in 1970, the year Sam Ferraro left the Racket Squad. The grand jury subpoenaed Ferraro immediately following his conviction, but even under a grant of immunity, he refused to testify regarding Duggan and was jailed for contempt.

For many years, Duggan had been close to the immensely wealthy Cordelia Scaife May, so it was possible that his money had come from her. The IRS scheduled an interview with Mrs. May, but shortly before it was to take place, she and Duggan were married in Nevada. As Duggan's wife, she could not be compelled to testify against him. Instead, we subpoenaed her financial records, which were maintained by Mellon family accountants. Her lawyer objected, invoking both the marital privilege and the Fifth Amendment. However, Judge Ralph Scalera agreed with us that the marital privilege applies only to testimony, not to books and records, and that the Fifth Amendment claim was personal to Mrs. May and could not be asserted by her accountant. In particular, an employee could not refuse to produce subpoenaed material belonging to his employer, and Mrs. May, having turned the records over to her accountant, had "little expectation of privacy" concerning them for Fifth Amendment purposes. Examination of the records quickly established that Mrs. May could not possibly have provided Duggan with any sizable amount of cash, as most of her expenditures were tightly controlled and monitored by family retainers.

Sam Ferraro finally provided the last piece in this puzzle. After three months in various federal, state and local prisons on contempt charges, he told our investigators that the racket payoff money had, in fact, gone to Duggan.

By this point, I was worried that Duggan might flee the country. I considered putting him under surveillance but decided not to risk accusations of harassment, as some had already unjustly characterized the case as a feud between the two of us. As a courtesy, we told Duggan's attorney on the afternoon of Monday, March 3, that we expected to seek an indictment the following morning.

On Tuesday, Ferraro gave his testimony under oath before the grand jury, which returned an eight-count indictment charging Duggan with failing to report more than $137,000 in payoff income from 1967 through 1970. When I returned to my office, my secretary met me with the news that Duggan had taken his life early that morning, apparently turning a twelve-gauge shotgun on himself at his country estate. This dreadful news was doubly ironic: Duggan might not have died if we had, in fact, put him under surveillance, or if we had not advised his attorney of the pending indictment.

It did not take long for conspiracy theories to surface over the circumstances of Duggan's death. Many of his friends and admirers were unable to accept the fact that he was a crook, and they cast about feverishly for some other explanation. No evidence ever came to light, however, to indicate that his death was anything other than a suicide.

Thereafter, based on further evidence given by Tony Grosso, we were able to indict Pittsburgh alderman Frank Bruno, a powerful Democratic political leader; District Magistrate Jacob (Jakie) Williams, a prominent Democratic leader in the African American community, and his brother,

Frank; Pronty Ford, a constable in Williams's area; and John Hammer, Ferraro's successor as Racket Squad chief. All were charged with accepting cash from Grosso to protect his illegal numbers operation.

I personally prosecuted Bruno, who was convicted of taking up to $3,000 a month from the ubiquitous Grosso. The trial was enlivened by Grosso's allegations that most of this money was actually intended for the office of Sheriff (and Allegheny County Democratic Party Chairman) Eugene Coon, who vehemently denied the charges. We began investigating them, but evidence was hard to come by and the inquiry died, though Coon's animosity toward me did not. Ford was also convicted, and Hammer pleaded guilty; the Williams brothers were acquitted. Tony Grosso had his sentence reduced from ten years to three, of which he served nearly two and one-half. The book on the Grosso payoffs and the corruption in the district attorney's office was finally closed.

MEANWHILE, ALLEGATIONS of corruption in the administration of Governor Milton Shapp and the state legislature had begun to surface. Following up on allegations made, but not supported, in the spring of 1974 by Representative Martin Mullen, a showboating Philadelphia Democrat, we began investigating potential kickbacks from contractors. Information obtained from various engineering and contracting firms that had done business with the state, especially the General State Authority, showed highly suspicious correlations between political contributions and contract awards. But no testimony could be developed before the grand jury to tie the two together. Outside the courtroom, however, we helped to revise the procedures for the awarding of state professional contracts. Ultimately, the General State Authority was abolished.

Our next inquiry struck pay dirt. Republicans in the General Assembly had raised allegations of impropriety against Frank C. Hilton, who, as Governor Shapp's secretary of property and supplies, headed the state's buy-sell-lease agency. In August 1974, our grand jury subpoenaed Hilton to produce relevant records and to testify about a $603,000 insurance contract between the state and Gulf Insurance Company of Texas. A state Justice Department official had described the contract as "a waste of the taxpayers' money" because it insured the state against risks from which it was already protected by the doctrine of sovereign immunity. David Oppenheim, the agent who had written (and received a $78,000 fee for) the contract, was a controlling stockholder in a firm that held a majority interest in Keystone State Bank. Hilton had borrowed $20,000 from Keystone, and the unpaid balance was paid off at the time the insurance contract was issued.

Before the inquiry could get very far, Governor Shapp cut his losses by firing Hilton, ostensibly because Hilton had lied to a press conference about who had paid off the Keystone loan. Our grand jury returned a perjury indictment against Hilton on similar grounds. The indictment alleged that it was actually Oppenheim who had paid off the loan. Testifying under a grant of immunity, Oppenheim confirmed a $31,000 kickback to Hilton. The grand jury returned a superseding indictment against Hilton adding extortion and income tax charges to the perjury counts.

At the trial, Keystone officials testified that a check drawn on Oppenheim's account had been applied to pay off the Hilton loan. The balance of the kickback had gone directly to Hilton. A former Hilton aide attested to other kickback schemes. Oppenheim confirmed that he had made the payments, under pressure from Hilton, because "I felt that it was like an investment, a relationship that would get me a lot of business in the future—from the commonwealth, through Mr. Hilton."

This set the stage for our concluding witness, Governor Milton J. Shapp, who testified to the falsity of Hilton's grand jury testimony. We were accused, with some justification, of showboating by calling Shapp to the stand, but he did corroborate that Hilton had lied to the grand jury. The defense offered no case, and Judge Gerald Weber found Hilton guilty on all counts and sentenced him to five years in prison. He was the first Pennsylvania cabinet member to be convicted since 1938.

An even more explosive case involved state senator Frank Mazzei, a former member of the minor judiciary and an adversary of mine since the Constitutional Convention. One of the most powerful Democratic politicians in the state, Mazzei was slated to be elected Senate majority leader when we indicted him in October 1974 on two counts of violating the Hobbs Anti-Racketeering Act. The charges related to kickback payments totaling $20,000 made to Mazzei by a Pittsburgh firm, BMI, Inc., in connection with two leases negotiated with the state's lottery office and the Department of Labor and Industry.

BMI and bank officials testified that the payments had been made and that the senator, rather than the state agencies, had set the terms of the leases. Mazzei was quoted as saying that "it was the practice on all state leases that 10 percent of the gross . . . be used for the Senate Campaign Committee." My closing argument pointed out that state taxpayers had paid an extra $20,000 for these leases. A guilty verdict was returned. Chief

Judge Rabe F. Marsh meted out a five-year prison sentence, fined Mazzei $20,000 and ordered him expelled from the Senate. The Third Circuit Court of Appeals stayed this order, however.

The state constitution provided that "[n]o person hereafter convicted of embezzlement of public moneys, bribery, perjury or other infamous crime, shall be eligible to the General Assembly, or capable of holding any office of trust or profit in this commonwealth." A 1916 Pennsylvania Supreme Court decision had held this to mean that, upon conviction and sentencing, expulsion from office was automatic. The Senate, however, not only did not expel Mazzei, but proceeded to appoint him head of its Transportation Committee, vice chairman of the Appropriations Committee and, the unkindest cut of all, a member of the Law and Justice Committee! Lieutenant Governor Ernest Kline issued a ruling that Mazzei's expulsion would require a two-thirds vote. The Senate then adjourned, while Mazzei took a paid leave of absence.

This was more than I could digest, and I went far beyond my mandate as U.S. attorney in an effort to force the legislature to expel the convicted senator. Typical was a May 1 Law Day speech before the Washington County Bar Association, where I asked: "What kind of example does this travesty set for today's young people, for the dispossessed of our society and for defilers of the law? It is this type of lawlessness that will bring this nation to its knees far more quickly than even the highest imaginable percentage rise in the rate of crime in our streets. It cannot and must not be tolerated." Mazzei was ultimately expelled by the Senate.

OF COURSE, OUR OFFICE handled many matters that did not involve racketeering or public corruption. Illegal drug traffic, for example, was one of my priority targets. We worked closely with state and local authorities in our antidrug efforts, which had a special meaning to me as a parent. We obtained federal convictions of most of the identified black heroin kingpins and also shut down the so-called Lebanese Connection, which distributed Middle Eastern heroin. Seizures of marijuana by the Drug Enforcement Administration (DEA) were increasingly frequent, and a significant number of clandestine drug laboratories were seized and shut down.

This period saw a rise in environmental litigation, and one pathfinding case in this area literally walked in our door. On a fall afternoon in 1970, two Penn State professors, David Nixon and John Zavodni, accompanied by backpedaling television cameramen, showed up at our offices. The professors had spent the summer on a sixty-five-mile canoe trip, sampling the waters of the Monongahela and Ohio Rivers. Having had the Allegheny County Bureau of Tests analyze the samples, they brought us more than 500 of them, together with written evaluations of their properties, and demanded that we prosecute industrial polluters of these rivers under the 1899 Rivers and Harbors Act (sometimes called the Refuse Act). They fully expected us to dismiss their concerns but hoped to gain some notoriety for their cause—a cleaner environment. We received them cordially and, concealing my abject ignorance of the law they were citing, I promised to give their request every consideration.

I asked Jim Seif, an ardent environmentalist whose mother had been a friend of Rachel Carson's, to look at the law and give me some advice. He reported that the Refuse Act, which obviously antedated the rise in concern over the environment, was primarily designed to deal with obstructions to navigation. However, the United States Supreme Court in 1966 had held it to apply to "all foreign substances and pollutants." The act had already been used to elicit a guilty plea in a pollution case in Manhattan. Its unique "bounty hunter" provisions entitled citizens who reported violations to 50 percent of the fines assessed.

After analyzing the evidence, we filed a total of seventy-three criminal counts against Pennsylvania Industrial Chemical Company (PICCO), United States Steel Corporation, Jones & Laughlin Steel Corporation and Wheeling-Pittsburgh Steel Corporation, charging them with illegally polluting the Ohio and Monongahela Rivers with a variety of chemical substances and solid materials, all in violation of the 1899 Refuse Act. I am sure that counsel for the defendants were as baffled by the charges as we had been by the allegations when they were first brought to our attention. Equally surprised, I suspect, were Messrs. Nixon and Zavodni, who, in theory, would be entitled to half of the maximum $182,500 in fines called for by the act if all the prosecutions were successful.

In the first jury trial in history under the bounty provisions of the Refuse Act, PICCO's lawyer pulled no punches: "[W]e would have lost World War II because of this stupid interpretation of the Justice Department. All industry would have to close down." The case seemed a real mismatch, but the jury returned a guilty verdict, and we had chalked up another first. On appeal, the Third Circuit threw out the conviction, partly on the basis that the government had forfeited the capacity to invoke the 1899 act through years of nonprosecution. The Supreme Court, however, overturned this holding and returned the case for a new trial. By this time, the 1972 Water Pollution Control Act had been passed, and the 1899 act was all but history. The defendants all ultimately pleaded no contest, and the two professors and Mike Watts, director of the Bureau of Tests, shared a modest bounty of $10,000.

These prosecutions did more than help clean up our rivers. They also proved that interested citizens had a place in the law enforcement process. Sharing the pride of the two professors who had made this case possible, Jim Seif and I worked up a set of guidelines for citizens who might wish to emulate them in chasing down polluters for their own bounties. The guidelines received widespread publicity, and we sent out over 500 copies across the nation.

This exercise occasioned a delicious practical joke on Seif. We fabricated a letter informing him that 834 mason jars containing contaminated water from the Scituate Reservoir in Rhode Island were being shipped collect to our office. Would Seif please send the $500 bounty by return mail? A bogus call slip informed Seif that Railway Express had phoned, asking what to do with a crate addressed to him that was leaking furiously. While Seif grabbed his dictating machine to get off a frenzied reply ("the Scituate Reservoir is not a navigable body of water," "the bounty is not due until after conviction," etc.), we huddled outside his office for as long as we could contain ourselves, then burst in. Jim was so relieved that he barely had a chance to express his ire.

In civil rights, perhaps our major forward step was in the area of police brutality. No civil rights charge had ever been brought against a police officer in western Pennsylvania for using excessive force against a suspect. We brought such a charge against Robert Hutzler, a Pittsburgh police officer notorious for his mistreatment of African Americans. While the case was disposed of by a plea of nolo contendere and Hutzler's resignation, it sent a signal to the law enforcement community. (During my tenure, our office also hired its first female assistant U.S. attorney—not without some grumbling by a few local male lawyers—and only its second African American prosecutor.)

Other successes included the obscenity conviction of Michael Kutler, who owned three of the most notorious "adult" theaters in downtown Pittsburgh. This type of operation had been the object of repeated fruitless enforcement efforts by the Pittsburgh police and the district attorney. A $500,000, eight-state bankruptcy scam masterminded by Maurice Olen and Ivan Ezrine was also brought to heel. Finally, the Secret Service cracked major counterfeiting cases involving currency, coins and stamps. One of these had a humorous sidelight. The seizure of $500,000 in counterfeit $20 bills had been splashed across the front pages of both Pittsburgh newspapers, replete with pictures of Special Agent in Charge Tom Smith and me behind an enormous stack of the counterfeit currency. In the federal cafeteria the following day, I sought to pay for my lunch with a $20 bill. The alert cashier refused, saying, "Oh no, you don't. I saw your picture in the *Post-Gazette* with all that counterfeit money!" She quickly relented with a smile and agreed to accept my (genuine) currency.

THE U.S. ATTORNEY'S office engaged in various efforts to assist youth. Among other things, we taught a criminal justice course at Westinghouse High School, a mostly black inner-city institution. We tried to give the students a more conceptual view of a system most of them knew only from street level. Ironically, some of the assistant U.S. attorneys who participated got as much out of the program as the students did, enhancing their own street-level perceptions.

Outside the office, Ginny and I both participated in a yearlong study of youth problems commissioned by the Health and Welfare Association of Allegheny County. Our thirty-seven-member panel of students, youth workers, "street people," educators, social service providers, civic, religious and business leaders, judges and law enforcement officials sought to understand and tackle some of the root causes of unrest among area youth. Our report called for better communication in the schools, better teachers, curricula more sensitive to student needs, enhanced job development programs, evenhanded treatment by police, more accessible leisure activities and better health services, including information concerning abortion, birth control and venereal disease. Over my dissent and that of fourteen other members, the report also advocated the legalization of marijuana. To me, our most important conclusion was that young people should be allowed and encouraged to participate in the management of institutions serving them.

Another extracurricular activity brought me into sharp conflict with local law enforcement officials and sportsmen's groups. Following the killing of a police officer by a young woman with a concealed handgun, I was outraged over the easy accessibility of these weapons and took a very hard line against them. In an article published in *Juris*, a Duquesne University Law School periodical, and later reprinted widely, most prominently in the *American Bar Association Journal*, I called for much tighter regulation of the sale of handguns. In particular, I argued that prospective owners should have to show why they should be permitted to purchase handguns, rather than law enforcement officers having to establish why they shouldn't. I also called for fingerprinting and photographing of applicants. This proposal earned the vehement opposition of the Western Pennsylvania Chiefs of Police Association and a wide variety of sportsmen's groups.

THIS PERIOD MARKED the beginning of my education in the relationship between public officials and the press. Reporters have an insatiable appetite for information on criminal investigations. The temptation to leak such information is great for every law enforcement official, particularly when reporters offer to portray the policeman or prosecutor in a favorable light. But the job of law enforcement is to gather evidence for presentation in court, not in the media. The Federal Rules of Criminal Procedure absolutely prohibit the disclosure of grand jury information, and simple fairness and due process militate against the disclosure of information that would violate the privacy of any citizen. Such disclosure can prejudice the rights of citizens under investigation. It can also adversely affect the integrity of the investigation itself. Investigative targets, especially of the more sophisticated kind, are even more hungry than reporters for snippets of information about ongoing inquiries.

We were frequently accused of leaks, but to my knowledge, no member of my staff was ever guilty of one. We did learn to accommodate the news media without engaging in improprieties. For example, our press releases, many of which I wrote myself, spelled out, in plain English, most of the actions we undertook in court. When we expected particularly newsworthy witnesses to appear, we often suggested that reporters "hang around the grand jury room." On occasion we even told them, "If you had been outside the grand jury room this morning, you might have seen so-and-so." We "loaded up" public documents with as many facts as we could, so that reporters were not left in the dark, and I often suggested questions to reporters that would elicit responses designed to serve our legitimate law enforcement purposes. None of this violated any statutes, rules or codes of conduct. It did, however, help get our message out to the public.

On the lighter side of our dealings with the press, I enjoyed taking "revenge" for a fulsome *Post-Gazette* article labeling me the "Silver Knight of Area Law Enforcement," over which I took a good bit of razzing. The writer, Bill McCloskey, described me as appearing in court in an "ill-fitting but expensive suit." I had my son John type a letter identifying himself as "Anatole Deegan, Mr. Thornburgh's tailor," complaining bitterly about McCloskey's description and threatening to consult a lawyer. I waved it off, saying, "Oh, Bill. He sues everyone!" Finally I took pity on him, and we shared a good laugh.

MY TIME AS U.S. ATTORNEY was the happiest of my professional life. It was also a relatively calm and stable period for our family. As I wound up my service, John was seventeen, David sixteen, Peter fourteen and Bill eight.

Peter continued to be special in more ways than one. Almost always cheerful and mercifully unaware of the full extent of his limitations, he worked to extend his capabilities in every possible area. He taught us to be as patient as he was, and we celebrated as a family his every accomplishment. On occasion, he was an understandable source of embarrassment to his brothers, but that was equally true of the rest of us. Peter, in many ways, became the conscience of the family, somehow bringing out our very best. Through him we learned to be more tolerant and appreciative of diversity and more committed to the general welfare of persons with disabilities.

When he was fourteen, Peter learned to take the public bus to school, which opened a new world to him. (He had earlier, to my surprise, mastered a two-wheel bike, giving him increased mobility within the neighborhood as well.) The riskiness of this step was illustrated on one occasion when the bus broke down and all passengers were instructed to "take the next bus." Peter dutifully climbed aboard the very next bus, which was not headed toward his school. After a considerable period of time, an all-points bulletin over the bus intercom enabled the driver to spot him and return him to safety. Such episodes made his brothers and me skeptical about Peter's somewhat hazardous endeavors, but Ginny, refusing to limit his horizons, constantly encouraged him to live as much of a mainstream life as possible. Indeed, the risks of his doing so were dwarfed by his increasing degree of independence.

Ginny, in the meantime, took on more and more responsibilities in advocacy for the mentally retarded. She and her fellow advocates embarked on an aggressive program of unannounced visits to public and private facilities for the mentally retarded, extensively documenting their shortcomings for presentation to the state bureaucracy and legislative committees. In many cases, changes resulted, but the deficiencies were daunting indeed. Ginny eventually was to visit many such institutions in the state.

On the political front, we all watched in horrified fascination as the Watergate hearings unfolded. I was particularly appalled to learn that Attorney General John Mitchell, whom many in the beleaguered law enforcement community had viewed as a champion, had been involved in discussing some of the more bizarre schemes hatched by G. Gordon Liddy and company to violate the civil rights of Americans. This breaching of the wall between the rule of law and partisan politics felt like a betrayal and left many of us in the Department of Justice in a state of despair.

I have often been tempted to think that President Nixon might have preserved his presidency and a deserved place in history by taking full responsibility for the break-in as soon as it was discovered. Perhaps, as many observers have suggested, there was too much else to hide, but I suspect that it was the hubris of the "President's men" that blinded them to such a self-evident resolution.

On the Pennsylvania political scene, both Pittsburgh mayor Pete Flaherty and, despite gathering clouds of corruption, Governor Shapp were elected to second terms with little difficulty. And John Heinz was elected to the House of Representatives, where he began a long career of public service.

5

Serving in
Washington, D.C.

Favorable publicity regarding our prosecutions, especially of corruption and racketeering cases, led to some curiosity as to my personal agenda. After the first round of corruption convictions, Sherley Uhl, chief political writer for the *Pittsburgh Press*, wrote a column projecting me into races for mayor, district attorney, congressman and senator. Others indulged in similar speculations. While flattering, these made me an even more inviting target for those, such as Governor Shapp and Sheriff Coon, who sought to lay all of their problems at the feet of a "political" U.S. attorney.

The guesswork came to an end in March 1975, when Attorney General Edward Levi called to ask if I wished to serve as an assistant attorney general in Washington. To the surprise of most, and the disappointment of some, I did. It was hard for my family and me to leave a city we loved, but I simply could not pass up this opportunity. I would be heading the Criminal Division, which had borne a good deal of criticism during the Watergate affair. Much was expected of our team.

Considerable local acclaim greeted my appointment. While the praise was somewhat embarrassing, I was delighted to have put our U.S. attorney's office on the map. Moreover, my time there had both developed my lawyering skills and given me insights into the challenges of public management. I felt fully prepared to accept my new responsibilities in Washington.

My June 12 confirmation hearing before the Senate Judiciary Committee was uneventful, despite adverse testimony from Sheriff Coon, still smarting from the Bruno case, and a Pittsburgh-area builder, Jack Nard, who had pleaded no contest to tax charges brought by our office. Subsequently, he conducted a two-decade vendetta against me and all others responsible for what he perceived to be a gross miscarriage of justice. Allegheny County District Attorney John Hickton, Duggan's successor, lodged a letter protesting my appointment, but did not testify.

On July 8, 1975, I was administered the oath of office, joining an able and personable team. Antonin Scalia headed the Office of Legal Counsel; Rex Lee, the Civil Division; Scott Crampton, the Tax Division; J. Stanley Pottinger, the Civil Rights Division; Tom Kauper, the Antitrust Division; Wally Johnson, the Lands and Natural Resources Division; Mike McKevitt, the Office of Legislative Affairs; and Glenn Pommerening, the Justice Management Division. Other important officials included the solicitor general, Bob Bork, and the head of the FBI, Clarence Kelley.

Attorney General Levi had been recruited from the presidency of the University of Chicago, where he had previously served as dean of the law school. A man of undoubted integrity, independence and intellect, Levi was a superb choice as attorney general during this difficult period in the department's history. Slight and soft-spoken, with a wry sense of humor, he seemed to regard his prosecutors with bemusement. His top aide, the deputy attorney general, was Harold "Ace" Tyler, formerly a judge in the Southern District of New York. Judge Tyler was a bald, debonair, good-humored Wall Street-type lawyer, who had, I suspected, somewhat looked down his nose at me when we first met because of my University of Pittsburgh law degree.

Jim Seif and Jay Waldman joined me as special assistants. Jim had charge of administrative operations, while Jay tended to the more substantive side, eventually becoming a deputy assistant attorney general with oversight responsibility for organized crime, official corruption and narcotics matters.

Within the Criminal Division were sections dealing with organized crime and racketeering, narcotics, management and labor, government regulation, internal security, fraud and general crimes. All were headed by department veterans with an understandable suspicion of someone from "the field." Ginny had captured this tension accurately as we were leaving

Pittsburgh. "For six years," she said, "you have been complaining about 'the department.' Well, Buster, *you* are now 'the department'!" The point was well taken. My challenge was to use the insights I had obtained away from Washington to make our division an effective working partner of U.S. attorneys' offices across the nation.

I began by putting my two principal aides to work on a top-to-bottom review of the division's management structure. This resulted in widespread and sometimes wrenching personnel changes, including the replacement or reassignment of nearly all of the deputies and section chiefs. To support a stepped-up effort against public corruption, we also created a Public Integrity Section that could take charge of corruption cases that a U.S. attorney was unable or unwilling to handle. I considered the creation of this section the most important contribution of my tenure at the Criminal Division.

IN THE MIDDLE OF an otherwise bare desk on the first day of my new job lay a pale blue paperback volume containing the report of the so-called Rockefeller Commission, established by President Ford to investigate allegations of wrongdoing by the FBI and the CIA. The Church Committee in the Senate and the Pike Committee in the House were also investigating these matters. Our division's task was the narrow one of examining the evidence to determine if there was a basis for criminal charges. The political and policy matters were to be handled elsewhere. In the public's mind, however, this distinction was blurred. This project was to take up a considerable portion of my time.

The department had previously agreed that the CIA could investigate and dispose of any potential criminal charges against its employees. With the acquiescence of CIA Director George Bush, I immediately abrogated that rule and made CIA employees subject to federal prosecution on the same basis as any other federal employees. In October 1975, we impaneled a grand jury to assist in the inquiry.

Our investigation came to focus on three areas: (1) assassination attempts against foreign heads of state, such as Congolese president Patrice Lumumba, Dominican Republic strongman Rafael Trujillo and Cuban leader Fidel Castro; (2) testimony by former CIA director Richard Helms before a Senate committee regarding activities to overthrow the Chilean government; and (3) mail-opening programs directed at U.S. citizens corresponding with people in the Soviet Union.

We did not recommend prosecution regarding the assassination attempts. After I left office, Helms pleaded no contest to charges of misleading Congress in his testimony regarding Chile. We also recommended no prosecution regarding the mail-opening program, finding a continuum of presidential authority for it. Attorney General Levi was troubled by the ambiguity of this authority, a difficult question given the longtime practice of providing the chief executive with "plausible deniability" for such acts. However, he concluded that it would be improper "to indict a generation," referring to the wide acceptance of these practices since the beginning of the Cold War. The question of actual presidential authority for the openings he left, of necessity, unresolved.

We also undertook other inquiries into FBI activities, including a massive review of the infamous COINTELPRO operation to neutralize domestic political dissidents, but little individual criminal liability was established during my tenure. Later, officials were convicted of illegal break-ins in New York, but most were subsequently pardoned. There had been insufficient guidelines for these types of activities and a general lack of accountability for law enforcement and intelligence operations. Correcting these problems was a high priority for the attorney general. Despite some grumbling from the old guard, comprehensive guidelines for the FBI were ultimately implemented, and a new Office of Professional Responsibility was established within the department to deal with allegations of non-criminal misconduct. These initiatives created a new environment within the investigative agencies and signaled the final end of the J. Edgar Hoover era. This was a principal contribution, in my view, of Edward Levi's tenure as attorney general.

The number of federally prosecuted corruption cases increased from 63 indictments in 1970 to 337 in 1976, for a total of 1,598 during this period. I was proud of most of these, but there was some overreaction to the Watergate revelations. One regrettable, and highly overpublicized, investigation was undertaken largely because of intense election-year media and congressional pressure. Allegations were made that FBI Director Kelley had received gifts—mostly knickknacks—from subordinates and had arranged for some work to be done at his apartment, much of it during his wife's terminal illness. President Ford agreed with our conclusion that the charges were inconsequential and certainly not criminal and the director remained at his post. Clarence Kelley was the farthest type of person imaginable from the wheeler-dealer trying to cut corners and enrich himself at the public trough. These charges were indicative, however, of the post-Watergate mentality that had come to infect official Washington and was to recur time and again in years to come.

Also unfortunate were the allegations made in 1976 against Howard "Bo" Calloway, former secretary of the army and President Ford's reelection campaign manager, concerning actions regarding a ski resort in which he later acquired an interest. Publicity surrounding our inquiry prompted Calloway to resign as campaign manager, but no basis for criminal charges emerged. The matter underscored the vulnerability of careers in public life even to mere investigations into allegations of wrongdoing.

Such investigations were to help lay the groundwork for the mischievous special prosecutor or independent counsel statute, first passed (over the objection of Attorney General Griffin Bell) during President Carter's administration. Institutionalizing an office that had, up to then, been used only selectively was to have negative consequences for all succeeding administrations.

It was during my breaking-in period that a member of Congress first intimated that we had actually covered up wrongdoing by declining to prosecute a target of congressional inquiry. Many more such accusations were to follow; none were sustained. In this case, Senator William Proxmire (D-Wis.) had requested that we investigate the congressional testimony of Henry Kearns, former chairman of the Export-Import Bank, concerning the sale of stock in one of his businesses to a Japanese firm that had a number of transactions with the bank. We found that Kearns had been "perhaps less than candid with the subcommittee" but that there was insufficient evidence to support a criminal prosecution. The department later brought a civil suit against Kearns over the profits he had made on the transaction.

Not all the official wrongdoing that we investigated, of course, related to federal agencies or employees. In fact, the new Public Integrity Section had been created, in large part, to deal with state and local corruption that was beyond the reach of the normal law enforcement process. Two such cases involved state governors. Following the shock of Vice President Spiro Agnew's resignation in 1973 and the exposure of the seamy world of payoffs and kickbacks in Maryland, allegations surfaced about the conduct of Democratic governor Marvin Mandel, and the U.S. attorney's office in Baltimore launched an investigation. Mandel and five associates were eventually indicted for mail fraud related to the operation of a Maryland racetrack. After one mistrial because of an attempt to bribe a juror, the governor was convicted and jailed, although the conviction was overturned years later on the ground that the mail fraud statutes had been misapplied.

Charges were also brought against Arch Moore, the Republican governor of West Virginia, but an acquittal resulted. The case involved an alleged $25,000 payment to Moore to secure a bank charter. There was evidence of the payment, but arrests were made before the charter had been issued. I was told, perhaps apocryphally, that Moore's counsel had argued, "Ladies and gentlemen, that witness must have lied about that payment. You know Arch Moore. If he had been paid $25,000 to issue a bank charter, that charter would have been issued!" Justice prevailed years later, during my tenure as attorney general, when Moore, by that time governor again, was convicted and imprisoned on other charges.

ONE ONGOING DEPARTMENT project to which I attached myself was the recodification of federal criminal law. The U.S. Code had grown like Topsy over the years and contained many redundant and contradictory provisions. The recodification effort had begun with the National Commission for Reform of Federal Criminal Laws, appointed by President Johnson and chaired by former California governor Pat Brown.

It was generally agreed that 95 percent of the more than 799 pages of the bill resulting from that commission's report addressed noncontroversial matters. The case for reform could be easily made, under normal conditions, if the listener's eyes did not glaze over. However, these were not normal conditions. Memories of Watergate caused intense scrutiny of proposals even remotely connected to the abuses of that era. And the proximity of the 1976 presidential campaign caused otherwise responsible legislators to behave in unaccountable ways. The reform bill was alleged to endanger freedom of speech and of the press, workers' rights in labor-management disputes and official accountability in Watergate-type situations. These concerns were all highly exaggerated. Most other objections related to provisions already on the books that the bill would merely carry forward.

The Criminal Division mounted a somewhat lonely campaign for the bill, beating back attacks from all sides. Events overtook us, however, and Congress adjourned without taking action. Many of the bill's features, most notably establishment of the Sentencing Commission, abolition of parole and compensation of victims, were enacted in the 1980s, but the central task of comprehensive reform remains unfinished today.

Another focus of our attention was the use of false identification documents. The June 1976 report of the seventy-five-member Federal Advisory Commission on False Identification, which I chaired, put a price tag of $20 billion a year on the use of such papers. It also contained a number of other startling findings; for example, an FBI survey showed that of 500 random wanted persons, all had active aliases, and some had more than thirty identities. The commission set forth a series of recommendations for dealing with this phenomenon, though it declined to recommend a national identification card because of its perceived threat to privacy. In my view, the most important proposal was one to match birth and death certificates. I observed, "There are an awful lot of dead people walking around committing crimes." Little follow-up occurred to our report and this problem continues to plague our nation today.

A ruling that I made in 1975 opened the door for expanded public participation in political campaigns through political action committees (PACs). These committees originated in the 1940s, being first utilized by the CIO to get around the prohibition on political contributions by labor unions. The specific question presented to us was whether, under the post-Watergate election reform laws, corporations could pay the administrative costs of PACs that solicited funds from employees, or only of those that solicited from shareholders. The newly established Federal Election Commission asked us for an advisory opinion in a case involving SUNPAC, a PAC established by the Sun Oil Company, and we held that both types of solicitations were covered. Employers could not suggest to employees who should receive earmarked funds, could not pressure employees to contribute and could not themselves contribute to candidates. But we "would be disposed to decline prosecution" of a corporation that underwrote the operating expenses of a PAC. We characterized this corporate effort, aptly I believe, as one that "encourages its employees to participate in politics in general, including making personal contributions." The commission concurred with our views, and the corporate PAC, for better or worse, came into widespread use.

During this period, the department began to give significant attention to international matters. The worlds of commerce and finance were shrinking rapidly, and more American companies were doing business in different countries with different ethical and legal standards.

We broke new ground in a series of cases growing out of contracts entered into by Lockheed Aircraft Corporation around the world, allegedly aided by payments to officials of foreign governments. The investigations carried out by U.S. authorities were more or less routine. What was new was the interest of foreign governments in pursuing charges against their own officials. Naturally, they wanted access to the evidence we had developed. In response, our prosecutors and the State Department developed unique new legal procedures to simplify cooperation across borders.

These procedures were to ripen into a succession of Mutual Legal Assistance Treaties ("MLATs"). The forerunners of these treaties were executive agreements providing for exchange of evidence in criminal cases outside of the usual cumbersome diplomatic procedures. The first of these agreements, entered into with the Japanese government in March 1976, related to some $12 million in payments allegedly made by Lockheed in Japan. Similar agreements were entered into with the governments of Italy and the Netherlands, and this kind of cooperation soon became a staple of our growing international practice.

Also begun, but not finished before I left office, was an investigation into alleged influence peddling by Korean interests, involving a number of members of Congress. Many of these charges involved a businessman and Washington man-about-town named Tongsun Park. Very little resulted from the "Koreagate" investigation, in spite of the lurid stories and frequent headlines in the Washington media.

A number of "celebrity" cases did not raise important legal questions but did attract widespread public attention. My involvement in these matters was usually peripheral, but they indicate the wide variety of fare served up to federal prosecutors.

During his presidency, Gerald Ford was twice subject to assassination attempts by women—Lynette "Squeaky" Fromme, a Charles Manson disciple, and a deranged Sara Jane Moore. Both were convicted. In an interesting wrinkle, Fromme's defense wished to have President Ford testify at the trial. We were hard pressed to present a legal argument that would excuse him, since he was both target and prime eyewitness. The solution we reached was that the president would give a videotaped deposition in Washington. On the morning of November 1, 1975, a group of lawyers and technicians assembled in the Old Executive Office Building to videotape, for the first time ever, the testimony of the president of the United States in a criminal proceeding. All of us had a distinct feeling that history was being made.

Another West Coast extravaganza was the apprehension and trial of heiress Patty Hearst, following her abduction by members of a ragtag group known as the Symbionese Liberation Army. Hearst was convicted of bank robbery in a case involving few legal questions of moment.

The disappearance of former Teamsters boss Jimmy Hoffa attracted a great deal of public attention and FBI scrutiny. Although numerous leads were run down and a wide variety of theories advanced, none proved to be fruitful. To this day, the case remains unsolved.

An apparent mob-linked assassination took the life of Sam Giancana, a Chicago La Cosa Nostra boss who had figured in the Castro assassination attempts. He was later alleged to have shared the attentions of a woman named Judith Campbell Exner with President John F. Kennedy. In spite of the titillating prospect of some connection between his killing and his rather high-profile past, the FBI investigation prompted me to conclude that his demise was simply another "gangland slaying intended to settle problems within the syndicate."

Congressman Wayne Hays and his "secretary," Elizabeth Ray, became the subjects of a federal criminal investigation following the widespread publicity given to their relationship. It was claimed that the powerful chairman of both the House Administration Committee and the Democratic Congressional Campaign Committee had placed Ray on his payroll in exchange for sexual favors, thus defrauding the government. Grand jury proceedings were instituted, but no charges were brought, because the prime witness against the congressman would have been the somewhat unreliable and vulnerable Elizabeth Ray herself. Two newspaper reporters who could have corroborated Ray's testimony refused to cooperate with the investigation. Congressman Hays had resigned his seat following a House Ethics Committee inquiry and, in the final analysis, we felt further criminal proceedings would serve no purpose.

DURING MY TIME at the department, I could not avoid involvement in Pennsylvania matters. Governor Shapp continued to complain about "political prosecutions" even as more members of his administration were convicted of crimes. Early in 1976, as he was pondering his ill-fated run for the Democratic presidential nomination, the governor complained to columnist Jack Anderson about my activities. This was a bad mistake. Anderson sent a reporter to Pennsylvania for a month-long look into the charges and wrote, "We found systematic corruption, including organized crime links, throughout the Shapp administration. During his two terms, fifty-seven state officials have been indicted by grand juries." Moreover, Anderson wrote, federal and state authorities were conducting a total of twenty-one other inquiries involving associates of the governor.

Shapp was undeterred. Following the indictment of his close associate,

Egidio Cerilli, chairman of the Turnpike Commission, whom he nonetheless continued in his position, he gave a long interview to the Associated Press, stating, "I think our administration has done more to stamp out corruption than any previous administration in the recent history of this state." Subsequently Shapp's revenue secretary, George Mowod, was indicted on federal tax charges.

Robert E. J. Curran, U.S. attorney for the Eastern District of Pennsylvania, had had a stormy relationship with the Department of Justice. Curran ultimately resigned and unloaded a series of serious charges against me, most notably that I was "out to get" Philadelphia mayor Frank Rizzo. My response was succinct: "I have made no such statement or expressed any such desire with regards to Mr. Rizzo. We're not in the business of 'getting' people." A department inquiry found no evidence of any such vendetta.

Curran's successor, David Marston, stepped up the effort against corruption. He later secured the convictions of two of the most powerful Democrats in Philadelphia: Pennsylvania House Speaker Herbert Fineman and State Senator Buddy Cianfrani, chairman of the Senate Appropriations Committee. He also successfully prosecuted Democratic congressman Joshua Eilburg.

The 1976 race to succeed retiring U.S. Senator Hugh Scott touched our office as well. Contenders for the Republican nomination were former Philadelphia district attorney Arlen Specter and Congressman John Heinz. It had earlier been alleged that because of our close relationship, I was reluctant to pursue allegations that Senator Scott had accepted illegal payments from Gulf Oil Corporation of Pittsburgh. Heinz was also alleged to have accepted payments from Gulf, and Specter called upon me to probe those as well. My response in both cases was to point out that the Gulf matter was under the exclusive jurisdiction of the Watergate special prosecutor's office. Heinz went on to become Pennsylvania's new junior Republican senator.

In 1976, Jimmy Carter defeated Gerald Ford in the presidential election, and my tenure at the department drew toward a close. Shortly after the Carter administration came to office, Pittsburgh Mayor Pete Flaherty told me that he was looking for a position in Washington. I promptly introduced him to newly appointed Attorney General Griffin Bell with the words, "Judge Bell, I want you to meet my mayor. He ain't much of a lawyer, but he's a helluva politician!" Shortly thereafter, Pete Flaherty was named the new deputy attorney general.

I resigned effective March 12, 1977. In a farewell letter to Judge Bell, I stated: "There is not, and never has been, anything necessarily inconsistent between a forceful and aggressive law enforcement effort and the absolute observance of the civil rights and civil liberties of all of our citizens. A law enforcement effort which does not observe those rights and liberties can, in fact, be counterproductive to the best interests of a stable society. So, in the final analysis, it is an important part of our professional responsibilities to ensure that such is not the case." I was less sure that Judge Bell needed this advice than determined that he know my own views as I bade farewell to a calling to which, with great satisfaction, I had given eight years of my life.

ALTHOUGH PROFESSIONALLY very rewarding, the move to Washington had been traumatic for our entire family. We had been obliged to sell our beloved Pittsburgh home and exchange life in a community in which we were totally at ease for the peculiarities of life in the nation's capital.

In September 1975 John entered Bucknell University in Lewisburg, Pennsylvania. David was admitted to Sidwell Friends School as the only new member of the senior class, a very tough assignment that he handled with aplomb. He entered Haverford College in fall 1976. Bill attended the fine Horace Mann public school near our Washington residence.

During his year at Sidwell, David and several classmates conspired to carry off a traditional senior prank, in this case a nocturnal rearranging of desks within the school building to clog the entry to their classrooms. They were apprehended as burglars by D.C. police officers with drawn pistols and attack dogs. Taken to the local station house, they were each allowed the proverbial one phone call. David's awakened me about 2 A.M., and I set off for the station on foot, as Ginny, Peter and Bill had taken our car to New York to visit Ginny's mother. Although David had informed us that he and his cohorts were up to some mischief, we were unaware of the specifics.

Upon arrival, I discovered the miscreants handcuffed to their chairs and looking very sheepish indeed. Also present were other dads routed out of bed for the occasion, including newscaster Roger Mudd, father of Daniel, and Pennsylvania Congressman Edward "Pete" Biester, father of Eddie (who, being over eighteen, was actually lodged behind bars). My chagrin was the greatest, however, as I was, after all, the head of the Criminal Division of the U.S. Department of Justice! All ended well as school representatives showed up and exonerated the boys as mere pranksters, and David and I undertook the long walk home together. We didn't share the story with Ginny, however, until long after her return.

Peter's schooling continued at the Joseph P. Kennedy Institute, an excellent private school in northeast Washington, where he enjoyed the loving attention of the Catholic sisters and participated on the school's basketball team. He quickly mastered a new bus route—with a transfer at the White House, no less. He also became involved in a neighborhood Boy Scout troop thanks to a thoughtful neighbor, Dick Bienvenue.

The financial burden of Peter's schooling was eased by Ginny's dogged pursuit of his "right to an appropriate educational placement" under the Right to Education Act. After thorough research, she determined that the Trainable Mentally Retarded classes offered through the District of Columbia public schools could not offer such a placement and that Peter by law deserved to be educated at the Kennedy Institute. On her own, Ginny engaged and briefed a volunteer lawyer, and they ultimately prevailed on appeal.

Ginny's situation was the most difficult, as she was coming from a community where she was at the center of many activities to one where she knew almost no one. She eventually took a position as the Washington representative for Operation Crossroads Africa, arranging stays by African visitors. Friends were few and far between for Ginny during this loneliest time of our life together. Her salvation was that Jane Hooton Ince, my first wife's younger sister, lived not five minutes away from us. In a wonderful irony, Ginny and Jane became lifelong friends. Jane's parents, the Hootons, were as happy about this as we were.

We did not see our way clear to joining the fabled Washington social circuit, partly out of insecurity, partly because of my heavy workload, and partly because of a general aversion to the unreality of what passes for Washington society. One hilarious encounter at the White House did give us some satisfaction. As we awaited admission to a black-tie reception for administration officials graciously hosted by President and Mrs. Ford, we were surrounded by a clutch of "beautiful people," all of whom seemed to know each other and none of whom, understandably, gave us a tumble. When we reached the stiff-as-starch Marine guard outside the entrance, I handed him our invitation, whereupon he greeted us, "Oh, Mr. Thornburgh, sir. What an honor it is to meet you, sir!" I was dumbfounded until he followed up in a decidedly Pittsburgh accent, "I'm from North Braddock, sir. My mother sends me news clippings about you all the time!" Ginny and I returned our compliments and strode though the gawking crowd of real celebrities, feeling ten feet tall, into the inner reaches of the White House.

6

Running for Governor:
The Primary

LONG BEFORE I LEFT Washington, there was widespread speculation that I would seek the Pennsylvania governor's office in 1978. This
was fueled, in part, by Governor Shapp's charges of political prosecutions.
But the most potent argument for my prospective candidacy derived from
genuine public concern about corruption and mismanagement in state
government and the widely acknowledged need to "clean up Harrisburg."
Republicans, eager to end a two-term hiatus in control of the governor's
office, were determined to mount a serious campaign in 1978 and saw the
issue of reform as a viable one. My credentials as a prosecutor therefore established a strong claim to the nomination, at least in western Pennsylvania, where most of our efforts had been concentrated.

My longtime interest in public service, coupled with recent insights
into what I was to call "the dark underside of Pennsylvania government,"
made the possibility of running for governor intriguing. Moreover, reorga-
nizing an entrenched Justice Department bureaucracy and handling a $20
million Criminal Division budget gave me a claim to the necessary management background. That experience had been gained, however, at the expense of a nearly two-year absence from Pennsylvania. Furthermore, my
prosecutor's duties had (despite Shapp's claims) been nonpolitical. These
factors created a wide gulf between my political interests and both the
Pennsylvania Republican establishment and the community at large.

Pennsylvania presents a formidable challenge to any statewide candidate. With a sizable land area and then the nation's fifth-largest population (nearly 12 million), it demanded an all-out commitment. Furthermore, the state was not cut from whole cloth. It had seven separate television viewing markets and innumerable newspapers and radio stations, each fiercely representative of its own clientele. The state had been staunchly Republican from the end of the Civil War until the New Deal and had since been a swing state, its voters carefully examining candidates without slavish adherence to party labels.

Philadelphia and its suburbs represented the biggest concentration of voters, but the issues in the inner city were obviously quite different from those in the more affluent commuting counties. The broad center of the state was more conservative; it had a thriving agricultural economy as well as numerous small enterprises in smaller cities and towns, including Harrisburg, Williamsport, Sunbury, Lancaster, Lebanon and York. Over the rough divide of the Allegheny Mountains lay the declining cities of Johnstown and Altoona and the southwestern area of the state. This was the old iron and coal region, now in eclipse, centered around Pittsburgh, but encompassing numerous smaller communities and some good-sized cities as well. The northwest—sometimes labeled the "forgotten northwest"—was almost viewed as part of Ohio or New York, upon which it bordered. It claimed Erie as its principal urban center but was dotted with many smaller communities. The broad northern tier was made up of mountainous areas, dense forests and counties "with more bears than voters" until it gave way to the northeast, the former hard-coal region, with its cities of Scranton and Wilkes-Barre, now also in decline. Further down the eastern border with New Jersey were the Lehigh Valley cities of Allentown, Bethlehem and Easton.

To support myself upon my return from Washington, I rejoined my old law firm, now styled Kirkpatrick, Lockhart, Johnson & Hutchison, as a partner, with the full understanding that I would be assessing my chances of running for governor during the balance of 1977. In fact, I did little else during that period and was, I am sure, of only incidental value to the firm from the standpoint of lawyering. Once again, however, I was to benefit from its generous policy of encouraging its lawyers to pursue opportunities for public service.

Estimates of the cost of a successful campaign ran as high as $3–5 million, amounts that at first seemed out of reach. My college classmate, Evans Rose Jr., became a superb fund-raiser and supporter in this and many endeavors to follow. My own aversion to raising campaign dollars made me especially grateful that Ev seemed to enjoy it. Our initial goal was to secure commitments of $200,000 by fall 1977. While we fell short of that goal, we did well enough to continue and establish other criteria for going the distance.

In terms of a campaign organization, one crucial choice was whether to engage a professional campaign consultant or to rely on my own staff, engaging experts in particular areas as needed. Here, I took a leap of faith. I had been impressed with Jay Waldman's savvy intelligence and strategic insights, was convinced of his absolute loyalty and was comfortable with our ability to interact candidly. I was therefore delighted when he agreed to become my campaign manager.

By fall, for the all-important role of press secretary, we were able to recruit Paul Critchlow, a former political writer for the *Philadelphia Inquirer*, who had covered the latter stages of my stint as U.S. attorney and written one of the first stories to highlight our anticorruption activities for Philadelphia-area readers. An experienced newsman with a wide circle of acquaintances and the respect of his peers, Paul was to serve with distinction into my second term as governor. To head our research effort, we were fortunate enough to sign on Rick Stafford, a graduate of Carnegie Mellon's Graduate School of Urban and Public Affairs. Rick was a tireless worker and an imaginative thinker, and his relaxed style and sense of humor often eased tense situations. These, together with Jim Seif, who took on scheduling, and Murray Dickman, a classmate of Rick's who acted as our utility infielder, were the hard core of our campaign roster.

My contact with the Pennsylvania political establishment had been minimal. In December 1976, Ginny and I had attended the annual dinner of the Pennsylvania Society in New York. This event, initiated just before the turn of the century to provide wealthy Pennsylvanians and their wives with a pre-Christmas shopping excursion to New York, had grown over the years into a major political happening. Ginny and I knew few of the luminaries present and, from our dinner table far in the rear of the Grand Ballroom at the Waldorf-Astoria, we recognized even fewer of the black-tied leaders on the tiered dais.

On our way to Pittsburgh the following March, my son John and I made our first visit to a meeting of the Republican State Committee in Harrisburg. Many of those in attendance knew me, if at all, only by reputation. We met and greeted as many of them as we could. While the impact was negligible, we had gotten our feet wet at another of the ritual gatherings of the Pennsylvania GOP. (The committee would later decide to hold an open primary with no endorsed candidate, a result distinctly in my favor as the outsider.)

I began testing the waters statewide by accepting virtually all speaking invitations tendered. At the outset most of these were from the Pittsburgh area, but gradually they began coming from farther afield. The tone of these appearances was set by my very first purely "political" speech, given to the suburban Mt. Lebanon Council of Republican Women in March 1977. I described Pennsylvania as undergoing a "crisis in integrity" and "an epidemic of corruption and shoddy practices." State officials had been charged "in a wide variety of ripoff schemes." What was needed was "a maximum effort from top to bottom" to restore confidence and faith in state government.

At that time, a *Philadelphia Magazine* article handicapping the race established the odds on me at 20:1. The article's assessment: "Asset: He's bosom buddies with John Heinz. Liability: He's boring. Heinz money could make him an exciting candidate. Look what it did for John Heinz." The odds-on choice for the GOP nomination was state House leader Bob Butera of Montgomery County at 8:1. Other candidates were Senate leader Henry Hager of Williamsport and former Philadelphia district attorney Arlen Specter.

A major publicity coup came my way in late May, when I testified before a state House subcommittee on crime and corruption in the Shapp administration. The story was widely carried around the state and, together with speeches, panel discussions and press conferences, began to establish me as the candidate most fully committed to cleaning up the capital. My prospective candidacy was clearly developing into one designed to distance me from Harrisburg and the old-boy network, including, by implication, Butera and Hager. Specter had an equally vigorous record as a prosecutor, but some labeled him a three-time loser due to successive defeats in efforts to become Philadelphia mayor in 1969, be reelected district attorney in 1973, and gain the Republican nomination for the Senate in 1976.

During the summer I continued to sound out support around the state. June, for example, took me to Philadelphia for a series of meetings with leaders there, to Greensburg for a rally with former California governor Ronald Reagan, to the Governor's Club in Hershey, to the Indiana County GOP Women's Council, back to Philadelphia, to York County, back to Philadelphia twice again, to Valley Forge, to Bucks County, to Oil City, to Harrisburg and to Lancaster. The Greensburg appearance was especially encouraging. Describing Milton Shapp's Harrisburg as reminiscent of one of Reagan's old television shows, *Death Valley Days*, I received a standing ovation from the 1,200 guests and was encouraged to "go, go, go!" Other events included the Venango County fish fry; the annual Beaver County picnic; the Allegheny County Gateway Liner cruise on Pittsburgh's three rivers; and assorted other GOP picnics, Rotary Club and Chamber of Commerce meetings, as well as individual meetings with prospective donors and supporters. By now, all the candidates were in full swing, and many of these events were auditions for the right to represent the Republican Party in the election.

My exploratory effort was not without its debacles. In October, I was importuned to attend the Clarion Leaf Festival, at which upwards of 100,000 people were expected. After a lengthy drive, I arrived to find a scant welcoming committee huddled under umbrellas in the midst of a monumental daylong downpour. The show had to go on, however, and I was obliged to stand among a sparse crowd in the pouring rain for the length of a rather bedraggled and water-soaked parade of floats and marching bands.

Our fortunes had been boosted, on the other hand, at the Allegheny County GOP picnic in September, when our first "Thornburgh for Governor" buttons were displayed. At my insistence, they were gold with black letters, the Pittsburgh colors—much to the dismay of my advisers, who were trying their utmost to make me into a statewide personality.

We also received a major boost in September in the Philadelphia area: a positive front-page story by Steve Neal in the Sunday Review and Opinion section of the *Philadelphia Inquirer*, accompanied by an equally complimentary photo spread. The column, entitled "Tough Prosecutor Takes to Campaign," reviewed my career extensively, identified me as the front-runner for the Republican nomination and even included favorable quotes from Pittsburgh Democrats Pete Flaherty ("He really went after white-collar crime and organized crime") and John Bingler ("[H]e's got super integrity and would do his best to shake things up"). We had the story reprinted and widely distributed. A favorable profile written for the Associated Press by Bill Williams introduced the theme that was to dominate my governorship—the effort to develop Pennsylvania's economy. Even that reference took note of the need "to begin to turn a face to industry that we are not a state where you're going to get ripped off or shaken down." And a prominent Sunday profile by *Harrisburg Patriot-News* political writer John Scotzin quoted me as saying, "On the first day in office the next governor must get the word out to those interested in payoffs, bribery and kickbacks that they'd better clear out before sundown." On November 1, in a speech before the Republican City Committee in Bethlehem, I set out in detail my vision for the campaign. After reviewing the Shapp failures, I identified my core goals for Pennsylvania:

1. A sound and stable economic climate to provide jobs, business profits and tax revenues

2. Reductions in the vastly increased cost of welfare, with continued service to those genuinely in need

3. An honest and politics-free Department of Transportation to tend to pressing highway needs

4. Effective law enforcement against organized crime, drug trafficking, violence and official corruption

5. A review of the tax burden to ensure fairness and equity

6. An efficient and high-quality system of public education

I next recounted Republicans' opportunity to overcome the Democrats' 800,000-voter registration edge and hold on the governor's office and both houses of the legislature. It was the Democrats, I said, who had to "explain and seek to justify [their] shoddy leadership to our citizens next year." I added, "The machines are gone. The bloc votes [including labor and minority blocs] which have sustained the Democrats over the years are no more."

Not long thereafter, a bombshell exploded. On November 28, Deputy Attorney General Pete Flaherty, after only eight months on the job, resigned to explore running for governor, in spite of his previous commitment to serve the full four years of his appointment. His entry created a whole new ball game for Republicans as well as Democrats.

Soon after this, senior Republican senator Dick Schweiker began musing about becoming a candidate despite a previous disavowal of any interest in the race. Telephone polls indicated that Schweiker would be the front-runner if he entered. In December, Jay Waldman and I met with the senator and made it absolutely clear that we were in the race to stay. On January 4, Schweiker announced that he would not be a candidate after all because he had "no burning desire" to be governor. The real reason was, of course, that the consensus he had sought for his candidacy among party leaders was nowhere in evidence.

By now, it was clear that to win the GOP primary, I would have to build upon my base in western Pennsylvania while raising my profile in other areas. Specter and Butera were going to split the vote-rich southeast (Philadelphia and the suburban counties of Bucks, Montgomery, Delaware and Chester) but had almost no strength in the west. Butera was relying on his legislative colleagues across the state but had little additional support. Hager had bet all his chips on a somewhat bizarre "T" theory, seeking a swath of votes up through thinly populated central and northern Pennsylvania. Overall, geography was my strongest hope, as I was the only western candidate.

I OFFICIALLY ENTERED the race with a three-day blitz of the state, kicked off at a Pittsburgh rally on January 10, 1978. I began my speech here by lamenting:

a seven-year season of shame and shortcoming in Harrisburg . . . where over sixty persons have been charged with crimes relating to their conduct in office . . . where a dozen or so cabinet-level officials have been obliged to leave office because of criminal convictions or involvement in other wrongdoing [and] where, in the General Assembly, the speaker of the House, the man who was to have been the majority leader of the Senate and the chairman of the Senate Appropriations Committee have all been convicted of serious federal crimes. . . .

[H]ow can we teach our children respect for law and traditional moral values if the people who make and administer our laws cannot be relied upon to obey them?

How can we secure jobs for Pennsylvanians when extortion and kickbacks are viewed by many as a cost of doing business here?

These shortcomings, I noted, had cost Pennsylvania over 100,000 manufacturing jobs and created an adversarial relationship between government and business. Decline in the quality of public services had resulted as well and was nowhere more evident than in the Pennsylvania Department of Transportation (PennDOT), which, I said, "has become so bankrupt it cannot finish the highways it started, and so corrupt it cannot maintain the highways it finished."

I then set forth my commitments to a better economic climate, a stronger educational system, concern for crime and its victims and compassionate administration of health and welfare programs, with particular attention to those with mental or physical disabilities. Above all, I noted, "[I]t is a time for state government to learn to live within its means. . . . I know what it's like to live within a budget, and I think it's time that state government learn to do the same. . . . [W]e must recognize that there are limits to our resources. We cannot try to do everything lest we do all things badly. We must do those things which are important and do them well." With that, I had commenced the most important public undertaking of my lifetime. Over the next three days, we flew to Harrisburg, Philadelphia, the Lehigh Valley, Scranton, Erie, Johnstown and Altoona to make similar announcements.

Two matters now commanded our attention: financing and paid media. They were not unconnected, since most of the money we would raise would go into our television effort. This was a new experience for me. In the dozen years since my congressional campaign in 1966, television had begun to dominate the political process, and it had largely rendered obsolete (except as a basis for photo ops) much of the traditional face-to-face campaigning upon which I had cut my political teeth. We decided to engage New Yorker David Garth, the reigning guru of political television advertising, to handle this aspect of the campaign.

Ev Rose's fund-raising efforts were well in gear by the first of the year, in pursuit of $1.4 million for the primary. Substantial support came from Pittsburghers such as Elsie and Henry Hillman, Jack Heinz (the senator's father) and Dick Scaife. We began a series of major fund-raising dinners with an event in Pittsburgh supported by most of the leaders of the business and financial community. The $200-per-plate affair raised over $135,000. A similar dinner in Philadelphia attracted support from many business luminaries and lawyers who knew me from my bar association days. This $150-per-plate dinner added $80,000 to our coffers. Smaller events were held in other locales.

The issue of financial support was to be a major one. When Sherley Uhl of the *Pittsburgh Press* asked why we were soliciting campaign funds from wealthy donors, I gave the same answer as the legendary criminal Willie Sutton was said to have given when asked why he robbed banks: "That's where the money is." I told Uhl that contributors to my campaign could expect nothing more in return than the knowledge that they had made "an investment in good government"; there were no commitments and no quid pro quos. The bottom line was that a campaign for governor could cost $2 million or more, and I personally did not have that kind of cash. All other candidates were up against the same challenge. Later, in response to criticism of $25,000 contributions made by Jack Heinz and Henry Hillman, I pointed out that these were not just wealthy individuals, but people who had invested substantial time and effort to lead the Pittsburgh Renaissance. Their decision to support me, I said, was a source of great pride.

One more surprise was to come. On March 6, David Marston, who had been U.S. attorney for the Eastern District of Pennsylvania until fired by the Carter administration, announced his candidacy. This was a mixed blessing. On the one hand, as another Philadelphia-area candidate, Marston further diluted the appeals of both Specter and Butera. His anticorruption message, however, was in competition with mine, and he had the advantage of the widespread publicity that had attended his firing. Marston quickly became the story for national political reporters. This was frustrating for the rest of the pack; I observed semifacetiously that had I known he was going to run, I would have insisted upon being fired myself. Marston's late entry smacked of opportunism, and he was clearly not up to speed on many of the issues. He had, moreover, no organization to speak of, and he proved unable to raise sufficient funds to put any kind of message on television. His basic appeal, resting upon an 87 percent name recognition, was "Hi! I'm the guy Jimmy Carter fired because I was trying to clean up corruption."

In the Republican lists as well were two fringe candidates. Andrew Watson was a conservative and former chairman of the state's Constitutional Party; Alvin Joseph Jacobson claimed to be the only one in the race officially to be declared sane, as he brandished his discharge papers from a military mental hospital.

Heated primary battles were also developing in the race for lieutenant governor. For the Republicans, Bill Scranton, the thirty-year-old son of the former governor, was opposed by Faith Ryan Whittlesey, a hardball Delaware County commissioner. One of the thirteen Democratic candidates was one Robert P. Casey, a Pittsburgh schoolteacher with the same name as candidate for governor Bob Casey, the former auditor general. No gubernatorial candidate of either party chose to pair up with a running mate.

Our own battle quickly turned into a cross fire of carping and criticism. First to draw blood from our camp was the perennial issue of gun control. While serving in Washington, I had come to appreciate how vehement were the concerns about "the right to bear arms" expressed by hunters, sportsmen and many law enforcement officials, particularly in rural areas. It had become clear that proposals such as those I had advocated as an East Coast urban U.S. attorney would not fly everywhere. Butera and the other candidates circulated copies of my previous publications supporting tighter restrictions on handguns, and I was obliged to explain my position anew. We pointed out that Butera and Specter had once called for restrictions similar to those I had suggested. In the end, I relented completely and stated, "We need no additional gun control laws in Pennsylvania. Period." We also formed a committee that put out a brochure entitled "Why Pennsylvania Sportsmen Support Dick Thornburgh for Governor." It was not my finest hour.

Another glitch came with the disclosure that two of our volunteer fundraisers from the hard-coal region had been shareholders in a cable television company with others who were alleged to have organized-crime connections. This time the news media carried the ball, obviously delighted at discovering a connection, however tenuous, between "Mr. Clean" and the mob. We acted swiftly to separate the two from our campaign.

We were beginning to establish strong organizations in most of the counties and attract the support of leading GOP figures from key areas statewide. My schedule had become an endless succession of county dinners and candidate forums. My set speech was finely honed, including attention-getting lines describing the Shapp administration as "the crook of the month club" and a "cornucopia of corruption" and labeling PennDOT the "home of the three Ps—payoffs, patronage and potholes." I genuinely enjoyed the give-and-take with my rivals and the press.

When I was unable to attend such events, Ginny, or our sons John or David often filled in. Ginny also joined me in hosting many gatherings of volunteers, political officials and members of the press. She was indeed the "Super Saleswoman" described in one newspaper headline, and her tireless efforts across the state earned the admiration of countless Pennsylvanians. John, on leave from Bucknell for the fall semester, was to develop into my most reliable campaign aide, anticipating almost my every need and looking after such details as drafting thank-you notes and responses to personal correspondence. John also did valuable work putting together the campaign's "county books," crammed with research on every stop I made around the state.

By mid-April, David Garth's crews had produced three ads concentrating on my human qualities rather than the familiar hard-line prosecutor's image. One dealt with the industrial pollution case brought under the Refuse Act, one with a case brought against a confidence man who had fleeced elderly couples in a home repair scam, and one with Ginny's and my interest in the Home for Crippled Children. All of our spots were positive in nature. Butera's were more hard-edged, one describing Specter,

Marston and me as losers. The best ad in the primary, by common consent, was a folksy five-minute spot highlighting Pete Flaherty's record as a tax cutter and cost container and showing him in a variety of "real" settings with ordinary Pittsburghers. It included film shot at a cost of $47,000 by the U.S. Information Agency, but no one seemed to mind.

We also released a series of detailed position papers on major issues. One that had to be addressed this time was abortion, to which I had given little thought during my public life. I accumulated a variety of viewpoints before fashioning my own conclusion, first set forth in a May 10 interview with the *Allentown Morning Call*: "I am personally opposed to abortion except in cases of rape, incest or threat to the mother's life or health, and then only in a patient-doctor context. In these cases, I think it should be available regardless of the person's income. Where abortion is permitted in these limited cases, I believe that any state or federal medical assistance programs for which the person qualifies should be available to pay for abortion." This view I adhered to throughout my public career. My skepticism about "abortion on demand" was based upon my resistance to a view of abortion as simply another method of birth control, a view that I felt would only add to the already serious problem of casual attitudes towards sexual promiscuity. It also derived from my feelings about the sanctity of human life, based on our own experience with Peter. Years later, in a much more highly charged atmosphere, I was to be accused repeatedly of having changed my views on abortion, but the record clearly indicates my consistency in this regard from the very beginning.

On May 4, the five principal Republican candidates appeared together at the *Pittsburgh Post-Gazette* and laid out our cases. I emphasized the symbolic importance of electing a proven foe of corruption, my nationwide management experience and my private-sector insights into the state's economic problems.

As the campaign moved toward its climax, endorsements began to proliferate. The most important one for us was the May 10 nod from the *Philadelphia Daily News*. It noted, "Some may find it scary that Thornburgh has a ton of western Pennsylvania Republican money behind him. Big, big business money. But there doesn't appear to be a string on him. His record is one of integrity and independence. We endorse it and him." For a western Pennsylvania candidate, that kind of reception in Philadelphia was money in the bank. Both Pittsburgh papers endorsed me as well, as did the Pittsburgh Federation of Teachers. The Pennsylvania Rifle and Pistol Association, on the other hand, did not.

ON THE EVE OF May 16, election day, pundits considered the Republican primary too close to call. Indeed, it was not until after two o'clock on the morning after the primary that we were able to announce victory. Bill Scranton claimed the number two spot on our ticket. The Democratic nominees were Pete Flaherty and the improbable Robert P. Casey, the Pittsburgh schoolteacher who soon became known, with our assistance, as "the wrong Bob Casey."

The election results were, of course, carefully scrutinized. Statewide, I had received 325,376 votes; Specter, 206,802; Butera, 190,653; Marston, 161,813; Hager, 57,119; Watson, 48,460; and Jacobson, 7,101. On the Democratic side, Flaherty had gotten 574,899 votes; Casey, 446,146; Ernest Kline, 223,811; and Jennifer Wesner, 36,770. The vote was heavily regional. I had carried Allegheny County with 85,257 votes to Butera's 8,013, Marston's 7,277 and Specter's 1,650. Specter had carried Philadelphia with 54,987 votes to 11,790 for Marston, 10,342 for Butera and a mere 5,399 for me. Specter and I had thus obliterated each other on our respective home turfs, but he had to divide the rest of the southeastern vote with Butera (who carried all the suburban counties save Bucks), while I carried all but four of the counties west of central Pennsylvania (three went for Marston, Huntington County for Specter). One of our key regions was the hard-coal northeast. Lackawanna, Luzerne and Schuylkill Counties all gave pluralities to the Pittsburgh candidate, with Specter and Butera splitting the balance.

Ginny and I celebrated our victory with a reception at which our campaign staff presented me with a garish leisure suit and a pair of white shoes to mock my gray-flannel image. To everyone's surprise, I slipped upstairs for a quick change, festooned myself with a couple of Ginny's gold chains and reappeared as a more "with it" candidate. No one advised that the makeover should be permanent.

A postelection visit to Philadelphia generated a front-page picture in the *Daily News* showing me doing a fair imitation of a mummer's strut, the traditional Philadelphia dance step associated with the annual New Year's parade. It would take more than that in November, however, to turn around our miserable primary showing in the City of Brotherly Love.

7

The Victory!

A WEEK AFTER THE primary election, a massive "unity brunch" was held in the Harrisburg suburb of Camp Hill. Nearly 1,000 excited Republicans jammed the event. GOP National Chairman Bill Brock was there to describe our election as "absolutely crucial" to the Republican Party's hopes to regain the White House in 1980. All present left the event with a real sense of optimism about the fall campaign. But a number of bombshells were soon to fall.

The first resulted from our tactical decision not to disclose, during the primary, the financial contributions made to my campaign. When we made the filings required by law in June, the reason for our delay became apparent. The campaign had received $195,000 from the Heinz family—$75,000 in contributions and $50,000 in loans from Jack Heinz, Senator Heinz's father, and $25,000 in contributions and $45,000 in loans from Mrs. Clifford Heinz, his great-aunt. The loans were made, at my personal request through the senator, within the last three weeks of the campaign to finance Garth's closing television blitz. They amounted to about 20 percent of our total of $954,934 in contributions.

These disclosures were red meat for Pete Flaherty, who identified "big money" as his opponent and immediately accused the Heinz family of attempting to buy the governor's office. The media also criticized our delay unmercifully. While there was no legal requirement to disclose the contributions during the primary, we had said we would, and most viewed us as having been morally bound to do so. I offered the lame excuse that "mechanical problems" had prevented a timely filing and described again the Heinz family's longtime support of worthy causes. But for a campaign based on integrity, it was a rocky start.

At the annual meeting of the Associated Press managing editors at Penn State in late June, Pete shrewdly proposed that we each limit our general-election expenditures to $1 million. I rejected this limitation out of hand as a "clever strategy by a man who is already the front-runner and holds an 800,000 registration majority." Arguing that limiting expenditures was not nearly as important as revealing the source of contributions, I acceded to Flaherty's suggestion that we make full disclosures of our contributions on August 31, September 30 and October 31. Flaherty's response: "I'm glad Thornburgh has made another promise to disclose contributors. I hope he keeps this one." It was not a good day for our team.

Another flap soon provided more grist for the media. The extraordinary cost—$445,000—of our television effort, resulting in the embarrassing need to borrow from the Heinz family and compounded by Garth's seeming desire to run the entire campaign, had been a major irritant. After considerable anguish, I decided to replace Garth with John Deardourff. We stated that the decision had been "purely economic" and the parting "amicable." That the latter was pure fabrication was readily apparent, as Garth seldom missed a chance to take a shot at me, Jay, or Paul Critchlow. The switch also produced the first fissure between Senator Heinz and me. Garth remained a consultant to the senator, and both had expected that he would do the whole campaign for us. The change turned out to be for the best in the long run, but at the time it seemed to evidence further disarray in our camp.

No sooner had this controversy died down than a third arose, this time over the Republican State Committee chairmanship. Dick Filling, an amiable Lancaster businessman, had been the popular head of the committee for the fourteen months leading up to the primary and had wisely remained neutral in the spirited race for the nomination. Asserting the time-honored prerogative of the winner, I nonetheless decided to replace Filling with my own choice, Delaware County Councilman Harold "Bud" Haabestad, who had chaired our primary campaign in that populous county. Filling bowed out at my request but let it be known that he was available for a "draft." This laid the groundwork for a potential serious split in the party ranks.

Senator Hager and Representative Jack Seltzer immediately suggested that a compromise candidate be agreed upon. One party official observed, "It's a test of muscle. The Harrisburg crowd wants to teach some manners to Thornburgh" for failing to "consult" with the legislative leaders on the chairmanship.

It was in this mood that the "newly unified" Pennsylvania Republicans met in Lancaster on June 17–18. After considerable maneuvering among regional caucuses on Friday night and a final 2 A.M. meeting between Filling and Haabestad brokered by me, Filling agreed to step down, nominate Haabestad as his successor and assume undefined new duties. Bud was unanimously elected the following morning, and Filling eventually contributed to the campaign effort in Lancaster County in the fall.

This high-risk undertaking was designed to establish my control over the party, though at the very real peril of having my choice for chairman repudiated. But it also foreshadowed substantial other problems ahead with the "party regulars." My old friend Elsie Hillman had already warned me that some of them felt slighted by our "outsider" attitude.

On the substantive side, we were almost immediately bedeviled by the passage in California of Proposition 13, which established severe limits on taxing authority at all levels of government. Many self-styled experts within the Republican Party began to urge that we support a similar program in Pennsylvania lest Flaherty, who had made his reputation as a tax cutter, capture support from otherwise Republican fiscal conservatives. They had a point, but the differences in tax structures and economic conditions in California and Pennsylvania made me reluctant to advance a Proposition 13-type agenda without further study.

The last straw came in late July, when we received the results of a comprehensive poll that Bob Teeter had conducted after the primary. These results, shared with me only after some debate among the senior campaign managers, showed Flaherty with a thirty-two-point lead—55 percent to 23 percent. I was stunned. I had known we were the underdogs, but this deficit seemed almost insurmountable. As I was to learn, however, the questions and answers in this poll contained the seeds of the strategy that would govern the balance of our campaign.

It is perhaps appropriate at this juncture to examine Flaherty's and my respective images as the campaign got under way. Just after the primary, the *Philadelphia Inquirer* profiled both of us, and the headlines reflected some popular perceptions: "Pete Flaherty: A Natural Born Man of the People" and "Thornburgh: Warmth Beneath the Gray Flannel." Flaherty was the easygoing, unassuming former Pittsburgh mayor whose cost-cutting measures had included "turning in the mayor's Cadillac for a Dodge." I was the "steely-eyed prosecutor . . . big time crime buster . . . cold-blooded crusader," but underneath much warmer and happier than I appeared. The column took note of my efforts to loosen up on the campaign trail and adopt a folksier approach, without much apparent success.

Taking stock of the upcoming campaign, Paul Taylor, the *Inquirer's* chief political writer, said that Flaherty had neutralized the corruption issue by being the consummate outsider and rejecting Milton Shapp's endorsement the day before the primary. With corruption not an issue, Flaherty's record as a tax cutter overshadowed mine as a prosecutor. On ideology, Taylor only half-facetiously characterized the race as one between a moderate Democrat (me) and a conservative Republican (Pete) at a time when the country's drift was to the right. Geographically, we were both from the west, and Flaherty would benefit from the Democratic registration edge and his traditional appeal to Republicans (he had won both nominations in his 1973 mayoral reelection campaign). "It seems hard to imagine," Taylor noted, "Flaherty not taking a 200,000 vote plurality, minimum, out of Philadelphia." In addition, Pete had won all four suburban Philadelphia counties in his primary, while I had attracted only 10 percent of the Republican vote in that region.

On the crucial question of image, Taylor found me stuck with the gray-flannel curse in spite of being, in fact, "a relaxed, easy-going, compassionate man who can hold his own on an exchange on the respective merits of the Phillies and the Pirates." Flaherty was "Just Pete," the best politician in the state at "projecting himself as one of the guys," though vague on "hard, fine-tuning questions about government." The only advantages Taylor accorded me were my running mate and state history, finding an edge for the all-WASP, all-Yale team over "a couple of Irish-Catholics from Pittsburgh" and noting that Pennsylvania voters had "been religious about transferring the governor's office between the Republican and Democratic parties at regular eight-year intervals."

This was the rather discouraging lay of the political land as we entered the summer of 1978. I told our schedulers to book me wherever they could, and we began a regimen of days that started early and ended late, crammed with as many breakfasts, luncheons, dinners, picnics, rallies, news conferences, editorial board meetings and one-on-one sessions as possible, moving us around the state on chartered flights, through fair weather and foul. At our lowest moments, Ginny and I confided that our bottom-line goal was simply to avoid a humiliating defeat.

Jay Waldman was of a different mind, however. On July 7, he presented me with a strategic campaign plan that we were to follow to victory. As it was finally refined, this plan had six key points:

1. We had to make an immediate 180-degree turn from the primary, forsaking my status as the western candidate to make me the eastern one. Jay took note of Pete's poor showing against Schweiker in the 1974 Senate campaign and posited a maximum effort by Republicans in the Philadelphia suburbs. All of my efforts were to be skewed toward the eastern part of the state.

2. We had to identify my candidacy with the interests of the strong anti-Rizzo constituency forming in Philadelphia. (The Philadelphia ballot would include a referendum on eliminating the two-term limitation in the city's charter so that Frank Rizzo could seek a third term as mayor.)

3. We had to continue to stress the corruption issue, emphasizing Flaherty's past electoral support of Shapp and doing careful research to establish his ties with "organization" Democrats. (Flaherty himself was utterly free from any taint of corruption.)

4. We had to attack Flaherty's strength. Rick Stafford's team was to make a minute examination of his record as mayor, particularly his claims of good management and tax cutting.

5. The record of "the wrong Bob Casey" had to be given the same treatment, a task assigned to Nancy Watson, a volunteer in the Pittsburgh office.

6. Because of Flaherty's mixed record on dealing with African Americans and labor unions, two traditional sources of statewide Democratic strength, we were to make a special effort to court these groups.

One important breakthrough had come at the end of June when John Scales, my college classmate and Constitutional Convention colleague, agreed to chair Democrats for Thornburgh-Scranton. A former state senator, John was widely admired within the Democratic Party, which he had chaired from 1970 until he resigned in 1972 after a dispute with Governor Shapp. Flaherty recruited the disgruntled Bob Curran as a Republican supporting him, but the contrast between Scales and Curran could not have been greater.

In midsummer the Pennsylvania State Education Association (PSEA), a growing power in state politics, endorsed our team, while the state AFL-CIO went for Flaherty. Both had the capability to muster substantial resources across the state, and we were pleased to obtain the PSEA endorsement. We were more pleased, however, that other labor organizations did not flock to Flaherty following the AFL-CIO nod. The largest union of state employees, for example, the American Federation of State, County and Municipal Employees (AFSCME), did not endorse either candidate. We redoubled our efforts to corral the allegiance of those uncommitted labor organizations.

Despite these hopeful signs, we remained desperate for public attention during that baleful summer. Our "Philadelphia" strategy led me to participate (in a Phillies uniform) in a softball game between the casts of *Happy Days* and *Laverne and Shirley*, on the one hand, and a team of former Philadelphia athletic greats and politicians, on the other. The contest was held as a preliminary to a Giants-Phillies game. Few votes were captured, but a good time was had by the corporal's guard of Thornburgh enthusiasts who viewed our loss to the younger and better conditioned television stars.

One additional ignominy was in store. In September Ginny and I attended a fund-raising reception at Dutch Wonderland in Lancaster and afterwards watched the aquatic show. I was invited down to make an appearance and feed the dolphins. The emcee insisted that I try holding a fish in my mouth for a dolphin to grab, as he had done. Naturally, as I placed the fish between my teeth and leaned over one of the dolphins, flashbulbs popped. The next day an Associated Press photo appeared across the state with a story about my efforts to capture the dolphin vote. A Flaherty aide properly observed, "I always thought Thornburgh's campaign was fishy!" But it was statewide coverage.

Beset with "expert" advice from the old pros of Pennsylvania Republican politics, Jay Waldman decided to gather all the naysayers together for a broad-based critique of our operations. This ventilation of grievances probably bought us some goodwill. It was also another important reminder of how much "consulting" means to people involved in the political process.

IN PENNSYLVANIA, the fall campaign traditionally opens on Labor Day. Pete Flaherty jumped the gun by three days and set forth his bare-bones program in a two-page press release. His platform included calls for reducing the size of the legislature; introducing mechanisms for initiative, referendum and recall; and adding a zany constitutional requirement for a referendum if the legislature wanted to spend more than the governor had recommended (a proposal I later criticized as calling for a statewide "town meeting" every year on the budget). All of these were, it seemed, responses to the Proposition 13 mentality. We had ourselves finally taken note of this phenomenon by proposing a "Thornburgh amendment" that would constitutionally limit annual state spending increases by relating them to the rate of inflation.

After Labor Day, John Deardourff opened our television campaign with a superb five-minute "personality piece" that sought to reinforce my campaign themes and counteract some of the prevalent stereotypes of me and the Republican Party as hardhearted and uncaring. Other spots dealt specifically with the elderly, small business, agriculture, the "Thornburgh amendment" and economic development. The tag line for all our ads was "Dick Thornburgh . . . He'll Clean Up Harrisburg."

We did not try to match a paperback publication entitled "Pete," an impressive campaign biography that slickly recounted the mayor's accomplishments and was well stocked with photographs of the Flaherty clan. We concentrated instead on issues and summed up our case in a twenty-one-page document entitled "Making Pennsylvania Proud Again . . . What the People of the Commonwealth May Expect of a Thornburgh-Scranton Administration."

At this point several bizarre incidents threatened to throw us off our stride. The suspected perpetrator was my old adversary, Tony Grosso. Following his jail term, the renowned racketeer had sent me an Easter card, and in June 1978 he had sent a handwritten note wishing good health to my family and sharing some gossip about political figures. In a postscript, he had noted, "The price on you winning the governor's fight three months ago was 5–1 against you. Now it's down to almost even money. The price by election time will be 8–5 in your favor and you should win by more than 100,000 votes." He added, "You will make an excellent governor—hope you win it." At the time I was gratified to have anyone giving us better than an even chance, but I was puzzled by Tony's interest.

In September, the plot thickened. Leaflets were passed out in downtown Pittsburgh asking, "Want a nitwit for governor?" and quoting a book describing Flaherty as such. At a Steelers game shortly thereafter, the capacity crowd was treated to an unexpected aerial show as a light plane circled the stadium, trailing a banner with three messages: "A Nitwit Ruined Pittsburgh," "Mafia's Wango Capizzi Hosts Pete's Fundraiser at VIP Club" and "Thornburgh for Governor." (Flaherty had, in fact, canceled the VIP Club fund-raiser because of Capizzi's suspected involvement, which the club's owners vehemently denied.) Flaherty blamed us for the messages. I retorted that we were being set up. On consecutive days, front-page *Post-Gazette* stories identified Grosso as the perpetrator of these antics and uncovered what they called a "secret Thornburgh for Governor" headquarters near Grosso's South Hills restaurant.

Though amused, I adopted a posture of infuriation. I held a news conference denying any connection with Grosso or the "dirty tricks" and accusing organized crime of trying to sabotage my campaign. Both Flaherty and I made the ritual calls for an investigation. The hullabaloo continued for a week. Although I publicly identified these actions as efforts by Grosso to sabotage my campaign, I privately acknowledged that they were more than likely misguided efforts to help. We certainly gave him no encouragement. One of his comments to a reporter, however, I took to heart: "I bought every politician and cop in the state of Pennsylvania. If I could have bought Dick Thornburgh, I never would have got ten years and gone to jail. He wasn't for sale."

During the fall I routinely gave my all-purpose speech at two or three appearances a day. I had introduced a number of new lines, calling Pete Flaherty a "born-again independent" (referring to his prior support of Shapp) and questioning whether his oft-repeated commitment to "do for Pennsylvania what he had done for Pittsburgh" was a threat or a promise. The growing crowds at our events began to pick up my invariable tag line, "The only way to clean up Harrisburg is to clean it out . . . O-U-T . . . out!" Occasionally, at dinner events, I sang a takeoff on "My Favorite Things" from *The Sound of Music*:

> Nice big fat paychecks and liberal pensions
> Fringes and perks that we won't even mention
> Ample expense accounts minus the strings
> These are a few of my favorite things
>
> Cups of hot coffee and big Bloody Marys
> Made every morning by our secretaries
> Aides and assistants who treat us like kings
> These are a few of my favorite things

When the press writes nasty stories
And it makes us mad
We simply remember our favorite things
And then we don't feel so bad

All were amused save the occasional legislator with whom these jibes resonated.

Our research effort was now in high gear, fleshing out the concepts that Jay Waldman had sketched. Here we were greatly aided by a peculiar development. Not content to accurately describe his admittedly fine record as mayor of Pittsburgh, Flaherty began to exaggerate his accomplishments in almost every area. For example, he claimed to have cut real estate taxes. In fact, after being elected mayor in 1969, while still a councilman, he pushed through a 20 percent increase in city real estate millage. Thus, real estate taxes were higher for Pittsburghers when Flaherty left office than they had been before his election. He also claimed to have cut the mayor's staff in half. However, the cost of that staff rose 33 percent during his tenure. He claimed that Pittsburgh had been "on the verge of bankruptcy" when he was elected. In fact, the city had had an A-1 credit rating, which fell only after he left office, due to the financial consequences of his administration. He claimed to have built 125 playgrounds and 23 senior citizen centers; the actual numbers were 31 and 17. We released various publications summarizing these and other discrepancies. One was embellished with a photograph of a smiling and waving Pete Flaherty and Milton Shapp sharing a rear train platform.

The Philadelphia component of our campaign got its sea legs as well. Flaherty had stolen a march on us by coming out to oppose a third term for Mayor Rizzo, but we recovered by carrying the battle to the mayor's very doorstep. On October 3, I appeared in the courtyard of Philadelphia's City Hall to announce my opposition to a third term for the controversial mayor and to criticize his recent "vote white" advice to Philadelphia voters as "racially divisive and inflammatory." Surrounded by 100 or so hecklers sympathetic to the mayor, we could barely make ourselves heard over the shouting. This, of course, was just what we might have hoped for. Thereafter we were able to build a sizable constituency among the opponents of charter change. Well after the election, when Rizzo and I had made our peace, I was told that Rizzo himself had looked down on the chaotic scene from a City Hall window and said, "You know. I kinda like that guy. He's got balls!"

We got a needed morale boost when Mamie Eisenhower agreed to chair the statewide Citizens for Thornburgh-Scranton Committee. This endorsement lent some real magic to our campaign. A marvelous smiling picture of Mamie wearing a Thornburgh-Scranton button received wide circulation. Another assist came from within our official "family" when former governor Bill Scranton took to the campaign trail on behalf of our ticket.

The first media endorsement of my candidacy came out of Philadelphia, of all places, from CBS television affiliate WCAU-TV. While lukewarm, it represented a breakthrough in that previously hostile area. Meanwhile, we had begun to introduce negative television spots hammering away at Flaherty's record as mayor. Each ended with the query, "Can the man who drove Pittsburgh to its knees put Pennsylvania back on its feet?"

A statewide Gallup poll released on October 6 showed Flaherty holding a twelve- to fifteen-point lead (51 to 36 percent, with 13 percent undecided, among all registered voters and 51–39 percent, with 10 percent undecided, among likely voters). When a television reporter blindsided me with this news, I immediately thought of our own previously undisclosed July poll and determined that this was the moment to publicize it. "That's good news," I told the baffled reporter. "We've gained about twenty points on Flaherty since the summer! Now to close the rest of the gap." It was also good news that the Gallup poll had identified corruption, taxes and highway repairs as priority issues. More sobering was Flaherty's 49 to 32 percent lead in the vital Philadelphia suburbs (19 percent were undecided). To address this gap, we dispatched our "truth squad," an "Ask a Pittsburgher" team of five prominent Democrats, to the Philadelphia area for a stepped-up attack on the "real" Flaherty record. We also increased our commitment to negative television commercials in southeastern Pennsylvania.

As the underdog, I had agitated for debates and had agreed in July to two dates, which were now approaching. Of course, political debates, especially when televised, are not debates at all. They are vehicles for conveying images and themes, preferably in concise sound bites. The best advice to the televised political "debater" is to forget about the question, to the extent possible, and concentrate upon getting your message across. The opportunity for making a significant gaffe, or goading the opponent into making one, should also command attention. Most of all, the debater has to remember that television is a visual medium. In the Nixon-Kennedy debates of 1960, radio listeners famously called Nixon the clear winner, while television viewers gave an equally clear edge to Kennedy. As we prepared for our first debate, Frank Ursomarso, who had worked on President Ford's advance team, chimed in with some suggestions on this front (e.g., "Don't cross your legs . . . [it] may sometimes be perceived as effeminate"). On the substantive side, Rick Stafford prepared a massive binder containing a response to every question that might conceivably be raised.

The first debate was taped on October 10. Flaherty surprised everyone by appearing in shirtsleeves, apparently to enhance his "man of the people" image. (I later facetiously threatened to attend the next exchange in overalls.) I quickly took the offensive, telling the audience that "while Pete Flaherty was mayor of Pittsburgh, three things went up and three things went down. Taxes, spending and debt went up. And jobs, housing starts and the city's credit rating went down." I also chided Flaherty on "waffling" on a commitment to remove patronage from PennDOT and specified the kinds of cuts in state spending I would seek. For the first time, Flaherty admitted the full story about the record tax increases right after his election, but he unwisely attempted to blame them on his predecessor, Mayor Joe Barr. He also characterized me as being "in hock" to business interests and closed with a sly shot about my being the appointee of Richard Nixon and Hugh Scott.

Our team was, on the whole, satisfied with the outcome. Most stories identified me as the aggressor and highlighted Flaherty's admission regarding tax increases. Ginny and I watched the taped version on our fifteenth wedding anniversary at an enthusiastic fund-raising dinner at Lehigh University.

By now our campaign for the African American vote, normally heavily Democratic, had begun in earnest. A flyer entitled "Blacks Need Justice Now!" persuasively contrasted my record with Flaherty's on issues of particular concern to African American voters. We pointed out my hiring practices in both the U.S. attorney's office and the Department of Justice; my service on the Urban League board; our police brutality prosecution; my attack on Mayor Rizzo's racially divisive rhetoric; and my work on behalf of neighborhood legal services and youth services. In contrast, we provided generally negative reviews by others of Flaherty's record on issues such as employment, civil liberties and education. The piece was capped off by a charge by the respected Clarence Mitchell of the Washington, D.C., office of the NAACP: "Mr. Flaherty used his office as Mayor to create racial animosity to delay school desegregation." Democratic House minority leader K. Leroy Irvis added his appraisal of Flaherty as "anti-black." Flaherty began to fumble opportunities to gain support from African American voters, skipping a debate sponsored by the *Philadelphia Tri-*

bune, the city's largest black newspaper, and failing to overcome the skepticism of many prominent African Americans at the Family of Leaders dinner in the same city. At that dinner, I asked the audience to discard political stereotypes and to recognize that "[c]ompetition [was] on for black votes in Pennsylvania!"

Meanwhile, Flaherty's running mate created a major controversy by observing, in the course of a critique of overstaffing in the state's school systems: "Like what do we need special teachers for the hearing-disabled. Put those kids at the front of the classroom if they can't hear." Moreover, Casey, who had presented himself as the candidate of the "working man," unable to afford campaigning, was shown to have a net worth in excess of $200,000, a fact that Bill Scranton, himself a man of wealth, was nonetheless able to use to his advantage.

At our last major fund-raising dinner in Philadelphia, the word "momentum" was on everyone's lips. The dinner was addressed by former president Gerald Ford (who performed above and beyond the call of duty for us), as well as Senators Heinz and Schweiker. On October 25, our campaign got a big boost from the *Philadelphia Daily News*, whose endorsement reviewed my record on merit selection of judges and prosecution of corruption and white-collar crime, and even mentioned my misgivings about the Vietnam War.

Our second debate took place the evening of the day this endorsement appeared. Flaherty wore his suit coat this time and showed a lot more fire, though he seemed a little whiny. No new ground was broken, and there was a lot of bickering over statistics and Pete's record, but I was able to insert one new feature—criticism from Pittsburgh's present mayor, Dick Caligiuri, of Pete's "loner" posture. It was noted that Flaherty appeared to be perspiring, while I looked cooler—perhaps due to a last-minute lighting change that Frank Ursomarso suggested. The best news was the post-debate word that the *Pittsburgh Post-Gazette* had endorsed our ticket.

Two days later, the new Gallup poll showed that the margin among likely voters had shrunk to 4 percent—Flaherty 49 percent, Thornburgh 45. Most dramatic was the complete turnaround in the vital Philadelphia suburbs, where we now led, 53 to 42 percent. We had also gained substantially among women voters, turning a 49 to 40 percent deficit into a 49 to 45 percent lead.

The next day we flew to western Pennsylvania to attend the statewide NAACP convention in Mercer County. We also crowded as many black church services as possible onto our two remaining Sunday schedules, a new experience for Ginny and me. We will always remember the "Lion of Zion," the Reverend Leon Sullivan, bellowing against Mayor Rizzo during services at Zion Presbyterian Church in Philadelphia, just before introducing us to his congregation, an action that spoke almost as loudly. On October 30, Chuck Stone, the popular black columnist, issued a strong endorsement of our ticket. The following day, the *Philadelphia Tribune* and the *Pittsburgh Courier*, the largest newspapers of the African American communities in those cities, followed suit.

On October 29, we had achieved a wholly unexpected triple play, with all three of the remaining major newspapers in Pittsburgh and Philadelphia endorsing our ticket. By the beginning of November, we had the endorsements of twenty-five newspapers across the state, including a rare nod, for a Republican, from the *Scranton Times*. Flaherty had garnered only the endorsements of the *Lewistown Sentinel* and the *Uniontown Evening Standard*.

Earlier in the campaign, Flaherty had accepted endorsements from President Carter and Senator Ted Kennedy, but in general he had studiously avoided Democratic events to reinforce his image as "nobody's boy" and further distance himself from the Shapp administration. Organization Democrats had grumbled about their "loner" candidate, but a number of observers had attributed shrewdness and wisdom to his effort to "go it alone" during a time when voters were disillusioned with party politics. By now, however, clearly worried, Flaherty was beginning to show up at Democratic rallies and accept the contributions of party organizations. An attempt to avoid media coverage of his attendance at a dinner with Congressman Dan Flood, under indictment but still a power in the hard-coal region, brought down the wrath of the press.

Meanwhile, our new television spots featured interviews with Pittsburghers complaining about the job Pete had done as mayor. More telling criticism came in a widely publicized November 1 letter to Flaherty from Alice Barr, wife of the former mayor of Pittsburgh. In her letter, obtained with help from Elsie Hillman, Mrs. Barr not only validated all of our claims about Pete Flaherty's record as mayor but completely cut the ground from under his claims of misrepresentation in our media campaign.

On October 28, we had gained the endorsement of the 60,000-member Philadelphia Building and Trades Construction Council. Its president, Thomas J. Magrann, promised to deliver money and votes from the council's eighty-four locals, noting, "We want to support a man who is going to create jobs." On November 1 we announced the endorsement of

1,000-member Local 2274 of the Carpenters and Joiners Union in the Pittsburgh area. I also attended the annual dinner of the formerly hostile Philadelphia Republican City Committee and received warm greetings from the 1,300 guests. The following day we secured the approval of three black labor leaders representing 22,000 union members in the Philadelphia area: Earl Stout, head of District 33 of the AFSCME; Henry Nicholas, president of Local 1199C of the Hospital and Nursing Home Workers Union; and Alex Talmadge of Local 1291 of the International Longshoremen's Association. All promised financial support and poll workers. Finally, we secured the endorsement of the Philadelphia Federation of Sportsmen's Clubs, now satisfied with my watered-down position on gun control.

During the hectic last weekend, we crisscrossed the state and received several other welcome endorsements, including that of the student newspaper at the high school where Bob Casey taught (we saw to the distribution of 10,000 copies) and that of a tax-cutting group in Bucks County. As the icing on the cake of our efforts among African American voters, we announced the surprise endorsement of the Reverend Jesse Jackson, head of Operation PUSH (People United to Save Humanity) and former aide to the late Dr. Martin Luther King. Jackson's endorsement had been arranged by my old friend Nate Smith, now associated with Operation PUSH in Pittsburgh, who had never forgotten my help in his time of need. We flooded African American radio stations in Pittsburgh and Philadelphia with tapes of the civil rights leader's endorsement, urging black citizens to "vote strategically" and support my candidacy.

As the campaign drew to a close, Ginny and I shared a plane back to Pittsburgh with reporters Tom Ferrick Jr. from the *Philadelphia Inquirer* and Bob Dvorchak from the Associated Press. Both had been with us through thick and thin and had treated us fairly. As we cruised through the clear, starry night, I asked them who they expected to win. One of them replied, "Well, you've run a helluva race. You've made up a lot of ground and given Pete a real run for his money. But I don't think you're going to make it." "That's about how I see it," I responded. But Ginny and I knew how far we had come and hoped against hope that we could pull off a victory.

ON ELECTION DAY, we were off to the polls by 7:00 A.M. Ginny and I then sped to the airport for one last whirlwind tour of the state, going first to Philadelphia, then on to Steelton near Harrisburg, working the polls at each stop for some last-minute media exposure, before returning home at day's end, anticipating a long evening.

Shortly before 8:30 P.M., as I was dressing, John came to my door and said, "Dad, Walter Cronkite has just called you a winner." Dumbfounded, I finished dressing quickly and gathered up my family for the trip to our election headquarters, where pandemonium reigned. By 9:30, all three networks had called the election in our favor, and at 10:35, Pete Flaherty called to concede and offer his congratulations. It was almost an anticlimax.

The dimensions of the victory were astonishing. Statewide, we had outpolled Flaherty by 228,154 votes—1,966,042 to 1,737,888, a 53 to 47 percent spread. We had captured every eastern Pennsylvania county save Philadelphia, which we had lost by 34,875 votes, rather than the 200,000 predicted. Flaherty had held his two strongholds by margins well below those expected: Allegheny County by only 17,870 votes and the city of Pittsburgh by a mere 9,081. Exit polls showed us capturing an unprecedented 58 percent of the African American vote and 40–50 percent of the union vote. Moreover, after some recounts, Republicans had picked up a total of sixteen seats to gain control of the General Assembly, 102–100 (with one vacancy, which was filled by a Republican in a special election shortly after my inauguration), as well as three Senate seats to cut the Democrats' margin there to 27–23.

Our upset captured a good deal of national attention. The number of GOP governors had increased by 50 percent—from twelve to eighteen— and Pennsylvania was now the largest state in the nation with a Republican governor and two Republican senators. The *New York Times* featured me as one of the "New Faces on the National Political Scene" with, among others, the newly elected thirty-two-year-old governor of Arkansas, Bill Clinton. *Time, Newsweek* and *U.S. News & World Report* all featured stories and pictures.

But we had little time to bask in our victory. One of the first items of business was catching up on campaign finances. We had spent $2.4 million (compared to Flaherty's $1.6 million) and were left with a $170,000 debt, mostly in back pay to staff members. To liquidate the debt and provide a cushion for further political activities, we decided to hold a $100-a-plate fund-raising dinner in the Harrisburg area in early December. The event attracted some 2,200 of what one observer called "job-seekers, influence-seekers and just plain well-wishers." A shudder went through the crowd (and my close advisers as well) when I stated, with gusto, "The patronage plunder of the past will not recur."

This was true, but I could hardly claim full credit. The times had changed. The last time a Republican governor had succeeded a Democrat, in 1963 when Bill Scranton took office, some 50,000 state patronage jobs had changed hands and been filled largely at the behest of GOP county chairmen and other party officials. However, Governor Scranton had then extended civil service protection to many of those positions (in the minds of critics, to assure that the Republicans kept their jobs). During the Shapp administration, a public employees collective bargaining act had taken effect, and unions now gave many state employees additional job protection. Finally, the Supreme Court of the United States had recently held that public employees in non-policy-making jobs were entitled to First Amendment protection against being fired because of their political affiliation.

These developments combined to reduce that pool of 50,000 jobs to, as best we could estimate, about 900, mostly in the Harrisburg area. So my commitment to merit hiring and no wholesale firing was nothing more than yielding to the inevitable. It got us a lot of good press and praise from reform elements, but local party chairmen and others schooled in the old ways were unable or unwilling to recognize the new reality. The cry of "jobs, jobs, jobs" was to dominate the early days of my administration and to persist, at only slightly lesser volume, during my entire tenure.

Within days of the victory celebration dinner, Ginny and I returned in triumph to the annual dinner of the Pennsylvania Society in New York's Waldorf-Astoria Hotel. Where a scant two years earlier, we had been seated far in the rear of the massive ballroom, in 1978 we were at the center of the massive head table before the black-tie crowd of 1,300 business, financial and political leaders. My fifteen-minute speech focused on solving Pennsylvania's economic problems: "Government can and I hope will, in the next four years, offer the leadership, create the environment and act as a catalyst to enable productive forces in the great private sector in this state to move us forward. But the bulk of the task will be up to you."

IMMEDIATELY AFTER the election, Rick Stafford assumed the role of transition director. He established transition teams in the key areas of justice, education, commerce, labor and industry, energy and the environment, agriculture, transportation, personnel systems, budget systems, health and welfare, administrative and general services, and community affairs and intergovernmental relations. With cooperation from the outgoing Shapp administration, the transition process worked well and gave us some early insights into priority areas. The teams both offered substantive advice and served as a grapefruit league for certain contenders for cabinet positions.

I made my first staff appointments at the end of December, naming Jay Waldman executive assistant and legal counsel and Paul Critchlow director of communications and chief spokesman. Later Jim Seif became my administrative assistant and Rick Stafford our secretary of legislative affairs.

The first three cabinet members named were Bob Wilburn, president of Indiana University of Pennsylvania, as secretary of budget and administration; Ethel Allen, a black Philadelphia City Council member, as secretary of the commonwealth; and Penrose ("Penny") Hallowell, a Bucks County dairy farmer who had headed our Farmers for Thornburgh effort, as agriculture secretary. Allen and Hallowell were obviously rewarded for campaign efforts. Appointed as attorney general and adjutant general, respectively, were former U.S. Congressman Pete Biester of Bucks County and Lancaster Mayor Dick Scott.

The next three appointments included two Democrats. Dr. Robert Scanlon, executive director of Research for Better Schools, who had offered advice during the campaign, became education secretary, and Helen O'Bannon from Pittsburgh, the first woman to have served on the Public Utility Commission, became welfare secretary. Cliff Jones, former GOP state chairman and head of Pennsylvanians for Responsible Government, became secretary of the Department of Environmental Resources.

Two businessmen from smaller communities were nominated next. Ben McEnteer, a retired banker from Titusville, was named secretary of banking, and Walter Baran, a garment manufacturer from Frackville, was designated secretary of the Department of General Services, formerly the Department of Property and Supplies. Baran was the first Polish-American to serve as a Pennsylvania cabinet member.

The new secretary of transportation would face an awesome task in restoring operating efficiency and morale to the discredited PennDOT. Happily, I was able to turn to Dr. Thomas Larson, a professor at Penn State, a widely respected transportation expert and my mentor on highway issues during the campaign. James F. Bodine, a former bank president from Philadelphia who had exerted himself on behalf of the campaign was appointed to the top economic development job, that of commerce secretary. The final cabinet appointments before the inauguration were those of West-moreland County Commissioner William Davis, a tireless campaigner on my behalf, as secretary of the Department of Community Affairs, and Philadelphia lawyer Harvey Bartle III, an official of that city's reform group, the Committee of 70, as insurance commissioner.

The first round of nominees was very well received. Only O'Bannon and Jones drew any significant fire—she from Republicans because of her service as a Shapp appointee and he from environmentalists due to his work in industrial development. Both of these were fair criticisms, but we stuck to our guns, and all of our appointments were, despite ominous predictions, approved in short order by the Democrat-controlled Senate. It would later be apparent that I had guessed wrong on some of my choices, but given the time constraints and the variety of positions to be filled, this was nearly inevitable.

The full cabinet and key staff were not in place until March 7, 1979. By then I had recruited a former FBI colleague, Dan Dunn, as state police commissioner, a previously scandal-plagued position to which I had pledged the appointment of an outsider. (Sadly, Commissioner Dunn died in 1984, as did his successor, Cyril Laffey; FBI veteran Jay Cochran steadied the operation for the balance of my time in office.) To head the newly created Department of Aging, I appointed Gorham Black, a retired black army colonel who had served in the U.S. Department of Health and Human Services. My final three choices, made under increasing pressure, all were to be troublesome. As secretary of health, I chose Dr. Gordon MacLeod of the University of Pittsburgh School of Public Health; as secretary of labor and industry, Dr. Myron Joseph, an economist from Carnegie Mellon; and as secretary of revenue, Howard Cohen, a former federal official who was then at the Wharton School. My mistake in each case was hiring the resumé rather than the person.

Another key decision, resulting in snickers from some in the media and despair among some family and friends, was that I would use "Dick" as my official name for state purposes rather than the more formal "Richard L." My explanation was simple: "No one ever comes up to me and says 'Good morning, Richard L.' It's always 'Dick' and that's the way it should be for the governor."

The inauguration was held on January 16, 1979. We substituted a public reception for the customary parade, saving the taxpayers $250,000 and sending a signal of frugality. I was administered the brief oath of office by Supreme Court Chief Justice Michael Eagen, with my hand upon the 280-

year-old Bible of our state's founder, William Penn. In my inaugural address, the most important speech that I had ever delivered, I set out what I felt to be the "spirit of Pennsylvania," something to be seen "in Leon Sullivan as he preaches in the inner city . . . in the paintings of Andrew and Carolyn Wyeth . . . in James Michener's books and . . . in a Joe Paterno pep talk." While I noted "a saddening loss of belief in the ability of government and its leaders to serve the people," I stated that people wanted to believe in their government. What was needed, I said, was "strong, effective and forthright leadership." This I promised to provide, together with hard work, integrity, frugality, and "a sense of humanity that is blind to race and roots, to sex and color, but is mindful of political injustice and human need."

After the postinaugural festivities, we departed for our new home, the Executive Mansion. From six to eight that evening, we crowded in some 375 guests for cocktails and hors d'oeuvres. They paid $500 a person to help raise money to fund the day's activities and to build up some political capital in the Governor Thornburgh Committee. From the reception we went to the inaugural ball. What a thrill it was for me, Ginny and our four sons to acknowledge the roar of the 3,500 celebrants from a balcony high above. It was an unforgettable, if somewhat imperial, moment.

Ginny and I were even more exhilarated, however, by the prospects ahead. We would be able to engage in precisely the kinds of efforts toward which we had pointed our lives—efforts to help people improve the quality of their lives, to fashion specific solutions to the many vexing problems posed by modern society, to make government work better. In short, we would have the opportunity to make a difference for the better in our beloved commonwealth, to exercise the leadership and apply the resources necessary to make things happen.

8

A Rough Start:
Three Mile Island

A s we settled into the "Executive Mansion," one of our first items of business was to change its name to the "Governor's Home." As Ginny said, "Four boys and a black-and-white dog don't live in a 'mansion'!" The house had been unoccupied for several years following the 1972 Hurricane Agnes flood, and it became an immediate priority of Ginny's and mine to make it a source of pride for all Pennsylvanians. Committees were formed to provide advice and financial assistance in upgrading the public space in the building and redesigning the grounds. Many fine works of art were donated, and a series of exhibits highlighting Pennsylvania artists was arranged, thanks in large part to the exertions of Ginny's administrative assistant, Louise Curl-Adams. Outside, Wally Baran's Department of General Services built a handsome screened-in porch where our family, and the families of future governors, could enjoy a little privacy in the fresh air. The Governor's Home soon became a real political asset. We entertained there as much as we could, building bridges with cabinet members, legislators and interest group members.

John and David were off at college, but Bill, now thirteen, attended the nearby Harrisburg Academy and Peter the Harrisburg School District's special-education classes. The security detail drove them to and from school, and it was awkward for them to invite classmates over. We tried to normalize their situations as much as possible, but this was difficult, and, particularly in Bill's case, the unusual environment was to take a toll. Moreover, I fear that Ginny and I, both preoccupied with our exciting new responsibilities, gave Bill less attention at this time than we had given our other sons, and less than he deserved.

Peter's situation changed in other ways. We had always worked to heighten his self-esteem by providing him with his own chores to do—making his bed, setting and clearing the table, carrying out the trash—and he undertook these jobs cheerfully as a contributing member of the family. In the Governor's Home, of course, these tasks were performed by our attentive staff, and Peter's skills began to erode measurably. Before long, he was no longer able to set out the silverware and napkins properly, something Ginny had worked on with him for a considerable time. A complicating factor was Peter's charm. The staff not only did his chores for him but sought out other ways to "help" him. The state police officers included him in a lot of horseplay and good-natured boisterousness, well intended but hardly conducive to our efforts to raise a well-mannered young man.

THE PENNSYLVANIA General Assembly was somewhat chastened and defensive when I took office. The corruption that had played a major role in bringing me there had not been confined to the Shapp administration. In fact, federal prosecutions had removed from office most of the Democrats who had guided the legislature during the Shapp years—House Speaker Herbert Fineman and Senate Appropriations Chairman Henry "Buddy" Cianfrani (Philadelphia's most effective champions), as well as Senate majority leader-to-be Frank Mazzei. The Senate remained under Democratic control, however, as it had since 1970; the margin was 27–23. The longtime president pro tem was Martin Murray, from the hard-coal region of Luzerne County; the majority leader was Edward Zemprelli of Clairton. The Republicans were led by Henry Hager, with whom I had a somewhat prickly relationship. His whip, the gentlemanly Jack Stauffer of Chester County, made several substantive contributions to our legislative agenda.

The House, for the first time since 1974, was in Republican hands by a margin of 103 to 100. The speaker was H. Jack Seltzer of Lebanon County, whose family (unfortunately for a political figure) was in the baloney business. The majority leader, Matt Ryan of Delaware County, had nearly perfect pitch in counting the votes within his caucus. Both Seltzer and Ryan became good friends of ours. The minority leader was K. Leroy Irvis of

Pittsburgh, the state's leading African American legislator, a veteran of the civil rights wars and a friend of mine since the Constitutional Convention. His second in command was Jim Manderino of Monessen, a bear of a man with a fine legislative mind and a fierce partisan instinct. We circled each other in mutual respect during most of my tenure.

The Republican leaders in both houses were, for the most part, willing to back to the hilt all but our most controversial proposals and in some instances displayed uncommon courage. Moreover, the climate at the outset of my administration appeared to be favorable for legislative cooperation. The initial euphoria was quickly dampened, however, by the hard realities of one of America's most partisan legislative environments, the narrow margins in each house and the austere economic and fiscal prospects faced by the state. Every legislative triumph was to be a struggle. My style of governing may have contributed to this problem. A 1983 article in *Congressional Quarterly* noted, "The Legislature is almost everything that Thornburgh is not—rambunctious, belligerent, colorful, given to passionate debate and rarely entirely free of the scent of corruption." Our strategy of being more respected than liked was largely successful, but it did, from time to time, make the atmosphere less congenial.

Our interaction with the press corps perhaps deserves some attention at this point. While I was governor, my family and I were subject to intense and constant scrutiny. I had always prided myself on my open, easygoing relationship with reporters. But for the governor of a major state, the rules, I quickly learned, are quite different. Access had to be carefully controlled and strategically utilized. The risks of indiscretion were great. I remember being told, "Don't write or say anything to anyone that you would regret seeing in the headlines the following morning." The denizens of our newsroom were probably no better or worse than those in other state capitals, but they were constantly on the prowl and mightily suspicious of anything handed to them. Sometimes they carried their principles to absurd extremes, as when several reporters regularly declined to attend our annual Christmas party for the press.

By far the most common criticism voiced during my tenure related to my personality and style of governing. The press's most frequently used adjective seemed to be "aloof." Tom Ferrick of the *Inquirer* may have captured this characteristic best, observing, "He did not want to be seen as one of the boys. This might have been a legacy of Thornburgh's background as a U.S. attorney, where he spent a lot of time prosecuting some of the boys."

A ROUGH START: THREE MILE ISLAND

JAY WALDMAN quickly established himself as our key strategist and tactician, while Jim Seif took charge of scheduling, correspondence and briefings for the many events I attended. Rick Stafford, the majordomo of our internal think tank, was aided by our Office of Policy Development, most notably its heads, Walt Plosila, Bob Benko and Harold Miller. Other key staffers were Bob Wilburn; deputy counsels Robin Ross and Richard Glanton, both from the campaign; George Seidel, our legislative lobbyist, formerly with the PSEA; and Paul Critchlow. A good staff can make the executive look good, and my staff in Harrisburg was superb.

Cabinet meetings were few and far between, but I well remember our first, where Jay stunned the newly minted appointees with his somewhat exaggerated admonition, "Fire all the incompetent staff in your department and most of the competent ones as well," in recognition of our sweeping mandate to clean out Harrisburg.

Every proposed policy position was examined and vetted from six separate viewpoints: Rick Stafford's shop, which would assess the issues, the views of relevant departments and agencies, and related history and experience in Pennsylvania and elsewhere. This review would result in a "pure" policy recommendation or set of options. Second, the lawyers would review relevant statutes and court decisions and provide an opinion on any anticipated legal, especially constitutional, pitfalls. The budget office would assess the proposal's budget impacts—costs or savings, potential sources of revenue and possible alternate uses of any funds saved. George Seidel, further, would review the legislative implications of the policy—where we could expect support or opposition, how we could maximize the former and neutralize or convert the latter, and what matters of timing we had to consider. Fifth, the press office would examine the media implications—who was likely to support us, who would oppose us and whether any of that mattered. Particular attention was given to our supporters in the press, to avoid surprising or disillusioning them.

Lastly, Jay Waldman would conduct a political assessment, determining whether the policy was consistent with our overall philosophy and campaign themes, how key supporters or interest groups were likely to react (and whether that mattered) and how the policy fit into the long-term big picture. Of course, final approval or disapproval of the policy was up to me, but often I had been so intimately involved in the process that a formal yes or no was not necessary. My infamous red felt-tipped pen had usually been liberally applied at several intermediate stages. The procedure was never as orderly as its description indicates, but it saved us many a mistake, and when we did not follow it, we frequently got into trouble.

An early example of such a glitch was the flap over my issuing a Gay Pride Day proclamation early in my first term. Apparently, Governor Shapp had routinely issued such a proclamation, so one arrived on my desk in due course, having survived the usually careful scrutiny of Jim Seif. Its issuance was greeted by howls of outrage from Republicans (and many Democrats) in the legislature as well as conservative religious and social organizations throughout the state. After some consternation, we supplemented it with a Family Pride proclamation and a statement attempting to clarify my attitudes. In it I set forth my "deep and continuing commitment to the right of privacy in this country—the right of all Americans to live their lives as they see fit, so long as they obey the law and don't infringe on the rights of others." I had seen the proclamation, "at a glance," to be in conformance with this commitment, but in retrospect, I regretted the use of the word "pride." I concluded, "But I signed the proclamation as it was given to me. It's done. It's time now to turn to questions that have a far greater impact on the people of this Commonwealth."

Controversy over gay rights, of course, was to increase as time went on. I was to be asked occasionally why my advocacy for civil rights in the racial, gender and disability areas did not extend to this group as well. While I certainly opposed any discrimination against gays in the enjoyment of their civil rights, my religious and moral beliefs constrained me from supporting their political agenda, which, in my view, often consisted of advocacy of special preferences and lifestyle choices to which I objected.

WITHIN TWO DAYS after the inauguration, Bob Wilburn and his budget office aides came to the Governor's Home to discuss the state's financial condition. Estimates of the deficit looming at the end of the fiscal year (which was to end on June 30) ranged from $20 million to $175 million, all of which had to be made up before we even began to chart a course for the 1979–80 fiscal year. Wisely, nearly all states have a constitutional requirement that each year's budget be balanced. They cannot run at a deficit and count upon future generations to pay off the accumulated debt. I was later to become a zealot in the effort to secure passage of a balanced budget amendment to the federal constitution. I have always thought that matching revenues with expenditures is a large part of what accountability in government is all about.

The state's deplorable financial situation required immediate attention for other reasons as well. Though tax rates for both businesses and individuals were near all-time highs, the state's debt had also reached a record level. The state's credit rating had been cut three times in the previous eighteen months, and the bankruptcy of its unemployment compensation insurance fund meant that we owed the federal government over a billion dollars. PennDOT was unable to draw down desperately needed federal highway funds because the state could not match them. As a consequence, our already pothole-filled highways were deteriorating further, and unfinished "roads and bridges to nowhere" dotted the state. On top of all this, our economy remained sluggish—the strength of our traditional manufacturing industries was eroding rapidly, and no plans were in place to revitalize our economic base. While statewide unemployment had fallen slightly in 1978, it had been the seventh highest in the nation in November and was still well above the national average.

First we had to seek a supplemental appropriation to keep the governor's office running, as the Shapp people had used up the full year's funding in six months. We also imposed a hiring freeze and began to take stock of a bloated bureaucracy. The budget was due in early March, so I set aside two full weeks to work on it. Because all of an administration's priorities are, sooner or later, reflected in the budget figures, the budget process is far more than just making sure all the numbers add up. It is at the very heart of the craft of governing. In our case, we were committed to avoiding any general tax increases, so the emphasis was on cost cutting and better management, on "doing more with less." Cabinet members were asked to lay out the situation in their departments and offer any help they could in taming the projected deficit. This procedure was a productive one, and I followed it each year thereafter.

The budget presentation on March 7 was my first address to the 253 legislators as a group. I opened by observing bluntly, "This is a no frills, no nonsense, no luxuries document. It is an austere budget." While state expenditures had increased an average of 10.6 percent per year during the Shapp administration, my spending plan called for an increase of half that amount, less than the rate of inflation. I also repeated my campaign pledge to open a new Washington, D.C., office "to fight for our fair share of federal dollars."

Next I reviewed the major program areas. We were able to propose some additional spending on top priorities. In particular, we squeezed out some extra economic development funding—$15 million for the Pennsylvania Industrial Development Authority (PIDA), token amounts for overseas offices to promote foreign investment in the state and exports by our manufacturers, and some business tax relief in the form of a continued phase-out of the requirement that corporations prepay 90 percent of their estimated taxes each year. We also proposed to increase promotional expenditures for our travel and tourism industry from a mere $60,000 to $1 million (New York's "I Love New York" campaign that year had a budget of $10 million). But these were only signals of good faith. Our principal economic development initiatives would have to await major study and review.

I made a strong commitment to law enforcement, especially antiracket and anticorruption efforts. We also took a "first step" toward the statutory goal of having the state cover 50 percent of the expenditures of local school districts, proposing a $115 million increase in the subsidy. (The 50 percent goal, I was later to realize, would constantly recede unless some ceiling were to be placed on total school district expenditures. We had to deal with this issue extensively in years to come, in an escalating battle with the powerful teachers' unions.) Human services expenditures were treated more generously than many had expected. We proposed the first increase in four years for those receiving general-assistance welfare payments—a modest 5 percent, but a signal of concern. For those with mental retardation and mental illness, the increases were greater, including a whopping increase of 14.5 percent ($20 million) for community-based living arrangements. I also made a commitment to tackle fraud in human services programs, which conventional wisdom considered to be "unmanageable and uncontrollable." And using state lottery funds, we proposed a new program to help senior citizens pay their utility bills.

I proposed to raise the revenues necessary to meet the continuing and crushing needs of the highway system by extending the 6 percent sales tax to the wholesale purchase of motor fuels. This would produce an additional $177 million for a maintenance catch-up program and would enable us to suspend further bond borrowing, which had brought PennDOT to its financial knees. We chose the sales tax extension over an addition to the existing cents-per-gallon tax because of its inflation sensitivity and ease of application. The price of gasoline at the pump was to double during the energy crisis of the early years of my administration, and we sought to offset the resulting projected decline in consumption by relating tax revenues more closely to prices.

Overall, through reprogramming and cutbacks in areas of lesser priority, we were able to propose a balanced budget without any general tax increase, much to the surprise of some. In the following weeks, we set about to build support for the budget, meeting with legislators, local government officials, industry representatives and other special-interest groups. However, this effort was very soon eclipsed by a problem no governor, anywhere, had ever had to face.

AT 7:50 A.M. ON Wednesday, March 28, 1979, I received a telephone call from the state director of emergency management, Colonel Oran Henderson. There had been an accident, he told me, at the Three Mile Island (TMI) nuclear power plant, located about ten miles downstream from us, in the middle of the Susquehanna River.

During my "breaking-in" period, I had visited the offices of the Pennsylvania Emergency Management Agency (PEMA). My cursory briefing from Colonel Henderson had made passing reference to TMI along with other nuclear power facilities in the state. This was the extent of my knowledge of the subject. I asked Colonel Henderson to find out more details and keep me and Lieutenant Governor Scranton, to whose office I had assigned prime responsibility for energy and emergency management, informed.

As we were later to learn, the problem had begun at 4:00 that morning, when vital cooling water started to escape through an open valve in the newer of the two reactors at the site. For the next two and a quarter hours, plant operators failed to close that valve and mistakenly shut off an emergency cooling system that otherwise would have operated automatically. The reactor core overheated, and the worst accident in the history of commercial nuclear power was well under way by sunup.

It later became clear that, while some of the reactor fuel heated to the point of melting, a disastrous "meltdown" was never close to occurring. Detectable amounts of radiation escaped into our air, water and even milk, but these amounts were limited enough that their impact, if any, on public health remains debatable to this day. And a massive evacuation of the up to 200,000 people residing in the area, with its potential for panic, injury and even loss of life, would have been far more dangerous and damaging than was the accident itself. But at 7:50 on that March morning, we knew none of this. The thought of issuing a general evacuation order entered my mind immediately and never left during the days to follow.

Some considered nuclear power the ultimate answer to our energy problems, a source of electricity "too cheap to meter," with a safety record second to none. I had neither reason nor inclination to challenge these assumptions. Nuclear jargon was a foreign language to me. Nevertheless, it was very clear that we had better start asking questions, analyzing answers and preparing for the worst. Because we were so unfamiliar with the state bureaucracy, and because in any case there was no bureau of nuclear crisis management, let alone a precedent, I assembled an "ad-hocracy," a team of close associates whose judgment and competence I trusted—Jay Waldman, Paul Critchlow, Rick Stafford and Bob Wilburn, among others. We also pulled together a support group of relevant state specialists—most notably Tom Gerusky and Bill Dornsife—whose judgment and competence were about to be tested under pressures that none of them had ever known before.

This ad-hocracy reported to me only periodically at first. I believed that it was important to conduct business as usual in the governor's office, and perhaps even more important to appear to be doing so. As the implications of the accident became more apparent, however, I began to cancel other appointments, and the ad-hocracy virtually moved into my office.

Our first task was to find out exactly what was happening. This was to prove far more difficult than any of us could have imagined. The utility (Metropolitan Edison), its parent company (General Public Utilities), state and federal regulators, and other groups and institutions issued increasingly contradictory assessments, telling the public either more or less than they knew of the accident and its consequences. Self-appointed experts exaggerated either the danger or the safety of the situation. The credibility of the utility, in particular, did not fare well. On that first day it sought to minimize the accident, assuring us, inaccurately, that "everything is under control" and that "all safety equipment functioned properly." When company technicians found that radiation levels in the surrounding area had climbed above normal, the company neglected to release that information to the public. It also vented some radioactive steam into the air for two and one-half hours at midday on Wednesday, without informing us or the public.

Thus it fell to Lieutenant Governor Scranton, at a 4:30 P.M. press conference, to tell the people of central Pennsylvania that "this situation is more complex than the company first led us to believe" and that there had indeed been a release of radioactivity. He stated that further discharges were possible, that we were "concerned," but that off-site radioactivity levels had been decreasing during the afternoon and there was no evidence that they had ever reached a danger point.

Although we continued to monitor what utility officials were saying throughout the crisis, we began to look elsewhere for more credible sources of information. Among others, we turned to those federal engineers and inspectors who had spent most of the first day inside the plant. Three of these experts briefed us that first night. Following the briefing, I pulled down a previously unread book, reassuringly entitled *We Almost Lost Detroit*, an account by John G. Fuller of problems at the Enrico Fermi nuclear power plant in Michigan. Paging through it, I lighted on the subject of core damage, and it immediately struck me that our federal "experts" had not even raised this issue.

In 1979, few people realized that an actual nuclear explosion—mushroom cloud and all—from a nuclear power plant isn't physically possible. The real potential catastrophe, as Fuller outlined, was the overheating of the reactor core to the point where it would melt down and burn through its concrete and steel containment, thereby releasing massive amounts of radioactive material that, silently but lethally, could contaminate the environment for miles around, and for centuries to come. The term "China syndrome" was derived from the theory that such a core would be so hot that it could actually burn its way through to the other side of the earth—to China. Ironically, the movie *The China Syndrome*, describing a fictional accident at a California nuclear power plant, was running for the first time in Harrisburg-area theaters that very week. Its script, incredibly, described a meltdown as having the potential to contaminate an area "the size of Pennsylvania!"

As the authors of a specially commissioned report on the Three Mile Island accident were to write much later, the second day of the crisis was an "interlude, a day for the drawing of deep breaths . . . a good time for Members of Congress to put in an appearance," which they did. Chairman Joseph Hendrie of the Nuclear Regulatory Commission (NRC) told a congressional committee in Washington that the TMI facility had been "nowhere near" a meltdown, although he had no basis for such a statement at the time. And the company, at its first full-fledged press conference since the accident, told reporters that the plant was "stable" and that the controlled release of limited amounts of radioactivity into the atmosphere should be terminated soon. Those in charge seemed to feel that the worst had passed, but I was not so sure. Company efforts to cool down the reactor were not working as well as expected, and a certain air of apprehension was beginning to affect all those actually monitoring the recovery.

Meanwhile, self-appointed experts and dubious eyewitnesses continued to feed us unsubstantiated stories about dead animals, along with exaggerated warnings and evacuation schemes. A poorly worded NRC press release prompted a ridiculous tale, given currency by NBC's Tom Brokaw, of radiation so powerful that it was penetrating four feet of concrete and spreading up to sixteen miles from the plant. Signs popped up in grocery store windows in neighboring states proclaiming, "We don't sell Pennsylvania milk." Public faith in the experts and institutions involved was obviously beginning to erode.

It was becoming increasingly clear to us that whatever credibility the governor's office had might constitute the last check against a possible breakdown in civil authority and the chaos and panic that would ensue. The time had come for us to put things in perspective, to establish that the situation was not as bad as some would have us fear, nor as good as some would have us believe. It was also time for me to become publicly involved in the effort. Late on Thursday afternoon, I gave a press briefing designed to reassure Pennsylvanians that, although there was no cause for alarm, we would remain alert. I was followed at the podium, however, by one of the NRC experts, who declared, to my astonishment, that "the danger is over," a comment definitely not in the script. I learned later that night that another on-site expert disagreed with this assessment and that water samples indicated that "core damage is very bad." Thursday ended on a somewhat edgy note.

Friday, March 30, was to become known as the day of the great evacuation scare—the day that illustrated not only the folly, but the very real danger, of trying to manage this kind of emergency from afar.

Early that morning, the shift operators at Three Mile Island became alarmed by the buildup of steam pressure on a valve. Without approval from anyone, they opened the valve and allowed the steam, along with a substantial amount of radioactive material, to escape into the atmosphere. It so happened that, at that precise moment, a helicopter was taking radiation readings directly above the plant's exhaust stack. Not surprisingly, they indicated a very high radiation exposure rate—1,200 millirems per hour. This rate would certainly have been high enough to warrant an evacuation if the readings had been taken anywhere off the plant site. But because they were taken directly above the stack, they were no more significant than any of those taken on the previous two days. Materials leaving the stack would be immediately dispersed.

Unfortunately, in the first manifestation of what I was later to call the "garble gap" between Harrisburg and Washington, the NRC's Washington-based Executive Management Team somehow thought that the readings had been taken off-site and therefore recommended that we evacuate all residents within a five-mile radius of the plant. Also unfortunately, the Washington group forwarded its recommendation to our emergency management director instead of to Tom Gerusky, our radiation protection director, who could have quickly corrected the error and spared central Pennsylvania a trip to the very brink of panic. And even more unfortunately, the emergency management director called a local civil defense director, who called a local radio station with the news that an evacuation order from the governor's office was imminent. I had yet to be informed of any of this.

Word finally reached me that a "Doc Collins" from Washington was advising an evacuation. I had no idea who "Doc Collins" was or by what authority or for what reason he was making such a recommendation—and I certainly did not intend to order the evacuation of thousands of people on such incomplete information. No matter how well planned, a massive evacuation had the potential to kill or injure people—especially the aged and infirm, babies in incubators, other hospital patients and even able-bodied persons who happened to be in the wrong place at the wrong time.

So I started asking questions again. My difficulty in getting answers was compounded by the jamming of our switchboard, thanks not only to the premature and erroneous radio announcement, but to the mysterious tripping of an emergency siren that soon had hearts pounding and eyes widening throughout the city. People began to throw their belongings into cars and trucks and to lock up their shops and homes preparatory to getting out of town. If ever we came close to a general panic, this was the moment.

I finally placed a call to the NRC chairman himself. By the time I reached him, his staff had discovered what Tom Gerusky had already told me: the evacuation advisory was a mistake. The NRC group withdrew the advisory, and I immediately went on the radio to assure our citizens that the alarm was a false one. The decision not to call for a general evacuation was, predictably, the one that came in for the most second-guessing later on. A related complication resulted from Congressman George Gekas's inability to obtain information from the administration, which led to a threat by Dauphin County Emergency Manager Kevin Molloy to order an evacuation unless a meeting was arranged with Bill Scranton. The meeting was held and tempers cooled. All of this reflected the intense pressure felt by us all.

Shortly after announcing that there would be no general evacuation, I was on the phone with President Jimmy Carter. It was time to go to the top.

Our two staffs had quite rightly put aside partisan interests while dealing with this crisis, developing the kind of friendship under fire that such incidents frequently promote. My first conversation with the president was therefore honest, open, direct and, above all, productive. I asked for, and the president agreed to send us, a high-ranking professional who could go to TMI as his personal representative, merge solid technical and management expertise with an on-site perspective, and report accurately and directly to the White House, to me and to the people on what was going on out there, what was not going on and why. His near-perfect choice for this task was Harold Denton, the NRC's director of nuclear reactor regulation, and Denton's arrival later in the day would represent a turning point in the crisis.

For the moment, however, the ongoing confusion and uncertainty troubled us deeply. We began to wonder if pregnant women and small children, those residents most vulnerable to the effects of radiation, yet relatively easy to move, should be encouraged to leave the area nearest the plant. We put that question directly to Chairman Hendrie, who answered, "If my wife were pregnant and had small children in the area, I would get them out, because we don't know what's going to happen."

Shortly after noon on that third day of the crisis, therefore, I recommended that pregnant women and preschoolers leave the area within five miles of the plant until further notice, and that all schools within that zone be closed as well. I also ordered the opening of evacuation centers at various sites outside of the area to shelter those who had no place to go. "Current readings," I stated, "are no higher than they were yesterday [but] the continued presence of radioactivity in the area and the possibility of further emissions lead me to exercise the utmost of caution."

Harold Denton arrived at the plant on Friday afternoon. A three-way hot line was installed there to connect him with me and with the president. Later that night Harold and I met for the first time, with Chairman Hendrie sitting in, and spent a full hour and a half reviewing the situation. It was quite clear that Denton's easy manner, apparent candor and ability to speak plain English as well as nuclear jargon would make him the world's most believable expert on the technical situation at TMI.

Earlier that day, Denton's colleagues in Washington had finally referred publicly to the theoretical possibility of a meltdown. Their statement was accurate but poorly handled and caused even that most credible of all Americans, Walter Cronkite, to lead Friday's *CBS Evening News* by saying, "We are faced with the remote, but very real, possibility of a nuclear meltdown at the Three Mile Island atomic power plant." One could almost feel the shudder going through central Pennsylvania.

At a press conference at 10:00 that night, I reiterated that there would be no evacuation at that time, but that we would reconsider the question as events warranted. Denton then put the facts in perspective and lowered the level of concern. I felt that with his help, we were finally equipped to handle the misstatements, second-guessing and false alarms that had come to characterize the whole affair. We did continue to cross-check his observations against those of my team, but we quickly became convinced of his complete credibility.

At about this point, the seeds of a vexatious controversy over the use of potassium iodide were being sown. This drug can block radioactive iodine from the thyroid, where it could cause cancer. It had been recommended in 1978 for use by workers and affected populations in a radiological emergency. Few pharmaceutical companies, however, had manufactured the drug in appreciable quantities. Federal authorities, goaded by HEW Secretary Joe Califano, had made a Herculean effort to secure over 237,000 bottles of the drug, the first of which were to be dispatched to the Harrisburg area on Saturday night. But despite Secretary Califano's recommendation, the drug was never dispensed from the warehouse where it was stored under armed guard. Secretary MacLeod observed that the bottles were unlabeled and unaccompanied by the necessary droppers and that some were caked on the outside with crystallized spillover from the hasty filling process. My own misgivings were more basic. I imagined the following conversation after a knock at the door by emergency management personnel:

Distributor: Here's your potassium iodide.

Homeowner: What's this for?

Distributor: Take it when the radioactive cloud comes.

Nothing, to my mind, could have been better calculated to produce a large-scale, uncontrolled evacuation.

Califano was later to testify before a Senate subcommittee that the doses were needed but the state refused to administer them. We were furious and agreed with the observer, quoted in Daniel Martin's book *TMI: Prologue or Epilogue*, who noted, "Califano's statement was irresponsibly uninformed and was tantamount to an accusation that the state was denying its citizens a needed anti-cancer drug." Our decision, concurred in by

Secretary MacLeod, Harold Denton and myself, was made with full possession of the facts at the site and not from a Washington office.

Yet another chilling story broke on Saturday evening, just as we had begun to catch our collective breath. Based on information from an anonymous NRC source in Washington, a wire service ran a news bulletin that read: "U-R-G-E-N-T . . . The NRC now says the gas bubble atop the nuclear reactor at Three Mile Island show[s] signs of becoming potentially explosive. . . ." This bulletin moved like a hurricane advisory across the bottom of prime-time television screens everywhere. In Harrisburg, people streamed out of downtown bars and restaurants. Our switchboard jammed again, and a herd of reporters stampeded into our press office, demanding to know if they should get out of town. Obviously we had to move fast.

We called Harold Denton at the plant, and he confirmed that there was no danger of an imminent explosion and no cause for alarm. Paul Critchlow banged out a three-paragraph statement reflecting this view and literally ran it down to the newsroom. Within minutes, stories quoting our statement, followed by an impromptu press conference with Denton, began to move on the wires. Meanwhile, President Carter's press secretary, Jody Powell, issued a statement that the president would soon visit the site himself. Together, these stories averted another potential panic.

The president and his wife arrived by helicopter the very next day, and after a briefing in which he displayed his background as a nuclear engineer, we toured the plant. In full view of the television cameras, the Carters, Bill Scranton and I, all attired in yellow booties, were ushered into the control room and given a quick summary of the plant's condition. Afterwards, before a massive gathering of reporters, the president gracefully thanked me for my efforts, stating that I had done a "superlative job" and that "because of the trust of the American people in him . . . potential panic and disturbance has been minimized." These images, beamed around the world, had the desired effect. If it was safe enough for the president of the United States and the governor of Pennsylvania, it had to be safe enough for everyone.

That evening I briefed leaders of the General Assembly on the situation. I was tired, and the members were frustrated at having been left out of the process for so long. However, Senate Minority Leader Hager said, "We had the feeling he was in control and the people were safe."

Harold Denton continued to oversee the cooling of the reactor core and to offer progress reports to a press contingent that was rapidly losing interest. On Friday, April 6, just ten days after that fateful opening of the most famous power plant valve in the world, I was able to tell our people in a statewide televised address that the crisis had passed and that those who had chosen to leave the area "can come home again."

YEARS LATER, I WAS asked to share some of the lessons I had learned from the accident. These proved to apply not only to unforeseen crises, but to the day-to-day problems of governing as well.

Lesson number one, I noted, was to expect the unexpected and be prepared to adjust accordingly. The Three Mile Island crisis in Pennsylvania was followed by three-mile gas lines, water shortages, floods, transit strikes, subway crashes and two serious hostage-taking situations in our state prisons. None of these could have been anticipated, and all disrupted our carefully planned schedules. It is important to limit those things that any executive should attempt to do within the time allowed, because some of the toughest of our battles are chosen for us. Good men and women must be in place to handle the planned agenda when the boss becomes occupied by items that were never planned for at all.

Lesson number two: When emergencies strike, a trusted ad-hocracy may be far more useful than an entrenched or untested bureaucracy. It was not in our job description to grill witnesses to a nuclear emergency and then to serve as a worldwide communications center, but it worked. A manager cannot be afraid to scramble the organization chart. In the familiar example of the Cuban missile crisis, President Kennedy's brother's advice weighed more heavily with him than that of the secretary of state or the joint chiefs of staff.

Lesson number three: Be ready to restrain those who think solely in terms of "doing something," regardless of its safety, wisdom or necessity. These people may be emergency personnel, bureaucrats, technocrats, academics, medical and other professionals, or even politicians. The impulse to act for the sake of action, or to test a plan or agency because it is there, must be firmly restrained.

Lesson number four: Be wary of "emergency macho"—the temptation to stay up all night and brag about it. While it is often important for a crisis manager to maintain a visible and reassuring presence, anyone making critical decisions affecting thousands of people owes them a mind that is clear and a body that is rested, to the maximum extent possible. I worked hard during the TMI episode to get my normal amount of sleep and to keep hours that were as regular as possible.

Lesson number five: Don't try to manage an emergency away from the site. Someone must be in charge on location whose competence and judgment can be trusted. In March 1979, most of our communications problems originated in Washington. Even Harold Denton, I was to learn, had been involved in generating the bogus evacuation recommendation sent up to us before he reached the site in person.

Lesson number six, an obvious one: Search for the facts, evaluate them and their sources over and over again, and communicate them truthfully and carefully to the people. Credibility can be as fragile as it is crucial in the cauldron of a genuine public emergency.

Lesson number seven: The media must be respected, but not relied upon, during a crisis. We developed considerable empathy with the more than 400 reporters from around the world who were assigned to cover TMI. Their frustrations in establishing reliable facts mirrored ours, and we often compared notes with them in an effort to ensure the quality of both their reporting and our actions. Not all of the reporting was reliable, however, and some was downright outrageous. For example, a British news organization reported that "the governor's wife, pregnant with their first child, has left the area." Of course, Ginny was not pregnant, we already had four children and she stayed in Harrisburg during the whole episode (as did the lieutenant governor's wife, who *was* pregnant with their first child).

Lesson number eight: Forget partisanship, for there is no Republican or Democratic way to manage a real emergency. In our stewardship of this most basic of public trusts, leaders inevitably survive or suffer together, and so do the people they are elected to serve.

Lesson number nine: Learn from history. The Fuller book on the Fermi plant, for example, proved most useful.

Lesson number ten was best articulated by that well-known American philosopher, Yogi Berra: "It ain't over till it's over." Within a year after the accident, furor arose over a plan to vent radioactive krypton gas into the atmosphere as part of the reactor cleanup. Public hearings on the safety of the plant almost turned into riots. One imaginative opponent donned a Superman suit and proceeded to "choke" himself on the front steps of the Capitol. I took the unorthodox step of asking the Union of Concerned Scientists, a well-known group of nuclear industry critics, to study the venting plan. When that organization concluded that the venting posed no physical threat to public health or safety or to the environment, the plan proceeded peacefully.

A key question following the accident was who would pay the estimated billion-dollar cost of cleaning up the damaged reactor. The first year of discussion mostly involved finger-pointing and political posturing. No specific plans were forthcoming from the utility, from industry or from the federal government. Because the ultimate safety of the site depended upon completion of the cleanup, and because the established institutions seemed to be at an impasse, I felt my administration had no choice but to develop our own plan. We announced it at the plant site in July 1981 after discussions with all interested parties. It called for $190 million (25 percent of the funding) to come from the federal government, $190 million (25 percent) from the nuclear industry, $245 million (32 percent) from the utility company, $90 million (12 percent) from insurance proceeds, $30 million (4 percent) from the commonwealth of Pennsylvania and $15 million (2 percent) from the state of New Jersey, home of General Public Utilities. The total was $760 million, in addition to the $274 million already paid.

The *Washington Post* noted editorially, "Gov. Richard Thornburgh of Pennsylvania has responded to the lack of urgency displayed by industry and the federal government by proposing his own plan for raising the necessary funds . . . Thornburgh's plan should be taken as a reminder that the cleanup of Three Mile Island is in danger of being forgotten by just about everyone outside of Pennsylvania." The *Pittsburgh Post-Gazette* later stated, "Gov. Thornburgh, who shouldered the unpleasant task that nobody else was willing to tackle, deserves commendation" for achieving acceptance of the plan. I had to sell it vigorously to the White House and Congress, to my fellow governors and to various utility and regulatory groups. Congressional lobbying was hampered by some partisan sniping from Democratic members, but, in the end, the essentials of the plan were adopted by all parties, and the cleanup could proceed. It was not to be completed until August 1993, more than fourteen years after the accident. And it took until the end of 2002 to dispose of the claims of 1,900 plaintiffs who unsuccessfully sought to recover for alleged damage to their health from the accident.

Meanwhile, protracted proceedings were held on the utility's application to restart the undamaged Unit I reactor. This question ultimately went to the Supreme Court of the United States and consumed thousands of hours of state time as we sought to ensure a maximum commitment by the plant operators to public health and safety and the integrity of the environment. Interestingly enough, two unrelated Pennsylvania reactors were brought on line during the post-accident period without any public outcry. This we took as a compliment to our continuous effort at keeping the public informed and aware.

In December 1979, some eight months following the accident, I visited the then Soviet Union with a group of governors. We met with leaders in the Soviet nuclear energy and emergency management programs, ostensibly to share some of the lessons of Three Mile Island (or, as our translator called it, "Five Kilometer Island"). To our discomfort, our Soviet counterparts regarded nuclear safety as a "solved problem," felt that TMI had been "overdramatized" and stated that Soviet reactors "would soon be so safe as to be installed in Red Square."

The rest, of course, is history. How hollow these boastful observations rang on April 26, 1986, when a far more terrifying event occurred at Chernobyl. One must wonder if the accident there might have been prevented if the people of the Soviet Union had been as free to question their authorities as were Americans following TMI. Without a free press, the Soviet people were not even aware that Chernobyl was dangerous and were not alerted to the accident itself until unusually high levels of radiation were detected in the Scandinavian countries and reported through their free press. Moreover, no right of free speech protected Soviet citizens who might have warned of danger, and no free elections were available to make the Soviet government accountable to its constituents. The contrast between the TMI and Chernobyl episodes was a reminder of how valuable our political institutions are, for all their shortcomings. In the view of many, the Chernobyl debacle was a major contributor to the eventual collapse of the Soviet Union in the 1990s.

In general, reviews of our handling of TMI were favorable. Neal Peirce, in a later piece entitled "Pennsylvania's Thornburgh: Extraordinary Governor," took note of "the Thornburgh style—the calm, deliberate method he brought to Three Mile Island and now applies to virtually every problem." Syndicated columnists Jack Germond and Jules Witcover noted the political implications, even saying, "Suddenly everyone is talking about how [Thornburgh] would make a marvelous candidate for vice president on the Republican ticket in 1980." There were, of course, critics as well, mostly focusing upon my unwillingness to order a "precautionary" evacuation in light of all the uncertainty. In time, I was to be labeled both "antinuke" (by the industry) and "pronuke" (by environmentalists) for various positions taken after the accident. On the theory that one should seek to please neither of these elements all of the time, I took these assessments to be a positive sign. In a May 1979 address to the American Society of Newspaper Editors, I called for "a middle ground between those who would abandon [nuclear power] and those who would expand it tomorrow. . . . The question is not yes or no, but how best we can use it and keep it under control. . . . [If] we can't prepare ourselves to control it, then we must prepare ourselves to do without it."

Meanwhile, we had to get back to the normal business of running the state.

9

Reshaping Pennsylvania's Economy

Returning to consideration of the budget, we found there were already Republican holdouts in the House. In view of our 58 percent electoral support from African American voters, Rick Stafford boldly made overtures to the all-Democrat Black Caucus, offering its members an opportunity to become more independent of their party leadership. A show of political muscle on the budget, we urged, would enable them to stake out much stronger positions on their own interests later.

Unfortunately for us and, I believe, for these members as well as their constituencies, partisan allegiance overcame their strategic sense. The caucus took a hard line against nearly every measure we proposed, and a unique opportunity for an increase in real political power for African American citizens was lost. The Democrats continued to take them for granted. Sadder yet, Republicans did not even try to follow up on our remarkable success with these voters, and no other Republican candidate has since approached the level of support we achieved in 1978. Meanwhile, I continued my personal efforts to work with black leaders on a variety of projects across the state.

After much maneuvering in both houses, our efforts to "retail" the budget finally succeeded. We cobbled together majorities in both houses on the morning of July 4, much earlier than in previous years. The $6.3 billion budget was passed in reasonably intact form except for the measures to fund our transportation program. The General Assembly replaced our proposed extension of the sales tax with a two-cents-per-gallon tax increase, which produced virtually the same revenues but was not responsive to inflation.

NEXT IT WAS TIME to focus on Pennsylvania's long-term economic problems. Dr. Samuel Johnson's observation that "nothing so concentrates the mind as the prospect of imminent hanging" accurately summarized our mental state as we turned to this issue, on which assessments of our stewardship would rise or fall.

WHAT WAS CLEARLY called for was a plan to help create new jobs and provide for economic growth. In early 1979 I assigned Walt Plosila to work with the state planning board, which had been dormant in the Shapp years, to frame such a plan. The board included legislative representatives; the secretaries of community affairs, agriculture, environmental resources, transportation and commerce; and leaders in industry, labor, agriculture, community affairs, planning and the media. Walt entitled its venture "Choices for Pennsylvanians" in the belief that it was individual citizens, the private sector and both state and local government, rather than some central government authority, that should make the choices affecting our development. I asked the board to review economic and community conditions in Pennsylvania and to propose a set of priorities, directions, policies and actions that could guide public and private economic development, community conservation and resource management efforts throughout the 1980s.

Over two and one-half years, the board systematically gathered data. It heard the views of citizens and interest groups at more than seventy regional and local meetings throughout the state. It also took public opinion surveys, distributed prepaid mailers and produced a sixty-minute public television documentary. It used an econometric model to project existing trends and alternative future scenarios. Its report, submitted in September 1981, provided action options to be exercised over a multiyear period by our administration, the General Assembly, local officials and the private sector. Although we had already begun to implement some of the board's conclusions, a definitive statement of our economic development policy was not to be finalized until March 28, 1983, well after my election to a second term.

Taking the time for this careful study was not easy. Conditions on the national scene were worsening. The "misery index" (a combination of unemployment and inflation rates) rose to new heights, a development that would help usher in the Reagan administration in 1980. We were swamped with demands to "do something." But we stuck to our game plan, knowing that only a long-run approach could even begin to turn around problems that had taken decades to develop. As stated in David Osborne's widely praised book, *Laboratories of Democracy*:

Pennsylvania Democrats vilified Thornburgh for what they perceived as a failure to respond. Their approach to economic development was the traditional one: smokestack chasing and social welfare spending. . . . Thornburgh wanted nothing to do with expensive subsidies or social welfare programs. Instead, he decided to commission an in-depth study of the state's economy. . . . As the recession deepened, the Democrats pounded Thornburgh unmercifully for his failure to act. Thornburgh and his top staff, who were known for their conservatism and their palace guard mentality, pounded back. The combination of the Democrats' severe pressure to act and Thornburgh's fiscal restraint and market orientation eventually produced perhaps the best economic development system in the country.

Politically attractive quick fixes were certainly tempting, especially during a period that encompassed my 1982 reelection campaign. But we constantly reminded ourselves that the state's problems were deeply rooted and required harsh medicine.

The comprehensive economic plan that I finally unveiled in 1983 was based upon certain premises that evolved during the "Choices" process. All of Pennsylvania's net new jobs in the past several years had come from small firms, those with fewer than twenty employees. This suggested a major reorientation in our economic development approach, heretofore focused on larger firms. Studies also suggested that trying to outbid other locales for factories resulted in the winning and losing of equal numbers of facilities. Even recruiting foreign companies was a poor use of available resources. An example was the much ballyhooed Volkswagen Rabbit plant, attracted by the Shapp administration with $40 million in 1.75 percent loans (with repayment to begin in 1998), $25 million in highway and rail construction, $3 million in training subsidies and five years of local tax abatement. This premier smokestack–chasing prize of the 1970s lasted but nine years, closing in 1987. Pennsylvania's loss of some 200,000 manufacturing jobs in the 1970s suggested that manufacturers needed to modernize, particularly by incorporating emerging technologies. However, most high-tech growth programs focused on new firms, not on more traditional businesses such as steel mills, coal mines and machine shops. The "spinning in" of new job-saving technology to old businesses would prove as important as the "spinning off" of ideas to start new firms. Moreover, contrary to conventional wisdom, businesses were not fleeing the Frost Belt to move to the Sun Belt (the South and Southwest). Only 4 percent of job growth in the Sun Belt was due to relocations from the Frost Belt, and there was equal movement in the opposite direction. The real difference in job growth came from the Frost Belt's greater plant closure rate and lower birthrate of new firms. An increased emphasis on knowledge-based industries demanded substantial increases in our ability to educate, train and retrain our workforce.

In the final analysis, it would be private-sector decisions to invest, expand or relocate that would dictate our economic success or failure. And to a great extent, growth would depend upon national and international economic forces beyond our control. Nevertheless, there was much we could do to encourage new and existing businesses.

THE FIRST PRIORITY was to improve Pennsylvania's overall business climate, which had been perceived negatively throughout the 1970s. High taxes, excessive regulatory burdens, insufficient availability of capital and a generally antibusiness mentality in the bureaucracy posed substantial hurdles to private-sector growth and thus contributed to the low credit ratings given the state by Standard & Poor's and Moody's. We had to upgrade these ratings and focus the attention of the business community on positive news about Pennsylvania.

One obvious assignment was to improve the tax climate. Pennsylvania's corporate net income tax rate was one of the nation's highest at 10.5 percent, and annual prepayment of 90 percent of the previous year's tax was required. Although tax considerations are far from wholly determinative of business decisions, tax rates are so visible that they provide an all-too-easy measure of business hospitality.

Our first steps in this area were largely symbolic. We continued to phase out the prepayment provision. We also introduced a Subchapter S provision that permitted small business corporations to elect to be taxed at the much lower individual tax rate (2.1 to 2.45 percent during my time in office). In another boost for small start-ups, we introduced loss carry-forward provisions that permitted taxpayers to offset early-year losses against later-year profits. The Subchapter S and loss carry-forward provisions had been recommended by the Small Business Advisory Council, which we established early and with which I met regularly.

These initiatives were but a prelude to our major undertaking: cutting costs to create the opportunity for significant tax reduction. I was convinced we could achieve substantial savings through better management and reduction of the notoriously bloated state bureaucracy. Pennsylvania government had grown too large and too costly; management was lax and accountability low. A Cost Reduction Study Team chaired by Wally Baran cut the cost of governmental operations by over $6.1 billion during my eight years in office, an amount larger than the entire 1978–79 budget. The savings averaged out to over $2 million a day.

One of our principal cost-saving steps was the gradual elimination of nearly 15,000 unnecessary positions. A state payroll totaling nearly 95,000 in January 1979 was reduced to just over 80,000 by December 1986. By 1987 we had the lowest per capita payroll of any state. Simple management of attrition accomplished the vast majority of reductions in force. Under the hiring freeze imposed at the outset of the administration, vacancies frequently were not filled, and managers reassigned remaining personnel to take up the slack. In addition, the introduction of modern technology often increased the productivity of whole units. The sizable drop in the workforce resulted in no appreciable diminution of state services and, in some areas, actually increased our responsiveness to the public. Despite claims that it hurt employee morale, I saw indicators to the contrary. For example, by 1985, nearly 50,000, or close to half, of our employees were contributing a record $1,850,000 to the State Employees Combined Appeal campaign, something I had encouraged from the outset of my administration. This was not the behavior of employees whose morale, as union bosses were often to complain, "was at an all-time low."

Other efforts to "do more with less" also cut costs substantially. Cost containment within the medical-assistance program saved over $1 billion during my two terms. Welfare reform saved $82 million a year, but most of that was plowed back into increased cash grants to the truly needy. Stepped-up antifraud and collection efforts and curtailment of error rates saved another $750 million in welfare costs. Increased tax enforcement efforts recouped $743 million, with annual delinquent-tax collections soaring from $59 million in 1979 to $230 million in 1986. Value engineering in highway construction saved $122 million. Savings of $57 million came from renegotiated cost allocations with the federal government, increased direct deposit of payrolls and the eventual upgrading of our bond ratings.

RESHAPING PENNSYLVANIA'S ECONOMY

Paper costs were reduced by $51 million, a new telephone contract was designed to save $31 million, and energy conservation projects saved $27 million. Some small changes were symbolically significant. For example, over time we cut the state's automobile fleet by 20 percent, eliminating 1,400 cars. This cut, together with fuel savings resulting from downsizing of the remaining fleet, saved $3.5 million over eight years.

The principal beneficiaries of these efforts were Pennsylvania taxpayers. Beginning in 1984, tax rates were reduced each year; the total cuts exceeded $1 billion. Both individual and corporate tax rates were lower when I left office than when I was sworn in, with corporate rates going from 10.5 to 8.5 percent and individual rates from 2.2 to 2.1 percent, visibly improving our business climate. As a bonus we also created a rainy-day fund to protect against unforeseen downturns in the economy and avoid future tax increases. We set aside $25 million for this fund in 1985 and another $25 million in 1986. After I left office, unfortunately, the fund was wiped out when increased state spending could not keep pace with even the record tax increases imposed by my successor. It was to be rejuvenated during the go-go 1990s just in time to help take up the slack when the economy faltered in the new century.

On the regulatory front, we created a procedure (later enacted into law) to ensure that regulations were reviewed with interested parties before promulgation, were written in simple English and did not exceed the mandate of the laws. In March 1981, an advisory committee of business lawyers, accountants and corporate service firms assessed the notoriously slow and nonresponsive operations of the Corporation Bureau within the Department of State. The resulting changes in its accessibility and response capability earned the deserved plaudits of the specialized, but influential, group that patronized it.

We also created a Small Business Action Center designed to help small businesses deal with the state bureaucracy. Equipped with know-how and forms, the center provided one-stop aid in unsnarling red tape and overcoming delay. It coordinated as well a unique staff of skilled "expediters" throughout major state departments who were to respond within two working days to business inquiries. In addition, we put up the required state match to secure thirteen of the federal Small Business Administration's new Small Business Development Centers, whose consultants, recruited from the state's business schools, provided advice and assistance to budding entrepreneurs. By 1983, *INC.* magazine rated the commonwealth "Best of Show" in small-business assistance.

We heard regular complaints, particularly from small businesses, about the unavailability of capital to finance business opportunities. Since its creation in the 1950s, PIDA had served as a model for other states in providing low-interest loans for capital projects and prided itself on its 0.5 percent delinquency rate. We sought increased appropriations for PIDA every year, quadrupling the amounts available to borrowers. Eventually, $400 million in loans were dispersed to aid in industrial development and expansion. We directed nearly 50 percent of these new loans into the small-business sector and toward advanced-technology opportunities. These were riskier investments, to be sure, but helped to fill the gap for non-blue-chip borrowers.

An additional $25 million in capital funding at the local level came from a new Pennsylvania Capital Loan Fund established with resources redirected from the Appalachian Regional Commission. This fund provided the first state government working-capital loans; it also helped change banking behavior by educating the banks. Finally, we established a venture-capital program that provided over $40 million in seed grants for entrepreneurs out of a 1 percent set-aside from state and public school employee pension funds authorized in 1984.

Legislation phasing in statewide banking facilitated the provision of capital from the private sector. Previously banks could do business only in and contiguous to the county in which their principal office was located. Smaller banks resisted the change, but the legislature recognized that financial services were becoming increasingly globalized. As a subtle side effect, business leaders who served on the boards of these financial institutions developed more of a statewide awareness.

Bob Wilburn had engaged the Wall Street firm of Dillon, Read & Company to advise us on dealing with the credit rating agencies. Although skeptical at first, the experts soon began to enthuse over our fiscal progress, and before the end of my administration, both Standard & Poor's and Moody's upped our credit ratings for the first time in fifteen years. It helped that in 1985, the commonwealth had begun preparing audited financial statements in accordance with "gimmick-free" Generally Accepted Accounting Principles.

THE SECOND ELEMENT of our economic strategy was enhancing our traditional industrial base and relieving the pressure on the communities that had suffered as a result of its decline. Our successful Enterprise Zone Program, created in 1983, did not treat tax incentives as the moving force for increased investment. Instead, it emphasized community conservation and the building of strong local partnerships to shape strategies for particular communities. Initial planning grants of $50,000 were awarded on a competitive basis and followed by annual development grants of $250,000. Enterprise zones were also given priority consideration for a wide range of other state incentives, ranging from loans to infrastructure grants to highway funding. These zones were eventually designated in twenty-eight communities across the state, resulting in $228 million in private investment and the creation or expansion of nearly 700 businesses.

Though the state's economic problems transcended the plight of any one industry, that of the steel industry was the most dramatic. Pittsburgh had long been known as the Steel City, and the state was a historic leader in iron and steel production. I had pointed out that "when the steel industry sneezes, Pennsylvania catches cold." And by 1979, the industry was doing considerably more than sneezing.

From the end of World War II into the fifties, American producers could sell all the steel they could produce at any price. But foreign producers soon built more modern mills and began to compete effectively around the world, including within the United States. In 1959, steel imports into our country reached 5 million tons and exceeded exports for the first time in history. By 1978, imports had increased to 21.1 million tons. A principal reason for this reversal was the failure of American producers to modernize. By 1981, for example, only 21.6 percent of the steel in the United States was being made by the modern continuous-casting method, compared to 70.7 percent in Japan and 45.1 percent in Europe.

Between 1981 and 1985, the American steel industry accumulated losses of $7.25 billion, having developed over 300 million tons of excess capacity. Bethlehem Steel's plight was typical. A February 1981 report to its employees stated, "Bethlehem started 1960 . . . with more than three dollars on hand for every dollar we owed. . . . Today we owe almost four times as much as we have on hand." John Strohmayer, in his book *Trouble in Bethlehem*, identified the causes of this company's decline: shortsighted management not willing to invest in modernization; hostile unions pressing for ever-higher wages and benefits; outmoded and costly work rules; government pressure to contain prices and increase employee compensation; and unfair and often predatory practices of foreign competitors, many of which were government owned or highly subsidized and were not reluctant to "dump" steel in the United States at prices at or below their production costs. Nor were the problems confined to Bethlehem. From 1982 to 1993, U.S. Steel, suffering from many of the same woes, cut its output from

31 to 12 million tons per year and shrank its payroll from 90,000 to 18,000 nationwide.

In western Pennsylvania, where the steel industry had been born and flourished, it was in its death throes as the 1980s began. Between 1979 and 1984, roughly seven out of ten steel jobs disappeared, and the darkened hulks of once-prospering mills dotted the shores of the Monongahela and Ohio Rivers. Unemployment and its accompanying social ills plagued many of the mill towns, where jobs in the industry had been passed from generation to generation for well over a century.

There was very little we could do to bring back the steel industry. Most of our efforts had to be directed to developing new sources of employment. Almost immediately after I assumed office, however, we were pressured to participate in an effort to resuscitate the Wheeling-Pittsburgh mill in Monessen (Democratic legislative powerhouse Jim Manderino's hometown). We reluctantly agreed to make PIDA funding available as part of a federal-state-local bailout package, but the effort was fruitless. Thereafter, I resisted pleas for massive public assistance to "keep the mill open" in various communities where market forces dictated otherwise. These decisions proved to be wise in the long run but could be heartrending in the moment.

We did, however, support a level playing field for domestic and foreign steel producers, and we worked closely with steel executives and labor leaders facing unfair competition from abroad. For example, in June 1983 we met with top White House staff to urge restraints on specialty steel imports and in May 1984, I testified before the International Trade Commission in support of relief from dumping. The resulting "voluntary restraints" adopted by the Reagan administration were designed to cap steel imports at a level equal to 18.5 percent of domestic consumption and buy some time for modernization by American producers. But the problem persists to this day.

Our principal direct contribution to the mill towns was delayed until 1986 by our insistence on stabilizing the overall business climate first. The Renaissance Communities program targeted state grants to distressed communities; provided partial state funding for Strategy 21, a collection of capital projects in greater Pittsburgh that was devised by local business and governmental leaders; and made a series of $1 million planning grants to public-private community development organizations in the Monongahela, Beaver and Shenango Valleys, home to most of the communities impacted by the demise of the steel industry. This effort created, in effect, "super enterprise zones" encompassing entire regions. They could only succeed with grassroots involvement and the cooperation of insular communities in tackling regional problems. Funding at the outset was restricted to the planning effort. After consensus developed on strategies tailored to specific regional needs, as much as $100 million would be targeted to carrying out those strategies.

David Osborne, who generally found our economic development efforts praiseworthy, noted that fault was found (particularly among Democrats) with our slowness in assisting particularly distressed areas. I responded: "If I had come into office and made my first priority the areas of high unemployment, we would be nowhere today. First we had to get the fiscal situation straightened out, then we had to develop an intelligent overall economic development program. It was tough [but] we took the time to do this 'Choices' process and put something together that was not off the shelf and was not just one more glitzy incentive package." The problem was not our failure to seek timely and adequate funding for distressed communities, but our inability to make clear to these communities what our overall strategy meant to them. They felt their plight was being neglected, and we were to pay a price for this perception in my 1982 reelection campaign.

GROWTH IN ADVANCED technology, the third element in our economic development strategy, resulted in our most spectacular advances. To this day, Pennsylvania's achievements in this field are considered to be preeminent, and they have provided a role model for other state efforts.

The "Choices" process had identified an important underutilized economic development asset: our research colleges and universities and their reservoir of technological expertise. Pennsylvania was home to four of the top fifty graduate research universities in the country. It ranked fifth in the nation in both numbers employed in the technology field and total expenditures on research and development. The state also had the fifth-largest concentration of scientists and engineers in the country. Yet there was none of the kind of interaction and ferment that had given rise to advanced-technology growth in California's Silicon Valley or Route 128 in Massachusetts. We were determined to remedy this situation.

An existing state entity called the Pennsylvania Science and Engineering Foundation ostensibly provided science and technology advice to the governor. There was no evidence that it had had any appreciable impact on technology transfer, but we decided to make it our vehicle for greater commercialization of the state's advanced-technology capabilities. I renamed it the Ben Franklin Partnership, reasoning that Franklin, a Pennsylvanian, was "a scientist, inventor, businessman, educator, statesman . . . and a damned good politician as well!" In short, he evidenced precisely the skills that would be necessary to make this program work. I doubt very much if the enterprise would have enjoyed its unparalleled success had it continued to be called the Pennsylvania Science and Engineering Foundation.

The Ben Franklin Partnership sought to bring together education, business, labor and government to create new business and job opportunities in advanced technology. Challenge grants—state funds to be matched, at least three dollars to one, by the private sector—funded four regional Advanced Technology Centers, each at a major research university. Not a cent was to go for bricks and mortar. My 1983 budget request sought an initial appropriation of $1 million, which generated $3 million in matching grants.

Four principal characteristics distinguished the Advanced Technology Centers: Their activities were designed and implemented from the bottom up. No state master plan dictated their direction or operations, although their emphasis had to be consistent with the targets set forth in our 1982 advanced-technology policy statement. Second, they were tailored to the capabilities and needs of their particular areas. Third, their funding was highly leveraged, and matching funds had to be made available up front. And finally, they were competitive. Originally, only one-third of the state's annual contribution was distributed equally among them. The rest was awarded on the basis of program quality and the size of the dollar match.

Each center established its own areas of concentration based upon the strengths of its institutions and communities. The Northeastern Center, frequently acknowledged to be the best of the four, was located at Lehigh University in Bethlehem. It became an early laboratory for the application of computer-assisted design and computer-assisted manufacturing (CAD/CAM) technologies. Materials research, microelectronics and biotechnology were also on its agenda. The center purchased a former Bethlehem Steel laboratory for use as an academic and contract research facility and as a small-business incubator which provided inventors and entrepreneurs with rented space and common facilities to help speed their growth. One of my favorite stories involved a prospective tenant who was told there was no more space. Before departing, he noted a rather sizable coat closet and inquired as to its availability. In some disbelief, the center agreed to lease the space to him, whereupon he established a software operation that in time outgrew not just the closet but the incubator, eventually employing some twenty-four employees.

The Southeastern Center capitalized upon the existing University City Science Center (a consortium of local colleges and universities including the University of Pennsylvania, Drexel and Temple) and upon Philadelphia's vast medical research facilities. It focused on medical biotechnology and other leading-edge programs in the healing arts, as well as sensor technologies, materials research and space productivity and adaptability. A highly aggressive seed-capital program was initiated in this center, but it did not perform as well as its counterparts.

University Park, home of Pennsylvania State University, was the site of the Central and Northern Center. Programs in food and plant production and processing as well as mineral and materials research reflected the traditional strengths of Penn State in these areas. A new Biotechnology Institute was established, and programs in manufacturing and management control systems were initiated. A strong training component was included as well.

A precedent-setting cooperative undertaking by the University of Pittsburgh and Carnegie Mellon University (CMU) formed the basis for the Western Pennsylvania Center. CMU's strength in robotics and computer technology combined with the world-renowned medical center at Pitt to fashion a unique agenda. The program was strengthened when CMU won a spirited competition to become the locale of the Defense Department's $103 million Software Engineering Institute. The center also inherited the $100 million former Gulf Oil research facilities nearby. A strong focus on entrepreneurial assistance aided technology transfer in this hard-hit area. In particular, a private group, the Pittsburgh High Technology Council, worked closely with the center in "spinning off" start-ups.

Over the first ten years of the Ben Franklin Partnership, aggregate state funding of $220 million was matched by $780 million in private-sector funds, making it by far the largest such program in the country. A total of 1,700 companies were created or expanded, and over 400 new products or processes were developed. Forty-one small business incubators were established, attracting some 600 tenants. Enterprises connected with the partnership attracted $150 million in venture capital. One hundred thirteen colleges and universities ultimately participated in the program. The real payoff, however, was the 25,000 high-quality, future-oriented jobs created or retained in Pennsylvania. A later study estimated that Ben Franklin programs boosted the state economy by $8 billion from 1989 to 2001, returning more than $400 million in additional state tax revenue.

Even the critics of the program suggested that we were on the right track: the Pennsylvania Manufacturers Association called the effort "too academic," while some colleges and universities chafed at its "commercial" aspects.

By the end of my second term, the state had obtained other advanced-technology prizes. In 1986, the National Science Foundation, after an intense nationwide competition, decided to locate two of its five national engineering research centers at CMU and Lehigh. Our 1986–87 budget included $2 million for their support. The Lehigh center was to focus on structures-related industries, the CMU center on concepts, methods and design technologies to increase competitiveness. The foundation also selected Pittsburgh as the location for a $70 million supercomputer center to be run by a consortium of CMU, the University of Pittsburgh and Westinghouse Electric Corporation, and the National Aeronautics and Space Administration chose to locate its Bioprocessing and Pharmaceutical Research Center in Philadelphia.

JUST AS PENNSYLVANIA had to deal with an economy in transition during the 1980s, individual Pennsylvanians had to deal with careers in transition. Providing job training and retraining was therefore the fourth element of our economic development strategy.

This problem was multifaceted. One of the most difficult, yet understandable, barriers to change was a psychological one—the natural human commitment to the status quo, even when that commitment is unreasonable. Thus, in many mill towns of western Pennsylvania, individuals whose families had worked in the mill for generations were reluctant to try anything new. They preferred to stake their futures on the dwindling hope that the mill would "come back" and restore the employment that they viewed almost as an entitlement. The sad truth was that many of these jobs were gone forever—lost to more efficient, lower-cost operations elsewhere. It took the actual dismantling and leveling of the mills to convince many workers of that truth. Needless to say, the disruption of long-held expectations took a dreadful toll in terms of mental problems, substance abuse and disharmony in the home.

Change involving the introduction of modern technology was particularly threatening to many. The perception grew up that every Mr. Goodwrench would have to become Dr. Advanced Thinker with a Ph.D. and a white lab coat. Studies actually showed that the majority of jobs created through emerging economies required only a high school degree and two years of technical training. Still, these opportunities were viewed with suspicion.

A third difficulty was that traditional vocational education and training programs provided instruction in certain skills and trades with little prior evaluation of the demand for them. We decided to tackle this problem first, as it had implications for the other two. In 1982, I proposed a customized job-training (CJT) program designed to tailor training efforts to specific employer needs. Employers helped to select instructors and offered job training on site, in the classroom (often using Pennsylvania's community college system) or both. Often CJT was part of a larger package assembled as an incentive for plant relocation or expansion. The state paid the employer's job-training costs on condition that successful participants be guaranteed jobs. Funding for the program began at $1.9 million in 1982 and exceeded $12 million a year by the time I left office. CJT was responsible for over 42,000 Pennsylvanians being placed in new or upgraded positions with over 250 companies during that period. We encouraged the local private- industry councils that administered the federal Job Training Partnership Act to emphasize similar jobs-first commitments.

A typical CJT success story was the updating of the skills of some 200 workers at the Harley-Davidson motorcycle plant in York. Their manager praised CJT as "improving quality and reducing rework and downtime at our facility." Harley-Davidson, which had earlier sought trade tariffs on Japanese imports, used the protection to build up productivity through CJT and other programs and, in 1987, was able to ask the International Trade Commission to remove the tariffs.

The Bureau of Job Service also operated more traditional job-training services, through which more than a million persons were placed in jobs from 1979 through 1987. We focused particular attention on displaced workers.

It was in this connection that I had one of my most gratifying encounters with a satisfied customer. Late in my administration, I participated in a ceremony giving a new product award to a robotics firm that had manufactured a device with a touch so delicate that it could thread a needle. I made the rounds to congratulate all those involved and came, at last, to two men in white lab coats, standing at the back of the crowd. One of them said, "Governor, do you remember me?" I responded, "Gee, I don't think I do. Maybe you can help me out." He said, "We were steelworkers at Crucible Steel in Midland. You came there to present a check for a job-retraining program for those who lost their jobs when the plant closed. Well, we've been working for this company for two years." It was experiences such as these that made it all seem worthwhile.

As part of an overall education reform agenda, in 1985 we proposed a requirement that each new vocational education course offered be justified by local labor market information and be supported by local employers. Periodic review of both elements was to ensure that voc-ed courses were kept abreast of the changing needs of local economies. Here again, the goal was to match skills acquired in schools with those required in the marketplace and avoid the consequences of graduating, for example, some 10,000 cosmetologists a year, when we needed only a few hundred.

One major stumbling block to maximizing our human resources was the state AFL-CIO's constant partisan opposition. Often able to work with individual unions and their leaders at the local level, we failed to build a rapport with the statewide leadership of the umbrella organization because of its strong historic ties to the Democratic Party.

Business-labor cooperation did help solve the problem of the state's huge unemployment compensation debt to the federal government. During the 1970s, that debt had reached $1.2 billion; by the time I was sworn in, it was growing by $1 million a day. Knowing that any proposal we developed would occasion knee-jerk opposition from the AFL-CIO, we were content to have the union leadership fashion a proposal in direct negotiation with the business community. On July 21, 1983, I signed legislation that would reduce the debt through a combination of benefit adjustments and increased employer contributions. On May 7, 1986, we paid off the last of the state's unemployment compensation debt to the U.S. Treasury by wiring $31,989,631 to Washington, thereby eliminating the special 0.3 percent tax paid by some 200,000 Pennsylvania employers to retire that obligation.

WHEN I ENTERED office, the deplorable state of our highways and bridges posed not only a threat to the safety of travelers, but a substantial impediment to economic development. Pennsylvania's traditional designation as the Keystone State reflected its position astride the major transportation routes connecting the Northeast with the Middle West and the Upper South, the area within which most of the nation's economic activity still took place. These economic lifelines were severely threatened, with 40 percent of our 45,000 miles of roads and 25 percent of our 27,000 bridges in substandard condition. Upgrading our physical infrastructure thus became the fifth element of our economic development strategy. This task had to begin with a complete reconstruction of PennDOT.

The January 25, 1979, issue of the *Engineering News-Record*, the weekly "bible" of the construction industry, included a cover photograph of me and a feature story on Pennsylvania's highway situation. While those of us in public life normally court attention, in this case the publicity was most unwelcome. The story occasioned some mirth among my fellow graduates of the Yale School of Engineering. One of them, I was told, grumbled, "Wouldn't you know that the only way that guy would get on the cover of the *Engineering News-Record* would be as a politician?" The gist of the story was more ominous, however: "Stricken PennDOT is a textbook example of the fate that can befall an agency that becomes so infected with corrupt politics, graft, and inefficient management that it forfeits not only legislative and fiscal support, but the confidence of the public as well. . . . Pennsylvania's highway system is marked by such disrepair, disrepute and disarray that restoration seems all but impossible." With this assessment neither PennDOT secretary Tom Larson nor I could quarrel. But we set about, nonetheless, to try to accomplish the "all but impossible."

Working with a first-class team, we first tackled personnel problems. PennDOT had long been a patronage dump. For example, the maintenance manager in each of the state's sixty-seven counties had traditionally been chosen by the local party chairman, more to strengthen the party apparatus than to maintain the highways (in 1979, only one of the sixty-seven was a professional engineer). Many of the managers, in turn, essentially sold highway jobs for political contributions. Within three weeks of my inauguration, we announced that the managers would henceforth be chosen by a merit selection process featuring nonpartisan screening committees. Committee members largely represented civic-minded groups such as automobile clubs, chambers of commerce, leagues of women voters and labor organizations.

Wails of outrage, threats and promises of retribution emanated from Republican legislators and party chairmen across the state. In the words of the *Pittsburgh Press*, I "assiduously ignored" them. Mutterings were to continue throughout our administration, but in the final analysis, we succeeded. A whole new cadre of managers was recruited into PennDOT to undertake the massive deferred-maintenance tasks. The number of professional engineers reached a high of nineteen in 1983. And, as we departed, all the maintenance managers were brought within the protection of the civil service system. An era had ended in Pennsylvania.

Finances were the next problem on the agenda. Pennsylvania was dead last in the drawdown of federal highway funds and had lost some $474 million in federal aid due to inability to provide the necessary state match. During the Shapp years, our highway debt had reached $2.2 billion, the highest level in the nation, prompting our commitment to end bond funding of highway construction and to put the operation on a "pay as you go" basis.

This change would require a substantial bolstering of highway funding. Our efforts in the 1979 budget were only a finger in the dike. The following year, we launched a proposal to exchange six cents of the cents-per-gallon tax for a 6 percent levy on the price of gasoline at the pump, to take into account the rapid inflation of fuel prices. Despite an extensive public relations effort, we once again came up short and were obliged to accept a revenue enhancement package that left us about $100 million short of meeting our current needs. The next year, with both houses of the General Assembly in Republican hands, we finally secured passage of the oil franchise tax, a percentage tax on the wholesale price of gasoline and diesel fuel, to stabilize funding of the highway program. The revenue increase enabled us to leap from last into first place in drawdown of federal highway funds and to remain among the leaders throughout the 1980s. The final 70 miles of Pennsylvania's 1,500 miles of the interstate system were completed or under contract as I left office.

In 1982, a massive $1.4 billion, six-year bridge rehabilitation program was adopted. It was designed to repair nearly 1,000 of the state's "at risk" bridges and, not incidentally, provide an average of 20,000 construction-related jobs each year (one-third of the 60,000 created by our infrastructure-rebuilding efforts overall). The program particularly targeted some 200 deteriorated bridges that forced costly detours on important truck routes at an estimated cost to industry of $228 million a year. Funding came from a $36-per-axle tax on heavy trucks (which was accompanied by an increase in their allowable weights) and the state's share of the proceeds from a five-cents-per-gallon increase in the federal gas tax. In July 1986, a second Billion Dollar Bridge Program was signed into law, covering an additional 3,500 bridges at an estimated cost of $1.7 billion. This effort marked the largest bridge restoration and replacement program in the nation.

At the same time, highway debt dropped from $2.2 billion to $1.6 billion. To reduce the state's maintenance bill, more than 2,300 miles of state-maintained roads—those that were functionally local in character—were "turned back" to local jurisdictions for maintenance after being restored to good condition by PennDOT. This allowed for quicker attention to local maintenance needs while the state concentrated on roads with higher traffic volumes. It was in maintenance, particularly pothole repair, that we achieved our biggest breakthroughs, especially in my home area of western Pennsylvania, where the complaints had been the most vocal. As Greg Teslovich, manager of safety for West Penn AAA Motor Club, put it, "Potholes are nothing like they used to be around here."

By 1981, the public perception of PennDOT was beginning to change. At the dedication of the new Sewickley Bridge over the Ohio River near Pittsburgh, I was astonished but delighted when my first mention of this much-reviled agency was greeted by cheers and applause.

Finally, in 1982, our efforts were rewarded by the *Engineering News-Record*. In another cover story, the magazine featured Tom Larson as its Man of the Year and described PennDOT as "one of the best managed—and financed—public works agencies in the country." Rarely had such a quick turnabout been accomplished in state government, and Tom Larson was later recognized by the National Governors Association for his vast contributions to the transportation field. He went on to serve with distinction as the Federal Highway Administrator in the first Bush administration. He is truly one of the giants of public management. Overall, the value of state highway and bridge construction contracts increased from $180 million in 1978–79 to $1 billion in each of 1985–86 and 1986–87.

We also engaged in many infrastructure improvements not related to highways or bridges. One of the most vexing to me was the Capitol addition. Early in 1979, I looked out Bob Wilburn's office window at the lines of parked cars in the back lot and asked, "Can't we do something about this? How about putting all that parking underground?" Bob and Wally Baran subsequently developed plans for a handsome series of structures that provided not only underground parking and a beautified environment but also badly needed new offices to replace crowded and, in some cases, unsafe legislative quarters. The legislature approved the funding, and the project began.

It was, predictably, encumbered with controversy. A noisy legislator from Beaver County, Nick Colafella, concocted a bogus "granite-gate" scandal over purchases from the same quarry that had supplied the stone for the original Capitol. After hearings, lawsuits and exhaustive media coverage, the matter was finally laid to rest, with no wrongdoing ever having been shown. The building, when completed, drew mostly favorable reviews. *New York Times* architecture critic Paul Goldberger called it "perhaps the most ambitious work in the Classical mode in the United States in a generation . . . a design that manages at once to enrich the original capitol building and to defer to it." He concluded that Pennsylvania was "approaching the end of the century with its architectural values intact." To this day, however, not a single member of the General Assembly has so much as acknowledged my efforts to push this project to a successful conclusion.

New convention centers were provided for Philadelphia, Erie and Pittsburgh (the latter two having been commenced under the Shapp administration); a new airport terminal was constructed in Harrisburg to replace a truly shabby facility; and Pittsburgh's new International Airport was begun as a part of the Strategy 21 program. Investments were also made in the ports of Pittsburgh, Erie and Philadelphia, including an ill-fated joint investment to try to enhance CONRAIL's coal-exporting capabilities. In 1983 voters approved a $300 million bond issue to fund a comprehensive water resources loan program aimed at upgrading and developing dams, water supply systems and port facilities. To meet another urban priority, we committed more than $2 billion in federal and state funds to capital improvements in public transit systems and more than doubled state support for operating assistance, to $180 million a year.

All in all, the $20 billion in public funds that we committed in the 1980s was the biggest investment in infrastructure the state had ever seen. Our determination to upgrade physical facilities was cited time and again as a major plus in our efforts to attract new business and industry. The *Engineering News-Record* also noted a corresponding increase in private-sector infrastructure investment. In early 1987, it reported, "While 30 states across the nation suffered losses in contract award volume last year, Pennsylvania chalked up an enviable 21% annual growth rate."

THE FINAL ELEMENT of our strategy dealt with quality of life, not traditionally recognized as a significant factor in economic development, but important in attracting and retaining a skilled workforce. The following chapter describes many of our efforts in community development, environmental protection, crime prevention, education, human services, recreation and the arts.

We also worked to turn around Pennsylvania's negative image. Our efforts here did double duty, also benefiting our travel and tourism industry. In early 1979, we conducted a competition among leading Pennsylvania advertising agencies, inviting them to come up with a slogan to help convey the true assets of the state to potential visitors (and residents). We chose Ketchum's "You've Got a Friend in Pennsylvania" theme, complete with a lilting song and beautiful photographic imagery of landmarks and natural sites within our boundaries. The program was enthusiastically received. Thereafter funding for promotion of Pennsylvania travel and tourism was to grow steadily from its 1979 level of $60,000 to nearly $6 million a year. As a result, the industry became a major contributor to economic growth, employing over 200,000 persons by 1987 and pulling in a record $10.2 billion in annual revenues, over twice the 1978 level.

An interesting sidelight was the opposition of English teachers and other grammatically aware citizens to our use of the term "you've got" as opposed to "you have." Among those raising objections was nationally syndicated columnist James J. Kilpatrick. I responded with a letter, carefully researched by my staff, citing Shakespeare, a variety of songwriters such as Cole Porter and George Gershwin, and various slogans and jingles, all using "You've (or I've) got." Kilpatrick responded graciously in a "Dear Dick" letter and a column headed "Thornburgh to the Rescue; Slogan's Grammar Holds Up." Later, in my address to the Pennsylvania Society's annual black-tie dinner, I emphasized my triumph by singing excerpts from "I've Got Rhythm," "I've Got You Under My Skin," "I've Got a Crush on You," "He's Got the Whole World in His Hands," and "If You've Got the Time, I've Got the Beer." The matter was largely put to rest, although diehards continued to write, particularly after we put the slogan on the state's license plates.

Also on the quality-of-life front, we were able to trumpet Pittsburgh's 1985 designation as America's Most Livable City by the Rand-McNally *Places Rated Almanac*. This was a real eye-opener for those who still viewed my hometown as the "Smoky City." Throughout the 1980s, the *Almanac* consistently rated both Pittsburgh and Philadelphia in the top ten cities in terms of quality of life.

THE BIGGEST SINGLE contributor to Pennsylvania's economy was agriculture, and we paid it close attention. Nationally, people were moving off the land; the percentage of our population residing on farms was to decline from 40 percent in 1890 to about 2 percent a century later. Our state was no exception, although we still had the largest rural population in the nation and some 58,000 Pennsylvanians lived on family farms during my time in office.

In the 1978 campaign we had established strong working relations with leaders in the agricultural community. With their input, we were able to fashion a responsive legislative program and to secure the passage of over seventy pieces of legislation aimed at preserving the family farm and prime agricultural land. These included laws amending the inheritance tax provisions so that farm property could be more easily passed on to succeeding generations; protecting against unjust land condemnation practices; exempting family farm corporations from stock franchise taxes; and establishing a milk producers' security fund to protect dairy farmers from default by dealers and cooperatives. Symbolic actions secured a "right to farm" and established new agricultural districts. We also initiated new marketing programs—"Pennsylvania: We're Growing Better" and "Keystone Pride"—and pushed the increased export of our farm products.

THE DEMOCRATS did not take our advances lying down. Especially during the recession of 1982–83, they were highly critical of our failure to quickly turn around an economic situation for which their prior policies were largely responsible. After regaining control of the House of Representatives in 1982, they began to advocate a billion-dollar tax-and-spend program called PennPRIDE, largely developed by a Washington, D.C., economic development consultant. Although the program contained some useful components, which we were later to adopt, it was, as described by David Osborne, "the kind of program one gets when ten politicians sit down together to divvy up $1 billion; relatively unsophisticated, untargeted, and focused more on temporary relief than long-term structural change."

The House Democrats incorporated PennPRIDE into the 1982–83 budget without providing any funding source for it. Their goal was to maneuver me into not only agreeing to raise taxes, but taking the initiative to do so. The Republican-controlled Senate, by prearrangement with me, approved the budget intact, billion-dollar imbalance and all, and sent it on to me. Outraged at the Democrats' irresponsibility, I responded with a line-item veto including the legislature's own funding for the upcoming year. Faced with their own political extinction, the embarrassed Democrats came back four days later with a much scaled down budget and temporary tax increases (reduced in subsequent years at my initiative) to fund it. Nineteen days into the new fiscal year, I was able to sign our budget into law.

My use of the line-item veto, something that President Reagan had repeatedly urged as appropriate at the federal level, drew a great deal of attention. However, it failed to move Congress any closer to action on this useful mechanism of dealing with recurrent deficits in the federal budget. And, when ultimately enacted during the Clinton years, it was struck down as unconstitutional.

One item of compromise with the Democrats was a $190 million bond issue to fund a Pennsylvania Economic Revitalization Fund (PERF), authorized by the voters in a 1984 referendum. PERF was used to fund some programs adopted from the PennPRIDE agenda for infrastructure, education, parks and youth employment. Few bonds were issued, however, as we were able to provide for most of these initiatives out of general revenues.

THE NET IMPACT of our economic development strategy was most gratifying. We had created a future-oriented economic base with a higher number of jobs. Our unemployment rate, which had steadily increased to a high of 14.9 percent during the 1982–83 recession, declined steadily thereafter as the national economy improved and our strategy unfolded. By the end of 1986, it was consistently running below the national average. At 5.1 percent, our unemployment rate ranked forty-third in the nation when I left office. Equally important, our small-business start-up rate went from below the national average to well above it, while the deathrate dropped below the national average. This was doubly important because the thirty largest Pennsylvania employers saw their payrolls shrink from 1.2 million to 600,000 during the same period. Overall, our resurgent economy produced over 50,000 new businesses and over 500,000 new jobs; both these figures increased at rates nearly twice the national average. As I left office in January 1987, more Pennsylvanians were on the job than ever before. Moreover, we had cut the state's indebtedness by some $300 million, and we left it with a $350 million surplus.

Syndicated columnist Neal Peirce later described our strategy as "'the state-of-the-art in economic development programs in older industrial states." The Economic Policy Institute of Washington, D.C., called Pennsylvania's effort "the best single state economic development program in the country," and many others were to echo these findings. There were few accomplishments of which I was more proud during my eight years as governor.

With my mom and dad at an early age in our Rosslyn Farms home.

A longtime Pittsburgh Pirates fan, I never missed a chance to "get in uniform."

Ginny Hooton
Thornburgh
at the beach with
our three sons
just prior to her
fatal 1960
accident.

Ginny Judson on
our October 12,
1963, wedding
day with John,
age six, and
David, age five,
looking on.

Billboard from 1966 campaign.

With Pennsylvania Governor Bill Scranton. We later served together as
elected delegates to Pennsylvania's 1967–68 constitutional convention.

Western Pennsylvania's racket-busting United States attorney.

Action caricature of me as a vigorous prosecutor on the job.

Farewell tribute from *Pittsburgh Post-Gazette* cartoonist Cy Hungerford in 1975 as I left to head the criminal division of the Justice Department in Washington, D.C.

(Courtesy of the *Pittsburgh Post-Gazette*)

At my second inauguration as governor of Pennsylvania in 1983, I am sworn in by Chief Justice Samuel J. Roberts of the Pennsylvania Supreme Court.

Delivering a budget address to the Pennsylvania General Assembly in 1984.

(Above) Visit to the control room of the damaged Three Mile Island nuclear reactor on April 1, 1979, with President Jimmy Carter and Harold Denton of the Nuclear Regulatory Commission.
(Courtesy of Karl H. Schumacher)

(Opposite, top) Press conference on the Three Mile Island nuclear accident with President Jimmy Carter, Harold Denton and Lieutenant Governor Bill Scranton.

(Opposite, bottom) Presenting my $1 billion clean-up plan for the Three Mile Island nuclear accident with cooling towers in the background.

Greeting Pope
John Paul in
Philadelphia at
the outset of his
1979 visit.

Jimmy Stewart, a Pennsylvania native, receiving our first Distinguished
Pennsylvania Artist award in 1980. Ginny and I found him to be thoroughly
enjoyable during his overnight stay at the Governor's Home.

Greeting Penn State's legendary football coach Joe Paterno after his team
had won the 1986 national championship.

At the Great
Wall during
our 1980 trade
development
mission to
China.

Kicking off our "You've got a friend in Pennsylvania" travel and tourism promotion campaign in 1980.

With my family, celebrating our 1982 reelection triumph in a very tough year.

My swearing-in as attorney general of the United States on August 12, 1988, with, left to right, President Reagan, Ginny, Supreme Court Justice Antonin Scalia and Vice President Bush.

(Above) President-elect George H. W. Bush announcing his appointment of me to serve as attorney general in his administration in November 1988.

(Opposite, top) The *New York Times Magazine,* May 21, 1989, cover article "that put a great big target sign on my chest"!
(Courtesy of the *New York Times*)

(Opposite, bottom) Testifying before Congress, in this case during the hearings for the Americans with Disabilities Act, was part of my responsibility as attorney general.

(Above) Meeting with reporters after my successful 1988 argument before the United States Supreme Court, which sought to authorize post-accident employee drug testing in the railway industry.

(Opposite, top) Meeting with Soviet Justice Minister Veniamin Yakovlev during our 1989 trip to Moscow to promote the Rule of Law.

(Opposite, bottom) Speaking to disability advocates after the signing of the American with Disabilities Act on July 26, 1990. A great day!
(Courtesy of Lisa Kelly, LA Photos)

(Opposite, top) Former U.S. attorneys general and Ethel Kennedy gather at the Department of Justice in 1989 to celebrate the 200th anniversary of the creation of the office.

(Opposite, bottom) At my desk in the Department of Justice.
(Courtesy of Michael Geissinger)

(Above) Ginny and I enjoy a meeting with the Reagans.

(Above) With President
Bush in the Oval Office
while serving as attorney
general.

(Left) With General Colin
Powell, chairman of the
Joint Chiefs of Staff.

Following our audience with Pope John Paul during which Ginny and I discussed plans for the 1992 Vatican ecumenical conference on disability.

(Opposite, top) Visiting a Somali refugee camp in Kenya while serving as undersecretary-general of the United Nations.

(Opposite, bottom) With fellow panelists who examined legal aspects of the O. J. Simpson murder trial on CNN's *Larry King Live*.

(Above) My Yale roommates and I visit with President George W. Bush (Yale 1968) in the Oval Office in the spring of 2001.

Vacationing in Maine.

Family reunion in Pennsylvania in the summer of 2001.

10

A Governor's Agenda

In addition to economic development, my administration focused on four other key areas: social services, education, crime and quality of life. On October 2, 1979, I presented my first substantive agenda to the General Assembly, outlining our goals in these areas. This agenda, supplemented and amended from time to time, was our road map throughout my time in Harrisburg. Stating it at the outset also provided benchmarks against which our accomplishments could be measured—a course that was not without risk.

One of the first problems we chose to address was welfare reform, which combined fiscal and humanitarian concerns. The federal Aid to Families with Dependent Children (AFDC) program, which was actually funded 45 percent by the state, was the primary system of welfare cash assistance. The General Assistance (GA) program, funded 100 percent by the state, provided cash assistance to those not covered by AFDC (about 20 percent of those receiving public assistance). From 1970 to 1979, the number of persons receiving GA benefits had increased from 49,000 to 154,000, and the annual costs had risen from $88 million to $274 million. With only about 5 percent of the nation's population, Pennsylvania had about 20 percent of its GA population. Strong suspicions existed that people were actually moving into the state to take advantage of our generous GA eligibility standards. At the same time, GA benefits had not been increased since 1975, during a period of ravaging inflation.

Over 75 percent of those receiving GA benefits were single or childless persons between the ages of eighteen and fifty-five. Almost 57 percent of them were employable. While "workfare," public employment of those welfare clients who were able to work, was just coming into vogue, it was relatively untested, and I was suspicious that it might spawn costly new bureaucracies. Welfare Secretary Helen O'Bannon suggested a different solution: removing from the GA rolls those recipients who were able-bodied and employable. The savings could fund not only increased benefits for those who remained eligible for assistance—the "truly needy"—but job training and job placement. I set forth this new concept in my October speech to the legislature: "[W]e are not humanitarians when we allow able-bodied men and women to cash welfare checks, while the more helpless among us live in fear of starvation and winter cold. . . . I believe the time has come when we must take the burden of job-hunting out of the hands of state bureaucrats, and place it on the shoulders of the able-bodied unemployed themselves. . . . With appropriate exceptions, I believe the time has come when we must take able-bodied men and women off our welfare rolls." In our 1980–81 budget presentation, we estimated that this proposal would save $34 million in its first year. By diverting $26.9 million into increasing GA benefits from $381 to $429 a month for the very old, the very young and those with disabilities who were unable to work, we could enable these recipients to attain a minimally acceptable standard of living. The remaining savings would be used to provide job training and job placement for those removed from the rolls.

This proposal created a firestorm of controversy. Most Democrats, the liberal press, civil rights and civil liberties groups and leaders in the African American communities mounted an immediate and strident attack upon what soon came to be known as "Thornfare." On the other hand, there was also positive editorial comment from around the state.

Our proposal was not enacted into law until the Republicans gained control of both houses of the General Assembly in the 1980 elections. Even then, it was much watered down. The bill that reached my desk for signature on April 8, 1982, allowed able-bodied recipients three months of GA eligibility per year, provided they made themselves available for public-service employment through state and local agencies—a kind of modified workfare requirement. Tax breaks were also provided to encourage the private sector to hire able-bodied GA eligibles. We considered this outcome an acceptable compromise.

As the economic downturn continued, so did the criticism. The *Philadelphia Inquirer* adopted a very hard line against the reforms, even blaming them for the city's homeless problems, although most homeless persons would not have been eligible for GA even under the former law. Following one of my meetings with community activists in North Philadelphia, a group of protesters pelted me with eggs. But the effort was worth it. A major reallocation of state resources had been accomplished, providing a more rational basis for dealing with those in need at a time of scarcity in public funds.

Aided by improvements in the economy, the program was moderately successful. According to the magazine *Public Welfare*, Pennsylvania shared with Massachusetts the best track record in reducing welfare caseloads and moving welfare recipients into jobs. Over 200,000 welfare recipients secured employment through the implementation of "Thornfare" from 1982 to 1986. Moreover, 100,000 GA recipients had been placed in "workfare"—our Community Work Employment Program (CWEP)—even though our two largest cities, Philadelphia and Pittsburgh, under heavy public-employee union pressure, had steadfastly refused to participate in it. Their nonparticipation struck me as particularly egregious in view of the enormous needs of these cities for the very type of cleanup and maintenance jobs that CWEP workers typically performed. Over my eight years in office, our cost savings on welfare enabled us to increase GA benefits four times by a total of 25 percent for those entitled to continue receiving them.

In 1985 our Department of Insurance authorized an innovative program by Blue Cross of Western Pennsylvania and Pennsylvania Blue Shield to provide health care coverage for children of families in need. "The Blues" paid the administrative costs of the Caring Program for Children and matched the donations of sponsoring groups such as churches and civic organizations. By 2002 the program, the first of its kind in the nation and a forerunner of the national CHIPs program, had served some 80,000 western Pennsylvania children and been replicated in twenty-five other states. Blue Cross of Western Pennsylvania's special programs of health insurance for the unemployed, pioneered two years earlier, had already served some 30,000 families.

At the low point of the 1981–83 recession, we adopted innovative programs to help unemployed persons meet their mortgage payments. Our Health Care Cost Containment Program also established an important cost-comparison mechanism to aid all citizens in making decisions about health services. Programs for the homeless increased the stock of both interim and permanent housing available for those seeking shelter.

Considerable progress was also made in child support collections. By seeking to make the absent parent rather than the taxpayer responsible for the support of dependent children, we struck yet another blow for a more sensible welfare system. Using techniques such as intercepts of federal income tax refunds and unemployment compensation checks, our Department of Public Welfare secured delinquent payments in a highly cost-effective manner. In 1982 and 1983, Pennsylvania led the nation in child support collections.

Secretary O'Bannon pursued our reform efforts with great vigor and ran a tight ship at her department. She was a particular favorite of Ginny's and mine and I was disappointed that she was unable to relate better to members of my staff, with whom she seemed to have one run-in after another. I finally decided to make a change at Welfare in my second term. Helen was succeeded by Walter Cohen, whose performance was equally first-class.

Although editorial and interest-group mutterings about our welfare reform measures continued into the 1990s, only halfhearted efforts were undertaken to repeal or modify "Thornfare" and restore the status quo ante. Indeed, our "radical" reforms looked pretty tame compared to bipartisan welfare reform legislation enacted by the Republican-controlled Congress and signed into law by President Clinton in 1996.

ANOTHER AREA OF great personal interest to Ginny and me was the providing of additional assistance to citizens with mental retardation and chronic mental illness. A principal concern here was the movement of as many persons as appropriate out of institutional settings into the community, where their everyday lives would be more consistent with those of other citizens.

Before I took office, a suit had been filed on behalf of persons with mental retardation to close down the notorious Pennhurst facility in Delaware County and disperse the residents into the community. The court held for the plaintiffs and elevated their right to live in a noninstitutional setting to a constitutional level. As I entered office, the commonwealth had appealed the constitutional basis of the holding, and the future of Pennhurst was uncertain. I was firmly committed to shutting down Pennhurst, a symbol of second-class citizenship for Pennsylvanians with mental retardation. However, I was also determined to prosecute the appeal to overturn the far-reaching constitutional basis for the court's holding. My double-tracked approach confused and angered many of the advocacy groups with which Ginny and I had worked over the years and imposed a heavy burden on our administration to show good faith in closing Pennhurst.

On both fronts we were successful. The United States Supreme Court ultimately ruled that there was no constitutional basis for the Pennhurst plaintiffs' claim, and we converted the facility into a much-needed residence for veterans. The dispersal of citizens with mental illness and mental retardation during our administration exceeded all expectations. More than 6,000 persons were moved out of institutions into community-based settings—a 31 percent reduction in the institutional population. In 1985, for the first time, state funding for community-based services exceeded that for institutional care. In my final budget, we achieved approval of a five-year, $243 million plan to further the trend toward community-based services for those with mental retardation.

One difficulty with the community placement of persons with mental illness was the paucity of support mechanisms in the community. Many of today's homeless are mentally ill persons deinstitutionalized into an inhospitable world with which they are unable to cope. Striking a balance between their civil rights and their well-being constitutes a continuing challenge to our society.

To further normalize the lives of Pennsylvanians with disabilities and integrate them into mainstream society, we also supported centers for independent living, attendant care programs and supported work initiatives. We doubled the appropriation for early-intervention programs for children with disabilities, and our Bureau of Vocational Rehabilitation led the nation in successful job placements for persons with severe disabilities.

BY THE 1980s, the abortion issue had moved center stage in most political arenas, and Pennsylvania was no exception. A vocal group of pro-life advocates within the General Assembly, with the assistance of interested national organizations, succeeded in passing what they described as the country's strictest limitations on women's access to abortion. Enormous speculation arose as to how I would react. Although not a strident pro-lifer, I continued to believe that abortions should be limited to cases of rape, incest or serious danger to the life or health of the mother.

After agonizing over the question, I decided to veto the bill as too burdensome to those wishing to exercise the legally available right to undergo an abortion. I pointed out eleven specific constitutional and practical infirmities in the bill and invited the General Assembly to address these in the hope that we could reach agreement on a suitable bill.

My action caused a firestorm. Women's groups and pro-choice adherents (including the bulk of those in my family and administration) were pleasantly surprised. The pro-life forces were incensed; I even received a personal phone call from John Cardinal Krol of Philadelphia expressing his dismay over my action and its timing (the day before Christmas). But roles were soon to be reversed. True to my word, we worked with the General Assembly to craft a revised bill, which I signed on June 12, 1982. This action elicited praise from my former detractors and scorn from my former supporters. By then I was firmly convinced that, politically, abortion was a no-win issue. This assessment freed me to follow the dictates of my conscience. Portions of the Pennsylvania statute were later declared unconstitutional by the United States Supreme Court in a 5–4 decision that did little to clarify this vexing legal, moral, religious, medical and political issue.

VETERANS ASSERTED a special claim on our interest. Not having been a member of the military myself, I was determined to exhibit particular sensitivity to those who had served our nation in time of need. We upgraded and expanded the Erie Soldiers and Sailors Home, extensively renovated the Hollidaysburg facility (a former state mental hospital) and, as noted, opened a third veterans center at the former Pennhurst site. All in all, we expended some $13 million to expand and modernize these facilities.

We also established unique Veterans' Outreach and Assistance Centers (VOACs) at five locations around the state. These storefront, one-stop facilities were run by veterans' organizations and provided veteran-to-veteran counseling on job opportunities, veterans' benefits, drug and alcohol problems and medical and family concerns. We also set up a registry for Vietnam veterans exposed to Agent Orange, providing a much-needed database to aid research into the effects of that substance.

For all these efforts, I was honored by the Pennsylvania Department of the American Legion as "a true friend of the veteran and a true patriot." In 1992, I received the highest award of the national American Legion at its convention in Chicago, a treasured recognition of our special exertions on behalf of this important constituency.

BY THE TIME I left office, Pennsylvania had the most generous program for senior citizens in the nation, providing over $1 billion annually in benefits—more than double the level of any other state. The driving force behind this accomplishment was the extraordinary growth in proceeds from the Pennsylvania lottery. Established by Governor Shapp in 1972, the lottery came to full maturity during the 1980s. In 1984 it became the first state lottery to exceed $1 billion in annual sales, thanks to careful management and shrewd promotion. Administrative costs were consistently held to less than 3 percent. The proceeds went to some 550 senior centers, to attendant care programs and to free public transportation.

But the two most significant forms of assistance to the elderly were the original Shapp administration property tax and rent rebate program and the PACE (Pharmaceutical Assistance Contract for Elderly) prescription drug program introduced in 1984. I was reluctant to support the PACE program in its original form because it threatened to bankrupt the lottery fund. A political flap ensued, but we finally achieved a copay provision that made recipients responsible for the first $5 (later $6) of the cost of each prescription. I approved the bill as amended. My concerns about the fiscal integrity of the program were portrayed as opposition to it by the Democrats, who were particularly incensed when I later appeared in television advertisements to promote it among senior citizens.

PENNSYLVANIA HAD the sixth-largest public school system in the country, enrolling about 1.8 million students, and an extensive network of public and private colleges and universities. Education took by far the largest share of the state's budget, with subsidies to elementary and secondary school systems commanding the lion's share. This had become a contentious area; arcane formulae were devised to assure "equitable" distribution of public support among 501 school districts. Strong and politically effective teachers' unions, school board associations and administrators all had lobbyists in Harrisburg.

We had maintained a positive relationship with most of these players during the 1978 campaign, securing the endorsement of both the PSEA and the Pennsylvania Federation of Teachers (PFT), the two principal teachers' unions. These good feelings continued into our administration, and the educational community initially appeared satisfied with our efforts to increase state funding for local school districts. As noted previously, all interested parties were committed to dividing the costs of elementary and secondary education equally between the state and the districts. We had taken a step toward that goal in the 1979–80 budget.

In the 1980–81 budget, however, our determination not to increase taxes obliged us to "pause," as I put it, in our march toward the 50 percent funding goal. Though state funding continued to increase, tension began to build between our administration and the PSEA over the rate of progress. Under more aggressive leadership in 1981, the PSEA drafted a detailed plan to press the administration and the General Assembly for vast increases in the state subsidy and for the $400 million in tax increases necessary to fund them. Their plan, liberally salted with provocative and inflammatory language, referred to the need to "knock legislators out of office when they oppose us. . . . The same goes for the Governor." I found the union's attitude and tactics objectionable in the extreme.

On March 16, 1981, we met with reporters to denounce the PSEA's "secret plan" to pressure public officials into increasing the state subsidy and raising taxes. The union's officials were at first embarrassed, then livid, at our public disclosure of their internal documents. I had acquired a formidable enemy. During my 1982 reelection campaign, the PSEA went all out to defeat me in spite of only lukewarm enthusiasm for my opponent. When I was reelected despite the union's efforts, its political clout was somewhat diminished, but our frosty relationship continued. In contrast, we continued to work with PFT leaders.

In 1983, the National Commission on Excellence in Education produced a report entitled "A Nation at Risk" that sent shock waves across the nation. It concluded that "a rising tide of mediocrity" was sweeping our schools and threatening our leadership in industry, commerce, science and technology. Nearly 40 percent of the nation's seventeen-year-olds could not draw inferences from written material. Only 20 percent could write an essay, and only a third could solve mathematical problems that required several steps. The commission concluded, "For the first time in the history of our country, the educational skills of one generation will not surpass, will not equal, will not even approach, those of their parents." We already knew that 2.6 million Pennsylvanians were so lacking in basic mathematics and reading skills that their ability to get or hold a job was severely impaired.

Bob Wilburn, who had taken over the post of education secretary when Bob Scanlon chose to return to the private sector after my reelection, pitched into a lively reform effort. In October 1983, only months following the commission's report, I unveiled our "Agenda for Excellence." It was designed to raise standards, strengthen curricula, increase student achievement and make teachers more effective. It called for the eventual commitment of an additional $100 million a year in state educational funding.

Acting upon the premise that students wanted to be engaged, not indulged, we set out to increase the number of credits needed for high school graduation from thirteen to twenty-one. We tripled the requirements in science and mathematics and added a requirement that each student complete two courses in the arts and humanities. And we required each school district to offer at least one course in computer science.

To help "at risk" students, our TELLS (Testing for Essential Learning and Literacy Skills) program tested students in the third, fifth and eighth grades for proficiency in reading and mathematics. More important, it provided state funding for remedial instruction to help students who needed it before poor study habits and low expectations stunted their ambition. From 1984 to 1987, more than 800,000 students were tested. Some 230,000 of them were discovered to be in educational trouble. This posed a staggering challenge to already overburdened school systems.

Unfortunately, the educational lobby's insistence on "equitable" funding for all districts subverted our plan to fund remedial programs by having "the dollars follow the child." Eventually, all remedial funding was subsumed within the subsidy formula. The educational lobby also objected to the TELLS program because it provided an outcomes-based method of actually measuring school performance; this was anathema to those committed to the status quo. The program was to be abandoned when our administration was succeeded by one more favorably inclined toward the teachers' unions.

Gifted students fared better. We created an Honors Incentive Program, a more demanding four-year curriculum preparing them for an honors test and resulting state scholarships. Moreover, we expanded our Governor's Schools, which provided free college-level instruction in the summers for especially talented tenth and eleventh grade students. Governor Shapp had established such a school for the arts; we added programs for science, agriculture and international affairs and proposed one for business. We also increased support for pregnant teenagers seeking to complete their high school education and provided assistance for students with drug and alcohol problems.

New approaches were also taken to teaching. Teachers were tested to ensure their competence in basic skills and in their major subjects. A one-year induction period was required before permanent certification was accorded. Alternate routes to teaching for noncertified persons with "life experience" qualifications, first provided for in 1972 but seldom used, were vigorously promoted. Continuing professional-development responsibilities were imposed on both teachers and administrators. We failed to muster enough support for a merit pay plan, but we did give cash grants of up to $5,000 to Pennsylvania's "Teacher of the Year" finalists, theretofore recognized only with a certificate of appreciation. These awards were discontinued after I left office, and the leveling instincts of the teachers' unions were so ingrained that talk of merit pay was simply out of the question.

It never made much sense to me, as noted by my colleague and friend, Tennessee governor (and later U.S. secretary of education) Lamar Alexander, that "the very best of our teachers could not earn a single extra dollar for superior performance in the classroom." Overall, teachers' pay rose steadily; from 1982 to 1987, average Pennsylvania teacher salaries increased from $19,482 to $27,422, well above the national average. But the truly outstanding men and women in that often underappreciated calling deserved more. Our inability to reward excellence in this area was a great source of frustration to me.

It is difficult to assess the long-term impact of educational reforms. Certain short-term indicators were positive for our programs; the dropout rate decreased by nearly 15 percent between 1982 and 1986, and college entrance scores slightly increased by 1987. But my sense was that the other social maladies that vaulted into prominence during the 1980s and 1990s— violent crime, drug abuse, sexual promiscuity and the despair caused by broken homes—were of such magnitude that they had a tendency to override whatever marginal improvements might have been made in the classroom.

On the higher-education front, I urged the consolidation of the fourteen state-owned teachers' colleges into a single university system, in an effort to simplify their administration and to foster centers of excellence rather than having each campus attempt to cover every specialty. Legislation creating the new system was signed into law in 1982. A decade later, the American Association of State Colleges and Universities characterized the system as providing both "enhanced academic quality and overall institutional effectiveness." Ginny and I were filled with pride when Governor Tom Ridge in 1997 appointed our son John to the board of governors of the State System of Higher Education.

Pennsylvania's 4,000 public libraries, particularly those in economically distressed communities, were another focus of our attention. In the first five years of my administration, state library aid increased by 75 percent. And in my 1984 and 1985 budget requests, I sought funding, for the first time in our state's history, for adult literacy programs. In 1986, the General Assembly finally voted the first $2 million for this important effort, and it has become an ongoing and increasing commitment.

Perhaps my most enjoyable moments in the educational field came when I went into the classroom myself. As often as possible, I took on the role of teacher in both elementary and secondary schools across the state. The curiosity of the students, manifested in the great variety of their questions, never failed to inspire me. Ginny always said she could tell when I had been in the classroom by the smile on my face at the end of the day.

DURING THE 1970s, public concern over violent crime increased considerably, and with reason. In the first six months of 1979, reported crimes in Pennsylvania rose a staggering 13.1 percent. Early in my administration, I declared, "The first civil right of every American citizen is the right to be free from fear in our homes, on our streets and in our communities." Accordingly, we beefed up the state police and established new units to fight drug trafficking and organized crime.

We also established a cabinet-level Department of Corrections and pushed for needed expansions to the correctional system. No correctional facilities had been built in Pennsylvania since 1960, and our jails and prisons were overcrowded. Appropriations for such facilities are never the public's favorite, especially when resources are scarce and demands for social programs are on the increase. However, when the legislature proposed longer minimum mandatory sentences for certain violent offenses, we saw our opportunity. As the price for our reluctant support (I was always wary of mandatory sentences), we asked for and got a 30 percent increase in prison capacity—3,000 new cells at a cost of $300 million—to make the tougher sentences credible.

Tough sentencing appeared to have a demonstrable effect on offenses involving firearms. I believed strongly that the criminal use of firearms would only be deterred by the certainty of punishment, in most cases a substantial prison term. We thus proposed, and the legislature adopted, a law calling for a minimum mandatory five-year sentence for any violent crime involving the use of a firearm. We also arranged for private funding of billboards and television ads proclaiming, "Commit a crime with a gun in Pennsylvania . . . and you've shot five years of your life!" Robberies involving firearms had reached a ten-year high in 1981, the last full year before the new law took effect, and both assaults and murders involving firearms had skyrocketed in the previous four years. All of these numbers dropped dramatically after the law went into effect. Unfortunately, funding for the advertising campaign was discontinued within two years, and firearms offenses began to inch up again.

On October 29, 1981, a prison hostage-taking incident chilled us all. Joseph "Jo Jo" Bowen, a thrice-convicted murderer, and other armed inmates at the state's maximum-security Graterford Prison took thirty-six hostages, including three guards and three civilian employees, following a failed escape attempt. This was an occasion to apply the lessons learned from Three Mile Island. Patience was the order of the day, and we established close communications with Graterford. The major breakthrough was the assistance of *Philadelphia Daily News* columnist Chuck Stone, a frequent spokesman for the African American community, who had arranged for a number of suspects to turn themselves in to police in the past. At our request, Chuck became the intermediary between the state and Bowen and finally secured his surrender and the safety of the hostages. We were most gratified by an *Inquirer* editorial entitled "Calm Leadership Averted a Tragedy at Graterford," which noted, "Governor Thornburgh deserves much credit. . . . [He] put himself in charge instead of passing the buck to others, as governors in other states have done in emergency situations with tragic consequences." In April 1983, a lesser hostage-taking incident at the State Correctional Institution at Pittsburgh was also resolved without loss of life.

We made little progress on the increasingly severe problem of juvenile crime. According to a study by noted criminologist Dr. Marvin Wolfgang of the University of Pennsylvania, only 20 percent of apprehended juvenile offenders committed some 68 percent of serious juvenile crimes. In 1985, I proposed categorizing as a "dangerous juvenile offender" any juvenile over fourteen who had been a defendant at least once after turning twelve and was charged a second time with a serious crime. We proposed shifting to these juveniles the burden of proof on whether they should not be tried as adults. We also argued for permitting victims and the public to attend their hearings and for establishing a statewide registry of photographs, fingerprints and criminal histories of chronic offenders, to be disseminated where appropriate. The legislature took only partial action on these proposals. I was to renew many of them later as attorney general of the United States.

I cut back substantially on the use of pardons and commutations for convicted criminals, restricting both to cases of clear injustice rather than handing them out as good-conduct medals. Governor Shapp had commuted 255 life sentences and freed the offenders. I reduced that number to a mere seven, most of whom were incurably ill or otherwise incapacitated.

I signed only four death warrants under Pennsylvania's restored death penalty statute, all of them after intense internal review. Those condemned in August 1985 were John Lesko and Michael Travaglia, convicted five years earlier of four murders, including that of a police officer, and Keith Zettlemoyer, convicted of the 1980 murder of a witness scheduled to testify against him in a robbery trial. A year later I signed a death warrant for Leslie Beasley, convicted in 1981 for killing a Philadelphia police officer. In signing the warrants, I observed, "As one who values the sanctity of life, I do not approach this matter lightly, but I also recognize that it is the respect for innocent life which underlies our imposition of the maximum deterrent and penalty for those who would murder in cold blood." None of the warrants, the first signed in Pennsylvania in twenty-three years, were carried out prior to my leaving office, as successive appeals generated a new round of delays.

Our sentencing proposals did not fare well. I recommended establishing maximum and minimum sentences to increase uniformity in sentencing, and abolishing parole for newly convicted felons. The General Assembly, still wed to the status quo, did not act on either of these proposals. On the other hand, under a "guilty but mentally ill" law enacted with our support, an insanity finding would no longer occasion a verdict of innocence and release of the offender into the community. Impaired individuals would now be held in mental hospitals after conviction. (We also moved aggressively to improve the discredited Farview State Hospital for the Criminally Insane.)

By the time I left office, the number of serious crimes had decreased by some 19 percent since its high-water mark in 1981. In fact, our rate of serious crime was the fifth lowest in the nation and the lowest of any large state. We had also taken other important steps in the criminal justice area. One of these was enacting a law pushed by Mothers Against Drunk Driving (MADD), an impressive grassroots organization, to tighten procedures and increase penalties for driving under the influence. Another was establishing a Rape and Domestic Violence Fund, financed by additional court costs in criminal cases. One and a half million dollars a year went to fund locally operated rape crisis centers and domestic violence programs after this legislation was passed. Finally, we secured the passage of one of the nation's first Victim's Bills of Rights.

State and federal efforts against white-collar crime and public corruption also continued. There were two major white-collar prosecutions during my eight years in Harrisburg. The first derived from an attempt to "fix" the increasingly lucrative state lottery. Every evening, on television, the daily lottery winners were determined by drawing three numbered Ping-Pong balls from a transparent container. The balls were kept aloft by air currents circulated inside; each time the top was opened, one would be blown into position and extracted. The drawings were held at the studios of WTAE-TV in Pittsburgh. Employed there was a popular announcer named Nick Perry. One evening Perry and his accomplices, including lottery official Edward Plevel, arranged to have all the balls save those bearing the number 6 injected with a white paste to weigh them down. They heavily bet the guaranteed winning combination of 666 and reaped a handsome return.

Word on the street, however, quickly spread that the fix was in. Revenue Secretary Howard Cohen's investigation failed to uncover any wrongdoing, but reporters kept up a drumbeat of speculation. Suspicious myself, I asked state prosecutors to coordinate a more in-depth look at the case. Perry, Plevel and four others were later convicted for their role in the fix and Cohen resigned, to be succeeded briefly by Bob Bloom, and then by Jim Scheiner who turned in an outstanding performance in this vital position.

The second attempted scam had unexpectedly far-reaching and tragic consequences. Early in 1983, an opportunity arose to recover from the federal government overpayments made by state and local governments under the Federal Insurance Contributions Act (FICA). West Coast businessman John Torquato Jr. suggested that his corporation, Computer Technology Associates (CTA), perform the project. Torquato was the son of a former Democratic boss of Cambria County who had been convicted of corruption in the 1970s; he was also related to the jury-tampering couple I had encountered in my early days as U.S. attorney. The younger Torquato beat a path to various officials to seek the recovery contract. When I heard of this, I immediately ordered discussions to be terminated. Torquato encountered a more favorable reception from State Treasurer Budd Dwyer. A former teacher and state legislator from Meadville in Crawford County,

Dwyer had been elected treasurer in 1980 in the Republican sweep and was seeking reelection in 1984. He was a large, heavy-set, garrulous individual with close political ties to the PSEA. He was also an adroit politician who had cultivated a rather sizable following within the Republican Party.

I had already had a couple of run-ins with Dwyer over his efforts to enhance his own image by embarrassing me and my family. The first grew out of a trip I took to Europe in January 1984 to promote foreign investment in the state. Ginny accompanied me, and Dwyer suggested to the *Philadelphia Inquirer* that she had sought to travel at state expense, even though our press release prior to the trip had expressly stated that she would pay her own expenses. Although Ginny had repeatedly requested that my staff advise her of the amount of reimbursement required so that she could write a check, the story was too juicy for the scandal-starved press to pass up. Ginny was mortified, and I was furious.

Dwyer soon added an allegation that we had abused the security detail provided by the state police. They had transported our son Bill to and from Deerfield Academy in Massachusetts since his enrollment there in the fall of 1981, and once they had driven David to Cambridge, where he was attending Harvard's John F. Kennedy School of Government. Again the explanation was a simple one, but unheeded by the press. The security detail provided its services to all members of our household as the officers deemed necessary for our protection. Ginny and I neither asked for nor (as we were to regret) questioned these services, which were no different from those provided to our predecessors.

The third occasion for Dwyer's attention to our family involved our giving Bill a telephone credit card to facilitate his keeping in touch. A female friend had secured the number and, after she and Bill had stopped dating, used it to run up a sizable unauthorized bill. Dwyer leaked this matter to the *Inquirer* as well, but we were tipped off by a friend and commenced our own investigation before the story was published. Thanks in particular to Dave Runkel, who had by that time succeeded Paul Critchlow as press secretary, we were able to issue our own report on the matter and to recover some $3,200 in unauthorized state billings from the family of the young woman.

John Torquato cut a deal involving Dwyer, state GOP chairman Bob Asher and Dauphin County GOP chairman Bill Smith (Torquato's attorney). CTA would receive a $4.8 million contract from the treasurer's office to handle the FICA business; in exchange, payments of $100,000 each would be made to Dwyer, his reelection campaign and, through Asher, the

Republican State Committee. The conspiracy required, among other things, the passage of legislation authorizing the state treasurer to handle the FICA recoveries. I signed the bill under the impression that this was to be an in-house operation. When we learned of the contract award to CTA in May 1984, we raised strenuous objections.

State Auditor General Al Benedict, an acquaintance of Torquato who was running against Dwyer in November 1984, gave all this information to the FBI. The FBI seized CTA's records from Torquato's California office, and the U.S. Attorney's Office announced indictments against Torquato and David Herbert, a former employee of the Department of Labor and Industry who had been fired for his role in the contract award. Dwyer was reelected but was soon indicted, along with Asher and Smith. In 1986 all were convicted. Ironically, Benedict was later convicted of job selling.

The "business as usual" approach taken by these officials indicated that we still had a long way to go in establishing higher standards for the conduct of state business. Asher's involvement was particularly troublesome to me. He was one of the state's most effective political operatives, had chaired my 1982 reelection campaign and had succeeded to the party chairmanship with my strong support. I felt thoroughly betrayed by his involvement in this seamy affair. At the same time, the fact that state officials had not escaped prosecution and conviction sent a strong signal that federal authorities (with our cooperation) were still on the lookout for criminal conduct.

Dwyer's conviction produced one of the most grisly and bizarre events of Pennsylvania's always unpredictable political history. On the date upon which he was to be sentenced in January 1987, three days after I had left the governor's office, Dwyer called a press conference. After reading a rambling statement that partially sought to hold me responsible for his conviction and disgrace, he drew a large revolver from his briefcase, placed it in his mouth and fired, instantly killing himself before horrified reporters and a bank of television cameras.

In other efforts against public corruption, we wasted little time in impaneling Pennsylvania's first statewide investigative grand jury pursuant to legislation enacted during the 1978 campaign. We also appointed an inspector general to deal with any remaining vestiges of PennDOT corruption and mismanagement. Finally, we adopted new policies of suspending public employees charged with wrongdoing and of firing those convicted. Later, a comprehensive code of conduct for state employees incorporated these sanctions as well as requirements for full financial disclosure and prohibitions on outside income.

On the civil justice front, the legislature enacted, with our support, a new "no fault" law that simplified divorce proceedings and reduced the number of contrived trials. We were unable, however, to secure legislative support for merit selection of judges. We did establish statewide and county judicial nominating commissions to fill vacancies, which produced some excellent recommendations and helped introduce much-needed diversity into our judiciary. I was to appoint Pennsylvania's first Hispanic judge; the first woman and only the second African American to sit on the Superior Court; the first black judge in Dauphin County; and the first black woman to sit on the Allegheny County bench. Almost all of our merit appointees survived the partisan elections that followed their selection.

During the early 1990s, Pennsylvania Supreme Court Justice Rolf Larsen, against whose election I had campaigned in 1978, was convicted of charges relating to the misuse of prescription drugs and was impeached after a messy investigation. Even this tawdry affair did not provide the long-awaited catalyst for meaningful judicial reform. Pennsylvania remains one of the handful of states to elect all of its judges on a partisan political basis.

CONSERVATION AND environmental concerns had a prominent place on our agenda. From the days of Governor Gifford Pinchot onward, our state had prided itself on its commitment to the environment, which was carefully monitored by numerous sportsmen's groups and environmental advocacy organizations.

The Department of Environmental Resources (DER) oversaw 3.5 million acres of state parks, forests and gamelands; 45,000 miles of rivers and streams; and 4,000 lakes. All of these contributed to Pennsylvania's national reputation for excellent hunting, fishing and camping opportunities. We increased the number of DER personnel and secured record funding for preservation of our 113 state parks, covering 270,000 acres. The Youth Conservation Corps, created by the Democrat-controlled House in 1983, provided jobs for disadvantaged 18-to-21-year-olds on public lands and facilities under DER supervision, largely maintaining and restoring park facilities. And PennDOT's ambitious Keep Pennsylvania Beautiful program enlisted citizens across the state in an annual spring pickup effort along our highways. The number of participants grew from 8,000 in 1979 to 350,000 in 1986, and that year 60,000 tons of litter or trash were retrieved.

On waste disposal, the aftermath of TMI was initially our main concern. Gradually, however, we came to focus on the wider needs of the commonwealth. The NIMBY (Not In My Back Yard) syndrome made it extremely difficult to site disposal facilities, particularly for toxic or hazardous wastes. In the fall of 1985, we proposed a ten-year, $250 million resource recovery and recycling program to encourage counties to cut reliance on landfills by more than half. The Democrats in the House, however, refused to move the proposal. We did carry out one of the most aggressive Superfund programs in the nation and created our own Toxic Waste Investigation and Prosecution Unit to proceed criminally against those charged with illegally dumping these dangerous wastes. And in 1986 we proposed and won passage of a twenty-year, $100 million program to reclaim nearly 15,000 acres of abandoned strip mines, to be financed in part from increased mining fees.

One of our most stubborn environmental challenges was a long-smoldering underground mine fire in Centralia in north central Pennsylvania. For two decades, outcroppings of smoke and occasional flames had bothered this community, but concern increased during the 1980s. When a young boy was reported to have come close to falling into one of Centralia's fiery holes, media attention became focused upon the town. We were puzzled as to what to do. The most logical solution was to move the townspeople elsewhere, for there seemed to be little practical prospect of extinguishing the fire. However, the inhabitants had no desire to leave their homes, and officials were concerned about who would pay for such a move. Ultimately, after examining an astronomically expensive and far from guaranteed plan to try to extinguish the flames by building huge ditches, we agreed with the U.S. Department of the Interior to fund a relocation program. Centralia became a ghost town.

An unexpected threat arose in the Reading area, where homes were found to have been invaded by radon gas. We funded the installation of monitoring equipment, but little else could be done to deal with health concerns and declining property values in the area. Once again, media interest was high, and the state was criticized for its inability to solve the problem once and for all.

On the positive side, we played a leading role in the still-ongoing effort to clean up the Chesapeake Bay. Pennsylvania's commitment of $10 million to the project was premised on the fact that a considerable amount of runoff affecting the bay came from fertilizers used on Pennsylvania farms. Thereafter, we promoted the use of low-till farming and fewer fertilizers as our major contribution to saving the bay.

In this age, environmental awareness and citizen activism collide with the imperative of economic growth and the waste and pollution that inevitably result. The most that can be attempted is to strike a good-faith balance between these interests on a case-by-case basis. Criticism of our administration from both industry and environmental activists indicated that we did about as well as we could in this respect. However, I was deeply gratified to receive, at the end of my tenure, the Gold Medal of the Pennsylvania Fish and Game Protection Association. Since I was only the third governor, along with Gifford Pinchot and James Duff, to be so honored, I felt we had conducted our administration in the proper Pennsylvania environmental tradition.

I considered the arts to be the soul of our state, and we set out to support and recognize Pennsylvania artists from the first. We substantially increased state appropriations in support of the arts and, through the Pennsylvania Council on the Arts, vastly raised the visibility of our artistic treasures. The first annual Distinguished Pennsylvania Artists Award was presented in 1980 to actor Jimmy Stewart, with whom we had a delightful visit. Subsequent recipients were author James Michener, vocalist Marian Anderson, author John Updike, entertainer Bill Cosby, pianist Byron Janis and painter Andrew Wyeth, Pennsylvanians all and a pleasure to honor in the capital.

All was not always sweetness and light with the artistic community, however. One run-in left some hurtful scars. In June 1980, as part of our continuing series of exhibits at the Governor's Home, we invited a group of photographers to display their works. For some reason, the works were not adequately previewed, and after they were displayed, we discovered that a few included explicit frontal nudity. With groups of schoolchildren and families constantly touring the home, we felt these to be inappropriate and removed them from the exhibit. This decision was met by cries of censorship and actions by other artists to remove their works as well. Naturally, the news media had a field day with the controversy, and it occasioned a flood of mail, both pro and con.

We also worked to celebrate our state's ethnic diversity, creating a Heritage Affairs Advisory Commission made up of one representative from each of our identifiable ethnic or nationality groups. Its twenty-eight members kept me advised of their constituents' concerns and enabled us to arrange for appropriate proclamations and ceremonies to honor their national observances and significant historical figures.

Of our many distinguished visitors from abroad, none was more lovingly received by Pennsylvanians than Pope John Paul II, who came to Philadelphia in 1979. Mayor Frank Rizzo and I extended our official greetings upon his arrival, and the pope responded with a hearty "God bless Pennsylvania!" As the Holy Father and John Cardinal Krol, with Rizzo and me in their wake, proceeded down the red carpet at the airport, a crowd of well-wishers let out an earsplitting cheer. Rizzo turned to me and observed with obvious envy, "He don't have to run for election every four years!" You could always count on "the Riz" to put things in perspective.

A particularly rewarding initiative for me was the establishment of the Keystone State Games in 1982. The games were held first at Penn State and thereafter at various venues across the state. Each year they began with the carrying of a symbolic torch by relay from the Capitol steps. Amateur athletes competed in thirty different team and individual events. The games were generously supported by the business and financial community and added one more bit of luster to the state's proud athletic tradition. By 1996, over 175,000 athletes had participated in regional and statewide competition, and the program had been expanded to include a winter component and special events for seniors. Many competitors had gone on to the Olympics, some to win a variety of medals. On the event's fifteenth anniversary, I was honored as the "Father of the Games."

Elsewhere on the sporting front, I particularly remember attending a rare encounter between the Steelers and their cross-state rivals, the Philadelphia Eagles. As I made my way to my seat, a gaggle of reporters asked who I was going to root for, and I dutifully replied, "I can't take sides when two of our great teams meet one another." At that moment, around the corner came legendary Steelers owner (and lifelong Republican) Art Rooney, who offered effusive greetings and added, "I sure hope you'll be rooting hard for us today." I heartily responded, "You bet I will, Mr. Rooney!" The reporters rolled their eyes and put me down as just another political windbag, I am sure.

The 1979 World Series matched my beloved Pirates with the Baltimore Orioles. The series opened in Baltimore, and when Maryland governor Harry Hughes threw out the first ball, he was greeted with the traditional boos and catcalls indicating fan displeasure with politicians interrupting their game. Baseball Commissioner Bowie Kuhn was upset at the occurrence and summarily banned politicians from throwing out the first ball in the future. Thus, when the series moved to Pittsburgh, I was denied an opportunity I had awaited for a lifetime. I was heartbroken, but Pirates owner Tom Johnson, a founding partner of my old law firm, devised a solution. Mrs. Danny Murtaugh, widow of the popular former Pirates manager, threw out the first ball, but Ginny and I were seated next to her. The public address system and the giant letters of the electronic scoreboard identified us as accompanying Mrs. Murtaugh and added that we were celebrating our sixteenth wedding anniversary that night. Three Rivers Stadium rocked with cheers in tribute to the widow of our beloved manager, and Ginny and I were pleased to sail in her wake. Years later, Ken Burns's memorable public-television series *Baseball* included footage of that event, with Ginny and me clearly visible. Thus I took my small place in baseball history.

One effort that failed was the attempt to privatize the state's vast liquor monopoly. Established following the repeal of Prohibition, the much-derided state store system had become a monument to inefficiency, inhospitality and occasional corruption. Pennsylvania was one of only three states in which state government completely controlled the retail sale of both liquor and wine. By the 1980s, the system had annual sales of nearly $750 million. It operated through 725 retail outlets and was overseen by the highly politicized Liquor Control Board (LCB), which was suspected of bribery, extortion and shakedowns. I had stated its transformation to a private, consumer-oriented system as a goal in the 1978 campaign, but our efforts were largely rhetorical until, early in my second term, I then presented a detailed plan to accomplish that goal. Poor service was driving many customers out of state for their purchases, causing a loss of revenue, while expenses continued to rise. I hoped that declining profits, if nothing else, would sound the death knell for this dinosaur.

We proposed to auction off the retail outlets to the highest qualified bidders, permitting each successful bidder to open one additional outlet during the transition period. Wine-only licenses would be issued to separate stores or grocery outlets, and wholesale licenses for both liquor and wine would be sold to private purchasers. All proceeds would be earmarked for additional aid to education. A loan fund would be established to help present LCB employees purchase retail outlets. No individual or corporation could purchase more than ten outlets during the initial five-year period.

Media response was favorable (no doubt influenced by the prospect of increased advertising revenue from private retail outlets). But our legislation was stymied by a strong, if somewhat odd, coalition of organized labor, especially the powerful state store employees' union; Bible Belt "drys," opposed to liquor in general and fearful of more convenience to consumers; and organizations like MADD.

In the waning days of our administration, we achieved a minor, if temporary, victory. Because of some convoluted maneuverings, the legislature did not renew the charter of the LCB in December 1986, my last month in office. We immediately filled the void by enacting our entire reform package by administrative order, to take effect on June 1 of the following year. With undisguised glee, I affixed huge symbolic "For Sale" signs to retail outlets. Predictably, our opponents sought redress in the courts. While the matter was under consideration, Governor Bob Casey wasted little time vacating my order. I took some small consolation from the observation in the *Harrisburg Patriot* that "the attempt did bring about noticeable improvement in the State Stores."

DURING MY EIGHT years as governor, I had numerous opportunities to travel, both at home and abroad. Some trips were goodwill visits sponsored by the National Governors Association (NGA) and the like. Others were efforts to open export markets or attract new investment in Pennsylvania. In addition to these international marketing efforts, we worked to make our business community more aware of the need to compete overseas. As a result, we received a Presidential "E" (for excellence in exporting) award from Commerce Secretary Malcolm Baldrige in May 1982. (I was later to serve on the Advisory Committee of the Export-Import Bank, urging more assistance to small businesses.)

The first of our trips abroad was to the Soviet Union with an NGA delegation in November 1979. Our hosts fed us a depressing diet of propaganda about the glories of their system and their desire for peace. And we took note of the expressionless faces of Soviet citizens on Moscow's drab streets. On the other side of the coin, we had a most moving encounter with a group of "refuseniks," Russian Jews systematically denied their right of exit. Ginny and I were to become heavily involved with the refusenik cause. We also saw many impressive museums and war memorials and were struck by a strange paradox: a proletarian society seemingly unable to put two bricks together evenly in the construction of an apartment building was remarkably skilled at the delicate art of restoring and preserving historical sites.

In March 1980, we went with representatives of a number of Pennsylvania firms to the People's Republic of China (PRC) in an effort to help open up new markets. Ours was the first full-scale state delegation to visit China since the preceding year's normalization of its relationship with the United States.

Our first days in Beijing were devoted to sightseeing and ceremonial visits, including one with Vice Premier Li Xiannian, the number three man in the PRC government. Our business delegation began complaining that the trip was too "political." The next day, however, as we made the rounds of the ministries in the areas in which they expected to do business, we were told at nearly every meeting that I had been seen with Vice Premier Li on television the night before. No better entree could have been arranged. At meetings with representatives of the chemical, metallurgy, foreign trade, electric power and railways ministries and of eight trading corporations, our business colleagues had ample opportunity to discuss their interests in doing business in China. Five years later, many had made real progress in entering this often intractable market.

On this trip we also stopped in Tokyo for a dizzying round of meetings with representatives of the Foreign Ministry, the Finance Ministry, MITI, the Japan External Trade Organization (JETRO) and numerous corporate giants. Pennsylvania had established an office in Tokyo during the Shapp administration, but it appeared to have produced few results. Though we hoped our visit would raise its profile, we could see that any progress in this direction would be over the long run.

We returned to China in December 1983 under the auspices of the NGA. Once again we stopped in Japan on the way, this time to finalize the commitment of $18 million from the Federation of Japanese Electric Companies to help fund the TMI cleanup. This contribution gave us important leverage in bringing potential American contributors into line. In Beijing, by far our most significant meeting was one with Premier Zhao Ziyang, who was more than willing to consider our inquiries concerning increased trade and investment as well as the dilemma of Taiwan. Little did we suspect that a scant six years later, Zhao's relatively moderate counsel in response to unrest would make him one of the most prominent political casualties of the Tiananmen Square student demonstrations.

We established an economic development office in London, subsequently moving it to Brussels for cost reasons. Early in 1984 we returned to Europe to wrap up negotiations respecting some English and German investments in Pennsylvania. By this time, the press and the Democrats were becoming increasingly skeptical about my foreign travel, and the tangible results of this mission were a much-needed antidote.

We flew first to Frankfurt to meet with representatives of Neoplan. This bus manufacturer had won a competition to supply 1,000 vehicles to sixteen Pennsylvania transit authorities, at a total cost of $157.8 million, and had pledged to open its next plant in Pennsylvania. At the conclusion of our visit, we were able to announce that the company would locate this facility in Honeybrook, Chester County, creating an estimated 400 jobs in the area. Although commenced with much fanfare, the project was later to founder because of labor problems.

We thereafter met with travel and tourism interests in Stuttgart to promote Pennsylvania as a destination for German tourists, distributing the first 500 copies of a newly printed German-language brochure extolling the virtues of our state. In Blomberg we met with representatives of Phoenix Elektrizitaetsgesellschaft, a manufacturer of electronic components, which had expressed an interest in locating expanded facilities in our state. At the end of our visit, we announced that Phoenix would soon break ground in the Harrisburg area for a facility to house its corporate headquarters and an expanded U.S. manufacturing plant. These operations, eventually employing 125 people, were just the type of advanced-technology business we were seeking to help grow in our new future-oriented economy.

In England we touched base with two further prospects for Pennsylvania investment: PKS-DIGIPLAN, an electronics firm in Poole, and Ace Belmont International Caravans, a manufacturer of mini-mobile homes for vacation use, in North Humberside. In due course, we secured a commitment from PKS-DIGIPLAN to locate its American sales and marketing headquarters in Lancaster, with plans to employ up to 200 people within three years.

Notwithstanding pretrip misgivings about our "junkets," the results of our efforts were well received at home. Although Democratic senators Ed Zemprelli and Craig Lewis had stated, "We doubt seriously . . . that any of this will be translated into jobs for unemployed Pennsylvanians," the contrary was clearly the case. We were quick to acknowledge that all these negotiations had been under way for some time, but pointed out that my personal involvement helped bring them to a favorable conclusion.

By far the most exciting journey that Ginny and I took during my service as governor was one to Africa in the summer of 1986. The AmPart (American Participant) program, run by the United States Information Agency (USIA) to share the American experience with those in other countries, had asked me to give a series of lectures on management in government and Ginny to share her experiences in the disability field.

Our major stops were in Kinshasa, Brazzaville, Nairobi and Harare. U.S. Ambassador Alan Lukens noted later that our meetings with Denis Sassou-Nguesso, then president of the People's Republic of the Congo, and other dignitaries "contributed significantly to the present thaw in bilateral relations." Our African colleagues seemed to find the scale of my experience at the state level—dealing in millions rather than billions—particularly relevant to their own situations.

For her part, Ginny visited many health care and rehabilitation facilities, learning much about the conditions of the disabled in Third World nations. The chief surgeon of Kinshasa's major clinic told her, "[W]e shall remember your warmth, your love and humanitarian concern." Indeed, whenever she traveled with me, she took every opportunity to try to help persons with disabilities. In Guangzhou, China, for example, she was most disturbed by conditions at an institution for people with severe physical and mental disabilities. The presence of flies on open sores of the residents was a particular hazard to their health and comfort. Seeking the aid of resident representatives of Beatrice Foods, which was setting up a joint venture to manufacture snack food and soft drinks for Hong Kong and Chinese markets, Ginny left $500 with them to arrange for some screening to be provided to the facility. She later learned that the project had been carried out—a small but symbolic act.

USIA officials were generous in their assessment of our African trip. An article in *USIA World* referred to me as "a public diplomat of the highest order"; it also commended Ginny's "sincere interest and her deep feelings toward the people she met everywhere" and concluded that "her favorable impact will not soon be forgotten."

In Harare, I had addressed the Institute of Directors, a nearly all-white group of local CEOs, and learned much about the discouraging attitudes of the white community toward change in Zimbabwe and South Africa. Moreover, all the African leaders with whom I had met had expressed concerns over apartheid. Accordingly, one practical result of our trip was the issuance of much stricter guidelines for Pennsylvania investments in companies doing business in South Africa. During the 1990s, of course, the world was to witness the extraordinary transformation of that country into a true democracy and the end of its harsh regime of racial segregation. Zimbabwe, on the other hand, remains stalled in the autocratic hands of President Robert Mugabe.

A generous gesture by President Sassou-Nguesso provided a more amusing coda to our trip. Just before I left Brazzaville, a sizable wooden crate was delivered to the ambassador's residence. It contained two large elephant tusks, intended as a gift for me. Rather than return to the United States with objects that might incur the wrath of environmentalists, not to mention our government, I asked Ambassador Lukens to dispose of them as he saw fit. Later in the year, Sassou-Nguesso visited the United States and stopped in Harrisburg to visit us. We went to the airport to welcome him, and out of the corner of my eye, I could not help but notice a large wooden crate being lowered from the cargo hold. Predictably, the box contained the tusks that I had "forgotten." After the president's visit, I offered the well-traveled tusks to the state museum, where, I assume, they repose to this very day.

We journeyed to the Middle East in November 1980 under the auspices of the Federation of Jewish Agencies of Greater Philadelphia. The prime purpose of the trip was to strengthen the already significant economic ties between Pennsylvania and Israel. As the first Republican official to visit Israel since President Reagan's election, I was careful to be quoted that the president would strongly support Israel, "out of a realization that it is in the American national interest." We were also able to meet with some individuals who were related to or knew some of the refuseniks we had encountered in Russia the year before.

Israel left us with a number of significant impressions. First, an image remains in our minds of the map of the Middle East, with tiny Israel in the midst of its historic enemies. Second, we will not forget the greenery of the reclaimed lands, in contrast to the desert all around. Third, having seen the West Bank settlements, fortified in many cases, and their hardy inhabitants, we found it difficult to envision these areas being relinquished in the course of any peace process. Finally, the fact that the Israelis were obliged to spend 25 percent of their GNP on defense augured for continued dependence on massive U.S. aid and assured more of the economic uncertainty that has characterized the nation since its outset.

All this travel brought home the fact that, like it or not, neither Pennsylvania nor the United States can ignore the world around us. I hope we were able to communicate to our fellow Pennsylvanians the importance of engaging this challenge; all Americans must become active world citizens if we are to survive and prosper ourselves.

ONLY FOUR OF MY original cabinet members remained in the administration for its entire eight years: Transportation Secretary Tom Larson, General Services Secretary Walter Baran, Banking Secretary Ben McEnteer and Adjutant General Dick Scott.

The first to depart was Secretary of the Commonwealth Ethel Allen, who violated our ban on accepting honoraria for outside speaking engagements and resigned before the end of her first year. Bill Davis took over this position and served until mid-1985, when Rob Gleason succeeded him. Labor and Industry Secretary Myron Joseph, whose management style I found much too academic for the hurly-burly of Harrisburg, also departed within a year. He was succeeded by Charlie Lieberth, Barry Stern and Jim Knepper for stints of two years or so each. Health Secretary MacLeod left shortly after the TMI incident, during which his erratic behavior had depleted my confidence in him. He was succeeded by Arnold Muller. Shirley Dennis, an outstanding African American leader, took over the Department of Community Affairs from Bill Davis in late 1979 and served thereafter through my second term.

Environmental Resources Secretaries Cliff Jones (to the Public Utility Commission) and Pete Duncan (to the Game Commission) departed during my first term, to be succeeded by Nick DeBenedictis. Sandy Stengel, who had succeeded Jim Bodine as commerce secretary, also left at the end of my first term. He was succeeded by Lancaster businessman Jim Pickard, who had been active in my reelection campaign and served during the balance of my tenure. Bob Bittenbender succeeded Bob Wilburn as budget secretary in my second term and later served Governor Tom Ridge in a similar capacity. Bob Wilburn left in 1984 to head the Carnegie Institute in Pittsburgh. His immediate successor as education secretary, Peg Smith, left after eighteen months to become superintendent of the Hempfield School District.

Harvey Bartle, who succeeded Pete Biester as the state's last appointed attorney general, turned over his prior portfolio as insurance commissioner to Michael Browne. In mid-1983, Browne was followed by a succession of acting commissioners until George Grode took over the post in 1985. Gorham Black left the Department of Aging in early 1985 and Penny Hallowell the Department of Agriculture shortly thereafter, to be ultimately succeeded, respectively, by Alma Jacobs and Dick Grubb. The new Department of Corrections was headed by Glen Jeffes through 1986.

Hallowell's leaving was most regrettable. From a longtime Bucks County farm family, he had been an early and faithful supporter of mine and was widely respected in the agricultural community. For some unaccountable reason, he committed a minor shoplifting offense in the fall of 1984, seeking to conceal a tape cassette on his person during a visit to a store where he was actually purchasing more expensive items. I had to advise Penny to depart lest he be pursued by questions about the incident during the balance of his tenure.

Staff changes took place as well. Few of the original inner circle lasted the full eight years. After serving me in a variety of capacities since 1970, Jay Waldman departed in 1985 to join a Philadelphia law firm. Paul Critchlow moved to New York, where he eventually became senior vice president for communications at Merrill Lynch. Jim Seif, who had served me since the 1966 congressional effort, left to become regional administrator of the federal Environmental Protection Agency. He was to serve as environmental secretary in the administration of Governor Tom Ridge in the 1990s. Murray Dickman took over the administration side upon Bob Wilburn's departure until he joined Rite Aid Corporation briefly in 1985. He subsequently joined me at the Department of Justice and the United Nations. Rick Stafford left in 1983 for a stint in investment banking but returned in 1985 to succeed Jay as chief of staff. He later became executive director of the Allegheny Conference on Community Development in Pittsburgh. Legislative Secretary George Seidel departed for private-sector lobbying endeavors and was succeeded by Tom Usiadek. Our Washington office, originally headed by Gwen King, was overseen by former congressman Jim Nelligan when Gwen was tapped for duty in the Reagan White House. One of the highest ranking African Americans in Republican circles, Gwen later served as commissioner of the Social Security Administration. The D.C. office became widely respected on Capitol Hill during Gwen's tenure and provided a significant return on our investment.

To almost all of those who served with me, I owe a substantial and continuing debt of gratitude. The value of their service to the Commonwealth of Pennsylvania is measured best by the quality and prestige of the positions they assumed following that service.

11

The Politics of
the Governorship

Throughout my time in the governor's office I was active in groups such as the NGA, the Republican Governors Association (RGA), the Coalition of Northeast Governors (CONEG), the Appalachian Regional Commission and, by appointment of President Reagan, the Advisory Commission on Intergovernmental Relations (ACIR). Many of their sessions were rather tedious, but they gave me an opportunity to work on broader issues and to enter some important national networks.

My principal focus within the NGA was the federal deficit. The states had a major interest in deficit reduction and debt containment. After grappling with the specifics of the federal budget and enduring the partisan opposition within the NGA to President Reagan's "new federalism," I became convinced that a balanced-budget amendment to the United States Constitution was the only answer, and I began working to gain NGA support for such an amendment. At our summer 1982 meeting, the matter was debated but never brought to a vote. The 1982 elections then reduced the ranks of Republican governors and brought to office several articulate opponents of the amendment, such as New York's Mario Cuomo. It was not until February 1985 that the NGA finally called for a federal balanced-budget amendment, together with a line-item veto for the president (already available to forty-three state governors) and a requirement for a capital budget separate from the budget for current expenditures.

I took the governors' resolution to ACIR that summer. This organization usually occupied itself with "safe" issues, such as improving management in government and fostering better federal-state-local dialogue. However, it directed its staff to study the states' experience with balanced-budget requirements, the line-item veto and capital budgeting and to determine the feasibility of their use at the federal level. Completed after I left office, the study found "significant evidence that constitutional rules, including those that require expenditures and revenues be in balance, can be effective instruments for influencing fiscal behavior." To this day, however, the balanced-budget proposal languishes, as successive Congresses have been unable to muster the two-thirds majority required to send it to the states for ratification. A statute designed to achieve the same result was found unconstitutional by a 6–3 vote in the Supreme Court in 1998. Even the NGA, at the urging of Governor Cuomo, watered down its support for the concept in the 1990s.

Governor Cuomo and I had another dustup in 1985, this time over the deductibility under federal tax laws of state and local taxes. President Reagan proposed the elimination of this $36 billion tax break as part of his tax reform plan. Because New York was a high-tax state and Pennsylvania a low-tax state, the deduction favored New York taxpayers to the disadvantage of their counterparts in our state. In fact, I argued, Pennsylvanians were actually subsidizing beleaguered New York taxpayers. Testifying before the House Ways and Means Committee, I stated, "The choice is simple: either to continue a tax break, which benefits only one-third of all taxpayers . . . or to provide lower tax rates for all taxpayers in all states. To me the answer is obvious." The clincher was that 85 percent of the benefits of the deduction went to the 15 percent of the populace in high tax brackets. Nonetheless, no change was enacted.

My work in the NGA had practical benefits for Pennsylvania. The good relationships I developed with many in the federal administration helped ensure that when Pennsylvania's issues warranted federal consideration, they received it. This was particularly helpful during the 1981–83 recession, when our state needed—and received—a fair amount of federal help.

In December 1984, I was elected RGA chairman, assuming office to find the organization somewhat moribund and its treasury bare. I hired a new executive director, Michele Davis, who instituted an annual dinner, attended by the president, at which we raised nearly a million dollars. Since this was three times as much as had been raised in any previous year, we were able to carry out a much more ambitious program and even aid some of our candidates financially for the first time. In 1986, when I served as RGA campaign chairman, traveling near and far in support of GOP gubernatorial candidates, we realized a net gain of seven statehouses (it would have been eight, but for the troubles which drove Arizona's Evan Mecham from office). To this day, I am proud when one of my former colleagues refers to me as the one who brought the RGA back to life.

WHEN U.S. SENATOR Dick Schweiker announced in early 1980 that he would not seek reelection, Jay Waldman made a pitch for my seeking the seat, largely on the theory of quitting while we were ahead. My job required making almost daily decisions that were bound to create controversy and alienate some constituents. This could not help but erode the goodwill built up during my first year in office. But since I was not enthusiastic about leaving the position after just a year and even less so about moving to the Senate, this discussion was largely academic.

My first choice as a Senate candidate was Bill Scranton, but he was not interested (largely, I suspect, because of his own gubernatorial aspirations). Arlen Specter wanted to run again, but it was not in our interest to create yet another power center within the party (a concern we shared with Senator Heinz). We were also wary of Specter's string of losses; he had not won a race since 1969. To head off a Specter candidacy, we enlisted Pennsylvania's GOP chairman, Bud Haabestad. The party people were not excited about Bud, however, since he was rightfully viewed as my candidate and as such was identified with the patronage drought. Sure enough, Specter captured the nomination. Our red faces were somewhat relieved by Specter's victory over Pete Flaherty in the fall landslide generated by Ronald Reagan's resounding defeat of Jimmy Carter.

I declined to endorse any candidate in the 1980 Pennsylvania presidential primary, which George Bush won. But I did campaign hard in the fall for the Reagan-Bush team, and we were rewarded with the biggest Republican sweep in years. The strength of the top of the ticket led us to victory in every statewide race but one and restored both houses of the General Assembly to Republican control. I was thereafter to describe Pennsylvania as "the most Republican state in the nation: the largest state with a Republican governor, two Republican senators and both houses of the legislature under Republican control!"

CONSIDERATION OF MY own run for reelection began in earnest in the fall of 1981. With nearly three years of governing under my belt, I was beginning to get a feel for the office and to derive considerable satisfaction from checking items off our agenda as they were accomplished. I did not want to quit midway through our ambitious agenda. And much remained to be done, most notably the final framing and execution of our economic development plan.

In April 1981, Bill Scranton disclosed that he intended to run an "independent" reelection campaign. I was somewhat baffled by what this meant, since the candidates for governor and lieutenant governor are paired on the general-election ballot and no primary opposition was in sight for either of us. There was speculation that Scranton was miffed because the Republican State Committee had not picked up his 1978 primary debts, or because he felt insufficiently included in the governing process (although he had been given more responsibility than any of his predecessors in office). We tried to shut down his "independent" fund-raising effort after complaints from our supporters. Finally, in February 1982, we agreed to use all funds raised by both committees in support of the ticket. By the time of his announcement for reelection, Scranton was stating that we would be running as a team.

On February 25, 1982, three-term congressman Allen Ertel of Williamsport announced his candidacy for the Democratic nomination. The Democratic State Committee quickly endorsed him, along with state senator Jim Lloyd for lieutenant governor.

My only previous contacts with Ertel had been unpleasant. At the time of the TMI incident, he had appeared at the Capitol seeking to hold a press conference. Thereafter, he had proposed a number of schemes to finance the cleanup but seemed more interested in talk than action. Although he was not well known statewide, his repeated election from a congressional district that was 60 percent Republican indicated that he was a viable contender. Jay Waldman concluded that he might well combine a good showing in central Pennsylvania with substantial margins in the cities to defeat me.

Ertel's announcement speech stated, falsely in both cases, that the state "had the second highest unemployment rate in the nation" and that "[w]hile the federal government has cut income taxes, the Thornburgh administration has raised them." Such exaggerations and falsehoods were to characterize much of his campaign. He concluded, "I reject Governor

Thornburgh's unmistakable conclusion that Pennsylvania's day has passed. I reject his blind allegiance to Sun-belt economics."

It was understandable that Ertel would try to hold our administration responsible for the state's economic throes as the nation slipped into a recession. Unemployment in Pennsylvania had reached nearly 9 percent in December 1981 and zoomed to an eleven-year high of 11.2 percent in January 1982. In September 1982, the last month for which figures were released before the election, it was 11.3 percent—the highest rate since the federal Bureau of Labor Statistics had begun to keep track in 1970. It was to reach 14.9 percent by January 1983. We consistently responded to Ertel's near-exclusive focus on the economy by noting the national character of our economic quandary, reminding voters that Pennsylvania was not "an island of unemployment in a sea of prosperity."

Despite Ertel's charges, national media observers were lavish in their praise of my first term. While welcome, their plaudits created what turned out to be unduly high expectations for my reelection. Jack Germond and Jules Witcover reviewed our accomplishments and concluded, "[I]f you were going to bet the farm this year, Thornburgh is your horse." They also expressed the view that our expected victory "would give charisma a bad name."

My campaign kickoff tour, on March 2–3, began in Philadelphia and continued on to Pittsburgh, Harrisburg, Wilkes-Barre/Scranton, Erie, Johnstown and Altoona. At each stop, I emphasized the accomplishments of my first term—an end to corruption, an end to "credit-card government," a reduction in the bloated bureaucracy, a refusal to raise taxes and the revitalization of PennDOT. I noted our increased support for education and for aid to senior citizens, veterans and others in need; our crackdown on violent crime; and our encouragement of "small and advanced technology businesses . . . the greatest source of potential new jobs." Somewhat weakly, I concluded, "While any increase in unemployment is unacceptable . . . in the last three years, unemployment in the Commonwealth has increased at a rate less than in the nation as a whole." In addition to continuing to work for better management, tax restraint and economic recovery, I pledged to reform the welfare system, end the state's liquor monopoly and fight burdensome and expensive twice-a-year auto inspections.

The Republican State Committee unanimously endorsed our ticket. Most, but not all, of the internecine tension surrounding the continuing patronage squabble and the 1980 Senate race had been neutralized by this time. Montgomery County GOP Chairman Bob Asher chaired my campaign, working closely with State Chairman Martha Bell Schoeninger, the first woman to head a major party in Pennsylvania.

The quixotic Alvin Joseph Jacobson, one of the 1978 primary contenders, appeared to have gathered enough signatures to place him on the GOP primary ballot, but sleuthing and legal arguments by our campaign counsel showed enough of those signatures to be invalid to cause his removal from the race. Thus the primary election was to be strictly pro forma.

Senator John Heinz was also seeking reelection in 1982. While we remained personally cordial, our staffs, each beholden to an ambitious political figure, had scrapped off and on since 1978, and our natural rivalry heightened as each of us became more successful. Early in the 1982 campaign, *Pittsburgh Press* reporter Sherley Uhl noted that we were both "presumed to be running either for president or vice-president in 1984, or perhaps 1988." These circumstances provoked an ugly confrontation that was to sour our relationship considerably.

The biggest attraction for prospective donors was President Reagan, and we secured tentative White House approval of a presidential appearance on my behalf at a $250-a-plate luncheon. Heinz demanded that the president reverse this decision and attend a luncheon or dinner on his behalf instead. White House Chief of Staff Jim Baker asked me if there was any give in our position. Upon my holding firm, he said they would flip a coin, and we were later told that we had won.

Shortly thereafter, the senator called to demand that I accede to the president's appearing at his event rather than mine. He claimed that I owed him this favor because of his family's support for me in 1978. I replied that while I had always been grateful for that support, I had never regarded it as making me a hostage to his demands. He had a weak opponent and unlimited personal financial resources, while I faced a tough race, and I was not willing to give up the president's drawing power. Ultimately, Heinz agreed to hold an afternoon reception where the president would "drop by" to meet his supporters.

Long after, some uncertainty was voiced as to whether the coin toss had ever really taken place. The Reagan White House was upset with Heinz's call for a midcourse correction in its economic policies. I had been a firm supporter of the president's programs and had urged his administration and Congress to undertake the same kinds of budget cuts we had undertaken in Pennsylvania. Many suspected that the president's attendance at my luncheon was intended to send a message that the administration would reward its supporters over its detractors. My allegiance to the president and his programs, however, was to have its costs throughout the campaign, while Senator Heinz's opposition to both reaped him substantial benefits.

Four developments gave our campaign a boost during the spring. Passage of our welfare reform bill, even in its watered-down form, was a major triumph. Not long afterward, we secured approval of our 1982–83 budget nearly two months before the deadline, the earliest passage in twenty years. By the end of the fiscal year, our austerity measures had also turned a predicted 1981–82 budget deficit into a slight surplus. The *Philadelphia Inquirer* praised this accomplishment in a lead editorial that concluded, "It couldn't all have been luck. There must have been tight management and careful counting of pennies along the way." Finally, I was able to fulfill my campaign pledge to cut the number of auto inspections to once a year.

The summer featured several odd incidents. The most bizarre involved Frank Hoffman, a young man on our campaign press staff. When an Ertel aide discovered that Hoffman had brought a tape recorder to an Ertel town meeting, the aide asked him to erase the tape, ostensibly because it might be distorted to alter Ertel's words. On July 28, Ertel took to the floor of the House of Representatives in Washington to complain that the meeting had been "bugged" and charged that the "secret taping" (Hoffman had concealed the recorder behind a newspaper) was a violation of Pennsylvania criminal law. The media quickly noted the absurdity of these charges. The editors of the *York Dispatch* sagely inquired, "How can anyone break the law by recording or reporting what goes on at a public meeting?"

In September, Ertel attempted to turn a ghastly tragedy to his political advantage. A guard at the Camp Hill state correctional institution turned an AK-15 rifle on thirteen members of his family during a weekend spree in Wilkes-Barre, killing them all. Ertel charged our administration with "responsibility for having hired, trained and armed this accused murderer." The *Pittsburgh Post-Gazette* described this as "about as low as a candidate can go," and other papers followed suit.

More annoying to me, however, were Ertel's day-in, day-out misrepresentations and exaggerations. I finally compiled a list of thirty-nine of the most recurrent and blatant of these. They included a claim that Pennsylvania "ranks last of fifty states" in attracting new business; an allegation that we backed user fees on locks and dams, when I had led a fight against them; a portrayal of Ertel as having opposed a $75-a-day tax break for congressmen, when he had both voted for it and defended it; references to cuts in state funding for mass transit, schools and programs for the aging, when we had actually increased funding for all of them; a claim that Ertel had been a volunteer lawyer for the Wilmington, Delaware, NAACP, when the director had never heard of him; and the constant use of fictional unemployment figures to paint the worst picture possible of our economic straits. Attempting to rebut these charges almost daily was exhausting for my campaign staff and, as intended by the Ertel camp, diverted us from emphasizing our own themes.

Our former friends at the PSEA joined in the fray, stating that I had "misled" them in 1978 and publicly comparing me and my "propaganda machine" to both Adolf Hitler and Joseph Goebbels. Robert M. Zweiman, national commander of the Jewish War Veterans, wrote me, "No political differences could justify such hideous comparisons, but in your case, they are completely unjustified. Your record of support for human rights and decency is well known and contradicts completely any relationship to these heinous historical figures." Even under media pressure, the PSEA refused to back down from its scurrilous characterizations, but it did not repeat them.

Our television advertising primarily reviewed the record of my first term. The ads were workmanlike but, in my view, not nearly so memorable as those done in 1978. Perhaps this was inevitable; my sense is that political consultants are far more energized when their candidate is an underdog.

Though Ertel had consistently asked us for debates, we had deferred a decision on this until the fall. Frankly, we saw no reason to give him such a forum. After the election, Jay Waldman was to tell David Morrison of the *Philadelphia Inquirer*, "When someone is as unknown as Ertel, it's not a question of 'Will he move up?'—but, 'When and by how much?' Our strategy was to retard his movement. We knew that we could never get any higher than where we started. So, at all times, we were running a campaign of containment." Declining to debate Ertel was part of this strategy. Predictably, Ertel accused me of "ducking" him, and editorial writers and columnists, always looking for controversy, echoed his complaint. In September we responded that we were unwilling to agree to debates until we were satisfied that a debate format could contain Ertel's "distortions and misrepresentations."

At the same time, we released my income tax returns for the previous five years, as we had done in past campaigns, and called upon Ertel to do the same. Ertel responded that he had already filed financial disclosure forms as a congressman, but we pointed out that these contained "omissions and inconsistencies." On September 21, he flatly refused to make his tax returns public, implying a fear of being "whipsawed" by charitable institutions that might seek contributions from him and his wife. Our response to this lame excuse was, "How can someone who can't stand up to the United Way stand up to the PSEA?" We then asserted that I was unwilling to debate Ertel unless his tax returns were made public.

The media soon began criticizing Ertel's "tax secrecy." On September 29, he released a thirty-page financial "summary" that included a consolidation of federal income tax information for the previous seven years, but not the returns themselves. This time, he added as an excuse the reluctance of his wife to let "everybody in the world . . . know everything in the world about us." This caused me a slight chuckle, as I knew my own wife's feelings on this matter. We responded, however, with a five-page press release focusing on integrity. Shortly thereafter, we pulled the plug altogether on the debate discussions, to mixed reactions by the media.

Two years later, when Ertel was finally obliged to release his returns in his race for attorney general, we were to learn the reason for his reluctance to do so in 1982. He had, in fact, paid no federal taxes whatsoever in 1980.

Another of Ertel's antics caused me to cancel a planned visit to the Little League Hall of Fame near Williamsport in the early fall. I had thrown out the first pitch at the Little League World Series in 1979 to former Chicago Cub shortstop Ernie Banks (who, surprisingly, did not hit it out of the park). I had also had a chance to meet announcers Red Barber and Mel Allen, as well as Bill Shea, for whom Shea Stadium in New York had been named. I was looking forward to my visit to the Hall of Fame until I learned en route that Ertel had shown up at the site, intent upon confronting me over the debate issue. We skipped the museum and went directly to Williamsport, Ertel's hometown, where I spoke to an enthusiastic crowd of some 300.

Meanwhile, important endorsements were forthcoming for our effort. The Democrats for Thornburgh-Scranton group was joined by a Small Business for Thornburgh-Scranton Committee. The United Chapters of the Polish-American Congress in Pennsylvania added their approval, as did three major statewide volunteer firefighters' organizations, the Fraternal Order of Police and the Pennsylvania Association of College and University Professors. Henry Kissinger appeared at a Philadelphia fund-raising dinner for us, attracting considerable attention.

The Family of Leaders, representing nearly 200 African American civic, business and fraternal organizations in the greater Philadelphia area, endorsed our ticket in September. We had no chance to replicate our 1978 majority in the black community because of the economic downturn and the furor over "Thornfare." We were determined, nonetheless, to make a serious campaign effort in this community.

On October 1, the first statewide poll, conducted for the *Pittsburgh Post-Gazette*, showed us with a 56–33 percent lead. (We were to regularly track the race with our own sophisticated polls.) It was a danger sign, however, that the poll showed voters with a far more positive view of both Heinz and me than of President Reagan. Thereafter, Ertel often referred to me as "Reagan's clone," and presidential hopeful Walter Mondale joined him for a swing through western Pennsylvania. Nonetheless, David Broder, in his election-year *Washington Post* assessment of our state, headlined his story "GOP Ebb Tide Hasn't Caught Thornburgh," though he warned readers not to expect a landslide because of strong opposition from the AFL-CIO and PSEA, my unwillingness to distance myself from the president and double-digit unemployment.

The PSEA and statewide AFL-CIO, both rabid in their opposition to the Reagan administration, had indeed endorsed Ertel (and Heinz), as had the UMW and, to my chagrin, the statewide Building Trades Council, despite the enormous positive impact of our infrastructure-building program on construction employment. AFSCME's approval of Ertel was not so surprising. The PFT, however, stuck with our ticket, and we had support from the Transport Workers Union and an unprecedented statewide endorsement from the two Teamsters councils. Other important labor endorsements came from International Longshoreman's Local 1291 in southeastern Pennsylvania; from Heavy Construction Carpenters Local 2274, Painters Local 327 and the Boilermakers Union, all in the Pittsburgh area; and from the National Union of Hospital and Health Care Employees.

Our first newspaper endorsement came, much to our surprise, from the *Philadelphia Daily News*, among our most strident critics throughout my first term. After cataloguing what they called "Thornburgh outrages" (most notably "Thornfare"), the editors nevertheless declared their support for my reelection, on the basis of "Ivory pure, effectively administered, fiscally sound government." In closing, they addressed me directly: "Forgive us this reluctant endorsement, Governor. . . . Competent, clean government is wonderful, but try to remember there are people out there . . . and desperate cities." We were also backed by WCAU-TV in Philadelphia and by newspapers in Lancaster, Harrisburg, Johnstown and Williamsport. An October *Reader's Digest* article gave us a major boost, highlighting our successes in cost cutting, welfare reform and better management. The *Wall*

Street Journal weighed in with a piece describing me as "one of the political phenomena of this recession year" and as having run "a clean, efficient and economical state government." The article included an interesting observation from Julius Uehlein, state AFL-CIO president: "If it weren't for the economic issue, I imagine he'd be invincible."

The *Post-Gazette*'s final poll was released on October 22 and showed us in the lead by thirteen points—52–39 percent—down from the twenty-three points reported in September, but still a comfortable margin. Unfortunately, the following days were marred by blunders and mishaps.

The first of these seemed, at the time, of little moment. After receiving the most welcome and newsworthy endorsement of Erie's Democratic mayor, Louis Tullio, my son John and I set off for some street campaigning in that community. Accosted by a woman who complained about her inability to get by on welfare payments, I noted, while munching on an apple purchased from a street vendor, that we had twice increased the level of those payments. This response did not satisfy her, and I finally threw out a line from one of our television commercials, which I had used frequently: "Things are tough all over."

Reporters took this to be a particularly callous response, made more so by my casting my apple into a trash basket at the end of our exchange. They interviewed the woman, a thirty-six-year-old unemployed nurse with a ten-year-old son, about her plight. While she did not blame me for the recession, she said, "It's Reaganomics and he's a Republican." She told reporters she had never heard of Ertel and would not vote for him, but he highlighted our exchange at every appearance as evidence of my not caring about the needs of Pennsylvanians hurting because of the recession.

The second wound, too, was largely self-inflicted. Each year of my first term, I had appeared at the annual convention of the overwhelmingly Democratic state NAACP to report on our efforts to assist black Pennsylvanians. I had been a member of the organization for nearly twenty years. As the date for the 1982 meeting approached, we were informed that the format called for a "debate" between Ertel and me. By that time we had firmly established our position on debates. I was determined to attend the meeting, however, and hoped that we could persuade the NAACP leadership that they owed me a forum for my annual report. After further negotiations the morning of the meeting, we were advised that an acceptable format had been arranged.

When we arrived, it was clear that we had been set up. A toss of the coin between Ertel and me was quickly arranged to set the order of appearance for the "debate." I won and proceeded to deliver my report to the 200 NAACP chapter leaders present. At the end of ten minutes, I was rudely interrupted and told to relinquish the floor to Ertel. I asked if I could complete my report by using time originally allocated for rebuttal. Told that I could not, I left by a side door and returned home. Thereafter, all hell broke loose. Ertel launched an attack on me, and the group's president, Dr. Charles H. Butler, observed that my action "will cost him at the polls." Others at the meeting eagerly sought out reporters, who were only too willing to hype the story. The following day's Sunday papers were filled with stories about my "walking out" of the NAACP meeting. Even our release of endorsements by Leon Sullivan and Jesse Jackson did not abate the furor. We subsequently determined that one of Ertel's campaigners, Barton Fields, a Shapp administration official whom we had fired in 1979, had apparently influenced the amiable Dr. Butler to revise the meeting format to create this confrontation.

The third incident was the most hurtful to Ginny and me personally. One of our television ads had been shot at Conroy School, Peter's old school in Pittsburgh. It portrayed me among some of the students, as the voice-over and visuals extolled our record on aiding persons with disabilities. The spot seemed fairly straightforward to me, and our record in this area was one of which I was justifiably proud. In the waning days of the campaign, about fifteen parents of children with disabilities appeared at Conroy with Ertel to attack me for "exploiting" their children for political purposes and failing to live up to our commitments to retarded citizens. We could only respond that consent had been obtained for use of the footage, which we felt might "show the parents of other handicapped children that it is possible to move out of an institutional setting into the mainstream of the community."

Dr. Gordon MacLeod endorsed Ertel at the end of the campaign, charging that I had "ignored vital public health considerations when those of us in central Pennsylvania were threatened by" TMI. We responded by observing of MacLeod: "As the crisis went on, he just seemed more emotionally distraught . . . finally, he did have to be excused from the crisis management process and eventually from the administration itself." The doctor's endorsement had no observable effect on Ertel's fortunes.

A more significant switch to Ertel's side was that of *Philadelphia Daily News* African American columnist Chuck Stone. In a column appearing two weeks before the election, Stone described me as a "decent and good person, a man of enduring amiability and a desire to do good that is transcended only by his peculiarity for doing well." He then recounted the faltering economy, my refusal to break with the president, "Thornfare," mandatory sentences, the PSEA's figures on lack of support for education and my "thermal-heated lust" for higher office as reasons to vote against me. He closed with a plea to "send a message to Mr. Reagan and the nation that the American people are mad as hell and they aren't going to take it anymore." About the same time, Lucien Blackwell, a Democratic Philadelphia city councilman, accused me of "wag[ing] war on the black community." The *Philadelphia Tribune*, the city's leading African American newspaper, however, decided "to reluctantly endorse Gov. Thornburgh . . . because the Democratic Party provides no real viable alternative."

Endorsements by other newspapers across the state continued to be heavily in our favor. Most important, of course, were the metropolitan dailies. The *Pittsburgh Press* called me "an able and effective leader [who] had kept most of his major campaign promises," while the *Post-Gazette* concluded, "[O]ne good term deserves another." When all was said and done, we had acquired the endorsement of every major newspaper in the state, save for the *Lancaster Intelligencer-Journal* and the *Valley News-Dispatch* in Tarentum, near Pittsburgh.

During the last week of the campaign, we attended get-out-the-vote events in both Philadelphia and Pittsburgh. The Philadelphia City Committee dinner was distinguished by a rare appearance by Billy Meehan, who gave me his personal endorsement. This was a significant gesture, as some in the crowd had booed me at a similar gathering in 1980 because of dissatisfaction with our patronage practices. My speech this time was interrupted by applause a dozen times.

In Pittsburgh, we held a festive rally for 1,000 of the faithful. I used the occasion to question how Ertel proposed to fund the $1.5 billion package of additional wages, benefits and school subsidies with which his supporters in the state employees' unions and the PSEA sought to saddle Pennsylvania taxpayers. We also arose before dawn to switch on a "Parkway Open" electric sign on the heavily traveled Parkway East, signaling the conclusion of a two-year rebuilding project. Tooting horns, waving motorists and handshakes among the construction workers marked the end of the biggest reconstruction effort ever undertaken in western Pennsylvania, six days ahead of schedule. The event was enlivened by the appearance of an Ertel supporter in a chicken suit, seeking to dramatize our reluctance to debate.

On the Sunday before the election, *Philadelphia Inquirer* reporter Larry Eichel took the measure of the candidates:

[T]he governor looks the part of a winner, if that means anything. He seems loose, relaxed and confident. As he travels from stop to stop, Thornburgh appears to be enjoying himself. He can be curt and standoffish with news reporters, but in the final days he has been chatting and joking with reporters who travel with him, telling stories and doing imitations.

Ertel, on the other hand, appears worn out and sometimes disoriented, bludgeoned into numbness by a brutal schedule. His emotions, he admitted recently, "were close to the surface." Unlike his opponent, whose camp is tracking the race almost daily with sophisticated polling, Ertel can go only by what he has heard, felt and seen. As the end approaches, he seems not to know what to make of it all.

Well aware of the Democrats' 678,000-voter registration edge and the relentless attack by our opponents during a period of severe economic downturn and increasing unemployment, we felt we had done all that we could to communicate our message. "Rightly or wrongly," observed Eichel, on the eve of the election, "the results . . . will be interpreted as a referendum on Reaganomics." With this conclusion, I was distinctly uneasy.

Election day found Ginny and me voting in Harrisburg. We had changed our registration to the capital in 1979 to show our allegiance to the community where we would be residing over the next four or, as we hoped, eight years. This move was viewed negatively, probably correctly so from a political standpoint, by Jay Waldman, who treasured our ballot identification with western Pennsylvania. After casting our ballots, we departed to Pittsburgh and thence to Philadelphia.

From the outset, it was clear that there was to be no landslide. Although we never fell behind, our lead was slim as a strong Democratic tide swept the country. All three networks early called me the winner but, about 9:30, CBS temporarily removed the indication that I had won from its map. It was not until 11:57 that Ertel conceded.

Just how tough it had been was not fully apparent until the next day. "Thornburgh Survives," said the headline in the *Philadelphia Daily News*. Our winning margin was 100,431—less than half our 228,154-vote edge in 1978. In Philadelphia, which we had lost by a mere 34,875 votes in 1978, Ertel had run up a winning margin of 150,131—a swing of 115,256 votes. This alone accounted for 90 percent of the statewide difference between our winning margins in the two years. We had also fared worse in the hard-coal region, losing Lackawanna (Scranton and environs), Luzerne (Wilkes-Barre and Hazelton), Schuylkill and Carbon Counties, all of which we had carried in 1978. On the other hand, Allegheny County voters "came home" to back their native son over Ertel by a margin of 250,836 to 244,391, and other western Pennsylvania counties also gave us stronger support than in 1978. We lost the city of Pittsburgh to Ertel by 30,539, thrice Flaherty's edge in 1978. The reason, as in Philadelphia, was the decline in our support among African American voters. Statewide our showing among this constituency dipped from 58 percent in 1978 to 21 percent in 1982. Erie County was a winner for us in a switch from 1978, thanks, I am sure, to Mayor Tullio's endorsement. We carried the Philadelphia suburban counties by better than two to one and ran well in south central Pennsylvania. I was the first candidate in fifty years to be elected governor of Pennsylvania while a president of his own party was in office.

The Democrats recaptured the state House and were to hold it throughout my second term. The Republicans solidified their control of the state Senate, however, by adding a seat. Senator Heinz scored a massive victory, capitalizing on the distance he had put between himself and the Reagan presidency plus the weakness of his opponent. In contrast, Democratic congressional candidates received 215,000 more votes than Republicans.

Nationwide, the number of GOP governors tumbled from twenty-three to sixteen as Democrats defeated nine incumbents, Republicans only two. In the ten largest states, those most affected by the economic downturn, seven of those races were won by Democrats, only three by Republicans. Of the three, our winning margin was by far the largest—nearly double the 52,295-vote edge of California's George Deukmejian and nearly twenty times Illinois governor Jim Thompson's 5,114-vote margin over Adlai Stevenson III, in a race not officially decided until after a recount. At the end of 1982, columnist-historian Paul Beers of the *Harrisburg Patriot* observed, "Dick Thornburgh had a 678,000 registration handicap and unemployment at a 40-year high of 630,000 jobless against him, but he . . . won by 100,431 votes, a margin just shy of the total vote of Dauphin and Cumberland counties. . . . It is true that 14 others for the governorship— including Milt Shapp twice and Thornburgh himself in 1978—won by bigger margins, but Thornburgh still pulled one of the most amazing vote switches ever in Pennsylvania."

Prior to the 1982 inaugural ball, Ginny and I hosted a $500-per-person reception at the Governor's Home. Much controversy surrounded this event, which was to help pay for the inaugural events and provide a cushion for the second-term political activities of the Governor Thornburgh

Committee. Democrats had earlier attacked the use of the home for "political" events and succeeded in having the State Ethics Commission "suggest" that the reception not be held there, even though no state dollars were involved. Ultimately, the commission was to drop the matter, but not without some embarrassment to us.

GINNY AND I continued to support the Republican Party and its candidates through campaigning and fund-raising, both in the state and across the nation. In my first term, these activities had helped dampen criticism from party regulars over the lack of patronage. They also kept us in touch with friends and supporters and gained us valuable political intelligence. And we used them to contribute to the political dialogue of the 1980s. We surely raised more money for local parties than any Republican in Pennsylvania history, and we got real satisfaction from seeing "our" candidates triumph. The 1984 effort for Attorney General Roy Zimmerman's reelection drew a special effort because his opponent was Allen Ertel, whose election would have made life most difficult for our administration. Also in 1984, I chaired our delegation to the Dallas GOP convention and, after some rumbling from one dissident delegate, delivered a unanimous vote for the Reagan-Bush ticket.

In 1985, pressure began to build for me to run against first-term senator Arlen Specter in his race for reelection. Never a favorite among conservatives, Specter had alienated some of the far right in Washington with his positions on such volatile issues as abortion. Moreover, it was pointed out, I would likely find myself at a political dead end when my second term was finished, as I was constitutionally barred from seeking reelection. Our polling data indicated that I could win a primary battle, but I decided not to try. I really did not want to serve in the U.S. Senate. I also felt that a primary challenge would be intensely divisive and would be a substantial distraction from my efforts to complete a successful second term. Moreover, a hard-fought general election was likely, as always, and I was not sure that I would be able to get "up" for it. Specter went on to win reelection and to serve two additional terms with distinction.

The 1986 campaign of most interest to me was Lieutenant Governor Scranton's effort to succeed me as governor. Scranton was unopposed in the primary. The Democrats nominated the "real" Bob Casey. Both candidates were from Scranton, but there the resemblance ended. Scranton was a true child of the sixties, having admitted during the 1978 primary that he had experimented with drugs while in college; he and his wife had also spent some time as disciples of the transcendental meditation movement and its leader, the Maharishi Yogi. The older, Roman Catholic Casey had strong pro-life views and was something of a classic New Deal Democrat. He also had strong ties to organized labor.

The race was a peculiar one. Although the economy was recovering strongly, Casey campaigned relentlessly against our "failed" economic policies. Scranton, rather than running on our record, seemed to concede Casey's argument and proposed his own new set of economic development policies. This neutralized his strongest issue and somewhat diminished my enthusiasm for his campaign. I suspect that Bill Scranton simply did not want to be viewed as Dick Thornburgh's candidate, although the Democrats' own polling data showed that I enjoyed a 72 percent approval rating. As the son of a beloved political figure, Scranton had two somewhat oppressive role models.

Scranton might yet have won but for one of the most effective, and distasteful, television advertisements ever to run in Pennsylvania. It was aired in the closing days of the race by Casey's campaign consultant, a then little-known Louisianan named James Carville. Opening with pictures of a long-haired, college-age Scranton with sitar music playing in the background, it then dissolved into a picture of the Maharishi Yogi while the voice-over recounted the lieutenant governor's youthful escapades. The "guru" spot was run only in conservative areas and not in either Pittsburgh or Philadelphia. It was buttressed by a last-minute mailing to all Republican voters statewide raising questions about Scranton's character.

On election day, Republican reaction was vividly evident. Scranton ran far behind the more liberal Specter and was "cut" by GOP voters in many areas. Even so, he lost by fewer than 80,000 votes. After his defeat, he left public life, separated from his wife and moved to the West Coast, where he entered upon a successful business career. He returned to Scranton in the late 1990s to remarry and manage the family's interests.

It always seemed to me that Bill Scranton could have neutralized the drug issue (which was, at least subliminally, raised in the "guru" ad) by becoming our administration's point man on the drug problem from the outset. By going to schools, telling students that he had experimented with drugs himself, that it was a bad idea and that they should avoid all forms of substance abuse, he could have created a credible image for himself as an opponent of drug use and negated any attempt to insert the issue into the campaign. Having survived the issue in 1978, however, he may never have anticipated that it would reappear with such dramatic consequences. Had

Scranton won the 1986 gubernatorial race, George Bush might well have seriously considered him as a prospective running mate in 1988. How fragile can be the dreams and prospects of those of us in the political calling!

Oddly enough, following the 1986 election, we enjoyed a period of effectiveness usually denied lame-duck governors. The reason was simple: another legislative pay raise had been proposed. I had, quite frankly, always supported higher pay for public officials as a matter of principle, but saw here an opportunity to accomplish some of our own goals. So I played hard to get and presented my own wish list to the legislative leaders as the price for my support. They delivered on nearly every item and, once I had assured myself by a phone call to incoming governor Bob Casey that he would not publicly blast all of us for the pay raise, I extended my support (or to be more precise, did not offer opposition) to it. Reporters were astonished at our ongoing success. I synthesized our attitude when one asked if we were "winding down" the administration. "No," I responded, "winding up!"

Two final speeches rounded out my valedictory effort. One pointed out how we had successfully challenged the following tenets of "conventional wisdom":

> Corruption and mismanagement had become a way of life in Pennsylvania.

> Reducing the size of government is like the weather—everybody talks about it but nobody does anything about it.

> You can't cut taxes and balance the budget at the same time in a state like Pennsylvania.

> You can't reform a welfare system to benefit both taxpayers and the poor.

> Tough anticrime measures don't really reduce crime.

> Pennsylvania will always be dependent upon its traditional "smokestack" economic base.

My farewell speech highlighted the fact that employment had reached an all-time high and unemployment a twelve-year low. I expressed my hope that I was leaving the state in better shape than I had found it, and my gratitude "for the opportunity to serve a state which I love and a people whom I cherish."

Editorial writers were most generous in their farewell appraisals, especially regarding our integrity and fiscal responsibility. I was particularly gratified at the assessment of Ed Guthman of the *Philadelphia Inquirer*, the most influential newspaper in the city where I had been a virtual unknown eight years previously. He noted, "Foes and admirers alike use the same adjectives—'decisive,' 'efficient,' 'perfectionist,' 'professional,' 'fiscally responsible'—to describe how he shouldered his duties." There were, of course, some negative appraisals as well. In some cases, frankly, I got the sense that reporters had sought these out for the sake of balance. I was leaving office with a 72 percent approval rating. And I am proud to say that my fellow governors, Republican and Democrat, when polled by *Newsweek* in 1986, placed me among the most effective big-state governors in the nation.

FOR THE MOST PART, my time as governor was highly enjoyable from a personal perspective. Many changes took place in our family, of course. John graduated from Bucknell in 1979 and began a career with Bell Atlantic that was to last until 1997. After a short stint as president of Penn's Southwest Association, a nonprofit economic development effort serving greater Pittsburgh, he carved out a successful career in the private sector. He was also elected to the board of directors of the Children's Institute in Pittsburgh, the former Home for Crippled Children where his brother Peter had received such loving care. In 1982 he married Sharon Kratz of Landsdale, Pennsylvania. Our first grandchild, their daughter Kendall Leigh, was born in 1984; our first grandson, Richard Lewis Thornburgh II, in 1987; their second daughter, Devon Virginia, in 1990; and their second son, Bradford Scott, in 1996.

David graduated from Haverford in 1981, taught eighth grade in Chicago for two years, then earned a master's degree in public administration from Harvard's John F. Kennedy School of Government. After this he worked first for CIGNA, then for the Small Business Development Center at the Wharton School. In 1994 he became executive director of the eastern division of the Pennsylvania Economy League, a good-government organization, which gave him a major opportunity to influence economic and community development in the Philadelphia area. He married Rebecca McKillip from Hollidaysburg, Pennsylvania in 1984. Their first daughter, Blair Elizabeth, was born in 1989 and their second, Alice McKillip, in 1992.

Peter's life underwent a major change as a result of our concern about the unnatural surroundings at the Governor's Home. In 1981, following his "graduation" from the Harrisburg public schools and a stint working at Goodwill Industries, we came to realize that he would benefit by living away from his parents. With considerable pangs of uncertainty, we arranged his move into a group home about fifteen minutes away, where he had his own room and shared common facilities with five other clients. He also began to work at the Center for Industrialized Training (CIT), a workshop in nearby Mechanicsburg. Peter went through another blossoming period that made it clear we had done the right thing. He was able to join us on weekends and, sometimes with friends, for special occasions and official events.

One reminder of Peter's continuing vulnerability came in the winter following his move. To kill time between his two buses on the way to work, he usually stopped for a cup of hot chocolate at a local café. On one particularly cold morning, his glasses fogged up as he came into the restaurant and he laid them aside, then left without them. When he realized his mistake and returned to the cafe, he was unable to find the glasses on his table; a helpful waitress had given them to the checkout person, but Peter did not ask anyone about their whereabouts.

By this time the bus had left. Notwithstanding the cold, Peter set off on foot by the route his bus usually followed, a trip which stretched some ten miles ahead of him. After two or three miles, he was observed by Hilda Gibble, a retired schoolteacher, who knew there was something strange about a young man walking without one of his gloves in such bitter cold weather. Peter was still clutching his bus transfer in his bare right hand. Her teacher's instincts were, of course, correct, and she bundled Peter into her car for delivery to work. Peter suffered severe frostbite on one of his fingers, but no permanent harm.

It was our youngest son, Bill, whose life was most challenging during this period. After he finished eighth grade, Ginny and I decided he would be better off away from a community where his parents were constantly in the public eye. He visited several boarding schools and finally decided on Deerfield Academy, but he was not happy there and missed his family and friends. We finally consented to let him return home and spend his senior year at Harrisburg Academy. He graduated in 1985 and went on to Bucknell, but he did not stay there, and by the fall of 1987 he seemed to have lost all confidence in his academic ability. Over the Christmas holidays, he told us that he intended to join the U.S. Navy's submarine service, and on February 18, 1988, he reported for duty. We strongly supported his decision and, as it turned out, it was a sound one. He qualified as a sonar technician and served with distinction for six years, including a stint aboard the U.S.S. *Baton Rouge*, a Los Angeles–class nuclear-powered fast attack submarine out of Norfolk, Virginia. In early 1994, he returned to college, this time to Penn State. He graduated in 1997 and embarked on his own career in the Pittsburgh area.

Ginny, of course, continued working on the issues closest to her heart throughout my terms as governor, engaging in advocacy for persons with disabilities throughout Pennsylvania. One very important project that she started was completed after we had left Harrisburg: the dedication of a cemetery for institutionalized people, who had previously been identified only by number upon death. She felt it very important to accord these persons a dignity in death that was often not forthcoming during their troubled lives. She also served, by appointment of President Reagan, on the President's Committee on Mental Retardation. Meanwhile, I served as a founding director of the National Organization on Disability (NOD). In 1985, we were, with Peter, honored as the Family of the Year by the Pennsylvania Association of Retarded Citizens.

12

Harvard and a Return
to Washington

On January 20, 1987, Ginny and I attended the inauguration of Governor Robert P. Casey and thereafter left Harrisburg—somewhat sadly, but with a real sense of accomplishment and excitement about what the future might hold. We were headed, somewhat surprisingly, for Boston.

I was to have several unexpected opportunities. Secretary of State George Shultz asked if I would be interested in becoming administrator of the Agency for International Development, and Attorney General Edwin Meese asked if I would consider appointment as director of the FBI. I had no strong desire to take on the important AID responsibility toward the end of the Reagan administration, and the ten-year term of the FBI appointment called for a commitment I was not ready to make. I thus respectfully declined both offers. Predictably, the FBI feeler was leaked, but it was only a one-day story. Thus ended my second courtship with this respected institution (the first having occurred toward the beginning of the Carter administration).

In November 1986, I had attended a conference at the Institute of Politics (IOP) at Harvard's John F. Kennedy School of Government. Shortly thereafter, the retiring IOP director, Jonathan Moore, called to ask if I were interested in his position. After a whirlwind series of interviews, I was named the new director in early January. I was honored that the announcement of my appointment called me "a very successful governor and practicing politician who, like President John F. Kennedy, whom the Institute memorializes, has a deep personal commitment to public life and government as a high calling."

I also rejoined Kirkpatrick & Lockhart, which had opened an office in Boston. I had maintained contact with my former colleagues during my time in Harrisburg, my major contribution being a raucous rendition of "Mack the Knife" à la Louis Armstrong at their 1981 retreat. I am sure colleagues who did not know me were relieved that I was not then a member of the firm. Once again, however, I had very little time for the practice of law. My other pursuits included service on the boards of Rite Aid Corporation, ARCO Chemicals and Merrill Lynch.

The IOP was a unique and fascinating place. It offered fellowships for public figures who were between jobs or on sabbatical; lectures, panel discussions and seminars with persons of prominence; and opportunities for Harvard undergraduates to conduct their own programs and write and publish on political issues. As I told the *Harvard University Gazette* in an introductory interview, I hoped, as the first director who had been an elected official, to instill in students more enthusiasm for the electoral process and a recognition that "holding public office . . . is an honorable profession." I emphasized careers in state and local government. My bottom line was very specific: "If during my tenure here I can divert a dozen or so of the best and brightest Harvard students from careers in investment banking into the electoral process, I'd consider it a job well done."

Illustrative of the value added by my background was an experience with a class that had chosen our Pennsylvania welfare reform initiative as a case study. The top team of briefers in the class was to make recommendations to me on their world-class welfare reform program. When I entered the classroom, I began,

Whew, what a day! I just had a call from Three Mile Island and had to dispatch the state police to deal with some antinuclear demonstrators there. As I left the office, I heard from one of our correctional institutions where a hunger strike is being carried on by some inmates who claim their religious practices are being inhibited by the administration's policy. Then, just as I got into the car to come here, an aide broke the news that he had me scheduled to meet with the United Way in Philadelphia and an Erie County Republican gathering on the same evening. Next I learn that Representative Trello won't vote for our budget unless we agree to rebuild three miles of highway in Coraopolis. Now, what is it that you're here to talk about?

With each blow, I could see the students blanch as the relative priority of their briefing dropped lower on the busy governor's agenda. The subject to which they had devoted weeks turned out to be a mere blip on the screen of the state's problems. Of course, after the initial shock wore off, we had a spirited and productive discussion of welfare reform, but I doubt if any of those students will ever forget that lesson in context.

In the spring of 1987 I addressed the Wednesday Group, a moderate Republican organization in the House of Representatives, on a "post-Reagan America." I focused on two promising areas where the GOP held the high ground. The first was fiscal integrity, including a balanced-budget amendment, adherence to the targets set by the Gramm-Rudman-Hollings Act and reduced government spending. The second was a renewed commitment to strong state and local governments and a turn away from the centralizing impulses dominant since the 1930s. I also recommended that the GOP embrace its role as the party of business, rather than bobbing and weaving to avoid that label. My closing set forth an ominous scenario: "I believe that traditionally and historically there are real differences between the two parties. The 'difference gap' is being closed because of the emulation by Democrats of what Republicans have accomplished in the past. If imitation is the sincerest form of flattery, we should be flattered. But I would hate to see our thunder stolen." One could well argue that this is precisely what happened in the post-Reagan era. The Republicans failed to produce on their principles, and the Democrats preempted them in the presidential elections of 1992 and especially 1996. Only by a return to these themes in 1994 did Republicans temporarily interrupt the tide. By 2000, these principles had nearly become the conventional wisdom for both parties, one of the reasons that the presidential election that year between Al Gore and George W. Bush was so close.

During this period I also appeared before the Senate Judiciary Committee on behalf of my former Justice Department colleague, Bob Bork, who had been nominated for the Supreme Court. His nomination, an ugly battle fought upon rigid ideological lines, was not aided by his numerous and forthright writings in a variety of areas. My testimony related more to his personal characteristics and was little noted. The nomination was ultimately defeated after an effort that established new and negative norms for the consideration of judicial appointments.

Pennsylvania matters did not entirely escape my attention at this time. Governor Casey and his team were seeking to discredit our accomplishments and to focus more attention on their own agenda. The highly successful "You've Got a Friend in Pennsylvania" effort was scrapped for a limp campaign with the mystifying theme "America Starts Here." An attempt was made to downgrade the widely acclaimed Ben Franklin Partnership until its stakeholders rebelled. In a particularly spiteful bit of foolishness, Labor and Industry Secretary Harris Wofford charged, without proof, that his predecessor, Jim Knepper, had shredded department records before leaving. In June 1987, the administration undertook a concerted effort, at taxpayers' expense, to document "deficiencies" incurred during my tenure. Eventually, even the *Philadelphia Inquirer* took Governor Casey mildly to task. These and other negative reactions finally brought an end to the "Thornburgh bashing."

Back at the IOP, I was working to put together a program of serious research into elective politics. Professors Dick Neustadt of the Kennedy School and Dick Fenno from Rochester proposed creating a center for studying elected politicians and their careers, with an ultimate goal of attracting more and better-qualified people to public office. Unfortunately, some of the IOP's senior advisers were lukewarm about the project, and it ultimately foundered, though I felt it would truly have put the IOP on the map. Another effort, the creation of a clearinghouse of information useful to women candidates, also lost much of its steam after my departure.

During our time in Cambridge, Ginny worked as Harvard's first disability coordinator, serving as advocate for all Harvard students, faculty and staff who had physical, mental or sensory disabilities. This role often put her at odds with the university bureaucracy, but her charm and tenacity usually carried the day. She capped her accomplishments with the publication of the university's first guide to services for persons with disabilities.

ON JULY 9, 1988, I received a message to call A. B. Culvahouse Jr., counsel to President Reagan. The likely purpose of the call was evident. Edwin Meese had announced his intention to resign as attorney general, following a stormy tenure marked by two investigations of his conduct by an independent counsel. Former assistant attorney general Bill Weld had told me that he had recommended that President Reagan appoint me to succeed Meese. Frankly, I had not expected this recommendation to count for much, as I knew Weld was in disfavor with the administration for criticizing Meese. My law enforcement, political and management record, as well as my good relations with the president and vice president, did seem to make me one of the logical candidates, but I was hardly expecting Culvahouse's call.

After meetings with Culvahouse and Ken Duberstein, the president's chief of staff, I met with President Reagan on July 12, and he formally requested that I serve as his attorney general. In announcing my nomination, he described me as "a tough minded crime-buster . . . [and a governor who] won tough mandatory jail terms for violent and repeat criminals. He was in the forefront of the war against drugs, cracking down on drug traffickers and creating preventive education programs." For my part, I promised to help "implement the priorities of the Reagan-Bush administration" and "to follow the evidence wherever it may lead" in the aftermath of the Meese investigations.

Initial responses to my appointment were highly favorable, with the exception of some predictable partisan criticism from Pennsylvania and a distinct lack of enthusiasm on the part of both right-to-life leaders and the more strident pro-choice people. The *New York Times* opined, "Mr. Thornburgh, who made his reputation fighting public corruption, brings an ethical dimension that has rarely been in greater demand." *Time* and *Newsweek* both described my appointment as "Mr. Clean goes to Washington." On the substantive side, many articles praised my strong record as a prosecutor and administrator. I was soon to realize, however, that overly positive reviews were no favor when they gave rise to impossible expectations.

I resigned from my law firm again, and from the corporate boards upon which I served, and took a leave of absence from the Kennedy School. Upon my departure, Dean Graham Allison praised both my work there and my commitment to public service. As something of a token Republican at the IOP, I was gratified by his kind words as well as by my good relations with most of the people there. I had greatly enjoyed my brief tenure and would have stayed much longer if this unexpected opportunity to become the nation's chief law enforcement officer and a member of the president's cabinet had not intervened. For a lawyer, being attorney general is the job of a lifetime. As I delighted in repeating in years to come, "They made me an offer I couldn't refuse."

Some of the policy views I had articulated over the years differed from some of those advanced by the Reagan administration. This and other perceived inconsistencies have caused some observers to wonder aloud whether I am a liberal, a conservative, a former liberal turned conservative, or some other permutation of these labels. In fact, I have always resisted these attempts to label my political philosophy. This has frustrated both political opponents and pundits, who invariably seek to paint the subjects of their scrutiny with as broad a brush as possible. It has also given rise to criticism that I have changed my views over the years on certain issues.

My rejoinder to the latter has always been that my views have, by and large, remained constant; it is the political spectrum itself that has shifted. For example, being strong on civil rights and racial equality (as I have always been) was a "liberal" stance in the 1960s. Today it is a given for any responsible public figure. On the other side of the coin, the pathbreaking welfare reform proposal that we pursued in Pennsylvania in the early 1980s was denounced by liberal observers as "radical" and "reactionary." By the end of the century, however, it had been overshadowed by much more stringent congressional enactments approved on a bipartisan basis and trumpeted by Democratic president Bill Clinton as a major achievement.

Another factor contributing to some observers' frustration in attempting to assign me an overarching political philosophy has been my almost constant involvement in the executive branch. Legislators are free to opine on almost any issue that catches their fancy and to propose solutions to any issue that appears on their radar screen. While the executive branch also must respond to current public concerns, governors or cabinet members are much more restricted to "playing the hand that is dealt them." Management and practical responses to developing day-to-day situations occupy much of their time, often requiring more pragmatism than dogma.

Further confounding any attempt to pigeonhole my political philosophy, I have indeed held some views that are classically "liberal" and others that are similarly "conservative." Among the former are my support of civil rights initiatives, such as the Americans with Disabilities Act and the ill-fated Equal Rights Amendment; a longtime commitment to providing legal counsel to the indigent; support for self-determination for Puerto Rico and the District of Columbia; strong support of anti–hate crime laws and prosecutions; and advocacy of an effective UN. Balanced against these are classic "conservative" causes, such as support for a limited, constitutional death penalty; opposition to abortion upon demand; vigorous prosecution of antiobscenity laws; and resistance to legalization or decriminalization of drug offenses. Devising a simple label for such a varied menu would challenge even the most astute analyst. All this prompted one intimate to characterize my position as "Keep 'em guessing."

Finally, there is the phenomenon of compromise. Too many Americans now trust no one in high public office. "They all lie," too many citizens think. "They constantly compromise and sell out their principles." During my public life, I found the vast majority of those with whom I worked to be decent and honorable men and women of integrity and commitment, often serving at great personal sacrifice. How do we come, as a nation, to so disrespect such persons?

I believe it is because we fail to make an important distinction. Those in high office occasionally do lie or compromise their principles, and such behavior deserves public condemnation. But "politics," as has been observed, "is the art of the possible." And constructive compromise is the essence of the craft of politics. While no one should compromise on matters of principle, compromise in pursuit of principle is a necessary part of the political process, often prompting those in public life to properly forgo the lesser for the greater good.

As for whether I agreed with every element of the Reagan and Bush agendas, I have always been of the view that the president sets the agenda for his administration. If subordinates do not accept that agenda, their proper course is to resign and be replaced by someone loyal to the president. Fortunately, I never faced any differences of such magnitude. Those that I did face are discussed in the following chapters; in each case, I remained completely comfortable with continuing to serve the president in question.

Another speculation that periodically arose throughout my public career was whether my ultimate goal was to become president myself. Anyone achieving high office in a major state is assumed to aspire to even higher office. Such speculation about me had followed our upset win in 1978 and the notoriety resulting from TMI. Among some of my senior staff members, there were stirrings about a potential presidential or vice presidential candidacy in 1980. I did go to the 1980 Republican convention with some thought of being taken seriously as a vice presidential contender, but my heart wasn't in it. It all seemed so improbable. Being among those consulted by Governor Reagan as to whom he should choose as a running mate seemed about as close to the process as I should properly be.

Those of us who seek public office do, of course, aspire to the highest level possible. We are, by definition, ambitious individuals. For some reason this is looked upon with suspicion, but I have never apologized for it. I was indeed ambitious to do the very best that I could at the highest level I could achieve.

Nevertheless, I had little or no interest in the presidency. Having already achieved a position far beyond my expectations, I was never, in my mind, able to project myself beyond the office of governor. Even when former fellow governors such as Republicans Pete du Pont and Lamar

Alexander and Democrats Bruce Babbitt, Mike Dukakis, Bob Kerrey and Bill Clinton entered into serious competition for the presidency, I did not envision myself doing so. I thought that my record in office was at least as good as theirs, but I never viewed myself in the same light as they apparently viewed themselves. My short-lived exploration of a presidential campaign in 1988 was utterly halfhearted. And the rumors of a vice presidential nod that year were more a source of amusement than anything else. I never heard a word from the Bush camp on the subject. Nevertheless, after a number of other prospective nominees had been told they were off the list, many reporters assumed I was among the finalists. Eventually, of course, Senator Dan Quayle of Indiana was chosen. It was later reported that I had, in fact, been under serious consideration, polling data having shown that I would help the Bush ticket carry Pennsylvania. As it turned out, however, who occupied the number two spot appeared to be of little consequence in the ultimate Bush victory.

My lack of interest in becoming president did not, of course, mean that I did not have a political agenda. Ideas and programs alone would never carry the day. Dealing with political forces, including parties and special interests, was part of the process, and I enjoyed it. But I never had to slant either my political maneuverings or my policy positions toward a potential presidential campaign, and I considered this liberating. Even at this late date, I feel compelled to protest having been unfairly measured against other people's goals for me, rather than those I set myself. On the wall of my office in the State Capitol was mounted a framed quotation from Pennsylvania author John O'Hara's novel *Ten North Frederick*: "Any son of a bitch who thinks he'd like to be President of the United States ought to try being Governor of Pennsylvania for a few years." Far from expressing any aspiration of mine, this was a reminder of just how tough my present job was.

Analysis of political careers and motivations is a difficult task, to be sure. But a little less glibness and more attention to the actual record in the context of the hurly-burly and give and take of our political process would surely help.

MY RETURN TO Washington was an eye-opener. For the past eleven years, I had not been immersed in the day-to-day intrigue that characterizes the upper levels of our federal government. My previous service at the subcabinet level also had not prepared me for the scrutiny and suspicion focused on those in more prominent positions by the 1980s. Worse, there was far less of the civility and mutual respect that I recalled between federal officials, on the one hand, and the press and Congress, on the other. Relations had become more and more antagonistic during the Reagan years.

On August 5, the morning of my Senate Judiciary Committee hearing, I got a taste of the new climate. The *Wall Street Journal* ran a strange story alleging that while serving as assistant attorney general, I had participated in a scheme to withhold from Congress information on the involvement of Manuel Noriega in drug trafficking. (I suspected, but had no proof, that this story had come from a former strike force leader who strongly opposed my redirection of our efforts against organized crime.) I had very little recollection of the Noriega matter, but at the hearing I took note of the eternal conflict between Congress and the Justice Department over the sharing of files related to ongoing criminal investigations—a matter that was to haunt my tenure as attorney general from start to finish. It happened that U.S. District Judge Mark Wolf of Boston, who had served as an aide to Ed Levi, was watching the hearings on C-SPAN. He recalled the matter well, knew that I had had nothing to do with any improper withholding of information and was thoughtful enough to telephone me at the lunch hour to that effect. I cleared the matter up at the outset of the afternoon session, and the balance of the proceedings was largely uneventful.

Conservative Republicans raised the principal concerns about my nomination. Senator Gordon Humphrey of New Hampshire, for example, pressed me on the abortion issue. My response was direct: "I think *Roe v. Wade* was wrong, but it is now the law of the land." Only if the proper case presented itself would the department seek to challenge the ruling, and, in such a case, I "wouldn't hesitate to proceed." I had to remind him that I was the Thornburgh in *Thornburgh v. American College of Obstetricians and Gynecologists*, in which the Supreme Court had ruled, 5–4, against overruling *Roe* in a challenge to the law regulating abortions that was passed while I was Pennsylvania's governor. Other senators, Republicans and Democrats alike, seemed more relieved at Meese's departure than enthusiastic about my arrival. Senator Ted Kennedy's support, largely a product of our recent IOP affiliation, sent a positive signal to other Democrats. My nomination was unanimously approved by the Senate.

I was sworn in on August 12, but Ed Meese stole the headlines by ordering extension of the independent counsel statute to members of Congress. This somewhat petulant act reflected his own encounters with the independent counsel process, which had resulted in no prosecution but had severely crimped his tenure as attorney general. While I too opposed the independent counsel statute, I eventually vacated the Meese order on the ground that two wrongs don't make a right. Supporters of Meese's action argued that the worse the process became, the more likely it was to be repealed! This was not an area where reason bested emotions.

TO MY REGRET, Jay Waldman could not join me at the department, as he was assuming a well-deserved seat on the U.S. District Court in the Eastern District of Pennsylvania. Robin Ross came aboard to serve as my executive assistant and Murray Dickman to handle personnel and administrative matters as well as deal with the White House and the Hill on sensitive items. From Harrisburg also came Barry Stern, Henry Barr, Dick Weatherbee, Barry Hartman, Barbara Drake, Cuyler Walker and Bill Snyder. Predictably, these folks were tagged "the Pennsylvania Mafia" and were resented by some of the entrenched bureaucracy. Such tension between the attorney general's staff and the civil servants in the department is typical. Nevertheless, a cadre of people who "know the boss" is absolutely essential in managing a large operation, particularly in the early days of a new regime.

One amusing sidelight to my return was the apparent consternation at the *Washington Post* as to my proper name. I was used to the conflict over "Richard" and "Dick" from my gubernatorial days, but the *Post*'s concern reached a much higher level. "Leaked" to me was a solemn document resolving the issue as follows:

In the matter of Richard L. or Dick Thornburgh, we decide that his official use of the first name of Dick as governor of Pennsylvania and attorney general of the United States is of sufficient consistency and duration to warrant our use of it as his name in the *Washington Post*. We find Jimmy Carter and Jim Wright to be precedents, even though they established their first name usages at earlier stages of their career (*sic*). We are confounded by the case of Robert J. or Bob Dole, but note that it is not at issue here. We will continue to judge each future case on its own merits.

Justice [Ben] Bradlee's suggestion that we also explain to readers what Thornburgh has done with his name is ruled moot because [Ruth] Marcus has done that in the *Post*. The suggestion of Tom Wilkinson, of counsel to the court, that we have readers vote on this by coupon . . . is denied.

By unanimous vote of the three-judge panel: Bradlee, Downie and Silberman.

It must have been a slow news day at the *Post*!

When Secretary of Defense Dick Cheney was reported to face a similar quandary ("stuff is coming across my desk signed Richard B., but I still sign Dick," he said), I sent him a limerick advising him to stick with Dick. As reported by columnist William Safire, "That advice from counsel did it; Mr. Cheney's formal name is no longer Richard, but Dick (his friends call him Secdef)."

MY CONTACT WITH President Reagan during the remaining five months of his presidency was infrequent. I was quite fond of the Reagans, however, and regarded him as perhaps the best intuitive politician ever to serve in the office, despite his obvious lack of the policy "wonk" instincts that possess so many of us in public life. And Nancy Reagan always went out of her way to be gracious.

I also enjoyed a cordial relationship with the vice president, but my continued service in a Bush administration was by no means assured. For this reason, Ginny remained in Cambridge, enjoying her job at Harvard. Until the summer of 1989 we commuted on weekends, and for the most part I had to take on the Washington social scene as a bachelor. Ginny's absence gave me an excuse to avoid many otherwise unappealing events, but it was still second best. One occasion she was obliged to miss was a dinner at the home of Katharine Graham, publisher of the *Washington Post*, in honor of Nick Brady's and my arrival. Mrs. Graham, regularly numbered among Washington's true power brokers, was always most gracious to Ginny and me, although we were never among her intimates. After the election, news articles speculated that I might be replaced, but on November 19, President-elect Bush asked that I stay on as attorney general. He then spelled out his principal goals for me, all of which were priorities of my own as well:

Install a "Bush team" in the Department of Justice and compatible legal counsel in the other departments.

Undertake more outreach and a "kinder, gentler" approach on civil rights matters, and secure more African American appointees.

Aggressively prosecute savings and loan and other white-collar crooks.

In cooperation with the new drug czar, keep the pressure on drug traffickers, with particular attention to Mexico and other Latin American countries.

Work with White House Counsel Boyden Gray on the appointment of "strict constructionist" judges who would "interpret and not make" laws.

Prepare especially for potential Supreme Court appointments.

Look for opportunities to strengthen the power of the executive branch through court cases or legislation.

Help in a coordinated effort to deal with ethical problems.

The first two months of the Bush administration were given over to the transition, including the filling of important positions within the department. Though a list of suggested candidates for major appointments came from the White House, the ultimate appointees came more from the ranks of seasoned and respected lawyers, consistent with my desire for a more professional, less political department. A real triumph was the recruitment of U.S. Court of Appeals Judge Ken Starr to serve as solicitor general. Bill Barr headed the Office of Legal Counsel; Dick Stewart took over the Environment and Natural Resources Division; Stuart Gerson was named to head the Civil Division; Shirley Peterson became the first woman to lead the Tax Division; and Jim Rill took charge of the Antitrust Division. Gene McNary took over the Immigration and Naturalization Service (INS), Mike Moore the Marshals Service. Holdovers included Bill Sessions at the FBI, Jack Lawn at the DEA, Ed Dennis at the Criminal Division and Rick Abbell, later replaced by Jimmy Gurulé, at the Office of Criminal Justice Programs. Carol Crawford headed our Office of Legislative Affairs but was soon succeeded by Lee Rawls. On the staff side, three months into my responsibilities, I recruited Dave Runkel from the IOP to join me as press secretary. Unfortunately, we had already lost valuable time in establishing a decent working relationship with reporters covering the department.

13

Battling White-Collar Crime

On October 7, 1988, I addressed the staff of the department to spell out my priorities: a vigorous assault on drug trafficking, a continued focus on organized and white-collar crime and stepped-up activity in the civil rights, antitrust and environmental fields. I also asked that the department "speak with one voice" to the public, the press and Congress so as to avoid giving aid and comfort to our critics, and closed with my familiar request that there be "no surprises . . . whether it's good news or bad, I want to hear it first from you and not from some other source." Both these requests were to be misinterpreted in later days.

My highest substantive priority for the department at this time was white-collar crime. The excesses of the 1980s had left a substantial inventory of challenges in the area I frequently identified as "crime in the suites." The crest of the savings and loan scandal was about to break. Operation Ill Wind, involving serious allegations of procurement fraud in the defense industry, was ongoing. Insider trading and junk bond scams were in the headlines with increasing frequency. Money laundering had become big business as a result of the increasing amounts of cash generated by the drug lords. And official corruption persisted.

More often than not, these operations crossed state and even national boundaries and were thus beyond the reach of even the best state and local law enforcement agencies. Moreover, the operators were highly sophisticated, using modern technology to carry out elaborate deceptions and taking advantage of the highest-priced legal and accounting advice available. Investigators and accountants working for the FBI, the IRS, the Postal Service and the Securities and Exchange Commission (SEC) were among the few with skills to ferret out these illegal operations. Working hand in glove with experienced federal prosecutors, they painstakingly followed paper or electronic trails over months, if not years.

The wrongdoing in these cases was potentially subversive of important American institutions of business, labor and government. If citizens perceived that those who preyed upon these institutions were above the law, cynicism about our entire system could result. I was therefore gratified by the subsequent comment of one of the preeminent white-collar defense lawyers, Bob Bennett of Skadden, Arps, Slate, Meagher & Flom, that "in response to the perception of corporate excesses in the 1980s . . . the federal government had stepped up its prosecution of white-collar crime to perhaps the highest level in American history." That was precisely the goal I set in the fall of 1988.

Since these cases often involved high-profile individuals and organizations, they were of considerable interest to investigative reporters and legislative committees. Unlike our investigators and prosecutors, however, these reporters and legislators were not obliged to accumulate legally admissible evidence sufficient to prove specific criminal charges beyond a reasonable doubt before a judge and jury. They were free to publicize mere allegations of wrongdoing and often seemed to believe that, immediately following their revelations, those "charged" should be put behind bars without delay. When this did not occur, they accused law enforcement agencies of cover-ups or foot dragging. Seldom did considerations of due process intrude. In extreme cases, they demanded that special prosecutors be appointed to overcome the alleged lassitude or venality of law enforcement personnel. Ethical and due process considerations utterly preclude responsible investigators and prosecutors from responding to such allegations with progress reports on their cases. Unauthorized "leaks" that have come increasingly to be used for that purpose are equally improper.

THE MOST PRESSING challenge in the area of white-collar crime at the outset of the Bush administration was the savings and loan mess. Most Americans were as unaware as I was how this industry had changed during the go-go 1980s. (Pennsylvania, under Banking Secretary Ben McEnteer's sound leadership, had been able to avoid any major problems.) Our images were still of Jimmy Stewart's Bailey Building & Loan in the movie *It's a Wonderful Life*. Heavily lobbied congressional action and regulatory cupidity had, however, transformed the thrift business from a nurturer of the American dream of home ownership into a nightmare of excessive lending against vastly overvalued commercial and speculative properties from accounts now insured for up to $100,000. The Justice Department obviously needed to pursue those criminally responsible for the collapse of these institutions.

I convened a session of the government-wide Financial Institution Fraud Task Force to develop our plans. Given the obvious scope of the problem and the president's directive to make it a priority, a major new initiative was needed. We turned for our model to the Dallas Task Force, which coordinated all the relevant federal investigative agencies to tackle the large number of allegations regarding criminal activities in Texas savings and loans. Proposing to replicate this task force in twenty-seven cities across the country, we sought congressional authorization for about $50 million to fund 200 additional FBI agents, 100 new prosecutors and 30 additional attorneys. The White House lent its approval, and I presented our request to the Senate Banking Committee on February 9, 1989, just a month following President Bush's inauguration. We did not get the authority to hire our additional personnel until the beginning of 1990, but our redeployment strategy had already enabled us to jump-start the operation in many cities.

Meanwhile, the Justice Department and all others with responsibilities in this area were taking a heavy beating in Congress and the media for perceived previous inactivity. Part of this was bravado; the politicians and the press were obviously embarrassed over their own failure to spot the developing debacle in the thrift industry all through the 1980s. And some of it was plainly partisan, such as claims that we should have investigated and indicted Neil Bush, the president's son, for his involvement with a Denver savings and loan. In reality, those investigating the savings and loan cases never gave the department any evidence of criminal conduct on the part of Neil Bush, and we were not about to commence investigating him simply because he was related to the president.

Suzanne Garment's excellent book *Scandal* quotes Jerry Landauer of the *Wall Street Journal* on this process in general: "[I]n the capital these days a scandal isn't a scandal until important segments of the media 'discover' it. Once perceived, a scandalous situation is likely to dominate the news, for no newspaper editor or television executive wants to miss another Watergate. Then, as more newspeople pounce on the story, competitive pressures can overshadow fair play, resulting in overstated coverage that may not end until another 'scandal' comes along to divert the media's attention."

Criticism of our efforts reached a low point with the allegation by Democratic congressmen and party officials that 21,000 criminal cases growing out of the S&L scandals had been referred to the department without a single resulting indictment. In reality, the 21,000 figure covered all financial institutions, not just savings and loans, and included a multitude of cases of tellers lifting a couple of dollars from the cash drawer. Moreover, a sizable number of highly successful prosecutions had already been undertaken, and our redeployed units were beginning to have a real impact.

A principal problem in responding to such allegations was the lack of an adequate information system. I was horrified to discover that there was simply no database quantifying prosecutions, convictions or recoveries. I made a fervent plea to our prosecutors to help us produce accurate statistics, pointing out that otherwise we could not respond to irresponsible charges leveled at their efforts, and they would not receive adequate credit for their work. By the time I left the department, a much-improved reporting system was in place.

Its numbers told an impressive story. Our task forces obtained nearly 600 convictions, a 93 percent conviction rate, between October 1, 1988, and August 1, 1991, with 77 percent of those convicted receiving jail terms. Those successfully prosecuted included infamous operators such as Don R. Dixon and Woody Lemons of Vernon Savings and Loan; Jarrett E. Woods Jr. of Western Savings Association; Thomas Merrill Gaubert, Ed McBirney and Danny Faulkner, all involved in the collapse of institutions in Texas (where 40 percent of the nation's thrift failures occurred); David Paul of Miami's Centrust Bank; and Janet Faye McKinzie, Charles Knapp and Charles Keating Jr. of Lincoln Savings and Loan. Working with other agencies, we recouped substantial amounts that officers had fleeced from thrifts and also obtained recoveries from law firms and accountants involved in the losses.

Perhaps the best exemplar of the S&L rip-off artists was Don Dixon, about whom John M. Barry wrote in his book *The Ambition and the Power*:

Dixon had milked the Vernon Savings and Loan dry. [By 1986,] 96 percent of Vernon's loans, over one billion dollars' worth, were in default. Dixon had paid himself $8.8 million in salary and bonuses over a four-year period, while using company money to buy a $2 million home for himself in California. He spent another $800,000 of company money to maintain it for a little over a year and then sold it, at a loss, to a business partner. Vernon supplied the mortgage. And Dixon had not one airplane, but five: two jets, two propeller-driven aircraft, and one helicopter, along with six full-time pilots, all servicing this one 'thrift.' Dixon had taken over a solvent, respectable business and raped it.

On the whole, I believe the S&L mess cleanup was one of the most successful white-collar prosecution efforts ever undertaken by the department. But by the time the painstaking evidence-gathering process had been completed and the lengthy lawsuits had run their course, both Congress and the media had moved on. To this day, the department is often publicly characterized as having dragged its feet on the savings and loan scandal. In 1995, as the effort wound down, the Clinton administration noted that "[w]ith the help of the federal regulatory and investigative agencies, the Justice Department has achieved tremendous success in bringing to justice those who looted our nation's financial institutions during the 1980s." Perhaps, with the help of such long-overdue assessments, history may yet treat our efforts more positively.

THE NEXT SCANDAL involved a worldwide money-laundering and fraud operation conducted by the Bank of Credit and Commerce International (BCCI). This Luxembourg-based bank, owned largely by Abu Dhabi interests and doing business in some seventy-two countries, was a testament to the internationalization of the world's economy and financial systems. Its money-laundering activities were similarly a testament to the internationalization of crime, particularly drug trafficking.

BCCI's money laundering first came to light as a result of a three-year undercover investigation by the U.S. Customs Service in Tampa, Florida. An indictment charging BCCI and five of its officials with violations of the federal money-laundering statutes was returned in October 1988, shortly after I had assumed office. The bank pleaded guilty in January 1990 and forfeited $15 million in assets, the highest money-laundering penalty that had ever been exacted under federal laws. The Federal Reserve Board was also given authority to review BCCI's future operations. The BCCI officials involved were convicted in December 1990 and received jail terms of up to twelve years.

Further investigations were then undertaken by federal grand juries in other parts of the country and by authorities in many other countries where

BCCI conducted business. In the midst of these efforts, however, a media cyclone engulfed the entire matter, fueled in no small part by partisan and personal agendas developed through congressional hearings.

From the outset of the BCCI prosecution, I had used the bank as a prime example of the type of sophisticated operation that law enforcement had to face in tracing the flow of drug money. Sensitive to the ongoing nature of the investigation and the need to discuss only those facts already on the public record, we were able, nonetheless, to begin to alert the public and the industry to this important facet of the international drug-trafficking problem. I discussed the case with audiences across the country and with congressional committees.

In 1990, however, Senator John Kerry (D–Mass.) began alleging that the department had dragged its feet on the BCCI investigation and was indifferent to pursuing it to a successful conclusion. The Tampa charges were described as a "slap on the wrist" in spite of the unprecedented nature of the sentences. Vague allegations were also made about illegal CIA involvement with BCCI and its supposed influence on our decisions. Another source of complaint was the department's unwillingness to turn over its case files for use by other prosecutors and congressional investigating committees. The reason for this reluctance was well stated by Paul Maloney, deputy assistant attorney general in the Criminal Division, at a hearing before the Senate Banking Committee's Subcommittee on Consumer and Regulatory Affairs on May 23, 1991: "[L]aw enforcement suffers when an investigation is conducted in public. Sources dry up, persons who might be inclined to cooperate with the government are less inclined to do so, ongoing undercover operations may be compromised, and the targets of the investigation, having been apprised of what the government is after, have an opportunity to fabricate evidence, and coordinate their stories before they are approached by law enforcement agents."

Charges of law enforcement incompetence, or worse, at the federal level got a boost in the summer of 1991, when Manhattan District Attorney Robert Morgenthau's office produced a series of spectacular BCCI indictments under New York law. These eventually included as defendants such prominent persons as former White House counsel Clark Clifford and his law partner, Robert Altman.

Meanwhile, however, as a result of our own grand jury investigations, federal racketeering indictments were returned in December 1991. BCCI eventually pleaded guilty to these charges and related New York charges;

forfeited all of its assets in the United States, valued at some $550 million; and agreed to cooperate in related ongoing investigations. The back of BCCI operations worldwide had been broken. In May 1994, Swaleh Naqvi, the bank's former president, was surrendered to the FBI by officials of Abu Dhabi. He pleaded guilty to the criminal charges against him and received an eleven-year jail term after agreeing to cooperate in the continuing investigation. Abu Dhabi officials also made available considerable documentation that, it was hoped, would help in finally unwinding the complicated BCCI story. By 1996, the department's aggressive use of the forfeiture laws had recovered nearly $800 million, virtually all of which was earmarked for distribution to victims of various BCCI frauds through a Worldwide Victims Fund managed by court-appointed liquidators. Meanwhile, the more newsworthy of Morgenthau's indictments crashed and burned: a jury acquitted Altman in June 1993, and the charges against the aging and ailing Clifford were dismissed.

Once again, however, by the time these matters were resolved, media, congressional and public attention had moved on. In the public's memory, the splendid efforts of federal law enforcement authorities were buried by the more sensational unfounded charges made against them. Illustrative of the misinformation given to the public is an Oliphant cartoon that appeared in the *Washington Post* on April 5, 1992. Entitled "Emergency Meeting of the Board of Directors of BCCI," it depicts a sinister group gathered around a table. One asks, "Boss, does this mean we're all going to jail?" The response: "Relax, will ya? What about the savings and loans scams—Did anyone go to jail?" The implied answer is obvious, but the record in both cases clearly shows the contrary.

THE MOST SERIOUS challenge to the department's integrity in a major white-collar crime investigation during my tenure grew out of the inquiry by the U.S. attorney's office in Atlanta into activities of the Banca Nazionale del Lavoro (BNL). BNL is Italy's largest bank, with 424 branches; it is headquartered in Rome, and the Italian government owns nearly all of its stock. Its small Atlanta branch had extended over $5.5 billion in loans and letters of credit to benefit the government of Iraq and institutions that it controlled, all in violation of the bank's internal rules. The U.S. attorney's office began preparing charges against Christopher Drogoul, the bank's manager, and others in the Atlanta office. At this point our Fraud Section in Washington began to suspect that the culpability of persons in the bank's Italian offices might not have been adequately investigated. The Criminal Division subjected the matter to a full review beginning in January 1990.

The Italian government was concerned about the investigation. Like the Atlanta prosecutors, it took the view that the bank was the principal victim of Drogoul's operation and that senior officials in Rome were not implicated. The files of Italian Ambassador Renaldo Petrignani apparently show that he raised the matter with me at some time, but I have no recollection of any such discussion. In any event, whatever efforts the ambassador might have made to affect the department's proceedings were fruitless. I took no action whatsoever to influence the department's handling of the matter.

Once again, however, a congressional investigation preempted public attention. Representative Henry Gonzalez (D-Tex.) undertook a series of hearings and issued a steady stream of volatile reports accusing the department and, in some cases, me personally of a vast cover-up of illegal lending by BNL. Ironically, he characterized the review of the case in Washington as an attempt to limit the prosecution and protect Italian officials from facing charges, when it was just the opposite. Once again, CIA involvement was hinted at, and every action undertaken by law enforcement officials came to be viewed in its most sinister light.

On February 28, 1991, I announced that the Atlanta grand jury had returned a 347-count indictment charging ten persons with conspiracy, mail fraud and wire fraud in connection with more than $4 billion in loans and credit extensions by BNL's Atlanta office for the benefit of the government of Iraq. Those charged included Drogoul, two other bank employees, a Turkish-owned corporation operating in New York and its manager, an Iraqi government-owned bank and four Iraqi officials. As expected, reporters expressed incredulity over the length of the investigation, hinted at interference in our inquiry and, in one case, accused me personally of delaying the indictment.

Our most persistent nemesis in the press was noted *New York Times* columnist William Safire, who affixed himself to the BNL case like a leech and styled it "Iraqgate." Safire had, by this time, constituted himself a one-man Dick Thornburgh wrecking crew. Back at the end of the Ford administration, he had concocted a theory that I had quashed a potential prosecution of Georgia bank official Bert Lance, who was slated to become President Carter's budget director. According to Safire, I had curried favor with the Carter administration to advance my aspiration to become director of the FBI. In fact, the decision not to prosecute was made by U.S. Attorney John Stokes in Georgia in December 1976, at least three months before I had any discussions with the Carter administration about the FBI post. Safire had launched other attacks upon me, but Iraqgate was to prove the longest-running. His principal goal was for me to appoint an independent counsel to investigate the alleged cover-up and pursue those he supposed criminally responsible. I refused to do this, because of both my established misgivings about the independent counsel statute and the total lack of any basis for Safire's charges.

Drogoul pleaded guilty. However, at his sentencing hearing before Senior Judge Marvin Shoob in September 1992, he made new allegations of wrongdoing that resulted in his withdrawing his guilty plea and in Shoob's expressing the view that a cover-up had taken place. The judge subsequently recused himself from the matter, which ended with Drogoul's pleading guilty again in September 1993 and being sentenced to three years in prison.

My successor, Attorney General Bill Barr, in October 1992 appointed former U.S. attorney and federal judge Frederick Lacey to carry out an investigation of the entire matter. Filed on December 8, 1992, Judge Lacey's report found that "the evidence collected and developed . . . provided an insufficient basis on which to seek the indictment of BNL," and that the "decision to pursue a prosecution theory in which BNL-Rome was a 'victim' was entirely proper." Lacey examined in detail the allegations that I had attempted to obstruct the investigation and found that I had not. Instead, I had "sought to prevent disclosure he feared would damage a complex and important prosecution."

None of this slaked Bill Safire's thirst; he continued to insist upon the appointment of an independent counsel, lacing some twenty of his columns with diatribes against all allegedly involved in a BNL cover-up. Shrill charges also emanated from *U.S. News & World Report*. Its editor in chief, Mortimer B. Zuckerman, claimed that "[f]ederal investigators were blocked by Bush's attorney general, Dick Thornburgh, from traveling to Rome and Istanbul to track down those who had knowledge of the fraudulent loans to Iraq." This allegation is ludicrous on its face; no attorney general would become involved in the approval of travel plans for investigators. Judge Lacey's report confirmed that no such event had occurred.

The popular television program *60 Minutes* had chimed in with its usual sensationalized treatment in the form of an interview with Congressman Gonzalez on the eve of the 1992 presidential election. The program plowed no new ground but did elicit an observation from Mike Wallace that both Bill Barr and I might belong behind bars. The kickoff by Wallace set the tone:

Mike Wallace: What I hear you saying, Mr. Chairman, is that Dick Thornburgh, when he was attorney general, and William Barr, now that he is attorney general, have been involved in obstruction of justice.

Congressman Gonzalez: Yes, sir.

Foreign Policy subsequently published a study by Kenneth L. Juster entitled "The Myth of Iraqgate." Juster noted that "unproven allegations about . . . White House interference in the BNL investigations, and efforts to obstruct congressional investigations were repeated in the media so often that they were often regarded as established facts." Stuart Taylor Jr., in a November 1994 *American Lawyer* article entitled "Mediagate: Anatomy of a Feeding Frenzy," noted that every one of the allegations and innuendoes of criminality was "unsupported by credible evidence in 1992 and has since been proven false." He noted that the stories had resulted in "the smearing of innocent officials and the spread of cynicism about government, the media, and public affairs." Safire's columns were styled "some of the worst yellow journalism ever to appear under a prominent byline"; *60 Minutes* was accused of airing, "with no hint of skepticism, outlandish charges by sources of low credibility"; Gonzalez's charges were labeled as "magnified and unfounded"; and Judge Shoob's "error-plagued innuendos of a Justice Department cover-up and clamoring for a special prosecutor" were identified as giving "the scandalmania a patina of apolitical respectability." What Taylor called "[t]he biggest lie of all" was "to say that attorneys general Dick Thornburgh and Bill Barr rigged a cover-up by obstructing justice as Gonzalez (also on *60 Minutes*) and Safire asserted, without qualification, and as others, including Judge Shoob, the *New York Times* and the *Washington Post* hinted more circumspectly."

The matter should have finally been laid to rest by an exhaustive 119-page report prepared by John Hogan, counselor to Attorney General Janet Reno, in late 1994. The report characterized the case as "one of the most complex fraud cases that the Department has ever confronted" and, in essence, adopted Judge Lacey's findings. It found no basis for the appointment of an independent counsel and concluded: "I have found no evidence of corruption or incompetence in the conduct of the investigation. On the contrary, the work of the Department and other agencies has by and large been thorough, persistent and careful." Most important to me was the specific finding that "[t]he decision not to indict BNL or personnel of BNL outside the Atlanta agency was not politically influenced."

ABC-TV news correspondent Robert Zelnick thereafter recounted his own efforts to rebut the conventional media treatment of the BNL matter. Astoundingly, the *Washington Post* had rejected his submission to its Outlook section on the basis that it was only interested "in an article establishing the culpability of the Bush administration."

PERHAPS OUR MOST bizarre white-collar encounter was the INSLAW case, which resulted in no prosecution but consumed an inordinate amount of time. INSLAW (the Institute for Law and Social Research) had been engaged in 1982 to provide management information software to the Department of Justice under a contract providing that the system was to remain the department's property. After this contract was terminated, INSLAW claimed that the department had "pirated" an enhanced version of the package and sued for damages, claiming ownership in the enhancements. The U.S. Court of Appeals threw out the claim in 1990.

By this time, however, INSLAW's owners, a couple by the name of Hamilton, had constructed the mother of all conspiracy theories and sought to discredit all who had come in contact with the matter, ultimately including me, by dint of my office. The media accorded INSLAW a measure of credibility because it was represented by former attorney general Elliot Richardson, who wasted little time in corresponding with me on the matter shortly after I took office. Having no desire to get involved in what I thought was a routine contract dispute, I dispatched it to the appropriate levels within the department, expecting to hear no more of it.

I did not count on the persistence and apparent persuasiveness of the Hamiltons and their counsel. The matter was taken up by media "heavies" such as Jack Kilpatrick and *Washington Post* columnist Mary McGrory, as well as by the staff of Representative Jack Brooks (D-Tex.), the powerful chairman of the House Judiciary Committee. Assistant Attorney General Mike Luttig patiently carried out a seemingly interminable negotiation with the committee's staff, who always seemed to find they had been denied "just one more" file or category of information. The matter came to a boil on July 18, 1991, when I refused to appear before a Judiciary Committee hearing on the 1992 budget authorization. Representative Hamilton Fish (R-N.Y.), the senior Republican member of the committee, had recommended that I not appear, given what he called the "confrontational approach to the oversight hearing" and "the unusual and unnecessary restrictions placed on your ability to present the Justice Department's views."

By then the INSLAW matter had ripened into a cause célèbre with claimed ties to the Iran-Contra scandal, BCCI, the alleged delayed return of the Iran hostages in 1981 and numerous other high-profile matters. The final act in this melodrama was charged to be the "murder" (later ruled a suicide) of an itinerant journalist, Danny Casolaro, in a West Virginia hotel, where he had allegedly gone to meet an informant who would be able to tie all the loose ends of this "scandal" together.

In 1992, Bill Barr was finally driven to appoint yet another special counsel, former federal district court judge Nicholas Bua, to review all the allegations. The judge's 267-page report, rendered in March 1993, discredited the Hamiltons' conspiracy theories, adding, "We cannot fail to note the degree to which William Hamilton's statements and assertions do not withstand scrutiny. We repeatedly encountered witnesses who, in a very credible way, denied making the statements attributed to them by Hamilton." But the story would not go away. Barely six months later, Mary McGrory was calling for Attorney General Reno to appoint an independent counsel to review the INSLAW claims once again. She added, for good measure, another call for an independent counsel to review the BNL matter. The Clinton Justice Department undertook the INSLAW review and reached conclusions similar to those of Judge Bua.

The *Washington Post* illustrated the staying power of these types of stories with a March 1993 editorial listing some chores for incoming Attorney General Reno. It cited INSLAW, BCCI and BNL as prime prospects for immediate attention. "If she certifies," the *Post* noted, "after investigation, that no wrongdoing occurred in the Justice Department with regard to these matters, she will be believed." Since she has, in effect, so certified, perhaps we have finally heard the last of these sorry exercises in media overkill.

Though all officials involved in these so-called scandals were eventually exonerated of any wrongdoing whatsoever, the scandals were enormously distracting, diverting substantial time and resources from our day-to-day responsibilities. Most of those targeted deeply resented the shoot-from-the-hip mentality that permitted these charges to gain currency. It is to their lasting credit that, in most cases, they faithfully persevered in carrying out their duties, despite the unjustified criticism.

THE MOST NOTORIOUS of the major scandals of the 1980s was, of course, the hapless Iran-Contra case. Fortunately, the department had relatively little involvement in this matter. It nearly caused the independent counsel law to self-destruct—which would, in my opinion, have been a positive outcome.

The 1978 statute providing for the appointment of a special prosecutor, later designated an independent counsel, to handle certain criminal investigations was one of the most wretched of the post-Watergate legislative excesses. The theory was that conflicts of interest might preclude the Department of Justice from fairly and impartially investigating and prosecuting certain classes of criminal defendants, most notably those serving at the upper levels of the executive branch. A specially designated panel of judges was to appoint each special prosecutor, and the statute specified the circumstances under which the attorney general would be obliged to seek such an appointment.

Though an independent prosecutor might be desirable under certain very unusual circumstances, in my view the appointment of such a prosecutor should be dictated by political necessity rather than by a statute designed to cover every conceivable contingency. If there is sufficient political or popular pressure to appoint someone outside the department to handle a particular case, that appointment should be made. If not, experienced career prosecutors within the department can handle the case.

I believe history bears out this view. The best-known special prosecutor of the 1970s was Archibald Cox, the first of the Watergate outside lawyers, who was appointed by Attorney General Elliot Richardson when it became politically unacceptable to leave the investigation to "regular" prosecutors. No statute or elaborate procedure was needed. On the other hand, the department at about the same time successfully investigated and prosecuted a sitting vice president, Spiro Agnew, who was obliged to resign after pleading nolo contendere to income tax charges growing out of the receipt of illegal payoffs. No special counsel was needed.

My objection to the institutionalizing of the special prosecutor was, to be sure, based in part upon my pride in the proven capabilities of our "regular" prosecutors. Even more important to me, however, was that the special prosecutor framework very nearly created two separate classes of criminal suspects—those identified in the normal course of a criminal investigation, and those targeted for special treatment before the evidence had even been gathered. Such a double standard seemed inimical to the

American concept of equal justice under the law. Worse, as pointed out by Carter Attorney General Griffin Bell's advisers, the act required appointment of a special prosecutor "to investigate government officials for alleged crimes that would not ordinarily be pursued by federal authorities."

In practice, the act was mischievous in the extreme, subjecting countless executive branch officials to enormous expense and mental anguish, even though the investigations most often resulted in no charges whatsoever. The worst excess was the second of two fruitless investigations of Edwin Meese. Although finding insufficient evidence to justify prosecution, independent prosecutor James McKay's report stated his opinion that Meese had indeed committed criminal acts. I considered this statement both irresponsible and unethical for a prosecutor.

The Iran-Contra case grew out of allegations that our government had secretly sold arms to the Iranians and used the proceeds to arm the Nicaraguan contras conducting guerrilla warfare against the Sandinista government. In 1986, an investigation was undertaken within the White House by a special commission headed by former senator John Tower (R-Tex.). A joint congressional investigating committee then held lengthy public hearings. It fell to independent counsel Lawrence J. Walsh, appointed at the request of Attorney General Meese, to determine whether there had been violations of any federal criminal laws, most notably the Boland amendment, which some interpreted to bar the furnishing of arms to the contras. While a good case was often made that the Walsh inquiry was an attempt to criminalize the political differences that had produced the Boland amendment in the first place, the investigation proceeded apace and produced a number of indictments, including that of Marine Corps colonel and ex-NSC staff member Oliver North, the alleged mastermind of the scheme.

I appropriately delegated most of the day-to-day matters relating to Iran-Contra to career lawyers within the Criminal Division. These experts maintained a very close liaison with the intelligence community in responding to Walsh's requests for documents. Thus, I had almost no direct personal contact with Walsh or his staff. One matter, however, was nondelegable. Congress had passed the Classified Information Procedures Act (CIPA) to deal with the problem of "graymail": defendants' demanding classified materials they claimed were necessary to their defense, hoping that the government would rather forgo prosecution than expose the materials to public view in court. Given the potential damage to national security, it was deemed too risky to leave it to individual judges to make determinations on such materials. CIPA directed the attorney general to determine whether requested material was of such sensitivity as to justify its withholding in the interest of national security.

In January 1989, as the cases were proceeding to trial, Judge Walsh asked to see me. He told me that he felt obliged to dismiss the substantive charges brought against North because the intelligence community had told him that disclosure in court of the evidence substantiating them would be harmful to national security. He proposed therefore to proceed only upon the charges relating to North's alleged false statements to Congress and some other miscellaneous matters. He did not ask that I intervene with the intelligence agencies or otherwise assist in the prosecution. I asked him only two questions: Had the intelligence agencies given him full access to everything he had sought? Was he satisfied that they had dealt with him in good faith? He answered in the affirmative and departed.

My only other contact with the case related to the obstruction of justice and false statement charges brought against one Joseph Fernandez, a CIA operative in Central America, who demanded classified documents in the course of his defense. After an extensive review and close questioning of senior representatives of the Departments of State and Defense, the CIA, the National Security Agency (NSA) and the NSC, I determined that release of the documents would be unjustified and filed the affidavit to that effect required by CIPA. Walsh appealed, claiming the ultimate authority to make this determination, but the appellate courts denied relief. I conducted yet another review and satisfied myself that, if anything, the prospective harm had increased in the interim. The case against Fernandez was thereupon dismissed on Walsh's motion. Walsh's final report harshly criticized my actions in this matter, as did a variety of pundits and columnists.

Walsh's costly and lengthy inquiry continued to collapse about him. While some guilty pleas were obtained, the convictions of North and former national security advisor John Poindexter were thrown out on appeal. Others charged were acquitted, and the whole matter finally wound down. A rather dismal parting shot was the indictment of former secretary of defense Caspar Weinberger on the eve of the 1992 elections in an obvious, and perhaps partly successful, attempt to discredit President Bush, who was later to pardon Weinberger and others before leaving office. Walsh's 566-page report on his $40 million investigation was finally released in 1993 but occasioned little notice. A *Washington Post* editorial found it "flawed by Mr. Walsh's readiness to characterize as crimes alleged acts by officials who were not tried or convicted of them."

Mostly in response to Walsh's excesses, the independent counsel statute was thereafter allowed to lapse, although it was revived during the later inquiry into the alleged wrongdoing of the Clintons in the Whitewater affair. Republicans, no doubt, held the view that what is sauce for the goose must be sauce for the gander. Once again, however, general dissatisfaction with the process caused it to lapse at the end of the Clinton inquiries. I believe it has lapsed for good this time, and that in the future an independent counsel will only be appointed in extraordinary cases like Watergate and Teapot Dome.

ONE OF THE FIRST matters to reach my office in 1998 was an investigation of fraud in the award of Defense Department contracts. Operation Ill Wind was the most intense inquiry ever undertaken into the multibillion-dollar area of military procurement. It had been kicked off by a September 1986 phone call from a small defense contractor to the Naval Investigative Services reporting that a consultant had offered to sell inside information on pending navy contracts. The contractor used a concealed microphone to record subsequent conversations with the consultant, and enough groundwork was laid for extensive court-authorized wiretaps and the execution of forty-four search warrants. These produced considerable evidence of wrongdoing in both Virginia and New York, and I assigned the case to the Eastern District of Virginia.

Assistant U.S. Attorney Joe Aronica and his team ultimately obtained the convictions of fifty-four individuals for schemes involving buying influence or seeking information about competitors' bids. Those convicted included corporate executives; Melvyn R. Paisley, a former assistant secretary of the navy; a former deputy assistant navy secretary; and a former deputy air force secretary. Among the ten defense contractors found guilty were such corporate giants as United Technologies Corporation, Loral Corporation, LTV Aerospace & Defense Company, Grumman Corporation and Litton Systems. More than $250 million in fines and civil penalties were recovered from those convicted, and a powerful message was sent to any who would attempt to "rip off" the nation's military establishment. Ironically, the most accurate evaluation of this effort came from Paisley himself, who had previously responded to a congressional committee's inquiry as to how to deal with corrupt contractors and military officials:

"You've got to hang them from a tree where everyone can see them." Janet Reno would call this "one of the most successful investigations and prosecutions ever undertaken by the Department of Justice against white-collar crime."

ONE RECOMMENDATION on my desk upon my arrival at the Department of Justice came from Rudy Giuliani, a former colleague from the Ford administration, who was then retiring as U.S. attorney for the Southern District of New York and would later become the highly successful mayor of New York City. His office had compiled an impressive record in insider trading cases and similar offenses on Wall Street, and he suggested we could do the same elsewhere if we established securities and commodities fraud task forces in major cities around the country. In January 1989, following this advice, I announced the establishment of such task forces in Chicago, New York, Los Angeles, San Francisco, Kansas City and Denver. Philadelphia, Salt Lake City and Newark were to be added later. These operations acquitted themselves well over the balance of my time in office.

In perhaps the most colorful of these proceedings, the FBI inserted undercover agents onto the floor of the Chicago Mercantile Exchange (Operation Hedgeclipper) and the Chicago Board of Trade (Operation Sourmash) to gather taped evidence of traders cheating customers. RICO and tax and mail fraud indictments were brought against forty-eight traders in the soybean, Japanese yen, treasury bond and Swiss franc pits in August 1989. Most of those involved were convicted.

Guilty pleas and record fines ended the era of high financial flying for Drexel Burnham Lambert and its junk bond impresario, Michael Milken. While criminal securities fraud proceedings had been initiated prior to my becoming attorney general, they came on for trial during 1990 and were a major preoccupation. Ultimately, Drexel pleaded guilty to six felony charges and was hit with a $650 million fine, leading to its bankruptcy and ending its preeminence in corporate financing. Milken's plea earned a ten-year jail sentence and $600 million in penalties. Thus ended a particularly sordid chapter in the "greed decade," which saw so many Wall Street highfliers unmasked as mere criminals.

At the other end of the scale was the successful prosecution of penny-stock king Meyer Blinder, head of Blinder, Robinson & Company, which grew to have offices in sixty-six cities in thirty-seven states before its downfall. Blinder was convicted in 1992 of racketeering, money laundering and securities fraud, sentenced to nearly four years in prison and barred from the securities business for life.

Other "celebrity" white-collar defendants successfully prosecuted included Cincinnati Reds baseball immortal Pete Rose (false tax returns), New York hotel and real estate magnate Leona Helmsley (tax evasion and mail fraud), televangelist Jim Bakker (mail and wire fraud) and sometime presidential candidate Lyndon LaRouche Jr. (mail fraud and obstruction of justice).

PUBLIC CORRUPTION continued to be a high priority. The Public Integrity Section had compiled an enviable record in the most sensitive cases. At the same time, U.S. attorneys continued to pursue corrupt public officials in their districts, often with spectacular results.

Perhaps the most regrettable cases of corruption are those involving federal judges. We had two such cases during my tenure. Judge Robert Aguilar of the Northern District of California was convicted of tipping off the subject of an FBI wiretap; the case was ultimately dismissed in 1996, conditioned upon his leaving the bench. Judge Robert F. Collins of New Orleans was convicted of accepting a $100,000 bribe in a case involving a reduced sentence for a drug smuggler. Such cases invariably cause no little anguish within the department, for the rule of law depends on judges who are not only independent but above suspicion.

Two of our most notable prosecutions involved prominent Republicans. Congressman Patrick Swindall (R- Ga.) was convicted in 1989 of perjury growing out of his alleged involvement in a money-laundering scheme. Former three-term West Virginia governor Arch A. Moore Jr., who had escaped conviction during the Ford administration, finally pleaded guilty to mail fraud, extortion, income tax evasion and obstruction of justice and was given a stiff prison term. I recused myself from this case, as I had come to know the sleek and colorful Moore during our respective terms as governor. I had even campaigned for him briefly during his run against Jay Rockefeller in 1984.

Federal investigators in South Carolina and California used imaginative sting operations to convict a raft of legislators for selling their votes. The practices had been long acknowledged but thought to be beyond the reach of law enforcement.

Not all our efforts in this difficult area were successful. Particularly troublesome were failed attempts to obtain convictions of two black Democratic congressmen, Floyd Flake of New York and Harold Ford of Tennessee. In each case, the Public Integrity Section authorized prosecution by the local U.S. attorney, but juries were not convinced that these popular elected officials should be convicted. The acquittals left the department open to completely unjustified and extremely upsetting charges of targeting black officials. However, these accusations were effectively rebutted by, among other things, the strenuous efforts of our Civil Rights Division, under the Voting Rights Act, to open up more elective posts for African American candidates across the country and our impressive overall record of convictions in the public integrity area.

14

Crime-Fighting in the
Department of Justice

"IF YOU WANT TO LOSE the war on drugs, just leave it to law enforcement."

I made this startling observation to audiences across the United States during and long after my service as attorney general. It was meant not to denigrate the dedicated efforts of law enforcement officials, but to remind listeners that no efforts to jail suppliers and dealers would obliterate a fundamentally demand-driven problem. The real answer to the drug dilemma lies in the creation of value systems that will not tolerate drug use and in the treatment and rehabilitation of those already committed to the drug culture. In these tasks, law enforcement is only peripherally involved. As my standard speech continued, the war against drugs "would not be won in the courtroom . . . but in the classroom . . . in our churches, homes and communities . . . [on] the field of values. And here we are truly engaged in a struggle for the soul of the next generation. We'll win the war on drugs when drugs go out of fashion, when the yuppie on the move no longer thinks it's hip to score from the corner supplier on his lunch hour. When drug-using rock stars and athletes cease being popular idols. When, in the inner-city school, the dealer with his gold chains and flashy car becomes an outcast rather than a role model for impressionable kids."

Nevertheless, drugs remain a formidable challenge for law enforcement. As I took the oath of office, I observed: "I firmly believe that unless we sustain a vigorous effort to make drug trafficking and drug abuse Public Enemy Number One, we could well stunt significantly the capacity of today's young people to contribute to a better quality of life in tomorrow's America." Fortunately, that area of law enforcement had been heavily emphasized during Ed Meese's tenure. It was basically well organized and soon had sufficient resources to carry out the aggressive effort needed.

One of my first directions to each U.S. attorney's office was to prepare a comprehensive report on drug trafficking within its jurisdiction. On the basis of these reports, we compiled a national profile of these illicit operations to present to the president. Delivered on August 3, 1989, this "Dun and Bradstreet" report presented the first complete and accurate picture of drug trafficking within the United States and provided a roadmap for subsequent enforcement efforts.

Many of my own antidrug activities related to a stepped-up international offensive. We focused on drug distribution networks rather than on the "buy and bust" approach, which had been of limited effect. The simple fact was that not one gram of heroin or cocaine was produced within the United States. To deal with the drug problem within our borders, we had to enlist the cooperation of those countries in which these drugs were produced and through which they transited.

Within two weeks after I assumed office, DEA Administrator Jack Lawn and I announced the results of a cooperative effort undertaken by the International Drug Enforcement Conference, a consortium of thirty North, Central and South American nations. This unprecedented month-long campaign had resulted in the seizure of 11 tons of cocaine, 1,200 arrests and the destruction of 244 tons of marijuana. But much more was on the agenda.

By the end of the year, work had just about been completed on the United Nations Drug Convention, which, for the first time, officially highlighted the necessity of international law enforcement efforts. In December, I traveled to Vienna to sign the convention on behalf of the United States and came to realize what an extraordinary opportunity it presented. The convention bound its signatory nations to criminalize all acts involved in producing and trafficking in illegal drugs, as well as money laundering by drug merchants, and to deal effectively with trafficking in precursor chemicals. They also had to provide for seizure and forfeiture of assets and profits of the drug trade, as well as for production of evidence, taking of testimony and extradition of offenders. Finally, they had to pierce the veil

of bank secrecy laws in tracing illegal international drug profits. I was subsequently to suggest this convention as a model for similar international
action to combat business crime, organized crime and official corruption.

Unfortunately, though the convention was ultimately signed by over
150 nations and ratified by over 100, it did not contain mechanisms for enforcing their commitments. On our end, such sanctions might logically
have included threats to cut off a noncomplying nation's foreign aid or ter-
minate its most-favored-nation trade status. These sanctions would have
been under the jurisdiction of the State Department, however, and that
department, responsible for balancing our nation's strategic interests on
many fronts, did not make the drug treaty one of its priorities. For example,
though our Senate swiftly ratified the UN Convention after I had testified
to its importance to law enforcement, the State Department and the drug
czar's office seemed unenthusiastic about urging the Andean countries to
follow suit.

On the Vienna trip, I also met with my counterparts in England, Switzerland, Germany and Italy and attended a TREVI meeting in Athens.
TREVI (Terrorism, Radicalism, Extremism, Violence International) was
the law enforcement counterpart to the European Economic Community.
Twice a year, it brought together justice and interior ministers and top police officials to discuss mutual problems and means of cooperation in dealing with cross-border challenges. The United States and Canada were
accorded observer status. One of our prime goals was to add antidrug efforts to TREVI's agenda. Given the rising level of concern in the world
community about drug abuse, it is not surprising that we succeeded.

The department had already developed a close connection with Italian
law enforcement authorities. On December 1, 1988, police on both sides of
the Atlantic moved in on the "Iron Tower" heroin-dealing apparatus, ar-
resting 75 suspects in the United States and 133 in Italy. The spectacular
"Pizza Connection" investigation, also carried out jointly by Italian and
American authorities, focused on heroin-dealing operations using pizza
parlor fronts along the eastern seaboard of the United States. Unfortunately, many Italian politicians of this period were suspected of having
Mafia connections. Italian prosecutors were ultimately to indict former
prime minister Giulio Andreotti on corruption charges related to Mafia
activities. The strong anticorruption effort of the "clean hands" prosecutors eventually brought to an end the long hegemony of the Christian
Democrats in Italian politics.

Not long after President Bush took office, I traveled to Bolivia, Peru and

Colombia, the sources of an estimated 90 percent of the cocaine consumed in the United States. The trip made clear various dimensions of the problem. In Bolivia, for example, the government's crop substitution program had generated little enthusiasm, given the ready markets and attractive prices offered by the drug cartels. Moreover, the incoming president, Jaime Paz Zamora, and his administration would have to deal with allegations of connections to drug traffickers throughout their tenure. In Peru, our DEA was attempting to establish a fortified outpost in the Upper Huallaga Valley as a base for field operations by Peruvian authorities against narco-traffickers. And Colombia was struggling to contain the Medellin and Cali cartels, the two biggest cocaine-producing entities in the world. In all three nations, the drug traffickers had essentially established a reign of terror.

Colombia had a particularly sorrowful and tragic history in this regard. In 1982, its government ratified a treaty authorizing the extradition of Colombian citizens to face drug charges in the United States. The treaty was not invoked until 1984, following the assassination of Justice Minister Rodrigo Lara Bonilla by narco-traffickers. When the constitutionality of the treaty was upheld in 1985, terrorists attacked the Supreme Court building, killing half of its members. The court proceeded to reverse itself on technicalities in 1986 and 1987, during which time another justice was murdered and two chief justices resigned under threats. Attorney General Carlos Mauro Hoya was kidnapped and found fatally shot in the head, and former justice minister Enrique Parejo was shot at in Budapest while serving as ambassador to Hungary. During this interval, Colombian law enforcement officials were said to have been regularly offered the grim choice of "plato o plomo" (silver or lead) to forestall their pursuit of the traffickers. Altogether 2,250 Colombian police were killed in action against narco-traffickers and insurgents during the 1980s. After I left office, I was to learn of threats against my own life from the Colombian drug cartels, as well as from Manuel Noriega, various mafiosi and the Irish Republican Army.

In a March 13, 1989, confidential letter to the president, I recommended that our government take the following steps:

Swiftly submit the UN Drug Convention to the Senate for ratification

Quickly resolve the standoff in the Upper Huallaga Valley of Peru

Assess the desirability of increasing our funding of and military participation in the South American antidrug effort

Condition any further assignment of U.S. drug enforcement personnel to these countries upon a weighing of our foreign policy interests
against risks to their safety and domestic enforcement needs

Encourage the upgrading of law enforcement capabilities in Bolivia,
Peru and Colombia to emphasize jailing major traffickers and seizing
their profits rather than seizing drugs and destroying laboratories

Encourage Peru's experiments in aerial eradication of coca and, if
these proved environmentally sound, encourage Bolivia and Colombia
to undertake similar efforts

Assist with crop substitution and other developmental programs
targeted toward current coca growers, especially in Bolivia and Peru

Renew our emphasis on extradition, including negotiation of a new
treaty with Peru and revision of the current treaty with Bolivia

Seek increased support from the European Community for antidrug
efforts in South America, in view of the increasing volume of South
American cocaine being imported to those countries

More effectively communicate our determination to deal with the
demand side of the drug equation by reducing domestic consumption
of illegal drugs

Most of these initiatives eventually found their way into administration
policy.

Matters in Colombia were brought to a head with the assassination of
presidential candidate Luis Carlos Galan on August 19, 1989. President
Virgilio Barco reinstated summary extradition powers under his state-of-
siege authority; to the surprise of many, the Supreme Court sustained
them. Within the year, twenty-five Colombians were made available for
trial in the United States, beginning with Eduardo Martinez Romero, a
member of the Medellin cartel, who later pleaded guilty to drug trafficking
and money laundering. We next demanded extradition of the dozen most
wanted traffickers under indictment in the United States, starting with
Pablo Escobar, the head of the Medellin cartel. Eventually, most of these
fugitives were run to ground, in one way or another. In some cases, substantial assets stashed in foreign banks were seized.

Barco's successor, President Cesar Gaviria Trujillo, in July 1990 put an
end to extradition for traffickers who would surrender to his government.
Within the year, Colombia was to adopt a new constitution that explicitly
prohibited extradition of its citizens. The Colombians assured us of their

determination to keep up the pressure on the traffickers. New police units and special courts had been created to deal with problems of corruption and incompetence, and extradition would remain an option for those who did not surrender. We pledged to extend technical assistance and urged early Colombian ratification of the UN Drug Convention and a mutual legal assistance treaty.

The problem of the Colombian drug traffickers would persist in spite of the imaginative efforts made in that country and in ours. There simply was not enough firepower or political will to put a stop to this sinister commerce through law enforcement alone. I still believe that the thing the Colombian drug lords fear the most is extradition to the United States, where they are virtually assured of long prison sentences. Extradition was resumed, I was pleased to note, in 2003.

Our antidrug efforts faced a particular challenge in Mexico, with which we share a highly porous 1,900-mile border. Substantial amounts of marijuana were grown in Mexico, and it was a suspected transshipment point for a variety of other drugs. Relations were particularly tense following the torture and murder of DEA agent Enrique "Kiki" Camarena in 1985. Our authorities suspected their Mexican counterparts of foot dragging, cover-up or, at the worst, complicity in the Camarena slaying. The U.S. attorney's office in Los Angeles had undertaken an aggressive investigation, and indictments of Mexican nationals had already been obtained when I assumed office.

Meanwhile, President Bush was seeking to build closer ties with the Mexican government, a process greatly enhanced by the coming to power of President Carlos Salinas de Gortari, an American-educated technocrat. Salinas and Bush hit it off well and, as a consequence, our contacts with Mexican law enforcement officials increased despite our edginess over the Camarena affair. I never had a particularly comfortable feeling about Attorney General Enrique Alvarez del Castillo, but we met regularly to try to promote cooperation. Continued requests came from both Salinas and Alvarez for evidence relating to alleged corruption within the Mexican government, material that we were reluctant to make available, for obvious reasons.

Relations were tolerable until a Los Angeles grand jury charged Dr. Humberto Alvarez Machain, a Mexican national, with administering drugs to Camarena to keep him alive while he was being tortured and questioned by Mexican drug kingpins. In the spring of 1990, Machain was rendered over the border to DEA agents in Texas and whisked to Los Angeles to face trial. It appeared that the DEA had been working with kidnappers in Mexico, even arranging passage to the United States for relatives of those involved and paying their rather substantial living expenses. None of this, needless to say, had been cleared with the department in Washington. We would never have granted that clearance, but Machain's presence in an American jail was now a fait accompli.

Attorney General Alvarez grimly demanded Machain's return, and our ambassador, John Negroponte, was understandably disturbed by the DEA's actions. Nonetheless, we decided that Machain's apprehension did not violate American law. As much as we disapproved of the DEA's methods, there was no basis for obliging it to disgorge such a significant figure in this important and gruesome case, especially in view of the heinous allegations against him. We therefore refused to return Machain and reiterated our request for further cooperation in the Camarena investigation. This led President Salinas to make some pointed remarks about national sovereignty at an Organization of American States summit meeting.

Subsequently, District Court Judge Edward Rafeedie, to our chagrin, threw the Machain case out on the grounds that the circumstances surrounding his rendition violated the extradition treaty between the United States and Mexico. The Ninth Circuit upheld the order, but the Supreme Court overturned it, and Machain's case was sent back to Los Angeles for trial. Judge Rafeedie had the last word, however: in December 1992, he dismissed all charges against Machain and criticized the government for its lack of proof in the case.

Another cause célèbre was the indictment of the president of Panama, Manuel Noriega, for drug trafficking and money laundering. These charges had been brought in February 1988, prior to my taking office, but they occupied a good deal of the department's attention during my tenure. Both President Bush and I wanted to be in a position to proceed with dispatch if and when jurisdiction was obtained, so, at the president's request, our department reviewed the case and confirmed that the indictment was sound.

December 1989 saw the launching of Operation Just Cause, our military invasion of Panama. It was provoked by the abuse of American nationals there, the unwillingness of Noriega to accept the results of elections held earlier that year and his continued involvement in drug trafficking. Noriega was apprehended within the Vatican legation after several days and was brought to Florida to face trial. Because of the prominence of the case, we assembled a special team of prosecutors to handle it.

The media focused on the notion that the trial might embarrass the CIA, the circumstances surrounding Noriega's surrender, the "head of state" defense, the alleged threats to a fair trial and the need for tight security. I responded that we were a nation committed to the rule of law, that the government recognized it had the burden of proving its case with legally admissible evidence, that Noriega was entitled to raise any defense available, but that I was confident we had a solid case.

Noriega was convicted in 1992 on eight counts of drug trafficking, racketeering and money laundering, and received a forty-year prison sentence. The biggest fireworks came when CNN broadcast tapes of Noriega's telephone conversations from prison. The monitoring of these calls by prison authorities was standard and was, in fact, consented to by all prisoners as a matter of course. But Noriega's attorneys, with little else to offer, succeeded in escalating media concern over an alleged violation of Noriega's rights or the attorney-client privilege until it dominated a whole news cycle. Ironically, CNN was later convicted of criminal contempt of court for using the tapes in violation of the trial judge's order not to do so. Faced with the threat of a heavy fine, CNN agreed in 1994 to apologize over the air for its defiance of the judge's order and to pay the costs of prosecution.

In the effort to rebuild Panama, the United States sought to create a police force and judicial and correctional systems worthy of their tasks. Our International Criminal Investigative Assistance Program (ICITAP), working with the American ambassador in Panama, assumed a lead role in this nation-building exercise. This was a little-noticed but potentially very important task for the department in a world wherein so many nations were seeking to establish the rule of law. We also began negotiating a mutual legal assistance treaty with the new government of Panama (which it ratified in July 1991) as well as an effective statute prohibiting money laundering.

Money laundering was another target in our attack on the drug trade (and other sophisticated criminal operations). It was coming to be recognized as a serious worldwide problem requiring bilateral and multilateral initiatives. We focused first on Switzerland. The fabled Swiss bank account, veiled in the utmost secrecy, had posed serious problems for law enforcement for decades. Some relief had been obtained during the 1970s when a Mutual Legal Assistance Treaty allowed evidence to be made available for American prosecutions. But the problem of money laundering had not been addressed by December 1988, when I made a trip to Switzerland.

On the eve of my departure, the *Wall Street Journal*'s lead editorial raised doubts about my mission, noting that the proposed Swiss money-laundering law was "causing distress to the established banking community, which fears the proposed law unworkable and dangerously broad." The *Journal* also noted critically, "The U.S. evinces an arrogant tendency to force others to live by its morality," and correctly noted our intention to seek cooperation from foreign authorities on a wide variety of white-collar offenses as well as drug crimes. We noted that the *Journal* showed, from time to time, a remarkable proclivity for looking out for its own!

During our meetings with Swiss banking leaders, I urged a "know your customer rule" that would oblige banks to make some inquiry of individuals showing up on their doorsteps with suitcases full of cash. Their banking system, I told them, was known around the world for its integrity and efficiency, and it would be foolish to sacrifice that reputation for the sake of handling a few more millions in drug-tainted dollars. However, the real impetus for a change in the government's attitude was the suspected involvement in a money-laundering operation of the husband of Justice Minister Elisabeth Kopp, expected to be the next president of Switzerland. Mrs. Kopp was obliged to resign. The legislature in 1990 finally passed provisions requiring banks to know who their clients are as well as the source of their deposits. These acts were supplemented in 1994 by provisions permitting banks to report suspected illegal activities without violating secrecy laws.

The Treasury Department's implementation of the Financial Crimes Enforcement Network (FINCEN) in May 1990 enhanced our own efforts to combat money laundering. FINCEN was created to collect, analyze and disseminate for law enforcement purposes financial intelligence gathered from federal, state, local, foreign and private-sector sources. A staff of 200 analysts and agents using state-of-the art computer technology to "follow the money" was often able to unravel complicated cash transactions and run to ground those responsible for illegal money movements.

The BCCI case was only one of several spectacularly successful prosecutions of money-laundering operations. Operation Polar Cap, the largest of these, identified an organization responsible for handling $1.1 billion for the Colombian cartels over a two-year period. The laundering had taken place through jewelry firms in Los Angeles, New York, Houston and Miami and was uncovered in a joint investigation by the FBI, the DEA, the Customs Service and the IRS. A total of 127 defendants were indicted, and our investigators seized $105 million in assets and ten tons of illegal drugs.

The 1980s and 1990s saw vastly increased use of the civil forfeiture statutes to seize the gains and instrumentalities of illegal drug trafficking. Federal laws allowing for dividing the contraband among the federal, state and local agencies participating in the confiscations provided a powerful new incentive for these often overly turf-conscious agencies to work together. The inventory of federally seized assets increased from $313.2 million at the end of fiscal year 1985 to $1.36 billion at the end of fiscal year 1990, with over $500 million having been turned back to cooperating state and local agencies and nearly $500 million having been used to help expand federal prison facilities. We even shared these assets with other governments. In 1991, as an outgrowth of Operation Polar Cap, I was able to publicly present oversized checks for $1 million, representing cooperation in freezing the assets of the money-laundering Banco de Occidente, to the beaming ambassadors of Canada and Switzerland.

The forfeiture program was not without its critics. Some saw the asset-sharing features as an incentive to overzealous law enforcement agents seeking to fill the coffers of local governments or police departments. In October 1989, I created the Executive Office for Asset Forfeiture to supervise these operations. Nonetheless, the *Pittsburgh Press* in early 1991 offered a scathing multipart critique of the program, concentrating primarily on the notion that property could be seized and forfeited even though no criminal charges had been filed, and on the plight of the "innocent owner." Civil seizure in this country, in fact, dated back to the beginnings of the republic, but its use in drug cases seemed to touch a sensitive nerve among some critics.

President Reagan had created the National Drug Policy Board (NDPB), which I chaired as successor to Ed Meese. Congress replaced it with the Office of National Drug Control Policy, headed by the so-called drug czar, effective in early 1989. The first drug czar was former education secretary William Bennett. He kept a high profile, but his policy statements varied little from those in our final NDPB report. Bennett wisely steered clear of asserting any direct jurisdiction over the department's law enforcement efforts and supported the sizable increase in DEA agents and prosecutors that we sought and obtained from Congress. Although our personal relations were cordial, our respective staffs did a great deal of circling about, and the czar had to be included in any major news releases or press announcements about drug law enforcement. Bennett appeared to tire of his responsibilities when the novelty wore off, and former Florida governor Bob Martinez replaced him in December 1991.

One of the most noteworthy drug cases prosecuted during this period unfolded virtually on our doorstep. After an extended investigation, FBI agents arrested Washington Mayor Marion Barry on January 18, 1990, at the Vista Hotel, where he had been videotaped smoking crack cocaine in the company of a female companion. (This sting had originally been scheduled for the previous day, which was Martin Luther King Day. I had to intervene personally to rectify this potential blunder.) Long suspected of using drugs, Barry chose to go to trial on his thirteen-count indictment. He was convicted on just one misdemeanor count of possessing an illegal drug and sentenced to six months in prison. We suspected an element of jury nullification, as Barry was a popular figure in the city's large African American community. One jury member, in fact, told CBS, "Maybe he's an addict, but he's our addict. Maybe he's guilty, but he's our mayor, and we're not going to send him to jail." Judge Thomas Penfield Jackson rated the evidence "overwhelming" in support of guilt on all but one of the charges. We were satisfied, however, that even the limited verdict vindicated our effort.

Inevitably, the Barry case unleashed new charges that we were "targeting" African American officials for selective prosecution. The best response to this came from Baltimore Mayor Kurt Schmoke, a black public official himself, who observed, "I saw that Arch Moore [the white Republican former governor of West Virginia] was sentenced to prison." Carl Rowan, a leading African American journalist, observed: "Marion Barry is not the victim of either white bigotry or excesses by the black policemen and black lawyers who were instrumental in his conviction and his stiff sentence. Barry destroyed Barry!" Even the liberal *Washington Post* columnist Colman McCarthy was to echo these sentiments in September 1994: "The reckless manner in which charges of racism are hurled around is befogging the air, decreasing visibility when bigotry really is happening. Who can, or will, pay attention to racial injustice if it is routinely exploited by politicians in a jam?"

The embarrassing conviction of Henry Barr, who had served with me in several capacities over the years, was further evidence of the department's evenhandedness in drug enforcement. Henry left the department rather abruptly in early 1989, and we soon learned of his alleged prior cocaine use in Harrisburg. Because of our close personal relationship, I promptly recused myself from the matter. Barr was indicted on drug charges and convicted in March 1991. I was, unnecessarily I believe, called to testify at his trial about matters that could easily have been stipulated for the record. The media had a field day with this case. Bill Safire, predictably, chimed in with a demand that a special prosecutor be appointed to handle the Barr case, although there was no showing that the regular prosecutor in Pennsylvania was taking anything other than an aggressive course. The most ludicrous bit of media overkill, however, came from Jerry Seper of the *Washington Times*, who quoted "sources in Pennsylvania" as saying that drug use had been widespread among my staff in Harrisburg, citing the conviction of Barr and, unaccountably, those of other Pennsylvanians who had no connection whatsoever with my administration. In reality, of course, Barr's conviction showed quite the opposite: that no one is exempt from prosecution for drug violations.

Early in my tenure, I argued before the Supreme Court an important case involving the Department of Transportation's requirement for involuntary post-accident testing of train crews for drug and alcohol use. Barraged with questions from the justices, I did not acquit myself especially well. However, the Court decided 7–2 in our favor, establishing new Fourth Amendment principles that struck an appropriate balance in favor of the safety of the traveling public. In the seven years following the decision, railroad accidents declined by 28 percent; from 1987 to 1993, the percentage of accidents involving workers who tested positive for drug use declined from 21 percent to 5.5 percent. The rules also enhanced the ability of employers to detect substance-abusing employees for referral to counseling and treatment programs. By 1996 nearly all Fortune 200 companies used drug tests to screen potential employees, and the share of positive test results had fallen from 18.1 percent in 1987 to 6.7 percent. (In a visit with baseball commissioner Bart Giamatti a few months before his death in August 1989, we both lamented the inability of the game to impose mandatory drug testing on players due to collective bargaining restrictions.)

The drug war is an unappetizing battle, first, last and always. Success can be measured only in relative terms. Nevertheless, our drug enforcement effort was generally well received, especially in its international aspects. At the end of my service, the Associated Press noted, "Thornburgh's most favorable reviews come for winning more international cooperation in the war on illegal drugs," while the *National Journal* observed, "With little fanfare, Thornburgh encouraged foreign regulators to take major steps in enforcing a worldwide crackdown on drug trafficking and money laundering." Drug use in the United States dropped significantly during President Bush's administration, continued to drop during the 1990s and remains less of a national scourge today than it was prior to his coming to office.

DURING THE 1980s, the department had continued its unrelenting pressure on organized crime in major cities across the country. President Reagan's first attorney general, William French Smith, had established a working group to coordinate efforts against organized crime in the United States, the "real" Mafia in Sicily, and the Cammora and the N'Drangheta elsewhere in Italy. We carried on these efforts with vigor.

A major accomplishment was the settlement in March 1989 of long-running civil racketeering charges against the Teamsters Union. The court appointed officers to administer the union, oversee elections and investigate corruption charges. Thereafter, a number of high-ranking Teamsters officials were ordered removed from office, and more than forty disciplinary charges were filed against others. The new leadership seemed committed to the cleanup.

A massive civil racketeering lawsuit was filed in February 1990 against the International Longshoremen's Association, several employers and dozens of alleged organized-crime figures for an attempted takeover of the New York and New Jersey waterfronts. In May 1990, in a major blow to the infiltration of legitimate businesses in New York, a far-reaching Manhattan indictment charged virtually the entire active hierarchy of the Colombo, Gambino, Genovese and Luchese families with rigging bids for $142 million in window contracts for the New York Housing Authority. In due course the U.S. attorney's office in Brooklyn even indicted and convicted John Gotti, the *capo di tutti capi* in the New York mob, thrice acquitted on state and federal charges.

A series of prosecutions in the Philadelphia area obliterated the Nicodemo ("Little Nicky") Scarfo organization, and we also brought charges against Scarfo-dominated labor organizations in the Atlantic City casinos.

In the course of the investigation of the Raymond Patriarca New England crime family, a court-authorized bugging device gathered unusual and fascinating evidence of the structure and practices of organized crime. An actual initiation ceremony was recorded. Four new members were instructed in the ways of La Cosa Nostra. After promising to kill those who threatened the organization or its members, they burned a holy card with the image of the Patriarca family saint, first pledging to uphold the code of silence and then intoning in Italian, "As burns this saint so will burn my soul. I want to enter alive into this organization and leave it dead." So much for those who claimed that there was no such thing as organized crime!

By the end of 1990, we were gratified by observations such as those made by veteran mob-watcher Selwyn Raab in a lengthy *New York Times* story. He noted the dismantling of thriving underworld organizations in Philadelphia, New Jersey, New England, New Orleans, Kansas City, Detroit, Milwaukee and St. Louis and concluded, "[M]ost of America's traditional Mafia families appear to be fading out of existence." Associated Press writers Rick Hampton and Larry McShane, in an article written shortly after I had left the department, examined the "Fortune 50" of organized crime leaders compiled in 1986 and found all but eight to be serving long prison sentences, retired, inactive, dead (or suspected so) or on bail. The battle against organized crime would continue, but I did begin to get the feeling that the "good guys" finally were gaining the upper hand.

While proud of this achievement, we did not rest on our laurels. In 1991 we decided that our definition of "organized crime" needed to be expanded. Rather than focusing solely on the traditional "families," we proposed to take aim at organizations like the burgeoning Asian gangs, the Jamaican posses and the inner-city Crips and Bloods, originally from Los Angeles, but reaching out to other cities as well. This effort is ongoing to this day.

TWO SPECTACULAR crimes of violence fell under the department's jurisdiction during my tenure. The first was the December 1988 terrorist bombing of Pan American flight 103 over Lockerbie, Scotland, taking the lives of 259 passengers and crew members and eleven residents of Lockerbie. The other was the mail-bomb assassination of Judge Robert Vance of the U.S. Court of Appeals for the Eleventh Circuit at his home in Birmingham, Alabama. In each instance, the FBI showcased the professionalism, tenacity and thoroughness that have made it the world's premier law enforcement agency.

Working well together after some minor jurisdictional disputes, British, Scottish and American investigators in the Pan Am 103 case first faced the challenge of gathering evidence scattered over 1,000 square miles of countryside. Search efforts by more than 1,000 police officers, military personnel and volunteers recovered some 100,000 pieces of the downed Boeing 747 jumbo jet. Masterful detective work then determined that a thumbnail-sized fragment of a circuit board in a radiocassette player contained traces of Semtex, an explosive activated by pressure at a given altitude. But where and how had the bomb been put aboard the plane, by whom and why?

Suspicions centered immediately on Middle Eastern terrorist groups, particularly the Popular Front for the Liberation of Palestine—General Command. This group, headed by Ahmed Jabril, had connections to Syria and Iran. American fire had downed an Iranian airliner the previous year, so revenge was a possible motive. Jabril and his confederates were also seemingly connected to a terrorist gang arrested in West Germany in possession of apparatus similar to that suspected of causing the explosion on Pan Am 103.

Then the debris from Pan Am 103 yielded items of clothing in which fragments of the timing device were embedded. The clothing was traced to a shop in Malta, where some of the flight's luggage had originated. At the same time, French authorities discovered pieces of a bomb device similar to that used in the Lockerbie attack in the wreckage of an exploded French airliner which had left Brazzaville in the Congo. A painstaking review of the evidence finally identified two Libyan intelligence officials, Abdel Bassett Ali Megrahi and Lamen Khalifa Fhimah, as the perpetrators of the bombing. They were simultaneously indicted by U.S. and Scottish authorities in November 1991. It was ten years before the Libyan government would turn the defendants over for trial, and only one was convicted (in a trial held under Scottish law in the Netherlands). Nonetheless, we felt that the outcome marked a milestone in our relentless efforts to apply the rule of law to international terrorism.

On December 16, 1989, a dreadful bombing claimed the life of Judge Robert Vance. A similar attack had killed civil rights leader Robert E. Robinson in Savannah, and pipe-bomb devices had been found unexploded at the Jacksonville, Florida, offices of the NAACP and in the mail at an Eleventh Circuit facility in Atlanta. At first some racial motive seemed likely, but there was little apparent connection between the various targets. The only clues readily available were the typewritten address labels on the packages. The FBI combed through thousands of typed letters directed to the Fifth Circuit (out of part of which the new Eleventh Circuit had been formed), then embarked on the equally demanding task of tracing the suspect typewriter. Finally, its owner was identified as Robert Wayne O'Ferrell of Enterprise, Alabama, a litigant in proceedings before Judge Vance. The media swarmed over O'Ferrell's small community, making it difficult to conduct a systematic search. Despite an exhaustive combing of O'Ferrell's home and office, his septic tank and a nearby pond, the typewriter was never found, and O'Ferrell was eliminated as a suspect. He was later to sue the FBI for damages.

Further FBI investigation led to Walter Leroy Moody Jr., who had also been involved in litigation before Judge Vance and had a previous conviction for an offense involving explosives. It was suspected that he had borrowed the typewriter from O'Ferrell, and his wife, Susan, subsequently testified that she had typed the address labels. Both Moodys were arrested. Taped jailhouse conversations provided additional incriminating testimony, and Walter Moody was convicted of federal charges and sentenced to life imprisonment with no possibility of parole. He was later convicted of the murder of Judge Vance in an Alabama state court and sentenced to death.

THE NEGLECT BY the criminal justice process of violent-crime victims and their families had long been of concern to me. In 1991, the case of *Payne v. Tennessee* gave me a unique opportunity to argue the cause of the victim.

The defendant, Pervis Tyrone Payne, had passed a Saturday morning injecting cocaine and drinking beer before entering the apartment of twenty-eight-year-old Charisse Christopher and making sexual advances, which she resisted. Police officers called to the scene encountered Payne leaving the apartment, covered with blood. He struck one of the officers and fled. Within the apartment, Charisse lay dead, having sustained eighty-four wounds from a butcher knife. Her two-year-old daughter, Lacie, had suffered fatal stab wounds to the chest, abdomen, back and head, and the murder weapon was found at her feet. Blood covered the walls and floor of the unit. Charisse's son, Nicholas, age three, had several wounds that penetrated his body from front to back. He miraculously survived, after seven hours of surgery and transfusions of 1,700 ccs of blood. When Payne was apprehended, blood on his clothes matched Charisse's. Three cans of malt liquor with his fingerprints were found on a table in the kitchen, and his baseball cap was snapped onto Lacie's arm.

A jury found Payne guilty on two counts of first-degree murder and one count of assault with intent to commit first-degree murder. It imposed the death penalty after hearing testimony from Payne's parents, a girlfriend and a clinical psychologist, all for the defense, and Charisse's mother, who testified to the effects of the murders on Nicholas: "He cries for his mom. He doesn't seem to understand why she doesn't come home. And he cries for his sister Lacie. He comes to me many times during the week and asks me, 'Grandmama, do you miss my Lacie'. And I tell him yes. He says, 'I'm worried about my Lacie'." In his argument to the jury, the prosecutor stated that Payne "doesn't want you to think about the people who love

Charisse Christopher, her mother and daddy who loved her. The people who loved little Lacie Jo, the grandparents who are still here. The brother who mourns for her every single day and wants to know where his little playmate is. . . . These are the things that go into why it is especially cruel, heinous, and atrocious, the burden that child will carry forever."

The Supreme Court of Tennessee affirmed the conviction and sentence. Payne appealed to the Supreme Court of the United States, claiming that the grandmother's testimony and the closing argument were prejudicial violations of his rights under the Eighth Amendment. In two 5–4 decisions, *Booth v. Maryland* (1987) and *South Carolina v. Gathers* (1989), the Supreme Court had held that the Eighth Amendment prohibits a capital sentencing jury from considering evidence on the personal characteristics of a murder victim and the emotional impact of the crimes on the victim's family. We felt these cases had been wrongly decided and filed an amicus brief in the *Payne* appeal.

We had a very heavy burden to carry, as we were asking the Supreme Court to overturn its own recent precedents. My argument went well, however. I urged that the harm done to survivors and to the community at large bore on the defendant's "personal responsibility and moral guilt," the Court's test in such cases. Moreover, under earlier rulings, the defendant was entitled to be treated as a "uniquely individual human being" and could present evidence of good character to mitigate other considerations at sentencing. I argued that the jury should be allowed to hear similar evidence concerning the victim.

The Court agreed. Its 6–3 decision explicitly overruled *Booth* and *Gathers* and held, "[I]f the State chooses to permit the admission of victim impact evidence and prosecutorial argument on this subject, the Eighth Amendment erects no *per se* bar. A state may legitimately conclude that evidence about the victim and about the impact of the murder on the victim's family is relevant to the jury's decision as to whether or not the death penalty should be imposed." As the majority noted, stare decisis, the principle that dictates against overruling previous decisions, "promotes the even-handed, predictable, and consistent development of legal principles, fosters reliance on judicial decisions and contributes to the actual and perceived integrity of the judicial process." However, the majority went on to say, "when governing decisions are unworkable or are badly reasoned, 'this Court has never felt constrained to follow precedent'." The opinion noted the particular need to act in constitutional cases, which are "practically impossible" to correct through legislative action. Indeed, if an opinion is to be overturned, it may be best to do it quickly, before it becomes the basis of a larger body of law. Justices Marshall and John Paul Stevens filed vigorous dissents. However, the majority did not find compelling Justice Marshall's arguments that the only thing that had changed since *Booth* and *Gathers* was the Court's makeup, and that its overruling of those precedents was an exercise of "[p]ower, not reason." It also disagreed with Justice Stevens's argument that victim impact evidence "can only be intended to identify some victims as more worthy of protection than others."

VERY LITTLE OF the violence that captures headlines and dominates most Americans' definition of "crime" falls within the jurisdiction of the federal government. About 95 percent of the nation's street crime is investigated and prosecuted by local authorities. Nevertheless, the American people in the 1990s made it abundantly clear that they expected us to "do something" about such crime. We accordingly prepared a legislative package designed to address those aspects of this problem that were within our reach. Included were provisions that would (1) create a "good faith" exception to the judge-made exclusionary rule that barred evidence obtained without a valid warrant; (2) cut short the seemingly interminable review of state death penalty sentences via the writ of habeas corpus in federal court; (3) establish a constitutional procedure for imposing the death penalty for certain federal offenses; and (4) extend the federal death penalty to cover a number of additional offenses (including those of the type involved in the Pan Am 103 and Judge Vance killings).

Over my three years as attorney general, our crime bill made progress first in one house and then in the other, but it never gained sufficient votes to pass. While many of our proposed reforms in areas such as the exclusionary rule, habeas corpus procedures and the death penalty were the subject of constant contention during my tenure, they were only to be passed by the Republican Congress elected in 1994; then signed into law by an increasingly "tough on crime" Bill Clinton.

In the spring of 1991, we convened a law enforcement summit meeting in Washington to highlight our concerns and bring together the experts—police officials, prosecutors, judges, correctional officers, academics and political leaders—for a three-day discussion. Most of those in attendance supported the essentials of our crime package. Unfortunately, there was virtually no press interest in the meeting, in spite of comprehensive briefings, elaborate press kits and the appearances of the president, the attorney general, the solicitor general and a Supreme Court justice, as well as most of the major leaders of the nation's law enforcement establishment. This was an example of how media silence can render substantive activity in Washington invisible. The summit did, however, result in three successful programs representing appropriate federal responses to problems essentially local in nature.

The first of these, Project Triggerlock, was announced on April 10, 1991, and was directed at the use of firearms by violent career criminals. Under this program, the most serious repeat offenders whose criminal behavior had not been deterred by state or local prosecutions were selectively prosecuted and subjected to tough federal penalties. State and local arrests were regularly screened to identify convicted felons who possessed a firearm at the time of arrest or were charged with an offense using a firearm. Those with the most serious previous criminal involvement were referred to the local U.S. attorneys' offices for prosecution under relevant federal laws. The toughest of these was the Armed Career Criminal Act, which mandated sentences of fifteen years to life for defendants with three prior felony convictions for violent or drug-related crimes. A study released by the Bureau of Alcohol, Tobacco and Firearms in March 1992 showed that each inmate incarcerated under this act had committed an average of 160 crimes a year—three crimes a week.

During its first year, Project Triggerlock more than doubled the number of federal firearms prosecutions to a total of 6,454 defendants charged. The average sentence received by a convicted Triggerlock defendant was seven years and the average for an armed career criminal was eighteen years, both without parole. Those convicted served far longer sentences than they would have under state or local laws. The point of this effort was not, as some charged, to clog the already busy federal courts with essentially state and local offenses. It was to incapacitate the most serious armed violent career criminals for extended periods and to potentially deter others from committing such offenses.

The second result of the crime summit was related to the controversial "Brady Bill," which sought to regulate the over-the-counter sale of handguns by imposing a five-day waiting period. This delay would ostensibly allow an investigation of the prospective purchaser. The bill was vehemently opposed by the National Rifle Association, which took the position that any attempt to regulate firearms was a threat to the Second Amendment right of citizens to bear arms. I had previously urged implementation of a point-of-sale system instead, so that gun dealers could access available information on purchasers immediately via touch-tone telephone.

At the summit I sought to deflect the criticism that the president had received for opposing the Brady Bill, pointing out, "[T]he records needed to make the necessary match-up between a potential firearms purchaser and his possible criminal past do not adequately exist. To put it bluntly: no matter what point of purchase, or 48-hour delay, or 7-day waiting period you might establish, you could not come up with the needed facts on a consistent basis." To help solve this problem, I directed the FBI to establish a complete and automated database of felons who are prohibited from purchasing firearms and authorized $13 million to help it clear up a backlog in processing arrest and disposition information. The Bureau of Justice Statistics was directed to develop voluntary reporting standards for state and local law enforcement and authorized to devote $27 million over three years to helping states improve their own criminal history records, upon which the FBI was largely dependent.

These steps did not, however, suffice to satisfy supporters of the Brady Bill. Moreover, most of the police present at the crime summit favored that bill. Therefore, at my urging, the president offered Congress a compromise: He would sign the bill as part of a package that included his anticrime proposals. Still no movement resulted, and no crime bill was ever to reach the president's desk. A waiting period for handgun purchases was ultimately mandated by a Democratic Congress during President Clinton's administration.

Operation Weed and Seed, implemented on a pilot basis just before I left office, was the final initiative resulting from the crime summit. It targeted high-crime neighborhoods and housing projects with efforts to "weed out" violent criminals, illegal gang activity, drug trafficking and related violence, then "seed" comprehensive social and economic development programs. The goal was to revitalize economically depressed and socially ravaged areas. All programs were locally designed; priorities were established at the grass roots and implemented by a number of different agencies. Four core elements were emphasized: community policing as a bridge between law enforcement and revitalization efforts; improved coordination between law enforcement and social service agencies, the private sector and the community; efforts to strengthen social infrastructure; and the provision of opportunities for economic development. Some forfeited real estate was rehabilitated for resale or rental to low-income buyers or renters. Eventually, some twenty cities participated in this popular program, and others adopted similar strategies. By the end of fiscal 1993, more than $25 million in department funds had been awarded, and the program had become a permanent part of the federal effort to build safer communities.

THE DEPARTMENT adopted a slightly lower public profile on pornography than it had in the Reagan administration. Attorney General Meese had put tremendous emphasis on this area, creating a Commission on Pornography and establishing an Obscenity Enforcement Unit. As might have been expected, these efforts drew a great deal of fire from the liberal community, including my former ACLU comrades, on First Amendment grounds. Their arguments found little favor with me, but we chose not to make this one of our major public-relations battles.

My particular focuses in this area were child pornography and the effects of hard-core smut on children, both of particular concern to me as a parent and grandparent. We worked hard for the passage of the Child Protection and Obscenity Enforcement Act of 1988 and sought to adapt our prosecutions to the rapidly developing technologies of "dial-a-porn," the computer and the satellite video.

Speaking to the National Conference of the Religious Alliance Against Pornography in October 1989, I set forth the department's priorities: vigorous prosecution of child pornography and obscenity by a specialist in each U.S. attorney's office; vigorous prosecution of dial-a-porn operations; and a national effort against producers and distributors of illegal hard-core videos. While acknowledging that some community clamor against pornography "has spilled egregiously over into artistic questions, threatening creative work that may properly deserve Constitutional protection," I reiterated that our focus was on the "indignity that occurs whenever perversion puts on its most vicious guise—that of an acceptable norm in society." By the time I departed, we had secured convictions against some of the major traffickers in this filth, including a host of those involved in mail-order distribution of pornography.

In 2002, I was to chair a National Research Council committee on how to deal with the explosion of inappropriate sexually explicit material available to young people on the Internet. Our report pointed out that neither law enforcement nor technology alone could be looked to for a quick fix to this problem, and that parents, teachers and librarians should play a much greater role in educating children about safe and intelligent Internet use. The *New York Times* described our effort as "one of the most thorough reports ever produced on protecting children from Internet pornography."

15

A Global Effort

THE ANTITRUST DIVISION and the Land and Natural Resources Division (which we renamed in 1990 the Environment and Natural Resources Division) had been heavily criticized during the Reagan years. Consistent with the media perception of the federal government's probusiness bias during the 1980s, these operations were considered to have been less than vigorous in promoting competition and protecting the environment, respectively. These perceptions were greatly exaggerated, but clearly some new messages were needed. In both cases, I believe, we achieved some limited success.

Speaking to the department's environmental lawyers in January 1991, I summarized the reasons for our commitment to environmental enforcement: "Environmental crime is, in fact, dirty white-collar crime—as insidious in its own way as the financial fraud we have lately uncovered. . . . It involves a similar betrayal of the public trust—often through a like evasion of regulations and accountability—and it is always a rip-off. Only here, the white-collar criminal is not ripping off our life savings. He is ripping off life itself, such life as our precious environment can fragilely sustain. And all out of greed."

Working with lawyers in the Environmental Protection Agency, headed by Administrator Bill Reilly, we chalked up our most measurable environmental success in stepped-up enforcement of the Superfund hazardous waste cleanup statute. We recovered $1 billion through Superfund actions in each of fiscal years 1989 and 1990, dwarfing the amounts recovered in previous years. We also aggressively enforced the Clean Water Act, bringing suits against forty municipalities for failure to maintain their water purity. The defendants included San Diego (which agreed to spend $2.5 million for sewage treatment improvements), Philadelphia (which paid a $1.5 million penalty and undertook to rehabilitate its sewage plant) and Phoenix (which was assessed a $450,000 penalty).

One of the first major criminal environmental proceedings to reach my desk related to the Rocky Flats nuclear weapons facility, located near Boulder, Colorado, owned by the Department of Energy but operated by Rockwell International Corporation. Rockwell entered a ten-count guilty plea in 1992 after nearly two years of negotiations. The plea resulted in an $18.5 million fine, the largest ever imposed for a hazardous waste violation.

An unfortunate aftermath to this proceeding was a congressional charge that it had been mishandled, in part because the grand jury was prohibited from issuing a public report condemning the conduct of certain plant employees. Attorney General Reno ultimately asked for and received an internal review; it showed, in her words, that "the prosecutors acted energetically and consistently with the highest professional standards." The report concluded, "There are serious consequences of politicized attacks on individual line prosecutors. . . . The Congressional maligning of the line prosecutors in this case provides strong incentives for prosecutors to stay away from politically charged environmental cases in the future." A subsequent review by the Clinton Justice Department also gave a much-deserved clean bill of health to the integrity of our overall environmental crimes effort, a priority during my tenure, but pointed out, once again, the vulnerability of the department to irresponsible congressional sniping and the need for attorneys general to resist attempts by these critics to browbeat their line attorneys.

The major environmental litigation during this period resulted from the oil spill from the tanker *Exxon Valdez* in Alaska's Prince William Sound. On March 24, 1989, this vessel dumped nearly 11 million gallons of crude oil into the pristine environment of the sound, causing enormous damage to the ecology and wildlife of the area. Cleanup efforts commenced at once, as did the search for the responsible parties. Criminal inquiries were begun before a federal grand jury in Alaska, and numerous civil suits were undertaken to recover the costs of the spill and compensate those who had been harmed. Much of this work was carried on within the Environment and Natural Resources Division, working with the EPA and the Departments of Transportation, Agriculture and the Interior.

An annoying side issue arose over Ginny's and my holdings of common stock in Atlantic Richfield Company and Mobil Corporation, valued at less than $33,000. Neither company was involved in the Exxon case, but both were part owners of Alyeska Pipeline Service Company, which had been investigated but not charged in the matter. I did not participate in the Alyeska investigation, and out of an overabundance of caution, I secured a waiver from President Bush under the applicable laws to permit me to continue to participate in the Exxon matter. Such was the climate in Washington, however, that it was regularly implied in the press and in partisan political circles that these remote financial interests impaired my zeal in pursuing the government's cause.

An early effort at a settlement of the Exxon case was aborted. Its terms would have included admission of guilt by Exxon, establishment of a $500 million fund for future claims for restoration, and payment of $50 million toward state spill response costs. (Exxon had already paid some $2 billion toward the cleanup.) Alaska Attorney General Doug Baily, however, after selective (and often erroneous) leaks of the terms to the press, objected to the settlement, ostensibly because it included a four-year moratorium on federal (not Alaska) civil suits against Exxon while the assessment went forward. One observer later characterized Baily's rejection as prompted more by Alaska politics than by displeasure with the terms.

On February 27, 1990, Exxon was indicted on two felony and three misdemeanor counts. By this time Alaska had a new governor, Walter Hickel, and a new attorney general, Charlie Cole. After much negotiation, during which I continuously emphasized the need for a substantial criminal fine, a $1.1 billion global settlement was agreed upon on March 13, 1991, twenty years to the day after the discovery of oil in Prudhoe Bay. This time we had the full backing of Alaskan authorities. Exxon Corporation and Exxon Shipping agreed to plead guilty to criminal charges and pay fines and restitution totaling $100 million plus an additional $1 billion in settlement of all federal and state civil claims resulting from the spill. The total was by far the largest amount ever paid as a result of environmental violations.

To our astonishment, the Alaska House of Representatives voted to reject the pact, and Judge H. Russell Holland in Anchorage subsequently refused to accept it, saying that the proposed criminal fine was too small.

Once again, the impression was given that we had made some sort of deal that benefited the corporate defendants. (It did not help that the president of Exxon told his annual stockholders' meeting that the fines would be tax-deductible.) Our negotiators eventually produced a package acceptable to the judge.

Our detractors engaged in nonstop criticism of the whole process. I gained the impression that many of them would be satisfied only if all of Exxon's assets were forfeited, all of its top officials jailed (if not executed) and the company itself forced into bankruptcy. In my view, the end result was a sound one, but the process reinforced my view that environmental litigation is a no-win situation, given the often paranoid attitude of some of the extreme environmentalists.

The difficulty in finally putting to bed anything in the environmental field was illustrated by our experience with the Florida Everglades. For years unsuccessful efforts had been made to cope with damage done to this vast area by drainage, urban development and discharges, including polluted runoff from cane sugar and dairy acreage. Finally, in 1988, U.S. Attorney Dexter Lehtinen brought an action charging the state of Florida and the South Florida Water Management District with violating the state's own standards. A settlement was reached with newly elected governor Lawton Chiles in July 1991. Under the settlement (called "a model for conservation everywhere" by the *New York Times*), Florida was to set aside 35,000 acres of marshland at four sites to filter polluted water before it entered the Everglades and was to reduce sharply the water's phosphorous content over a ten-year period. Farmers would also come under stiff new antipollution regulations. Years later, however, controversy continued and progress in implementing the agreement was meager.

One other proceeding brought me full circle in the environmental field. Federal prosecutors in the Western District of Pennsylvania brought an action in March 1989 against Ashland Oil Company for criminal violations of the Clean Water Act and the 1899 Refuse Act. The collapse of a forty-eight-year-old storage tank had damaged drinking water and plant and animal life by discharging more than 700,000 gallons of diesel oil into the Monongahela River, the very body of water where my career as an environmental prosecutor had begun nearly two decades earlier.

In December 1988, I collaborated with Commerce Secretary Bill Verity on a matter harking back to my experience with the Ben Franklin Partnership. Bill and I submitted side-by-side columns to the *Wall Street*

Journal calling for the relaxation of antitrust restrictions to permit more collaborative manufacture of products resulting from advanced-technology research and development. I noted that many foreign firms entered into cooperative production ventures, spreading the risks among several manufacturers. In the United States, such joint ventures were inhibited by our antitrust laws, in particular the provisions for private suits seeking treble damages and attorneys' fees.

We suggested two possible solutions. The first would provide government certification, limited in time and subject to periodic review, of joint production ventures deemed not to threaten competitiveness. The second would extend the antitrust waivers already available for joint R&D to joint manufacturing. While not protected from government actions to challenge anticompetitive behavior, cooperating producers would gain shelter from private treble-damage claims. The R&D exemption to this effect had permitted the formation (aided by $100 million in federal funds) of Sematech, a consortium of competing semiconductor companies researching advanced semiconductor design.

Both proposals were designed to eliminate artificial barriers to international competitiveness. They attracted a good deal of attention and earned mention in President Bush's first State of the Union address as examples of ways to increase international competitiveness in advanced technology. Although Bob Mosbacher, the new commerce secretary, supported the basic concept, it took considerable time to be enacted into law as the National Cooperative Production Amendments of 1993. Consumer advocate Ralph Nader and Senator Howard Metzenbaum (D-Ohio) led the opposition, and some within the Bush administration feared that the proposal smacked of "industrial policy," roundly condemned in the 1988 presidential campaign. In my view, this attitude caused a significant delay in our ability to compete in international markets at little or no political or economic cost at home. These were not the last imaginative proposals to be shelved or delayed by an overly cautious administration unwilling to advance new and different ideas in domestic policy.

We had more success in raising the profile of the Antitrust Division. Several important matters involved the airline industry. In June 1989, we faced down a $2 billion proposal by American Airlines and Delta Airlines to combine their computerized reservation systems, a move we said would reduce competition in both the market for air travel and the sale of computer services to travel agents. Together, the two competitors would have held about 48 percent of the market in computerized reservations. We also stopped USAir from acquiring additional gates at Philadelphia International Airport from Eastern Airlines, a move that Transportation Secretary Sam Skinner said would "raise serious competitive concerns at this airport and for the mid–Atlantic region." And a three-year investigation begun during my tenure resulted in a civil price-fixing suit in December 1992 against eight of the largest airlines and their data exchange system. The division described the suit as targeting "repeated exchanges . . . of price increase proposals and counterproposals, with the effect of raising fares to consumers." This arrangement was a classic target for trustbusters.

We took action leading to the abandonment or restructuring of a number of combinations that appeared likely to lessen competition. For example, we prevented two 1989 proposed joint ventures between Westinghouse and Asea Brown Boveri, a Swiss company, which we claimed would lessen competition in U.S. markets for electrical power equipment. We refused to allow Procter & Gamble, manufacturer of Pepto-Bismol, to acquire exclusive marketing and distribution rights to Maalox from Rhone-Poulenc Rorer; this transaction would have combined the nation's top two sellers of over-the-counter stomach remedies. And we derailed Gillette Company's attempt to acquire the non–European Economic Community razor blade business of Wilkinson Sword, which would have eliminated one of only four other suppliers of blades in the United States. We also supported legislation that increased the maximum fines in criminal antitrust cases from $1 million to $10 million.

The department won an important consent decree from the American Institute of Architects (AIA), ending its prohibition on members engaging in competitive bidding, discounting fees or providing free services. The AIA agreed to establish a comprehensive antitrust compliance program for its 280 member chapters and 54,000 members.

The division also broke significant new ground in dealing with international challenges. In Japan, a country notorious for not enforcing its own antitrust laws, we threatened bid-rigging suits against a number of Japanese firms that sought contracts from the U.S. Navy at its Yokosuka base. We were to collect over $34 million from 135 defendants in this undertaking, the first to elicit cooperation from Japan's Fair Trade Commission.

Our most prominent and controversial antitrust investigation centered on allegations of price fixing in the award of financial aid at over twenty of the nation's most prominent colleges and universities. In a nearly forty-year-old practice known as "overlap," the eight Ivy League colleges and, by 1990, fifteen other private institutions met each spring, just before final admissions decisions, to share information on financial aid to students who had applied to more than one of them. What I styled as a "collegiate cartel" agreed upon a uniform package of financial aid—grants, loans and part-time employment—for each student. The stated purposes were to avoid a bidding war for the best students and to meet goals of student body diversity and quality. We were concerned, however, that students and parents were being denied the benefits of competition among the universities in setting financial aid levels. As pointed out by a Dickinson College official in an article in the *Chronicle of Higher Education*, "By agreeing not to compete among themselves on the basis of price, the institutions had the opportunity to save substantial sums of money by pegging family contributions at the highest possible levels." This we regarded as a classic price-fixing scenario.

Substantial document demands produced howls of protest from the universities and their lawyers. However, the 1991 "overlap" meeting was canceled. On May 17, 1991, Jim Rill and I met with outgoing Harvard president Derek Bok and incoming president Neil Rudenstine. Both of them pressed the view that the antitrust laws were not intended to apply to either the practices in question or the institutions themselves. They also complained that the institutions would lose their special character if the pact on financial aid were abandoned. Finally, they stated a strong case for need-based aid to permit more minorities and other disadvantaged persons to attend these prestigious institutions. While I agreed completely with them on the last score, I pointed out that our proposed suit was not designed to discourage need-based aid, only prior agreement among universities on the amount of such aid in particular cases. Their claim that the resultant bidding wars would reduce the overall amount available to needy students would be of scant concern to families obliged to accept less aid. In some cases, receiving less aid might even deprive students of the opportunity to attend the school of their choice.

On May 22, 1991, we filed civil price-fixing charges in Philadelphia against nine of the universities and simultaneously announced a global settlement with eight of them. Brown, Columbia, Cornell, Dartmouth, Harvard, Princeton, the University of Pennsylvania and Yale agreed to forgo any future "overlap" meetings and "not to discuss or agree on future tuition or faculty salary increases," another practice in which they appeared to have engaged. Settling out of court enabled them to avoid private antitrust actions, with their potential for treble damages. (A Wesleyan College student had already filed a class action.) Only the Massachusetts Institute of Technology chose to contest the charges. It was later found to have violated the law but was awarded a new trial upon appeal, which prompted an out-of-court settlement by the Clinton administration in late 1993.

The global settlement did not quiet the chorus of shrill criticism emanating from the elite schools and their allies. High school counselors, however, noted that financial-aid competition would be good for students and their families.

MY TENURE SAW a huge increase in the department's activity in the international arena. The negotiation of extradition and mutual legal assistance treaties and executive agreements were high priorities as we sought more fugitives, evidence and forfeitable assets from abroad. Other meetings, conferences and negotiations focused on organized crime, money laundering, terrorism and narcotics. At various times I pursued these discussions in Greece, England, Switzerland, Germany, Italy, Spain, Ireland, Luxembourg, Scotland, Sweden, Hungary and Bulgaria.

One point of tension with the Italian authorities was the fate of Silvia Baraldini, an Italian citizen who had, some years earlier, been convicted of murder-terrorism charges in the United States in connection with the killing of a police officer. Italian political circles agitated for Baraldini to be returned to Italy to serve her sentence, but our correctional officials feared that she would immediately be released. I heard a plea on Baraldini's behalf from nearly every Italian official I encountered, but we steadfastly insisted that she remain in American custody. In 1999, the Clinton administration agreed to return Baraldini to Italy to serve out her sentence.

Meanwhile, in Greece, we were pressing for the extradition of terrorist suspect Mohammed Said Rashid, a member of the Palestinian May 15 organization (named for the date in 1948 when Israel was established). Rashid was implicated in one of the very first airplane bombing incidents, the 1982 explosion aboard a Pan Am 747 jet en route from Honolulu to Tokyo, which took the life of a Japanese youth and injured fifteen other passengers. We were unsure of the Greeks' ability to secure the kind of result we felt was justified by the symbolic importance of the deed. Our fears were well founded. Although Rashid was convicted and sentenced to fifteen years, he was released on grounds of good behavior after serving just over eight—hardly an adequate deterrent to such infamous conduct. Whether even these results would have eventuated without our remonstrances was questionable.

All these discussions were a little more diplomatic and pro forma than I would have preferred, but I was learning that law enforcement concerns were not always a priority in the multifaceted world of international relations.

In September 1990, I traveled to Seoul, Korea, for the first-ever gathering of twenty-four Asian and Pacific Rim attorneys general. I then stopped in Japan for discussions covering money laundering, asset forfeiture, chemical diversion measures and antitrust matters. At this time the Japanese lacked the essentials to deal with "criminal enterprises," including undercover investigative authority, witness immunity, conspiracy laws, a RICO statute, and forfeiture and money-laundering tools. Most of their cases depended on confessions, and they seldom got beyond the lower levels of criminal enterprises. They were most cooperative with American law enforcement efforts, however, and our relations remained good.

Tokyo had a treat in store for me: After hearing for years about Japanese baseball, I was finally able to attend a game. The stadium had a capacity of about 50,000, but only about 10,000 enthusiastic fans were on hand to see the Yakult Swallows defeat the Hiroshima Carp, 2–1. The season was winding down, young people were back in school and the Swallows were in last place. I later learned that it was the Yomiuri Giants, the other Tokyo team, that was the true Japanese baseball dynasty. One oddity: because Japanese fans are obliged to return foul balls to the field, there was none of the scramble in the stands that characterizes an American ballpark.

Twice I represented our administration at presidential inaugurations in Latin America: those of Uruguayan president Luis Alberto Lacalle in March 1990 and Guatemalan president Jorge Serrano Elias in January 1991. The latter marked the first transition from one democratically elected Guatemalan government to another since 1951. This period had seen constant insurgencies and containment efforts, including the violent and bloody tactics of death squads. We sought to impress upon Serrano and outgoing president Vinicio Cerezo our interest in human rights and cooperation in law enforcement endeavors, with particular attention to what appeared to be a burgeoning drug transshipment problem in Guatemala. I was to revisit the problems of integrity in law enforcement in Guatemala after I left public life.

The insights gained and contacts made during these trips were of considerable value in establishing and implementing the Department of Justice's international agenda. The Clinton administration's deputy attorney general, Jamie Gorelick, was later to acknowledge that "your work in the international arena while you were AG laid many of the underpinnings of our current effort." The effects that these experiences had upon me as an individual did not, however, become fully apparent until my later service at the United Nations.

BEGINNING IN LATE 1989, I became active in the effort to promote the rule of law in other nations. One extraordinary opportunity in this regard arose in the Soviet Union, which was in the throes of transformation. Premier Mikhail S. Gorbachev had undertaken to depart from the totalitarian past through *glasnost* (openness) and *perestroika* (restructuring). To help him create a "law-based state," the Soviet Ministry of Justice invited us to visit Moscow to discuss democracy, the rule of law and human rights. This gave us an unprecedented chance to participate in the truly revolutionary events occurring in the USSR. It would also mark the first visit ever by a sitting attorney general of the United States to the Soviet Union.

We had open-ended seminars with Justice Minister Veniamin F. Yakovlev, Procurator General Aleksandr Y. Sukharev and their colleagues, covering everything from federalism and our two-party system to the separation of powers, including the independence of the judiciary. At a later public appearance, Yakovlev and I spoke on the substance of our exchanges and signed a document committing each of us to follow-up action. Sukharev signed an agreement opening the Soviet wartime archives to our anti-Nazi investigators.

Our meeting with KGB chief Vladimir Kryuchkov at his headquarters office was a surreal experience for our FBI detail, who had spent their entire careers viewing this organization as demonic. He candidly sought our advice as to whether the intelligence and law enforcement roles of the KGB should be separated, and we discussed a number of current issues, including the potential for cooperation on drug trafficking, organized crime and terrorism. Perhaps the most assertive official we met was Vadim V. Bakatin, head of the militia, a no-nonsense individual obviously intent upon shaking up his organization. He acknowledged an increasing crime problem, including "organized crime," which was never precisely defined. He was particularly interested in our court-authorized wiretapping procedures; he had only known wiretapping to be used for intelligence gathering, and his eyes grew wide at the prospect of using it to produce legally admissible evidence of criminal wrongdoing.

Apparently, I was the first American cabinet member ever to visit the Supreme Soviet, and its members welcomed me warmly. Subsequently its chairman, Anatoly I. Lukyanov, spoke of the difficulty of introducing a human rights agenda at a time when public concern over a rising rate of violent crime had created pressure for a crackdown. He also aimed a few barbs at an increasingly free press.

Finally, I delivered a speech to law students at Moscow State University, seeking to tie together the accomplishments of our democratic system and the aspirations of the people of the Soviet Union. I pointed out the continuing need to cooperate on a transnational agenda, with particular emphasis on narcotics control and protection of the environment. I also mentioned two extraordinary heroes of our respective countries—Benjamin Franklin, publisher, printer, author, businessman, scientist, sage and founder of the University of Pennsylvania, and Mikhail Lomonosov, poet, chemist, physicist, linguist, artist and founder of Moscow State University. The two were contemporaries, although they never met or corresponded. I noted that they shared

the conviction that the unfettered human mind and enlightened government could open new horizons for their peoples and all mankind. . . . On his deathbed in 1765, Lomonosov said that he. . . . feared that all his good intentions would vanish with him. A quarter of a century later, and four months before his own death, Franklin wrote: "God grant that not only the Love of Liberty but a thorough Knowledge of the Rights of Man may pervade all the nations of the Earth so that a Philosopher may set his foot any where on its surface and say, 'This is my country.'"

I set forth a challenge: "Let us, gathered here today, resolve to do all we can to prove Lomonosov's last fears to have been unfounded and Franklin's last hopes to have been prophetic."

Shortly after our return, the Berlin Wall came down. The Cold War was soon to end. Gorbachev agreed to the reunification of Germany, and the last of the Warsaw Pact Communist satellites had been overthrown. Much of our effort in the Soviet Union, however, was overtaken by the final disintegration of the Gorbachev regime, culminating in the failed coup of August 1991 and the ascendancy of Boris Yeltsin. Of those we had met, Yakovlev was the principal survivor, becoming chief judge of the Court of Arbitration Appeals, the ultimate appellate court for commercial controversies. Many of the seeds planted by our discussions of the rule of law took hold, however, as I was to learn during subsequent visits to Boris Yeltsin's Russia in the ensuing decade.

Meanwhile, the department undertook similar missions to other countries seeking to shed their Communist and totalitarian identities. On visits to Budapest and Sofia in December 1990, I spoke with top officials and judges of their aspirations for the rule of law and greater human rights. Other representatives of the department conducted similar programs in Poland and Czechoslovakia as we sought to promote what I characterized before a Kennedy School Forum in May 1991 as "our most valuable export: the rule of law." At my urging, and after some congressional resistance, in late 1990 the department established an Office of International Affairs to focus these activities. I named Robin Ross as its director and Cuyler Walker as his deputy.

ONE VEXING PROBLEM that resolved itself during this period was the emigration of Soviet Jews. Progress on this issue had been one of the goals of our 1989 trip. Most of those we had met in Moscow a decade earlier had by now been permitted to emigrate, but we met with representatives of Soviet Jewish human rights groups as well as a group of refuseniks for a briefing on the status of those still denied that right. We also monitored interviews at the embassy of those seeking asylum, and we raised with Soviet officials our concerns over the status of emigration legislation. Later I raised by a letter to KGB chairman Kryuchkov the case of mathematician Vladimir Raiz, whose wife, Karmella, had visited our office. In 1965, Raiz had been denied permission to emigrate on the grounds of "access to state secrets." This objection had been dropped by his employer but not by the local authorities in Vilnius. Happily, my letter in early 1990 was soon followed by the grant of an exit visa, and the family was reunited.

Meanwhile, on our end, the INS had to assess the claims of individuals seeking to enter the United States as refugees using a worldwide standard: whether the person "because of persecution or a well-founded fear of persecution on account of race, religion, nationality, membership in a particular social group or political opinion is unable or unwilling to return to, or remain in, his or her country of origin." Congress established a ceiling of 50,000 entrants per year from the Soviet Union; I exercised my parole authority to admit others in late 1988, and the 1990 Lautenberg amendment made additional categories of émigrés eligible for admittance. It was not until the coming of the Yeltsin regime, however, that this long-standing problem was finally laid to rest so that all those wishing to emigrate could do so.

IN GENERAL, THE INS remained somewhat of a mystery to me throughout my tenure. Its role was somewhat ambiguous. On the one hand, as a law enforcement agency, it was responsible for preventing illegal immigration and, under the 1986 Simpson-Mazzoli Act, for sanctioning employers who hired illegal immigrants. On the other, it was responsible for facilitating legal immigration in a fair and equitable way and for evaluating claims for political asylum under highly technical legal rules often subject to the prevailing political winds. Many INS activities might have been better lodged within the State Department, but I had a distinct impression that Secretary Jim Baker was no more eager than I was to take on these challenges.

With a billion-dollar budget, the INS was one of the department's fastest-growing agencies. Its 17,000 employees included nearly 5,000 agents charged with policing 6,000 miles of land border; 1,600 investigative agents; 2,800 inspectors checking travel documents at points of entry; and 1,950 examiners processing applications for citizenship and various immigration benefits.

INS apprehensions along the borders totaled about 850,000 in fiscal year 1989, over 1,000,000 the following year and nearly 1,100,000 in fiscal year 1991. The rule of thumb, however, was that one or two persons cross the border illegally for every one apprehended. About 40 percent of the problem was in the San Diego area, followed by El Paso and Brownsville, Texas. By and large, those schemes that offered some prospect of stemming the flow were politically unpalatable. Legal ambiguities about the rights of illegal aliens under our Constitution made the agency's job still more difficult. The INS also had trouble on the recordkeeping front. During the period of Desert Storm, for example, it could not tell me how many Iraqis were in the United States. The travails of INS appear to continue to this day, compounded by post–September 11, 2001, concerns. In 2003, it was one of many agencies folded into the new Department of Homeland Security. Perhaps better days lie ahead.

16

The ADA and Other
Domestic Endeavors

T HE DEPARTMENT OF Justice had unique opportunities to contribute to President Bush's vision of "a kinder, gentler America." Nowhere were these opportunities more manifest than in the work to enact the landmark Americans with Disabilities Act (ADA), which secured the civil rights of 54 million Americans with disabilities. I take great pride in having served as the administration's point man in this effort.

Speaking for the administration before House and Senate committees in 1989, I stated our commitment to "attacking discrimination in employment, public services, transportation, public accommodations, and telecommunications." I noted the "anomaly of widely protecting women and minorities from discrimination while failing to provide parallel protection for people with disabilities." I urged a cost-benefit analysis of the bill, matching the burdens on business, for example, with the tangible benefits of empowering persons with disabilities. I closed by noting that people with disabilities "are all too often not allowed to participate because of stereotypical notions held by others in society—notions that have, in large measure, been created by ignorance and maintained by fear. . . . No particular court order or single piece of legislation can alone change long-standing perceptions or misperceptions; regrettably, attitudes can only be reshaped gradually. One of the keys to this reshaping process is to increase contact between and among people with disabilities and their able-bodied peers. And an essential component of that effort is the development of a comprehensive set of laws . . . to promote the integration of people with disabilities into our communities, schools, and work places." My testimony was well received by both the committee members and leaders of the disability community.

Protracted negotiations ensued within the committees, and I served as buffer between supporters of the bill and administration "hardliners" concerned about its impact on the business community. My argument to Republicans was that this was a different kind of civil rights bill—not based on quotas, preferences or set-asides, but designed to empower those with disabilities to enter the mainstream of American life.

Contentious issues included the minimum size of the workplaces subject to the discrimination provisions (ultimately pegged at twenty-five employees, to be phased down to fifteen within two years); the concept of "reasonable accommodation" to an employee's impairment, so long as such would not cause the employer "undue hardship"; the denial of benefits of the act to those illegally using drugs; the "readily achievable" standard for providing accessible public accommodations, so long as they would not cause an "undue burden," with particular provisions on the installation of elevators; limitations on litigation; and detailed rules on transportation and communications facilities. Each of these required careful review within the department, in tandem with White House Counsel Boyden Gray, a true champion of the rights of persons with disabilities. In this, as in other efforts, Chief of Staff John Sununu acted as the watchdog over efforts to expand the act's protection beyond that deemed absolutely necessary.

On July 26, 1990, President Bush signed the ADA into law. At Ginny's suggestion, a blessing was delivered by the Reverend Harold Wilke, an armless minister of the United Church of Christ and an old friend of ours. It was believed to be the first time that a bill signing was accompanied by a formal appeal to the Almighty. A crowd of some 4,000, most with disability of some kind or other, gathered in the bright sunlight on the South Lawn of the White House to share a true moment of achievement. The president was at his best, closing his remarks by saying, "[L]et the shameful wall of exclusion finally come tumbling down." He presented signing pens to all those on the stage, but Harold Wilke told him to give his pen (which he had accepted with his right foot) to Ginny Thornburgh in token of her vigorous efforts in support of the bill. The president thereupon sought me out in the front row and handed me the pen "for Ginny," which I promptly and proudly conveyed to her.

The signing was followed by a round of rallies, celebrations and picnics where I and others spoke in thanks and pride. I called the day one "of emancipation, not just for the many millions of Americans with disabilities who will directly benefit from this Act, but even more so for the rest of us now free to benefit from the contributions which those with disability can make to our economy, our communities and our own well being." The day was a high point of my tenure as attorney general, and I will never forget the celebration of what columnist David Broder called "arguably the most significant civil rights and social policy legislation to become law in more than a decade."

The department was responsible for framing the regulations implementing the new legislation. These were, to the surprise of many, completed on schedule and became effective on July 26, 1991, the first anniversary of the ADA's signing.

In speaking and writing on this subject, one of my favorite stories involved Ginny's and my friend the late Drew Batavia, a White House Fellow for whose assignment to the Department of Justice we had heavily lobbied. As a result of an auto injury, Drew had quadriplegia that left him with the use of only his head—including his very remarkable brain. He had received graduate degrees in law (from Harvard) and public health (from Stanford) before successfully competing for his White House assignment. I often described Drew's regimen: "When you go into Drew's office, just down the hall from mine, you are likely to find him tapping away at a computer keyboard with his mouth stick—25 words per minute at least five to eight hours a day. His computer and reading stands are on tables, raised to a level high enough to accommodate his wheel chair. At first glance, it looks expensive, but as Drew points out, virtually all employees have computers and telephones. How much does it cost to add a little height to the table legs? How much extra for a few wooden reading stands?"

"How much?" indeed, to provide the Drew Batavias of this world with the dignity of gainful employment and the rest of us with the benefit of their enormous talent. On the fifth anniversary of the ADA in July 1995, I was to coauthor an op-ed piece in the *Wall Street Journal* with Attorney General Janet Reno underscoring the fact that the predicted high costs to the business community of implementing the act had not, in fact, transpired. On the Act's tenth anniversary, Ginny and I and other advocates joined President George W. Bush for an inspiring White House ceremony awash in memories of the struggle to enact this milestone legislation.

Our Civil Rights Division also aggressively pursued a broad agenda in the disability field, most notably by combating zoning and other restrictions against neighborhood group homes. A landmark victory in Chicago was followed by one in Pittsburgh. Ginny and I were particularly heartened by these cases because we knew how important it was to Peter's well-being that he live in the community, rather than in isolation from the mainstream. In *Olmstead v. L.C. and E.W.*, the Supreme Court was in 1999 to interpret the Americans with Disabilities Act as requiring community-based treatment for those with mental disabilities such as Peter's. On behalf of myself and NOD, I had filed a friend of the court brief in support of this concept.

By now, Ginny was working full time in the disability movement as director of the Religion and Disability Program she had created at NOD. This interfaith program was designed to aid religious leaders in making their houses of worship more welcoming to those with disabilities. In years to come, she would establish herself as a national leader in this field, combining her faith and her advocacy for persons with disabilities in an effort that was to enrich the lives of many.

During a visit to Rome in December 1990, we had an opportunity to have a private audience with Pope John Paul. In what some might have characterized as a breach of protocol, Ginny began, "Your Holiness, I have a favor to ask you." Thereafter, she described to him the challenges faced by persons with disabilities in their congregations, then outlined a project for a worldwide ecumenical conference at the Vatican on religion and disability. At the end of our audience, the pope murmured to me, "Your wife is a very persuasive woman." The highly successful Vatican Conference on Disability was to take place in 1992. Quite an accomplishment for a Presbyterian!

I WAS DETERMINED to see improvements in the broader field of civil rights as well. Early in my tenure I met with prominent civil rights leaders, and I was often in contact with Jesse Jackson on issues of the day. There were some positive signs: my remarks at an Atlanta service honoring Dr. Martin Luther King Jr. led actress and activist Jane Fonda to write me a note saying, "Your presence and your words were an important and hopeful message of commitment by the federal government and the new administration to the ongoing civil rights effort." Moreover, lawsuits filed by minority employees presented opportunities to break down long-existing patterns of bias in Justice Department agencies themselves, and I encouraged their settlement.

Nevertheless, many of the other civil rights challenges that we faced had far less harmonious outcomes. Indeed, some were deeply contentious and sorely tested the relationships we had built with civil rights leaders. Ironically, one of the most difficult negotiations—that over the proposed Civil Rights Act of 1990—was roughly contemporaneous with the passage of the ADA.

In the spring of 1989, the Supreme Court handed down four employment discrimination decisions that rocked the civil rights community. *Richmond v. Croson* held that the city of Richmond's set-aside program for minority contractors violated equal protection requirements. *Ward's Cove Packing Co. v. Antonio* shifted the burden of proof to plaintiffs to show employment discrimination, holding that disparate impact in itself did not show such discrimination. *Martin v. Wilks* allowed white firefighters to challenge, under the Civil Rights Act, employment decisions made pursuant to a promotions quota set forth in a consent decree between the city of Birmingham and black firefighters. Finally, *Patterson v. McLean Credit Union* held that the Civil Rights Act of 1866 did not allow actions for discriminatory conduct (namely, racial harassment) after an employee had been hired.

Faced with a firestorm of reaction, which quickly focused on demands for legislative relief, the administration assigned John Sununu and Boyden Gray to handle damage control and asked the department to assume a supporting role on the technical legal issues involved. Over the next two years, administration policy seemed to ebb and flow, and Sununu, mostly because of the press of other matters, dipped in and out of our discussions and negotiations, often leaving Boyden and me somewhat at a loss as to the administration's precise goals. We knew that in general, it sought to be as responsive as possible to civil rights concerns without undercutting its bedrock beliefs. We knew also that on a personal level, the president was deeply opposed to racial and ethnic (as well as religious) prejudice, and that he did not want to be viewed as a foe of the civil rights community. Unfortunately, this was precisely how many did view him when this lengthy exercise was completed.

My first public foray into this controversy was an uncomfortable one. The Reverend Jesse Jackson invited me to speak on the subject at the annual conference of Operation PUSH, his umbrella organization for civil rights and social welfare initiatives. My remarks, delivered on June 27, 1989, were designed to put the court decisions and the administration's posture in context. Thus, I reviewed our efforts to reestablish a constructive dialogue with civil rights and minority groups, our support of the extension of the Fair Housing Act to allow monetary damages for discrimination, our stepped-up effort to prosecute hate crimes and our continued pressure to ensure that "one person, one vote" meant a maximum opportunity for African American representation in elected office at all levels of government.

Next, I suggested that the Court's decisions did not "conflict with the nation's fundamental commitment to ensure the provision of civil rights for all Americans." Nor did they "repudiate efforts aimed at achieving equal opportunity and protection under the law." Instead, they represented "attempts by the court to fine tune the complexities of enforcement of civil rights laws in America" and could "in the long run, through the certainty they lend to the legal process, place enforcement on an even firmer footing." I then delivered the real message of the day: that the president had asked that we monitor the implementation of these opinions in the lower courts to assess their impact on equal employment opportunities and, if needed, suggest any legislative or executive action required to resolve inequities. This was not the message that the audience, hostile from the outset, wanted to hear.

Senator Ted Kennedy and others quickly generated legislative proposals not only to overturn three of the four holdings (leaving *Croson* intact), but to break some new ground in the employment discrimination area. The administration was amenable to about 75 percent of the proposed package. We balked, however, at language that we felt might induce employers to adopt hiring quotas for fear of being sued. (In my confirmation hearings, I had stated my commitment to "removing barriers to qualified people who may have been excluded because of practices that arose in the past," but had opposed "artificial quotas [as] counterproductive.") The president wanted Congress to pass a civil rights bill that he could sign, but he was unwilling to sign a quota bill. Protracted negotiations followed, greatly influenced by liberal groups.

Boyden Gray, John Sununu and I spent hours over the next year or so dealing with Senator Kennedy and, occasionally, with other interested parties in an effort to iron out the kinks. At times, we must have resembled a gathering of Talmudic scholars as we pondered concepts such as "disparate impact," "business necessity," "manifest relationship to the employment in question" and "significant relationship to job performance." The whole discussion eventually deteriorated into a lawyers' debate over words and phrases. My own principal concern was the burden of proof, as I explained during an appearance on the *Today* show in July 1990: "[The Kennedy] bill gives the right to an individual to sue simply on the basis of an imbalance between the make-up of the employer's work force and the work force in the community in question. It then forces the employer to justify his practices. It finds him guilty until proven innocent with regard to any practices he has with regard to hiring. And this can become so costly and so difficult an operation for the average employer, facing the prospect of lawsuits and lawyers' fees, that it's going to compel him to throw in the towel and say I'll just do my hiring by the numbers. And that kind of quota isn't fair to the employees, isn't fair to the employer and it's certainly not consistent with the underlying theory of the Civil Rights Acts since 1964."

Finally, Congress passed a bill; the president vetoed it in October 1990, stating that he was taking a stand against quotas. Knowing the president's firm opposition to quotas, I was one of those who had recommended this veto. When the bill reappeared in roughly the same form before the 1992 election, he relented and signed it. The entire process was not particularly orderly and did not, in the final analysis, enhance the image of the Bush administration.

ONE OF MY MOST touching encounters followed the passage of the Civil Liberties Act of 1988. This law provided for $1.25 billion in compensation to the survivors of the 120,000 Japanese Americans interned during World War II—up to $20,000 for each of the American citizens shipped off to relocation camps. We invited nine recipients, aged 73 to 107, to a ceremony, together with the legislators who had sponsored the act and other interested parties. Most of the recipients were in wheelchairs or otherwise impaired. It was a very emotional experience for all of us, as justice was finally made manifest for those treated so callously in a time of stress.

On the other side of the ledger was an increase in hate crimes across the nation—physical or emotional attacks based on race, religion, ethnic background or gender. This had been a longtime concern of mine; when I was governor, we had secured the passage of Pennsylvania's Ethnic Intimidation Act. Organizations like the Aryan Nation and various "skinhead" groups posed a substantial challenge to local law enforcement. We participated in monitoring these groups and carried out over 100 successful prosecutions in more than twenty states, where federal jurisdiction could be established.

Much of our work was coordinated with the Anti-Defamation League of B'nai B'rith and with Morris Dees's Center for Human Rights in Birmingham, and was widely praised in the Jewish American community. Dees later observed, "The Justice Department under Reagan and Bush, to their credit, has done more than any prior Justice Department on record to prosecute white supremacists." Years later, frustrated by Clinton administration guidelines prompting a much less aggressive response to such groups, Abraham H. Foxman, national director of the Anti-Defamation League, wrote: "In the late 1980s violence by neo-Nazi skinheads was on the rise across America. At a meeting with Richard Thornburgh, then the Attorney General, we urged the Justice Department and the Federal Bureau of Investigation to place the skinheads on the F.B.I. watch list—to monitor their activities and vigorously apply the law. The Attorney General did just that and as a result violence by neo-Nazi skinheads declined significantly."

A particular civil rights challenge arose from the beating of motorist Rodney King by Los Angeles police officers on March 3, 1991. The public outcry over the videotaped beating was understandably great, and the accompanying demand for federal action was predictable. I had long felt that police misconduct of this sort was among the most corrosive influences in a free society and deserved to be dealt with vigorously. The invariable policy of the department in police brutality cases was to defer to local prosecution where it was undertaken with seriousness and dispatch. Nonetheless, the department had brought criminal charges for official misconduct against ninety-eight persons in the three years preceding the King incident, securing convictions in 75 percent of the cases that had reached the trial stage.

I instructed our Civil Rights Division to monitor the King prosecution closely. The police officers were acquitted in the state proceedings but were later convicted on federal civil rights charges during Bill Barr's watch. I also ordered a review of all allegations referred to the Civil Rights Division over the previous six years to see whether any patterns of police misconduct could be detected within particular jurisdictions.

During the redistricting process that followed the 1990 census, the Civil Rights Division was called upon to make numerous findings on the observance of constitutional "one man, one vote" guidelines. The most controversial of these determinations involved the efforts by some south-

ern states to create "safe" minority seats through imaginative configura-
tions of voting districts. Conservatives objected to these contortions as a
matter of principle, while Democrats charged that they also preserved
"safe" Republican districts. The matter was not resolved until the Supreme
Court's 5–4 rulings in 1996 that states could not use race as the predominant factor in designating legislative districts at the expense of compact-
ness and other traditional principles. The result was to undo a number of
the districts the department had approved.

Our department ceased the Reagan administration's practice of encouraging school boards to challenge court desegregation orders. This
earned us some plaudits from the civil rights community.

We worked to advance women's educational rights by supporting a
challenge to the all-male status of two of the nation's preeminent military
institutions, Virginia Military Institute (VMI) and the Citadel in South
Carolina. Our reading of the Fourteenth Amendment and the equal protection cases decided by the Supreme Court left little doubt that the exclusionary practices of these publicly supported colleges violated the rights of
women who sought to enroll there. Intense political pressure not to proceed
came from alumni, governmental officials and antifeminist groups as well
as from the schools themselves. We moved forward, however, and while
unsuccessful in the lower courts in the VMI case, we ultimately prevailed in
a 7–1 ruling by the Supreme Court in 1996. Shortly thereafter, the Citadel,
against which similar action had been taken, abandoned its efforts to retain
its single-sex status. By the turn of the century, both institutions were relatively comfortable with their coeducational status.

THE ABORTION ISSUE remained volatile. In November 1989, we filed
a brief in *Webster v. Reproductive Health Services* asserting the need to overturn *Roe v. Wade*. Yet another split response from the Court whittled away
at *Roe* but did not overturn it. After I left office, *Roe* was further eroded in
a case from Pennsylvania, *Casey v. Planned Parenthood*. This was a virtual
replay of the earlier *Thornburgh* case, but its slightly different result extended the state's authority to regulate abortions under *Roe*.

Public attention shifted during the summer of 1991 to the efforts of
pro-life groups such as Operation Rescue to obstruct access to abortion
clinics and to verbally harass both patients and medical personnel. Some of
the efforts suggested by feminist groups to restrain these undertakings
raised serious free-speech issues.

The department had already filed an amicus curiae brief in the Supreme Court in opposition to a Fourth Circuit decision, *Bray v. Alexandria Women's Health Clinic*, that used the Ku Klux Klan Act of 1871 to combat the efforts of the pro-life groups. Subsequently, on August 5, 1991, U.S. District Court Judge Patrick Kelly issued a preliminary injunction under the Ku Klux Klan Act against a range of activities being conducted by Operation Rescue in Wichita, Kansas. The United States was not a party to that action, but U.S. marshals carried out their responsibility of enforcing the injunction, although they considered its directions overly detailed. The U.S. attorney's office, however, also filed a copy of the amicus curiae brief in the *Bray* case with Judge Kelly, pointing out the erroneous legal basis of his order, while taking no position between the litigants in the Wichita case.

Judge Kelly proceeded to attack both the department and me personally in the media, even appearing on ABC-TV's *Nightline* and the *MacNeil/Lehrer NewsHour* to accuse us of having "given an imprimatur to what, in my view, is a license for mayhem." This was an unprecedented action for a judge in a case that he had under consideration. As Harvard Law School professor Mary Ann Glendon commented, "judicial ethics forbid a judge to make any public comment that might be reasonably expected to prejudice the outcome of pending litigation." Naturally, Kelly's appearance stirred a massive response from feminist and pro-choice groups across the country. We emphasized that we had taken no position in the case and that the judge's order was being enforced, but that we believed the court lacked the jurisdiction it had asserted. None of these fine points were appreciated, however, and the general public was left only with the vague impression that the Department of Justice and the attorney general were "supporting" Operation Rescue and "opposing" the judge.

Our position was never sufficiently explained until October 1991, when, in the midst of my later Senate campaign, feminist groups made it an issue in Pennsylvania. Senator Arlen Specter wrote a scholarly piece in the *Pittsburgh Post-Gazette* stating that I had "properly placed the rule of law above the policy viewpoint of the Bush administration by fully enforcing the court's orders . . . brought the full weight of the executive branch behind the court by condemning the demonstrators' violations of the court's order . . . and was consistent in raising in the Wichita case a legal issue that the Justice Department had already argued some months before in a similar case pending in U.S. Supreme Court."

In 1993, the justices ruled 5–4 in the *Bray* case that the Ku Klux Klan Act did not, in fact, give the federal courts jurisdiction over suits of this kind. By that time, however, my role as a villain had been irrevocably established among persons opposed (as, indeed, I was) to the harassment tactics of Operation Rescue.

THE BUREAU OF Prisons was among the department's fastest-growing agencies. Increases in serious crimes, stepped-up law enforcement and longer sentences stretched our prison capacity to the utmost during my tenure. The prison population exceeded 60,000 when I departed, well in excess of rated capacity. With sound advice from Director Mike Quinlan, we added 17,000 beds at a cost of $2.8 billion and secured congressional authorization for 42,000 more.

Nearly all prisoners will, at some time, return to the community. Their attitude, their skill levels and their ability to cope with that return are key. Funds invested in improving these factors are invested in halting the revolving door of crime. Despite the discouraging figures on recidivism, we wanted to give offenders every opportunity to rehabilitate themselves, so we emphasized access to drug treatment and rehabilitation, literacy programs and job training.

From fiscal year 1989 to fiscal year 1991, our drug treatment and rehabilitation budget grew from $2.25 million to $9.51 million, the staff for these efforts grew from 33 to 173 and the number of inmates participating rose from 3,800 to 9,000. For fiscal year 1992 we requested a budget of $21.76 million and a staff of 223 to serve a projected 12,000 inmates. Extensive urine surveillance programs were conducted at all sixty-seven institutions; positive findings decreased from 7.4 percent in 1985 to 1.9 percent in 1991 despite a growing population and increasing numbers of drug offenders.

Literacy efforts had begun in the early 1980s, with inmates not testing at a sixth-grade reading level being required to attend classes. The standard was later raised to the eighth-grade level and, by 1990, to the equivalent of a high school diploma. The sense of accomplishment among those completing their requirements was almost as important as the skill level achieved.

Every federal inmate able to hold a job was required to do so, and about 30 percent of our population at any given time held an industrial job. Our Federal Prison Industries constantly sought out new product lines and customers to maximize employment opportunities. Again, work habits and self-esteem were as important as the actual job skills acquired.

OUTSIDE THE SCOPE of our official duties, the department worked to contribute to our community. Our main focus in this regard was the public schools in the District of Columbia. Over 450 of our staff volunteered to teach in fourteen schools on law-related subjects. I taught one session of a seventh-grade class on American history at Stuart Hobson Middle School in the spring of 1990 and enjoyed it thoroughly. I was particularly pleased that the *Washington Post* quoted one of my students, Christon Hill, as saying, "They say he's not a good person . . . in the newspapers. . . . But that's false." This appearance and a second one the following year were widely covered on television, raising the profile of our effort. After I had left the department, the District's program head wrote that we had "touched the lives of many young people. Every day there is an employee—a secretary, special agent, assistant attorney general—of the Department in some school making a difference." President Bush later signed an executive order facilitating all federal employees' participation in such programs.

We also initiated the department's first day care program in long-overdue recognition of the changing nature of our workforce. Our child development center was officially opened about a year after I left office.

I WAS A MEMBER of four subcabinet groups established by the president: the Domestic Policy Council (DPC), the Economic Policy Council, the National Security Council (NSC) and the Council on Competitiveness. By far the most significant, and eventually the most frustrating, of these assignments was my chairmanship of the DPC—a chairmanship that, in retrospect, was probably not in my best interests.

In President Bush's words, the DPC was to "serve as the primary channel for advising me on the formulation, coordination, and implementation of domestic and social policy." Its members included the secretaries of health and human services (Dr. Louis Sullivan), housing and urban development (Jack Kemp), energy (Jim Watkins), transportation (Sam Skinner), commerce (Bob Mosbacher), agriculture (Clayton Yeutter and Ed Madigan), the interior (Manuel Lujan), veterans affairs (Ed Derwinski and Tony Principi), treasury (Nick Brady) and education (Lauro Cavazos and Lamar Alexander), as well as the administrator of the EPA (Bill Reilly), the director of the Office of Management and Budget (Dick Darman), the director of the Office of Policy Development (Roger Porter) and the White House chief of staff (John Sununu).

Although I already had a full plate as attorney general, I was intrigued by the prospect that service with the DPC would enable me to keep a hand in the types of issues I had dealt with as a governor. I considered the DPC's prime role to be dealing with areas where the interests of two or more cabinet-level agencies overlapped and possibly differed. Our job was not to take stands on issues, but to present the president with well-considered options, on the basis of which he could choose a course of action.

Our very first exercise, in May and June 1989, was of just this type—the framing of administration policy on reauthorization of the Clean Air Act. While primarily within the jurisdiction of the EPA, the issues involved affected other agencies as well, most notably the Departments of Energy, Transportation and Commerce. The council's sessions on acid rain, air toxics and ozone nonattainment resulted in decision memoranda for the president. On the basis of these, he was able to enunciate a coordinated clean air policy that greatly enhanced the administration's bargaining position with Congress.

During this exercise, it became apparent that John Sununu and Dick Darman were pursuing a separate, parallel process designed, it seemed, to keep the DPC within limits. While this did no particular harm at the time, it was a portent of the dominant influence that these two key aides were to exert over domestic policy. The two became increasingly unpopular with the cabinet as their role in policy making became more substantial. One observer was later to describe Darman and Sununu as "a domestic policy regency . . . who spurned information and advice, were imperious and secretive, and operated with a top-down style that cut off ideas from below." This was a far cry from what Roger Porter had earlier described as an optimum: a system "designed to expose the president to competing arguments and viewpoints made by advocates themselves rather than . . . filtered through a staff to the president."

Over the next year and a half, a wide variety of issues reached the DPC. Many of these resulted in decision memoranda that gave the president meaningful options for action. Others, however, did not. One example was national health policy. Typical was a meeting on October 15, 1990, where Sununu fenced in Dr. Sullivan's suggestions with a requirement that all proposals be "revenue neutral" and an admonition to work largely through the private sector and the NGA. Few particulars were to result.

It gradually became apparent that domestic policy was a relatively low priority for the administration. The president's successes in bringing the Cold War to an end, in dealing with Premier Gorbachev to reduce international tensions and in framing the extraordinary global coalition that contained Saddam Hussein clearly overshadowed the challenges of dealing with economic and social problems at home. One of the president's aides told me of having warned him that reporters would probably accuse him of being more interested in foreign policy than in domestic issues. "Yes," the president was said to have replied, "and they would be right." Moreover, the increasingly recalcitrant and partisan Democratic opposition that controlled both houses of Congress had far more say in domestic than in foreign affairs. Was it any wonder that George Bush preferred to deal with Gorbachev, British prime ministers Margaret Thatcher and John Major, and French president Francois Mitterrand than with Majority Leader George Mitchell and Speaker Tom Foley? When asked what the administration wanted from Congress, John Sununu is alleged to have responded, perhaps facetiously, "To go home."

Some of us, most vocally Jack Kemp, chafed under this relative inattention to domestic affairs. However, White House decision makers clearly did not take DPC proposals seriously. The DPC itself seemed to be falling into disuse as Operation Desert Shield consumed the fall of 1990. On November 15, I sent a memorandum to Sununu asking for "a more active (and indeed pro-active) role for the DPC" in "shaping new initiatives designed to further an agenda based on the President's values and principles." I suggested initiatives such as child care vouchers, choice in education, repeal of the Social Security earnings limits and tenant management of public housing. Sununu's only response was a call to say, "Just keep on doing what you've been doing." Although piqued, I did not carry the effort further. This was probably a mistake—for me and for the administration. The DPC was, for all intents and purposes, a dead letter.

The coup de grace for an aggressive domestic policy effort came on March 6, 1991, when the president addressed Congress following the astonishingly rapid victory over Saddam Hussein. After basking, justifiably, in this triumph, the president turned to the domestic agenda. He began with a clarion call to action, asking Congress to "move forward aggressively on our domestic front." However, he then limited the specifics to a new highway bill and his long-stalled crime bill. My heart sank. What an opportunity had been missed to outline a bold and comprehensive domestic program. Even if it had foundered on the shoals of partisan opposition, such an agenda would have clearly etched the differences between the parties and defined the issues in the 1992 campaign. In retrospect, I believe this is the moment I began to suspect that George Bush would not be reelected in 1992.

In fairness, as Roger Porter pointed out in a *Wall Street Journal* op-ed piece in late 1994, President Bush "faced larger majorities of the opposing party in Congress than any elected president in U.S. history," and his domestic agenda was thwarted by Democratic opposition at every turn. Many of his proposals found their way into the victorious House Republicans' widely heralded "Contract with America" in 1994, but they were never clearly articulated by the Bush administration.

My work on the NSC was limited, as most of the purely legal issues were handled at the deputy level. I was involved in the final briefing sessions on the Panamanian invasion and a flare-up in the Philippines, which occurred on Vice President Quayle's watch during an absence from Washington by the president. In a teleconference with representatives of the Defense and State Departments and the CIA, assessing how to preserve the government of President Corazon Aquino without committing the United States to a purely military response, the vice president acquitted himself well.

The vice president also chaired the Council on Competitiveness. The most noteworthy undertaking of this group was in the area of civil justice reform. At my suggestion, we enlisted Solicitor General Ken Starr to head a task force to make recommendations that would confront head-on the problems of our overly litigious society. The task force report addressed many issues: overuse of pretrial discovery; excessive punitive damages; the neglect of alternate dispute resolution; the desirability of an "English rule" under which the losing litigant pays both parties' legal fees; and the problem of product liability claims that had driven up losses, legal fees and insurance premiums for American businesses, making them less competitive worldwide. After I left office, the vice president unveiled the task force's recommendations in a speech to the ABA, which, not surprisingly, took him to task for "lawyer bashing."

The Economic Policy Council had relatively little impact. Our department's interest in its activities was largely limited to antitrust and environmental matters. Happily for me, I was not involved in what was, to my mind, the administration's single biggest blunder: agreeing to a sizable tax increase to resolve the budget stalemate of 1990. Most voters were understandably mystified by this move and many felt betrayed, remembering President Bush's noteworthy 1988 declaration, "Read my lips, no new taxes!" Given the parlous international situation, I would guess that the president's negotiators felt a deal was necessary to keep the government from shutting down. I also suspect that Darman and Sununu were enchanted with the notion of getting the best of the Democrats in these negotiations.

In retrospect, this was the beginning of the end for the Bush presidency. The fragile commodity of credibility was devalued overnight. Substantively, I believe the budget agreement laid the basis for the nation's strong fiscal performance during the 1990s by producing increased revenues and reducing the deficit. Politically, however, I believe Bush would have done better to refuse to go along with any budget that contained a tax increase, shutting down the government if necessary. Ironically, President Bill Clinton later did take this approach. In 1995 he refused to go along with GOP budget demands and placed the blame for the two ensuing government shutdowns on a recalcitrant Republican Congress. This strategy contributed in no small part to his 1996 reelection.

17

Criticisms:

Fair and Unfair

Mʏ sᴜʙsᴛᴀɴᴛɪᴠᴇ ᴡᴏʀᴋ at the department was consistently interesting and challenging. The nonlegal aspects of the job were even more challenging and were ultimately to frustrate me enormously. Tangles with other officials, interest groups and the press demanded sizable amounts of energy that could better have been spent elsewhere.

One set of battles involved my appointments to key positions within the department. At the beginning of the Bush administration, the most important post I had to fill was that of deputy attorney general, the department's chief operating officer. Intent on finding the best possible person for this crucial position, I made one of my first and most costly mistakes.

White House staff suggested several names, but I fastened early on to Bob Fiske, a former U.S. attorney from the Southern District of New York. Bob was generally regarded as one of the top litigators in the country. Moreover, he was a personal friend, he knew the department well, and his Republican credentials as a Ford appointee and Bush contributor seemed to be in order. He appeared, in short, to be an ideal choice. The eventual defeat of his appointment underscored the harshness of the Washington environment as well as my own naiveté in seeking to act without laying the proper foundation.

Bob Fiske had formerly chaired the ABA committee that had for many years evaluated potential appointees to the federal bench. At the time of Bob Bork's nomination to the Supreme Court, the committee was highly politicized, and although it eventually found Bork qualified (with Fiske speaking in support), there were dissents and considerable ill feeling regarding its proper role. In addition, Fiske was accused of giving the names of prospective nominees to various liberal interest groups for their evaluation.

Conservative members of the Senate Judiciary Committee, encouraged by conservative think tanks and legal foundations committed to strict constructionism, chose to see a Fiske appointment as the new administration's affirmation of the approach that had resulted in Bork's nomination being rejected. They were also determined to mount a charge against the ABA itself and saw Fiske as a symbol of that group. I failed to take the appropriate soundings and thus missed the opportunity to rebut this case until far too late. A complicating factor, I suspect, was my failure to court the support of the White House staff, specifically Chief of Staff John Sununu.

By the summer of 1989, Sununu's opposition, it was reported, had solidified (partly, I suspect, because of a desire to "put me in short pants"). In addition, fourteen conservative Republican senators sent the president a letter opposing Fiske's nomination. Finally, Bob asked that his name be withdrawn from consideration. I raised the matter directly with the president, making a strong plea based upon fairness, but made little headway, although the president had recently told the assembled U.S. attorneys that he hoped to "see Bob Fiske joining our ranks here soon." Sununu later confirmed that the decision against Fiske was final. Ironically, newspaper accounts later indicated that opposition to Fiske was softening just as this decision was made. The president later sent me a handwritten note expressing his dismay that Fiske had been "done in by rumors, fiction and half truths," but adding that "there would have been too much blood letting if we had proceeded."

In the final analysis, I was driven to agree with the editorial writers of the *National Legal Journal*: "Sometimes it's a wonder anyone would even consider relinquishing—even briefly—a successful legal career to enter public service. . . . [Deputy attorney general] is a job for which Mr. Fiske is perfectly suited: few in this country have the knowledge and integrity he has gained in his years in the law. [H]e is an extremely capable and reasonable professional whose addition to the Department of Justice would give it a new level of quality. The public deserves no less." But neither the public nor the department got what it deserved. And, as will be seen, the consequences for the department, and for me personally, were severe.

No sooner had the Fiske matter blown over than a controversy came to a head over the appointment to head the Civil Rights Division. I had believed that appointing Bill Lucas, an African American, to this position would send a powerful signal of commitment to civil rights. No conclusion could have been farther from reality.

The White House had suggested Bill for an appointment in the Justice Department because of his extensive background in law enforcement and his status as a former Democratic elected official who had switched to the Republican Party. Bill came from a humble background and had seen firsthand the ravages of second-class citizenship. He had worked on the New York City police force, as a civil rights troubleshooter in the Kennedy Justice Department, as an FBI special agent, as a sheriff and as Wayne County executive, the equivalent of a mayor, before changing parties in 1986. He was lacking in some scholarly skills, and critics belittled his knowledge of the intricacies of the civil rights laws. However, Bill Lucas had seen civil rights issues from ground level, not from the rarefied heights from which many intellectuals chose to attack his appointment. Moreover, I greatly admired his character and integrity.

The liberal establishment had chosen Lucas's appointment as its next big battle, using it, as it had used the Bork nomination, to hype its membership recruiting efforts. I saw the political stakes as quite different, however. No legitimate concern could be raised over the effect of the nomination per se on civil rights policy, since that would be enunciated by President Bush and me. I believe the real basis for the shrill opposition was that black Democratic politicians feared the dramatic consequences of having a high-ranking black Republican as a role model for disadvantaged urban African Americans, who could otherwise continue to be fed a steady litany of Republican wrongs to excuse the sad condition of their schools, communities and job opportunities (problems that had largely accrued under Democratic big-city mayors). These were high stakes indeed.

Bill Lucas's nomination was defeated. While he went on to serve the department well as director of the Office of Community Services, handling outreach to state and local governments and law enforcement groups, an opportunity had been missed to put someone with a real grassroots viewpoint into this important position. In a highly polarized political environment, Lucas had simply been demonized by the left, just as Bob Fiske had been demonized by the right. Fortunately, former New York state senator

John Dunne, one of the most decent men I ever encountered in public life, took the civil rights post and acquitted himself well.

PROBABLY MY single biggest blunder as attorney general was my handling of the Bill Gray affair. Inadvertently, I turned a matter of little consequence into a cause célèbre, as Washington measures such things.

During the spring of 1989, the department was conducting a number of highly sensitive investigations of public officials, including Jim Wright (D-Tex.), Speaker of the House, and Tony Coelho (D-Cal.), the House majority whip. To my considerable concern, unauthorized leaks from the department provided important particulars of these two investigations to the news media. Neither Wright nor Coelho was prosecuted, but both shortly resigned their congressional seats. All this generated a certain level of paranoia on the Hill.

After Coelho's resignation, Bill Gray was considered the leading contender for the Democratic whip position. Gray was a Philadelphia minister who had been elected to Congress in 1978. We had met during the campaign that year (I suspect that he helped my gubernatorial campaign to gain support among African American voters), and we had maintained a cordial relationship thereafter. There had long been media speculation about the congressman's finances, particularly his alleged commingling of church and political funds. I was aware that the U.S. attorney's office in Philadelphia was investigating his affairs, but knew none of the particulars and had no desire to become involved.

On Memorial Day, FBI agents interviewed Gray in connection with the Philadelphia investigation. In what FBI Director Sessions later called "a lapse," I was not notified of this action in advance. Instead, I learned of it via the CBS evening news, which cited unnamed department sources for the story. After the leaks in the Wright and Coelho investigations, this was the last straw. I was livid and responded in the worst possible manner in my determination to find out who was responsible for this one. From this I was to learn, painfully, that it is inadvisable to make decisions when one is furious.

Normally I would have asked our Office of Professional Responsibility (OPR) to try to ascertain the source of the leak. In this case, I directed Assistant Attorney General Ed Dennis to undertake a special criminal investigation, assigning FBI agents and an experienced prosecutor to it. On June 2, I told the Senate Judiciary Committee, "These unauthorized disclosures not only threaten to compromise ongoing investigations, but they give rise to the risk of focusing unwarranted public attention on persons who may not be guilty of any criminal wrongdoing." I pledged to fire anyone who had made such disclosures but noted that pursuing these investigations was extremely difficult without media cooperation.

My remarks were not well received by the media, which resented any attempt to discourage leaks, regardless of their effects on the integrity of investigations or the reputations of individuals. Moreover, my bypassing of the "independent" OPR provided ammunition for Gray's allies on Capitol Hill and other Democratic leaders, who viewed my actions with suspicion from the outset. Our office stated that Gray "is not the target of a criminal investigation by the Department of Justice" and that he and his office "have been fully cooperating with the Department . . . and the FBI." Nevertheless, because Gray was a Democrat and a Pennsylvanian, I myself was roundly criticized for the leak, allegedly motivated by partisan interest in damaging him. The ironic upshot was that my special, high-powered investigation into the leak came to be perceived as an attempt to cover up the facts. Demands for an independent prosecutor to investigate the leak began to emanate not only from the usual sources, but even from Republican House leader Bob Michel (Ill.).

Gray became majority whip, and the investigation moved off the front pages. Just before the end of November, the Criminal Division gave me its report. To no one's surprise, the investigators had been unable to identify the leaker, so no criminal prosecution or disciplinary action was possible. The media seemed to focus more on the estimated $224,000 cost of the five-month inquiry than on its outcome. However, Congressmen Don Edwards (D–Cal.) and Charles Schumer (D–N.Y.), often among our strongest critics, wrote me, "It seems to us that your department has taken thorough and adequate steps in Representative Gray's case to determine the source of the leak, albeit unsuccessfully."

According to the report (which, as was usual in closed criminal investigations, never was made public), the most likely source of the leak was actually Gray's own staff. This would have been typical; an enormous number of leaks originate from Congress. However, there was some evidence that department sources had confirmed it. Polygraphs undertaken to identify these sources produced vague and ambiguous responses from, among others, my aides, Dave Runkel and Robin Ross.

Just a few weeks before I received this report, Donald Ayer had been sworn in as deputy attorney general. Because of the controversy over Bob Fiske, this vital position had been unfilled for far too long. Robin Ross, my executive assistant, had come to act more and more as my de facto deputy, something that many in and out of the department had come to resent. When, belatedly, I addressed this situation, I once again succumbed to the appeal of a resumé. Ayer had impressive credentials but a quirky personality. Others in the administration warned me about him, but I foolishly charged ahead to gain his confirmation.

Ayer proved to have exaggerated notions of his responsibilities and to resent my confidence in Ross, Runkel and Murray Dickman. Soon developing a serious chip on his shoulder, he began taking actions independent of, or in conflict with, my wishes. Once he sent a letter to Boyden Gray containing recommendations for corporate sentencing guidelines that I had not even reviewed. We withdrew his submission for review, which prompted a round of media stories to the effect that Ayer had been overruled in seeking to impose tough guidelines on corporate criminals.

Ayer became highly upset that OPR had not been given the Criminal Division report on the Gray leak to review for potential disciplinary action. (OPR had been kept fully informed all along, and there was nothing left to investigate.) He was convinced that department rules mandated a referral to OPR and that I was required to recuse myself from the case because my top aides and I might have had access to the leaked information. On February 2, a full-blown *Washington Post* story made the identical arguments. At that point Ayer lost whatever credibility he had ever had with me, and the search began for a new deputy who would be both qualified and loyal.

On April 3, under pressure from Chairman Joe Biden (D-Del.) and other Judiciary Committee Democrats at our annual budget hearing, I relented and asked OPR to review the FBI investigation of the Gray case so that I might determine if any disciplinary action was justified. I also defended Dave Runkel, pointing out that he was only "following my standing instruction that no one in the department mislead the media." I concluded, "If . . . the media on occasion interprets the fact that we will not deny information or wave them off of a story as confirmation of an unauthorized disclosure, then that is an inevitable byproduct of our policy."

The OPR came up with nothing new, but its head, Michael Shaheen, insisted on further investigation, largely centered on Ross and Runkel. I was not willing to authorize this and believed it was unfair to further prolong the matter. After discussions with Biden and his House counterpart, Jack Brooks (D-Tex.), we agreed to refer the entire file to Solicitor General Ken Starr for a final determination. No small inducement to the chairmen's acquiescence, I suspect, was the fact that Shaheen was pushing for additional interviews of congressmen and senators, among others.

Ayer's "resignation" was announced on May 11. Bill Barr succeeded him and proved to be the deputy I had needed from the beginning. It was clear that Ross and Runkel had become liabilities, and they were reassigned on May 14. On May 16, Starr's report concluded "that the investigation conducted by the Department's Criminal Division was thorough and complete, and that no further investigation is warranted." Starr added that it was within my discretion to determine that no disciplinary action was warranted and noted that I had already taken corrective action, referring to the reassignments.

In a *Washington Post* interview on May 17, I tried to put the whole matter behind me by acknowledging that my choice of Ayer as deputy was "a mistake." Ayer retaliated by giving a wide-ranging interview to the *Los Angeles Times* that received prominent play. He described his "resignation" as "an act of conscience" and charged, "The attorney general was participating in an effort to prevent appropriate disclosure and evaluation through established procedures of the activities that earlier this week resulted in Robin Ross' abrupt removal from office." All this was not only arrant nonsense but betrayed Ayer's resentment of Ross. It was not clear what Ayer claimed I had done to "prevent appropriate disclosure" of anything whatsoever, unless it was to refuse to leak certain details of the investigation to the news media, a charge to which I would have readily pleaded guilty.

Ayer's departure did earn us some praise from the sometimes critical *Wall Street Journal*, which noted, "Mr. Thornburgh deserves credit for attempting to create a department that speaks with one voice in an Executive Branch that for years has weakened its institutional powers by speaking with too many voices." Most other editorial commentary was negative. The last news item to catch the public's eye in this sorry affair was the report that I myself had submitted to (and passed) a polygraph examination during the investigation. I had been more than willing to submit to the exam to help establish the credibility of the process.

The whole controversy could have been avoided if I had exercised better judgment from the very beginning: if I had been more alert to Fiske's confirmation problems and gotten a first-class deputy at the outset; if I had not been obliged to delegate so many of the deputy's duties to my aides; if I had heeded the warnings given me and had not "hired a resumé" in Don Ayer; and if I had not overreacted to the Gray leak and had assigned it, in the normal course, to OPR. I paid a high price for these lapses. By the time the matter was over, I was nearly on the ropes, being obliged to confirm publicly that I was not going to resign.

The underlying Gray investigation, incidentally, ended with a whimper. Criminal fraud charges unrelated to Gray were filed against one of his former aides over two years after the FBI's initial visit to the congressman. By that time, Gray had announced his intention to resign from Congress to become president of the United Negro College Fund, and I was a month away from leaving the department.

RELATIONSHIPS BETWEEN reporters and public officials in the nation's capital are unique. This was not something that I was able to turn to my advantage. Part of the difficulty was the nature of the department and its work. The Gray case, for example, grew out of our basic proposition that the business of the department is not everybody's business—most notably, not the business of the press. The conflict derives from a basic collision between important Bill of Rights provisions protecting the rights both of a free press and of individuals.

I tried to address these tensions in a speech to the Associated Press Managing Editors Association in October 1990, just after the peak of my own difficulties with the media. I assured the editors of our abiding commitment to freedom of the press. But I went on to point out that the public's insatiable appetite for "the truth, the whole truth and nothing but the truth" about criminal investigations was often at odds with the rights of individuals suspected of criminal involvement and with the effective conduct of criminal investigations. The proper role of the prosecutor is not to comment on pending investigations or to make a full public exposition of the evidence gathered, weighed and found wanting in the case of a prosecution not undertaken. It is "confined to the presentation of legally admissible evidence to a judge and jury in open court . . . through proceedings that identify specific defendants indicted for specific criminal acts." As noted by the Watergate Special Prosecution Force at the end of its investigations, "It would be irresponsible and unethical for a prosecutor to issue a report suggesting criminal conduct on the part of an individual who has no effective means of challenging allegations against him or requiring the prosecutor to establish such charges beyond a reasonable doubt."

Moreover, I noted, while prosecutors should "never hesitate to follow the evidence wherever it leads . . . we must never seek to carry investigation or prosecution beyond the point where the evidence ends—either out of personal motives or for political, ideological, economic or other purposes. . . . The courage to prosecute when the evidence is there must always be tempered by the courage not to prosecute when the evidence is lacking . . . regardless of pressures exerted in the name of some dubious, ill-defined right to know." We had to resist these pressures regardless of the inevitable charges of "whitewash" or "cover-up."

I closed by focusing upon the specific problem of leaks. "It may be unstylish today," I noted, "to suggest that any governmental process be kept hidden, in whole or in part, from public view. But that is precisely what I am compelled to conclude is appropriate for the continued impartiality and integrity of our criminal justice system." I pointed out the irreconcilable conflict between the protections guaranteed to individuals by the Fourth, Fifth, Sixth, Seventh and Eighth Amendments and the just claims asserted by the press under the First Amendment to access all departments of government. I added the observation of Justice Potter Stewart: "There is no constitutional right to have access to particular governmental information, or to require openness from the bureaucracy. . . . The Constitution itself is neither a Freedom of Information Act nor an Official Secrets Act."

All attorneys general must deal with these issues. My own relations with the media were made more problematic by the unreasonable expectations held out for my performance when I entered office. In addition, media perceptions of my ambition and qualifications for higher office did me no favor. In Washington, such talk merely raises one's head farther above the trench. In his classic account of the 1988 presidential campaign, *What It Takes*, author Richard Ben Cramer noted, "The only sure route to celebrity [for a political reporter] was to take somebody down." And the bigger the "somebody," the greater the celebrity. So arises the temptation to build some officeholders up so that they can later be "taken down" to maximum effect. While the following chronicle of my encounters with the news media is obviously a subjective one, it does not deviate too much from the norm in today's Washington.

Two basic ingredients were necessary for a full frontal media assault. The first was an initial series of positive press reviews, which we received, by and large, from August 1988 through the first half of 1989. Perhaps the culmination of these reviews, in both its tone and its consequences, was a May 21, 1989, cover story in the *New York Times* Sunday magazine. Subtitled "Dick Thornburgh, one tough Pittsburgh racket-buster, now is cracking his whip as Attorney General," it featured several flattering photographs, including one of me with Murray Dickman, Robin Ross and

Dave Runkel. The text reviewed my past record and recounted various of my efforts at the department, including moves to root out incompetence and waste and improve ethical standards. It predicted that I was likeliest to make my mark on financial crime and public corruption and portrayed me as both supremely confident of success and ambitious for higher office. Most of my advisers considered the article fair and mildly flattering. Dave Runkel, however, warned that it had put "a great big target sign" on my chest. Indeed it had, and it had done the same to Dave, Robin and Murray.

The second prerequisite for the attack was a credible source for negative appraisals. Ours was a presidential aide who had been accused of some minor impropriety at the outset of the Bush administration. As this technically fell within the overly expansive provisions of the Independent Counsel Act, I had little choice but to order a preliminary investigation. No further action was taken, but the aide evidently reacted very strongly (never considering, it appears, that if we had not complied with the act we might have subjected both him and ourselves to potential charges of cover-up). From that point forward, I had an implacable enemy within the White House to whom we could trace a number of unfavorable stories. In addition, early in my tenure we laid off eleven of the twenty-eight employees in the department's swollen press office. Most of those laid off had to be offered jobs elsewhere in our operations, and I suspect that they swiftly became first-class negative sources for reporters.

June 1989 saw the start of a year and a half of lemming-like negative stories, many replete with misstatements, others clearly traceable to ill-wishers. Few of them made new allegations of any substance. The headlines told the stories: "Sinking Star" (*National Journal*), "Thornburgh's Reputation Buffeted" (*Christian Science Monitor*), "Thornburgh's Image Shrinks and Shrinks" (*Philadelphia Inquirer*). I was called "the biggest disappointment in the cabinet" by the *National Journal* and "the Bush administration's first high level personnel problem" by *Time*. William Safire, in a column describing my "fall from grace," suggested falsely that I had toasted former Nazi officer (and then president of Austria) Kurt Waldheim at a dinner at the Austrian Embassy. The *Baltimore Sun* characterized me as "fighting to restore his reputation after a spate of bruising episodes that have rent his department's top ranks and raised questions about his integrity"; Newhouse News Service stated, "Some on the White House staff . . . are predicting he will be gone by Labor Day."

In June 1989, *Washingtonian Magazine*'s Owen Ullmann, called upon to grade the cabinet, had given me a B+ rating:

Strengths: He's not Ed Meese; solid legal judgment; squeaky clean.

Weaknesses: Dull; caught White House off guard by endorsing Bill Lucas for Brad Reynolds' civil-rights post.

Outlook: Has returned respectability to Justice; views more conservative than expected; rumored to be a top candidate for next Supreme Court vacancy.

By August 1990, Ullmann, reflecting the conventional wisdom, had reduced my grade to a C–:

Strengths: Preserves reputation as vigorous foe of white collar crime and government corruption. Still looks good in comparison with predecessor Ed Meese. Has strong defender in Bush.

Weaknesses: Bunker mentality approach to press relations results in poor public image. Reliance on old Pennsylvania aides proves disastrous. Occasionally panders to right-wing to soften moderate image and improve chances for Supreme Court seat.

Outlook: With strong credentials and easy act to follow, should have been big success. Instead, wins Disappointment of the Year award. Bush wants him to stay, but some in White House predict early exit.

BY FAR THE quintessential cheap shot was that of a *Detroit News* cartoonist who portrayed a glum Attorney General Thornburgh, attired in a big-game hunter's outfit, before a wall festooned with empty trophy plaques bearing the names of crime-fighting "failures." The only problem was that all of these but one (Ferdinand Marcos, who died before trial) turned out to be triumphs: "Mail Bomb Case," "S&L Cases," "Marion Barry," "Gotti," "Noriega" and "White Collar Crime." Included in the array of "failures," for some reason, was the special prosecutor's "Ollie North" case, from which the department had been effectively excluded.

I was more than once to pray for the strength to go about my daily tasks without betraying my hurt and resentment at these unjustified attacks. No prayer should properly seek redress for such slights, but I was not unwilling to ask divine assistance to enable me to carry on in my own endeavors without being preoccupied by the words and actions of others.

If we are truly to strengthen our system, we need a vigorous and courageous press. But the mean-spirited and hostile attitudes rightfully lamented by so many in public life today will only undercut that system. I had to agree with Mortimer Zuckerman, editor of *U.S. News & World Report*, who was to observe in a 1993 editorial, "[M]any journalists . . . are not only skeptical, which is their duty; too many of them are deeply cynical, which is destructive. . . . Increasingly, the public is conditioned to believe the worst." Determining the proper balance is a challenge worthy of sustained attention from us all—journalists, public officials and the American public. Its resolution will demand goodwill, common sense and decency from all concerned.

OVERALL, MY experiences with television were much more pleasant than those with the print media. My favorites were the talk shows, including the *MacNeil/Lehrer NewsHour*, the *Brinkley Show*, *Meet the Press* and *Face the Nation*. These programs were unfiltered and unedited, and their question-and-answer formats permitted complete responses and the opportunity to rebut erroneous charges as they were made.

My favorite pundits were Jim Lehrer and Robert MacNeil, who provided enough time for extended discussion of complicated issues and seemed less intent on playing "gotcha!" CBS's Leslie Stahl and ABC's Sam Donaldson were more acerbic and had an instinct for the jugular, but I still had the opportunity to give as good as I got. David Brinkley, George Will and guests such as David Broder were more cerebral and always a pleasure for thrust and parry exchanges. Ted Koppel of *Nightline* and the hosts and hostesses of the morning shows were more oriented toward sound bites, giving their guests less opportunity to deal thoroughly with events and issues, but my day in court was always assured. Obviously, the sound bites on nightly news shows did not allow for such response; neither did the print media, which could quote anonymous sources to their heart's content, leaving rebuttal, if any, to the next news cycle.

In radio, our main contact was with Nina Totenberg of National Public Radio. Unfortunately, Nina's overage of our activities was often unfavorable and sometimes rather snide.

My speech schedule was a busy one, and I enjoyed carrying our messages to a diverse group of audiences. Many of my texts had to be recycled for frequent use, but I always treated them as original works, adding updated facts and statistics and a local touch, if possible. Most of my appearances were well received; in a 1990 *American Lawyer* profile, Stuart Taylor Jr. described me as having "a confident but convivial presence, a solid grasp of the issues, a good sense of humor, and a politician's knack for impressing his audience." I also made it a practice to meet with newspaper editorial boards when I was traveling, so that they could question me at some length. I felt it was useful for them to see that the attorney general did not have horns or cloven hooves.

CRITICISMS: FAIR AND UNFAIR

ONE RELATIVELY minor but irksome instance of the media's relish for stories discrediting us involved my air travel. Our FBI security detail had warned us about the potential for embarrassment in the use of official cars and planes for personal matters, and we were naturally scrupulous about observing their rules of thumb. However, the FBI had also determined that I should not take commercial flights. This decision was the subject of intermittent controversy throughout my tenure, though it was based on security and communications concerns and on the greater flexibility that the use of government aircraft gave us in responding to opportunities as they arose. All this added up, however, to predictable suspicion on the part of reporters.

A vexatious example was my August 1989 trip to Honolulu to speak at the annual ABA meeting. Coming from Mexico City, where I had attended a summit meeting between President Bush and his cabinet and our Mexican counterparts, I flew to San Francisco to rest overnight. For some reason, our FBI plane was unable to fly us out the following morning. Some adept staff work turned up a U.S. Marshals Service four-engine Boeing 727 with bucket seats, which was normally used to transport prisoners, and this was pressed into service for our trip. After a most uncomfortable flight, I was whisked by car to the ABA meeting, delivered my somewhat uninspired speech, made a quick stop at the office of the U.S. attorney, then piled back on the plane for an equally uncomfortable flight home. The whole affair was an inconvenience, but I was gratified that the logistics had worked out.

I was utterly astonished to learn from our press office that reporters were making inquiries about the trip. Apparently, a disgruntled employee of the Marshals Service had leaked an exaggerated version of the matter, estimating the cost of the round trip to Hawaii at about $43,000 and creating the impression of some kind of boondoggle. We did not have cost figures at the ready to rebut this spin. Later, after John Sununu was forced out of office for, among other things, abuse of air travel privileges, this was to become the scandal of choice for the capital press corps.

It was small consolation that two reports rendered by the exacting General Accounting Office later gave me a virtual clean bill of health on my air travel. The first, in July 1990, examined my air travel and that of FBI Director Bill Sessions, nearly all aboard planes seized by the FBI from drug traffickers; it quibbled only with the cost-accounting methods followed. The report also noted that Ginny and I had paid for all her trips. We continued to reimburse the department for those trips until I left office. On

April 7, 1992, the second GAO report confirmed that all of my trips on military aircraft had been on official business and duly authorized.

PERHAPS THE MATTERS upon which President Bush and I worked most closely together were the appointments of two new Supreme Court justices. Early on I initiated an exhaustive search for potential candidates for the Court, so that the department would have recommendations ready if needed. We painstakingly reviewed the writings and, in the case of sitting judges, opinions of prospective nominees, but we applied no litmus tests. Our goal was to identify candidates who, as the president desired, would "interpret the law, not make it." We sought out, in particular, women and minorities to fulfill his wish to make the high court more representative.

Justice William Brennan, appointed by President Eisenhower in 1956, announced his decision to retire from the Supreme Court on July 19, 1990, after nearly thirty-four years of service. Two days later, we had briefing materials on over twenty prospective nominees in the hands of the president, John Sununu and Boyden Gray.

We quickly narrowed the list to four or five prospects. One prime contender was Clarence Thomas, a man of admirable personal and intellectual qualities and the president's highest-ranking African American judicial appointee. Judge Thomas had recently joined the U.S. Court of Appeals for the District of Columbia, sometimes referred to as the nation's second-highest court. But the consensus was that he had not yet served a sufficient stint as a judge. (As a side note, extensive judicial experience may not be crucial for a Supreme Court justice. Earl Warren, for example, had never served as a judge before being appointed to the Court. He was, however, a talented politician with strong leadership skills, which served him well as chief justice.)

Our two finalists were First Circuit Judge David Souter from New Hampshire, a particular favorite of Senator Warren Rudman, and Fifth Circuit Judge Edith Jones from Texas. The president at one point asked Boyden, "What about Dick? Shouldn't we consider him?" I was greatly flattered, but had given the matter little thought and was then in the throes of one of my more unpleasant bouts with the media. "The timing is not right, Mr. President," I told him, "but many thanks."

Both candidates met with us and with the president. The vice president and Sununu concluded that Jones was the best choice, while Boyden and I favored Souter. Both were eminently well qualified, but I felt that Jones had a bit of a hard edge that might work against quick confirmation. The president heard us all out and decided to appoint Judge Souter. The appointment was well received, and a speedy confirmation followed. Justice Souter, of course, turned out to be a much more liberal jurist than either the president or his supporters had expected.

We were not prepared for the furor accompanying the next appointment, which wrote a sorry chapter in the history of Senate confirmation hearings. Justice Thurgood Marshall announced his resignation on June 27, 1991. The president wanted to appoint a minority justice to take his place, and this time Clarence Thomas, the nation's best-qualified black Republican judge, was the leading contender. Thomas now had nearly two years of service on the circuit court under his belt and had acquitted himself well. Much to Boyden's dismay, however, I expressed concern that this relatively meager judicial experience might make his confirmation difficult. In response, the president asked that we look at others, especially Hispanic candidates. We focused on Fifth Circuit Judge Emilio Garza of Texas. However, Judge Garza had served even less time on the appellate court than Judge Thomas and was in obvious need of some more seasoning. Boyden and I therefore recommended Judge Thomas, and the president announced his appointment on July 1.

The initial response from quarters opposed to the president reminded me of the reaction to Bill Lucas's nomination. Judge Thomas was "not qualified," it was said, and his status as a representative of African Americans was suspect. These allegations, of course, were tame compared to those raised at the actual confirmation hearings, which occurred after I had left the department. The introduction of Anita Hill's sensational charges of sexual harassment reflected well on no one, least of all the Senate Judiciary Committee and its members. Justice Thomas was confirmed but was left with understandably bitter memories of the process. His tenure on the Court has been predictably conservative and considerably muted, giving rise to continued criticism from liberal pundits and politicos.

THE APPOINTMENT of judges to the lower courts, too, has historically caused contention between the Senate and the president. While the Constitution provides that "[t]he President . . . shall nominate, and by and with the Advice and Consent of the Senate, shall appoint" federal judges, many senators act as if the right of nomination belongs to them. A wise president appoints from a candidate pool created by senators or state leaders of his own party, except in the rare case where he has personal knowledge of an acceptable nominee. In general, the president defers to senators far more on district court appointments than on circuit court appointments.

Many senators use citizen merit selection bodies to screen potential candidates, often submitting the three top choices of these tribunals for presidential consideration. Some senators, however, insisted upon giving President Bush only one candidate, for whom they often fought tooth and nail. Unfortunately, in some cases there were good reasons of character or judicial philosophy for not acceding to the senator's choice. Long stalemates sometimes ensued, and many a floor vote was threatened to be withheld over a disputed appointment. On most occasions, the president was steadfast, often, I suspect, using the department as an understandable scapegoat.

To my knowledge, no candidate for any judicial office was ever asked his or her position on abortion or any other pending judicial issue. Such questioning, in my view, would have been not only improper but impractical, for no one could possibly anticipate the variety of issues that might come before a federal court. It is noteworthy that not a single person who was recommended, but not ultimately chosen, for a judicial position ever uttered a word about being asked improper questions. To my mind, this is strong confirmation that no such questions were asked.

Early in my tenure as attorney general, I had to address the ABA's role in judicial selection. Since 1952, presidents had submitted the names of potential nominees to the ABA Standing Committee on the Federal Judiciary for review as to "professional competence, judicial temperament, and integrity" as outlined in the ABA standard guide. Few candidates were nominated whom the committee did not rate as "qualified."

In 1980, the committee amended its standard to state that review was to be "*directed primarily* to professional qualifications—competence, integrity, and judicial temperament" (emphasis mine). A new section was also added: "The Committee does not investigate the prospective nominee's political or ideological philosophy except to the extent that extreme views on such matters might bear on judicial temperament or integrity." Theretofore no inquiry whatsoever had been made as to "political or ideological philosophy." In 1988, the criteria were further modified. The word "primarily" was deleted, but the "philosophy" language was broadened to read, "Political or ideological philosophy are not considered, except to the extent that they may bear on other factors."

Aware of the discontent over the assault on Judge Bork's "political

[and] ideological philosophy" and the feeling among many senators that the ABA was transgressing its legitimate sphere of inquiry, I met with ABA leaders and committee members in 1989. I told them I was concerned that they might be accused of trespassing in areas where they had no special expertise and hinted that we were rethinking the whole process. I also pointed out that leaks from their deliberations threatened to further discredit their role. The committee subsequently agreed to revert to its original charge of considering "professional qualifications—integrity, competence, and judicial temperament." (The department used these same factors in scrutinizing judicial candidates. We also examined their "judicial philosophy," declining, for example, to recommend the appointment of likely judicial activists. However, it was up to the White House to assess appointments from a political perspective.)

I regarded this change as a significant advance, not only for the process but for the ABA itself, which had come perilously close to forfeiting its important role in passing on professional qualifications. However, the liberal element that increasingly dominated the ABA's leadership apparently felt differently. By the time I left office, our differences were to be compounded by the "Thornburgh Memorandum" squabble, the ABA's insistence upon taking positions on political issues such as abortion, antidrug efforts and gun control, and my role in the Quayle civil justice reform proposals.

The clearance process was to become even more contentious over the years. The ABA's credibility sank so low in certain quarters that some senators welcomed ABA opposition to their judicial candidates. In 2001, the George W. Bush administration became so provoked with ABA politicking that it excluded the lawyers' group altogether from the clearance process.

Another series of issues brought us into conflict with the ABA and some of the more aggressive criminal defense lawyers, culminating in a showdown at the ABA meeting in July 1990. There, for the first time in memory, American prosecutors spoke with one voice in opposition to efforts to weaken their role.

The battle lines were most clearly drawn over the so-called Thornburgh Memorandum. The states, generally through their supreme courts, have traditionally issued codes of ethics to govern lawyers. Most of these are derived from model codes drafted by the ABA. They usually prohibit a lawyer from communicating with a party known to be represented by another lawyer in that matter unless he has the consent of the other lawyer "or is authorized by law to do so." This ban is modeled on an ABA provision labeled DR 7–104. In 1988, the Second Circuit held that a federal prosecutor had violated that rule by sending an informant to talk to a suspect who had retained a lawyer in connection with the investigation. While a revised opinion appeared to back off from this holding, sufficient concern existed to prompt my issuance of a clarifying memorandum in June 1989.

We were particularly concerned about organized-crime and white-collar cases. For example, the "general counsel" for an organization involved in drug trafficking may purport to be the lawyer for all involved. Often lower-level operatives seek to cooperate with the government in the hope of securing a lesser sentence or escaping prosecution altogether. Obviously, they do not want the lawyer for the kingpins to know of their cooperation. Literal application of the ABA rule would potentially disbar prosecutors for dealing with these operatives. Similarly, in white-collar investigations, corporate counsel often spread a blanket of representation over all knowledgeable employees, including potential whistle-blowers. Here, too, DR 7–104 could lead to disbarment of a prosecutor who approached a potential friendly witness. The Thornburgh Memorandum therefore stated that, prior to indictment, government lawyers and their agents are always free to communicate with persons known to be represented by counsel; such action was "authorized by law" and so would not violate DR 7–104.

The memorandum drew harsh criticism, and we knew that some show of strength would be necessary to head off an adverse ABA pronouncement. Along with leaders of the National District Attorneys Association and the National Association of Attorneys General, I called a press conference at which we stated, "The defense bar, with ABA sponsorship, is attempting to use rules of professional conduct to stymie criminal investigations and prosecutions." The ABA deferred action, but law review articles and the like continued to assault the memorandum. The Clinton administration was obliged to revisit the issue in 1994 after defense lawyers and the ABA renewed their concerns. Apart from some cosmetic changes, however, the Thornburgh Memorandum (now known as the Reno Memorandum) remained unchanged until Congress in 1998 enacted the McDade amendment, which brought all federal prosecutors under the more restrictive state ethics rules. The controversy, however, continues because the stakes are so high for the careers of individual federal prosecutors and the efficacy of major investigations.

This and other cooperative undertakings with fellow prosecutors no doubt contributed to the appraisal of the *Legal Times* that "[w]hen judged by his fellow prosecutors, Thornburgh emerged as a major hero, credited with helping unshackle them from burdensome restrictions, pouring in much-needed resources, and fostering unprecedented cooperation with state and local law-enforcement officials."

MY RELATIONS WITH the president were superb. Few men in public life possess such admirable personal qualities as George H. W. Bush. He is an intelligent, thoughtful and decent human being, loyal (sometimes to a fault) to those who served him, and he was accessible when needed on questions of serious policy import. While the president and I were not intimate and the occasions when I dealt with him directly on department business were fewer than might have been expected, he handled these with wisdom and an enviable style and grace. The president was particularly attentive in times of need. Handwritten notes or timely phone calls expressing his concern over nasty news articles were almost predictable.

Contrary to the advice of some of my younger aides and some junior presidential staff members, I did not make it a point to "be seen" around the White House or with the president. I felt that I had too much substantive work to waste time building a "key player" image. Perhaps, given the climate in the capital, this was a mistake.

Our serious legal business with the White House was most often handled through the Office of Legal Counsel. Particularly challenging were questions surrounding the commitment of military force in Panama and in the Persian Gulf and sensitive matters concerning foreign affairs. The Deputies Committee handled many of these without my personal involvement. Because of the unusual and sensitive nature of the department's role, the White House in general did not seek to interfere with our decisions.

My interactions with other cabinet members were episodic and usually cordial. Cabinet meetings were generally collegial but seldom momentous; most of the real work was done in far less formal settings. Cabinet members frequently sought advice from the department on legal matters, often informally. With some of them, most notably Energy Secretary Jim Watkins and EPA Administrator Bill Reilly, we worked closely on major investigations. And, of course, we shared law enforcement responsibilities with Treasury Secretary Nick Brady, whose department had jurisdiction over the IRS, Customs, the Bureau of Alcohol, Tobacco and Firearms and the Secret Service. We maintained solid working relations with all these agencies.

One of the most frequent criticisms of my stewardship of the department was my alleged inability to "get along with Congress." There was certainly a solid institutional basis to this perception. It was frequently my responsibility to defend the interests of the executive branch before that body, and some conflict was inevitable. Moreover, members of Congress had a nearly insatiable appetite for material within our investigative files. As discussed above, in most cases we were obliged to withhold this material to protect both the integrity of our investigations and the rights of persons who might be adversely affected by its premature or unwarranted disclosure. Thus there was always a little added tension. It seemed that on any given day, half the people on the Hill were annoyed about something happening in the department.

In addition, negotiating with the legislature was never something I enjoyed. In my experience, most of the time good staff with good information could work through any disagreements with legislators. My preference was always to have a top-flight legislative affairs office handle the work and inform me of any occasions when I needed to step in personally. This approach proved more successful in Harrisburg, however, than in Washington.

Nevertheless, we enjoyed remarkable legislative success in the area most important to the department in the long run. The three fiscal years that encompassed my term saw our appropriations soar to record levels. They went from $5.6 billion in fiscal year 1988, the year before I came to office, to $10.5 billion in fiscal year 1992, the year after I left, an increase of nearly 90 percent. This increase had important effects upon our key anti-crime resources in the field. For example, when I assumed office in August 1988, we had 2,544 assistant U.S. attorneys. By the spring of 1991, just before my departure, we had 4,396 such positions authorized, an increase of 73 percent in our most crucial prosecutive resource. Similarly, the number of FBI agents went up 9.4 percent, from 9,665 in 1988 to an authorized level of 10,577 by 1991, while DEA agent strength increased 18.3 percent, from 2,839 in 1988 to an authorized level of 3,358 by 1991. And the morale of all these professionals, not to mention the judges before whom we tried our cases, was substantially higher because of the long-overdue pay increases we relentlessly supported and won from Congress in 1990. Quite frankly, I did not mind our seemingly endless disputes with congressional committees or members or our reputation for not getting along with them, so long as they continued to provide us with the necessary tools to address our priority tasks. This, to their credit, they did.

One noteworthy failure was my inability, once again, to muster a constituency on Capitol Hill for the long-overdue recodification of the federal criminal laws. Federal criminal offenses now numbered some 3,000 and were scattered throughout all fifty titles of the U.S. Code in a most disconnected and irrational manner. They included such heinous acts as reproducing the image of Smokey Bear without authorization, wearing the uniform of a postman in a theatrical production that tends to discredit the postal service and taking artificial teeth into a state without approval of a local dentist. The code also described criminal intent in some seventy-eight different ways. However, neither of the Judiciary Committee chairs, Joe Biden and Jack Brooks, evidenced any interest whatsoever in recodification, and it never got off the ground.

In spite of our lobbying for judicial pay increases and our constant support for the appointment of more federal judges, we maintained, at best, only a coolly cordial relationship with the judicial branch. Perhaps this was simply a manifestation of the separation of powers, but I never got the sense that the judges were more than barely tolerant of our efforts. They resented the tide of drug and firearms cases resulting from our aggressive law enforcement efforts. They disliked the sentencing guidelines and mandates imposed by Congress. (I supported these, having seen too many cases of people in like situations receiving wildly diverse sentences. Regular review of the guidelines by the sentencing commission is the safety valve that has never been fully exploited.) And they were disgruntled by heavy criminal caseloads that crowded out and delayed the more interesting civil dockets. Surely more effective common cause can be made between the attorney general and the courts, but I was unable to find the key.

The professional staff of the department was our bedrock strength. I knew how important they were to our success, and I worked hard to keep communications open with those on our front lines, both in Washington and in the field. I met formally and informally with the various components of the department in Washington on a regular basis and visited fifty-four of the ninety-three U.S. attorneys' offices, some more than once. I also regularly attended the annual U.S. Attorneys Conferences, kept in close touch with the Attorney General's Advisory Committee of U.S. Attorneys and met frequently with the leadership of the federal law enforcement agencies: the FBI, the DEA, the Secret Service, the postal inspectors, the Bureau of Alcohol, Tobacco and Firearms, Customs, various military groups and others.

In view of this constant round of contacts and of my good relations with federal, state and local law enforcement personnel, I was always puzzled by the "inside Washington" characterization of my management style. Echoing their Pennsylvania counterparts, reporters constantly referred to my manner as "aloof," "inaccessible," "imperious," "abrasive," "rigid," "arrogant," "remote," "secretive" and the like. I did perhaps tend to treat the reporters themselves somewhat distantly because of the constant hammering we got from them. My relationships with most of our own staff and employees, however, were quite cordial, though I did insist upon the "no surprises" and "speak with one voice" rules and did not suffer breaches of them kindly.

In an otherwise fairly unfavorable article, Ruth Marcus of the *Washington Post* once noted, "Those who have worked with him praise Thornburgh as a smart, decisive, hands-on manager, who is a quick, well-informed study, legendary for his liberal use of a red felt-tipped pen to mark up documents. [Bill] Barr recounted a recent episode in which his office sent a 50-page, single spaced memorandum to Thornburgh for his signature. Thornburgh called one of Barr's deputies, Barr recalled, to question whether a case had been properly cited in one of the numerous footnotes." Stuart Taylor Jr., in his 1990 profile in the *American Lawyer*, echoed this description: "He works hard and conscientiously at his job, immersing himself in the details of the biggest issues, devouring memos and draft briefs down to the footnotes, adding marginal notations with a red felt-tipped pen. Getting to the office about 7:30 A.M. most days, Thornburgh often eats lunch at his desk, seldom leaves before 7 P.M. and often works on weekends. He keeps meticulous track of his schedule through a thick daily briefing book, crammed with background information about the people he will be meeting and the issues he will be addressing." On the other hand, Taylor's article quoted Ed Meese's solicitor general, Charles Fried, as saying, "Thornburgh's a very tough cookie, a much more authoritative and authoritarian personality than Meese. He will do things that need to be done, and that Meese could see needed to be done, but somehow would flinch from doing. He is a chief executive. He taught me something about political leadership. . . . He knows how to wield power." Taylor himself was to observe, "The most distinctive attribute of Thornburgh's leadership has been the firmness with which he has grasped command of his sprawling, 80,000 employee department, including the Federal Bureau of Investigation and other constituent agencies that had often operated semi-autonomously before his arrival."

WRAPPED UP IN our work and our family, Ginny and I had a somewhat limited social life. We found ourselves looking forward most to our Sunday afternoon walks and a rare "date" for a videotape of a favorite classic movie. These treasured times together were powerful reminders of how blessed we were to have a marriage that depended so little on the externals, but thrived on the simple intimacies of our continuing love affair.

We did come to enjoy the gaiety and elegance of the formal White House dinners given for visiting foreign dignitaries. I was also obliged to attend other "insider" events, such as dinners given by the Gridiron Club, the White House Correspondents, the Alfalfa Club and other organizations, where the self-styled greats and near-greats of Washington went to see and be seen. I found most of these events ordeals, but I tried to avoid being labeled antisocial by the cognoscenti. One of our great treats was to entertain family and friends in the President's box at the Kennedy Center, when available.

Peter, still living in his group home in Harrisburg, learned to take a Greyhound bus to and from Washington and did so about once a month for a four- or five-day visit. (He had also visited us often in Boston, with his first trip there marking his first solo plane flight.) We were to celebrate his thirtieth and fortieth birthdays in Washington. Although we were often "on his case" about table manners and personal hygiene, his forgiving disposition remained sunny, and he was always a joy to have visit.

Bill and I shared a particularly memorable experience on the Memorial Day following the 1991 Desert Storm triumph. The president had kindly invited cabinet members and their families to the reviewing stand overlooking the massive celebratory parade, and Bill, in his spanking Navy whites, was able to join me for it. Proud of his Navy service, I introduced him to Secretary of Defense Dick Cheney, Chairman of the Joint Chiefs of Staff Colin Powell, Chief of Naval Operations Admiral Frank Kelso and Desert Storm commanding general Norman Schwarzkopf—an unusual set of acquaintances for an ordinary seaman! Bill snapped off a proper salute to all his superiors.

Sustained by our love and our faith, Ginny and I had adapted well to the joys and hazards of official Washington. Little did we know that events beyond our control were once again about to reshape our lives.

18

Running for the Senate

On April 4, 1991, Sam Skinner called to tell me that Senator John Heinz had been killed in a small-airplane crash.

The news was devastating to all of Pennsylvania. John Heinz was easily the most popular politician in the state, all the more so because he had forsaken the life of easy wealth to which he had been born to seek a career in public service. He was also a bright, hard-working and principled senator who had earned the respect of many colleagues.

A special election would be held that fall to fill the vacancy created by Senator Heinz's death. To serve in the interim, Governor Bob Casey appointed his secretary of labor and industry, sixty-five-year-old Harris Wofford, a former aide in the Kennedy administration and ex-president of Bryn Mawr College. I knew Wofford slightly and regarded him as a classic 1960s liberal; he had a distinguished record in the civil rights area but was hardly a powerhouse candidate for the 1990s. Media reaction to the appointment was similar.

There was considerable speculation as to whether I would be a candidate to succeed Senator Heinz. I initially declined to discuss the matter, deeming it highly inappropriate while we were all mourning his loss. Nonetheless, I had to give it serious consideration, though I still lacked any strong desire to serve in the Senate. Bob Dole, the Senate minority leader, and Phil Gramm, chairman of the Republican Senatorial Campaign Committee, were desperate to hold on to this seat for the Republicans. They saw this as a prelude to a major assault on the Democrats' majority position coincident with President Bush's expected reelection. In most everyone's mind I appeared to be the logical candidate. Gramm, in particular, exhorted me to seek the seat; John Sununu chimed in, as did ranking Pennsylvania Republicans.

In making my decision, I focused almost entirely upon whether I wanted the position rather than whether I could win it. President Bush's standing with the public was still high following Desert Storm, and any Republican candidate was expected to reap a substantial coattail benefit. I also expected Pennsylvania voters to respond well to my candidacy based on what I hoped was a favorable recollection of my service as governor. Initial polling data were highly favorable as well.

Furthermore, things were not going to get much better at the Department of Justice. I felt I had done about as much as I could there and had gotten it into good order. Moreover, I had weathered the worst of the media and congressional attacks and finally emerged by early 1991 as what the *National Journal* called "Bush's Most Improved Player." Now might be as good a time as any to depart—particularly for what looked like pretty close to a sure thing.

There were some negative factors, however. For the first time in our life together, Ginny was not enthusiastic about my running for office. She was weary of having her husband battered by criticism and did not sense the "fire in her belly" that we both had brought to previous campaigns. She stated, of course, that she would support my decision, but some of her usual energy was lacking. John, David and Bill were noticeably quiet as well. And some caution was expressed by members of my staff and by Jay Waldman, my oldest and soundest political adviser, by then a judge. Jay took note of something no one else had raised with me. "You could lose, you know," he said. "The economy could go sour, and the president's popularity could plunge and take you or any other Republican candidate right with it." Finally, Senator Specter discussed with me the downsides of the job, especially the constant effort required to raise funds and the need to travel home frequently to tend to constituents. Fund-raising, in particular, had become an enormous burden; the average senator had to raise an estimated $2,000 per day, six days a week, over an entire six-year term, to secure enough money to get reelected.

By this time the pressure had grown to monumental proportions.

Other prospective candidates, most notably Congressman Tom Ridge of Erie, were getting restless. On June 4, I told the president of my intention to resign and seek the Republican nomination for the Senate seat.

AFTER I ANNOUNCED that I was leaving office, media reviews of my tenure were by and large favorable. I found some of the praise a bit exaggerated, but it was a welcome respite after close to two years of harsh criticism. Typical was the assessment of *Newsday*: "[Thornburgh] was credited with improving international relations in fighting the drug war and applauded for his support for the Americans with Disabilities Act. Thornburgh's Anti-trust Division got high marks for tough efforts to discourage anti-competitive practices by foreign companies, particularly in Japan. And, under his leadership, the Justice Department has brought more than 600 criminal cases against savings and loan officials." One of my early critics concluded on my departure that "Thornburgh's squeaky clean style succeeded in quickly restoring the department's tarnished image." Various other articles praised my role in the nomination of Justice Souter; my opposition to quotas; my replacement of errant staffers; and our white-collar crime, corruption, racketeering and environmental cases. I was even credited with improving my press relations. And, as *Business Week* put it, "Now, with John H. Sununu's White House crew developing a bad case of fumble-fingers, Dick Thornburgh is suddenly looking like one of the Administration's steadier hands."

No sooner had the euphoria of announcing my candidacy subsided, however, than a bombshell descended. Jack Trinsey, a bankrupt real estate developer and perennial political gadfly from Montgomery County, had earlier filed a challenge to the procedure for filling the Senate vacancy. Trinsey claimed that holding the election in November 1991 conflicted with federal and state constitutional provisions requiring that the candidates be chosen in a primary election. Little heed was paid to the case at first, but less than a week after I had signaled my intention to resign and run, Judge Edward N. Cahn filed an opinion agreeing with Trinsey's contentions and, in effect, postponing the election until the following year.

This left me in a dreadful quandary. Should I follow through with my announced intention to resign, when the election might be a year and a half away? On the other hand, could I continue effectively as attorney general under these circumstances? Although legal experts assured me that Judge Cahn's order would be overturned, this was by no means assured, and I had little desire to give up my cabinet post if there was to be no fall election. Thus I decided to remain as attorney general pending the outcome of the appeal and to resign only if the way was made clear for me to seek the Senate seat.

While I am not sure any other decision was feasible, this one made the summer of 1991 most uncomfortable. The positive image I had built up so painstakingly began to disintegrate. Democratic legislators now understandably viewed me as a partisan office seeker and treated me accordingly. This was the summer of the Operation Rescue case in Wichita, and special interests made it into a cause célèbre. The press also reacted very negatively, ignoring the fact that Judge Cahn's decision had given me good reason to change my plans. They treated me simply as a sitting attorney general running for office. I pointed out that Robert Kennedy had remained attorney general in 1964 until he had actually been *nominated* by the Democrats to seek a New York Senate seat, but the assault continued. The rules, I was driven to believe once again, are different for the Kennedys.

On August 6, the Third Circuit reversed Judge Cahn's decision and reinstated the November 1991 election date. Within a week, I formally tendered my resignation. President Bush's letter accepting it was most gracious: "[D]uring the last three years, when I had a tough call to make, I knew I could rely on your sound judgment and advice. That is, after all, the most important tribute that a client can pay his lawyer. So as you leave the cabinet, know that you carry with you the utmost thanks of your client for a job well done." The president asked whom I would recommend as my successor. I responded, without hesitation, that I hoped he would appoint Bill Barr, my trusted deputy, and I am happy to say that he did just that.

On August 15, three years to the day after I had first walked into the attorney general's office, I spoke once again to the assembled attorneys and staff. I went down the list of priorities I had set forth three years earlier and ticked off our record in each area. Drug arrests, prosecutions, convictions and asset forfeitures were at all-time highs; La Cosa Nostra families in major cities had been immobilized; a record number of white-collar crooks had been prosecuted; environmental and antitrust efforts had been revitalized; civil rights initiatives had produced the ADA and stepped-up efforts to deal with both discrimination and hate crimes; and expanded responsibilities had been assumed in dealing with violent crime and in promoting the rule of law around the world. We could all take great pride in these accomplishments.

PLANNING FOR THE campaign had proceeded in fits and starts. We had engaged President Bush's team, headed by Bob Teeter and Roger Ailes, to add some cachet to our effort, although I had never previously worked closely with either of them. Michele Davis, former executive director of the RGA, served as campaign manager, while Murray Dickman took charge of day-to-day arrangements and communication with our consultants on media, polling, fund-raising and the like. A number of colleagues resigned from the department to join us.

The president jump-started my campaign by inviting me to Kennebunkport for an overnight visit, then flying with me to Pittsburgh for the annual convention of the Fraternal Order of Police. His remarks to the FOP were most generous, and the Pennsylvania contingent quickly endorsed my candidacy.

Our fund-raising went well. President Bush appeared on my behalf at two events, Mrs. Bush appeared in Philadelphia and Vice President Quayle spoke in Harrisburg. In each case record amounts were raised. I also made successful fund-raising trips to Boston, New York and Los Angeles. All told, we raised some $3.7 million in a little more than two months.

We moved swiftly to touch our political bases in Pennsylvania, knowing we would have very little opportunity to put together our own grassroots organization. This was a downside of the two-month time frame for the campaign, which on the whole we had welcomed as an advantage in running against the lesser-known Harris Wofford. Most members of the Pennsylvania congressional delegation pledged their assistance, though Representative Joseph McDade from Scranton still bore me ill will for his indictment on federal corruption charges, a matter from which I had recused myself and in which he was eventually acquitted. The state committee, under Chairman Ann Anstine, was solidly behind our effort, and we counted on it to drum up support among the county and regional groups, whose efforts at the local level would be crucial.

Early polling data indicated that I had a sizable lead, based largely on name identification. I was perceived to be "honest, warm and friendly," as "concerned" and as someone who "gets things done." Ominously, however, my support was down and "soft" in southeastern Pennsylvania (the Philadelphia suburbs), due, we suspected, to ongoing controversy about abortion. Survey data also showed that "things are bad in Pennsylvania."

My first actual campaign event was an August 22 meeting at a Philadelphia senior citizens' center, an occasion of little substance but a lot of handshaking and folksiness. It was, however, punctuated by a portent of what was to come—sharp questioning on an alleged diversion of lottery funds during my service as governor into other than senior-citizen programs. This approach was to recur with increasing frequency throughout the campaign.

Our campaign leadership undertook its first comprehensive discussion on August 25, and our statewide kickoff tour began on August 29. It finished up the next evening at a special meeting of the Republican State Committee, which anointed me as the party's nominee.

My announcement speech touched upon all the themes we hoped to emphasize. A crucial paragraph, as it was to turn out, stated: "I will seek to serve as a strong and effective advocate for Pennsylvania in Washington. I know the corridors of power in our nation's capitol from my three years as a member of the president's cabinet. I know the people and I know the pressure points to pursue in the interest of my fellow Pennsylvanians. Washington, D.C., my friends, is no place for on-the-job training." Unfortunately, the "corridors of power" phrase was to be tortured by our opponents into a perception that I was defending the status quo rather than using my knowledge of Washington's ways on behalf of Pennsylvania's interests.

My announcement in Philadelphia was delayed by forty-five minutes, and nearly canceled, when AIDS activists from an organization called ACT-UP commandeered the podium, blowing whistles, waving placards, shouting and generally causing an uproar. My young grandchildren, who were present for what was expected to be a gala event, were visibly upset by these goings-on. At one point, our daughter-in-law, Rebecca, and little Blair were locked out of the room and surrounded by boisterous demonstrators until rescued by our staff. I was furious, particularly since I had had little or no contact with the AIDS issue, but clenched my teeth for television interviews, pointing out the importance of free speech to our nation and expressing the hope that these demonstrators would also allow me that right. Of course, as the demonstrators had planned, the news that evening was dominated by their antics rather than anything to do with my candidacy. We were to be beset with similar outbursts throughout the campaign. Whether these were directly orchestrated by our opponents was never quite clear.

Perhaps of greater concern was the distribution, within hours of the release of my announcement speech, of a detailed critique from the Wofford campaign. This was our first taste of the rapid-response capability fashioned by James Carville, Wofford's chief campaign consultant (the man who had hammered Bill Scranton so aggressively in the 1986 gubernatorial campaign), and his colleague, Paul Begala.

At the outset, Begala had set the tone of the Wofford campaign: "attack, attack, attack." He accused me of "sleeping through the S&L crisis, winking at BCCI, protecting lawlessness in the corporate suites at Exxon, putting a cocaine user in charge of the war on drugs," not to mention "courting the powerful and the privileged," and he described the race as "a fight between the forces of greed and the forces of families and working people." I was taken aback by this strident hyperbole.

I was, however, in awe of Carville and Begala's research and communications capabilities. Time and again, our well-reasoned and carefully crafted press releases were savaged within a few hours by broadsides from the Wofford campaign, equally well researched but injected with liberal doses of rhetoric and misrepresentation designed to preempt, if not obliterate, our message. Carville's two successful campaigns for Bob Casey had provided his team with a well-massaged Rolodex and instant entree to political reporters across the state, upon which they capitalized to the maximum by assiduous use of the fax machine. I developed a grudging admiration for their expert use of aggressive modern campaign techniques, even as I was being skewered by their frequently outrageous communiqués.

We initially concentrated on defining Wofford as a classic "tax-and-spend 1960s liberal" and emphasizing his ties to the Casey administration. We contrasted the reductions in both personal and corporate tax rates during my governorship with the unprecedented tax increases during Wofford's service as Casey's trusted adviser and cabinet member. Following his reelection in 1990, Casey had pushed through a record-high $2.8 billion tax increase, which upped personal rates from 2.1 to 3.45 percent and corporate rates from 8.5 to 12.25 percent. His administration had eaten up the $350 million surplus we had left it in 1987 as well as the $160 million rainy-day fund established for economic hard times. I also reminded voters of our widely praised economic development efforts. I added imaginative new proposals for national programs to deal with abandoned industrial sites and to extend the spirit of the Ben Franklin Partnership's advanced-technology initiatives across the country. Finally, I reiterated my record in dealing with violent crime. My constant theme was, "I'll do for Pennsylvania as a senator what I did as governor—create jobs, cut taxes and reduce violent crime."

In a normal campaign, all this would have excited some voter and media interest. But this was not a normal campaign. By mid-October, over 70 percent of the state's voters thought the country was headed in the wrong direction, and our message was subsumed in larger national issues. In their postmortem analysis, our pollsters identified this as a "'time for a change' election [where] many voted *against* the candidate they thought was the most qualified and would most effectively bring federal dollars to the state, namely, Dick Thornburgh" (emphasis mine). They found that an astonishing 24 percent of those voting for Wofford "feel that Thornburgh is more experienced and qualified to be U.S. Senator. . . . Thornburgh lost more ground than he gained from the voter's perception of his vast background and experience in government and in Washington in particular." So much for the argument that one can swim effectively against the kind of tide that was developing in 1991 and that broke in full force during the 1992 presidential election.

Carville and Begala's strategy of portraying me, the challenger, as the incumbent and Wofford as "the crusading outsider" was inspired. They hammered away at the "corridors of power" line as if I had made it the centerpiece of my campaign. (In fact, I never used the phrase again after my announcement speech.) We made a fatal mistake in overlooking that my whole public career had, in fact, been as a reformer—as a crusading prosecutor against organized crime and official corruption in western Pennsylvania, as a member of the post-Watergate Justice Department cleanup team, as a governor who restored integrity to state government and as the attorney general dealing with Ed Meese's legacy. Our public messages mentioned none of this, perhaps because no one but me on our campaign team had lived through all those efforts. The failure was thus mostly mine, and it was a costly one.

In our initial debate on September 6, Wofford displayed a pocket copy of the Constitution and asked, "If the constitution guarantees criminals the right to a lawyer, shouldn't it guarantee working Americans their right to a doctor?" Thereafter, his message focused almost exclusively on health care reform, paying heed to the colorful words of James Carville: "Reporters are like children in a school cafeteria. If you want them to eat spinach, don't put anything else on their plates." Wofford never laid out a detailed plan for health care reform and deftly protected himself from criticism of any particulars. I frequently asked him, "How much is your health care reform plan going to cost? And who is going to pay for it?" He never answered. And the journalists covering the campaign never put the questions to him themselves.

Ironically, I had spotted the health care issue as significant that summer and had asked Harold Miller, who was in charge of research for our campaign, to work on it. He produced some excellent thinking and some useful proposals, but we were not well positioned to use them until much too late. Our Washington strategists, most notably Phil Gramm, felt that we should not compete with Wofford on health care, especially as the administration had no plans to do anything about the issue. Instead, they felt, we should simply critique his proposals and establish our own issues as preeminent. They may have been right, but developments in Pennsylvania rapidly overtook this assessment. On October 30, barely a week before the election, we finally put out our own health care reform proposal, a fourteen-point plan addressing the availability, affordability and quality of health care for all Americans. But it was too little, too late.

My own sense was that health care was a surrogate issue fastened upon by voters who were anxious and uneasy about their economic future in a time of change. Importantly, many of these voters were Republicans. In 1982, we had weathered the storm of double-digit unemployment rates partly because they had principally affected industrial, blue-collar workers, most of whom traditionally voted Democratic anyway. This time, while unemployment was half what it had been ten years previously, anxiety was highest in normally Republican white-collar, middle-class, middle-income voters. The Wofford campaign masterfully capitalized upon Pennsylvanian's concerns about their own future, including the availability of decent, reasonably priced health care. Meanwhile, I defended President Bush's domestic policies, both in general and on health care in particular, as best I could. Despite my own issues with the administration's domestic policy agenda, it was not in my nature to disassociate myself from the president, and we may have paid a price for that loyalty.

Wofford's effort was enhanced immeasurably by a multipart preelection series in the *Philadelphia Inquirer* by reporters Donald Barlett and James Steele, later published as the paperback volume *America: What Went Wrong?* The authors recounted at length the problems of our economy and society, inferring the inability of those governing to tackle any of these effectively. Though rife with inaccuracies, their work harmed not only my campaign but President Bush's reelection effort in 1992 as well. The *Inquirer* in general campaigned against me, having opened its coverage in early September with a vicious column attacking nearly every aspect of my career as governor and attorney general in the most inflammatory manner.

Our television campaign was, by all accounts, uninspired. Following an initial "jobs" spot, two ads were designed to soften my image, focusing on the ADA and on the benefits provided to senior citizens by the expanded lottery while I served as governor. Later spots focused on crime and on our program for refurbishing abandoned industrial sites. "Attack" ads flagged Wofford's solicitation of funds from arms dealer Adnan Khashoggi while president of Bryn Mawr and his receipt of campaign contributions from shadowy savings and loan figures (including indicted Louisianan Edmund M. Reggie, whose daughter, Victoria, was later to marry Ted Kennedy). We also attacked Wofford's health care proposals, and one final spot set forth my own thoughts on health care. Wofford's attack ads focused on BCCI and my ill-fated Hawaii trip as attorney general.

Carville and company were adept at sidetracking us into debates about inconsequential matters. They were even better at enlisting reporters in their efforts. A prime example was the controversy they manufactured over my rejoining Kirkpatrick & Lockhart. When I left the department, I had no source of income. As I had done following similar stints in public life, I rejoined the firm as a partner. It was clearly understood that I would be available for little legal work before November 5. If I won, of course, I would withdraw from the firm once more; if I lost, we would have to make a more permanent arrangement. Meanwhile, I was most grateful for their assistance, office space and clerical aid.

The Wofford camp turned this arrangement into a cause célèbre. First, they convinced the media that the "normal" arrangement would have been for me to take an "of counsel" position. This is nonsense, of course. Lawyers and law firms have worked out a variety of relationships in these situations. Next, the Democratic State Committee, together with Ralph Nader's Public Citizen, filed complaints in early October with the Federal Election Commission, amid much fanfare, claiming that the firm was making an illegal campaign contribution by readmitting me to the partnership while I was an active candidate. I was greatly concerned about the potential embarrassment to the firm, but my partners seemed to take it in stride. Ultimately (long after the election, of course), the complaint was dismissed. For all this trouble, I had drawn down only $5,000 from my partner's account during the campaign.

Another damaging story could not be blamed on Carville or the media. For some unaccountable reason, campaign manager Michele Davis, in an interview with a reporter, referred to Pennsylvania as "a sorry-assed state." When confronted with the statement, I lamely opined that she must have meant Pennsylvania "was *in* a sorry-assed state." The *Inquirer* called for Davis's dismissal, and they were probably right. We were so short on qualified staff and so pressed for time, however, that I let the episode pass. It did nothing to allay the concern of many in the state that our campaign was being conducted by arrogant outsiders insensitive to their concerns.

The unfamiliarity of our press staff with the state and its reporters handicapped us in dealing with such flaps. After the campaign, this was one of the two biggest complaints I got, even from supporters. Our team seemed unable or unwilling to provide timely responses to legitimate inquiries, let alone take a proactive approach. Moreover, our outreach to party leaders and interest groups was deficient as well. Shortly before election day, for example, I was mortified to discover that no response had been made to the traditional League of Women Voters questionnaire, which was used in preparing a voters' guide for distribution by leading newspapers. A senior campaign official had characterized the league as "having its own agenda," which should not be dignified by response. Therefore, millions of voters received a guide noting "no response" from candidate Dick Thornburgh on the major issues of the day.

I suspect that some of our staff derived their attitudes from their experience in the hostile media and political environment at the Department of Justice. Campaigns, of course, are different, designed to maximize, not minimize, media coverage and to assiduously court the attention of special interests. But habits are hard to break. Overall, the members of our campaign staff were not the skilled, savvy operators of our previous efforts. There were no Jay Waldmans, Paul Critchlows or Rick Staffords among them. All were intensely loyal and hardworking, but I had asked many of them to assume responsibilities that exceeded their capabilities. Kit Seelye, the *Inquirer* reporter covering the campaign, put the ultimate question as, "Can an uncertain candidate [Wofford] with a sure-footed campaign overcome a sure-footed candidate [Thornburgh] with an uncertain campaign?" For any of the inadequacies of my campaign team, however, the ultimate blame had to rest with me.

Wofford and I engaged in two debates. I had hoped these would yield breakthroughs for our side, but in fact, Wofford gained substantially from the exposure and from holding his own in the exchanges. Moreover, our spin doctors were almost totally ineffectual.

While observers gave me the edge in the first debate, it enabled Wofford to introduce the health care issue to a significant audience. He also attacked the proposed North American Free Trade Agreement (it would put American jobs "on a fast track to Mexico"), most-favored-nation treatment for China (it would put additional jobs on "a slow boat to China") and my handling of BCCI, all frequent themes thereafter.

The second debate, on October 18, was more troublesome. Moderator Fred Friendly, a former CBS news producer, appeared somewhat addled, referring to the race as taking place in Massachusetts. He let Wofford set the agenda by getting in his lines about a constitutional right to a doctor in answer to the very first question, which was on gun control. When Friendly himself turned to health care, he first expounded on his own gallbladder attack and then launched into a discussion of Gaucher's disease. Wofford adroitly darted in and out of this mélange with glib assertions about his health care reform "plan." Next, Wofford accused me of seeking to "overthrow" the judge's order in the Wichita abortion case, and Friendly intimated that as attorney general, I had sent a message to the people of Kansas to disobey that order. My ire on this sensitive issue, I fear, was obvious, and my performance in the debate overall was sub par.

The first statewide poll, reported on October 1 by the *Pittsburgh Post-Gazette*, showed a substantial lead for me (50 to 38 percent, with 12 percent undecided). But on October 29, the second poll reported a statistically insignificant edge for me (45 to 44 percent, with 11 percent undecided).

More ominous signs came in late October with the editorial endorsements from the state's media outlets, a strong source of support in previous campaigns. The first reversal came from the *Harrisburg Patriot*, which concluded: "If you think the country is pretty much on the right course, Thornburgh is your man. If you think the nation has to address a number of serious domestic issues soon or face further economic and social deterioration, Wofford deserves your vote. . . . We fall among the latter group." The *Philadelphia Inquirer* wrote, "We are left, in the end, searching for the *why* of his candidacy. We are left wondering *which* Dick Thornburgh: The progressive corruption-buster of the 1970s? The popular tax-cutting governor who left office boasting of a surplus? The politicized and controversial attorney general who, just months ago, undercut a federal judge trying to stop law-breaking anti-abortion protests in Wichita? . . . It's time someone started rattling the gilded cages of Washington's political careerists. It's time for Harris Wofford." The *Post-Gazette* offered a particularly nasty personal appraisal, contrasting my earlier "relaxed" and "genuine" persona to an alleged "bloodlessness, even arrogance, that comes from an overdose of Reaganism."

Other major newspapers also endorsed Wofford, though a few of the second-tier papers stuck with me. We had lost a crucial edge, and the remaining steam seemed to go out of our effort. Ginny and I both had a feeling that the election was slipping away from us as we headed into the home stretch. But we were not prepared for the magnitude of the reversal we were about to endure.

On November 5, we voted in downtown Pittsburgh, then visited each of the polling places where we had voted in the past. To our chagrin, we saw almost no evidence of our campaign—few posters, almost no poll workers and only a scattering of literature. We began to put up "Thornburgh for Senate" posters ourselves as the morning wore on.

The returns were discouraging from the outset. By 11:00 that night, it was clear that we had lost, and I telephoned my congratulations to Senator Wofford. The final vote count was 1,860,760 to 1,521,986, or 55 to 45 percent. The most devastating difference was in the four Philadelphia suburban counties, traditional Republican-organization strongholds. We had lost three of these vote-rich counties—Delaware, Montgomery and Bucks—and eked out only a narrow win in the fourth, Chester. While local Republican candidates ran up an aggregate victory margin of over 80,000 votes in these four counties, we lost them by more than 12,000—a swing of over 90,000 votes. This area was the center of the angst belt that our polling data had identified and within the immediate media market of the *Inquirer*'s Barlett and Steele series. I also suspected the defection of some female voters over dissatisfaction with the national Republican position on abortion, although my own position on the issue was virtually indistinguishable from Wofford's and postelection analysis showed it to be a neutral factor statewide.

The election outcome had significant national ramifications. Pundits and experts wasted no time in analyzing its portents for the 1992 presidential election. Health care came center stage and prompted a scurrying about that did not end until President Clinton's own health care proposals crashed and burned in a Democratic Congress in 1994.

Somewhat to my annoyance, Greg Stevens, our media consultant, circulated an assessment after the election, largely exculpating his organization from major responsibility. Roger Ailes, on the other hand, at least called to "apologize." I, of course, had my own views on what went wrong.

1. The foremost problem was the anxiety of many normally Republican voters about the economy and the perception that a Republican administration in Washington was not sufficiently committed to addressing its problems.

2. President Bush's favorable ratings had plummeted to barely 50 percent by election day from a high of over 90 percent earlier in the

year in the wake of the Gulf War. My fortunes were inextricably tied to the president's popularity due to my cabinet service and his vigorous campaigning on my behalf. Our race provided a convenient vehicle to "send him a message." Jude Wanniski, the political economist, put it starkly: "The people of Pennsylvania voted against Bush, not Thornburgh." In this regard I was the canary in the coal mine for Republican prospects in 1992.

3. I had lost touch with Pennsylvania and the concerns of our citizens. I had been away from the state since 1987 and had not lived in Pittsburgh, my historic electoral base, since 1975. My credentials as a Pennsylvanian, and especially as the "western" candidate, were thus somewhat shopworn.

4. The campaign was too brief to plumb citizens' concerns and to involve them in fashioning responsible solutions. Wofford and his staff put the summer of our enforced inactivity to good use, while the inevitable perception arose that I was not sufficiently interested to begin serious campaigning.

5. Overconfidence on my part and on that of key campaign advisers, stemming partly from the initial favorable polls, caused us to rest on our oars at crucial junctures.

6. Our failed "get out the vote" effort relied almost exclusively on an expensive telephone solicitation effort by outsiders rather than the local volunteers we had used in the past. Wofford benefited from having the Casey organization and local Democratic committees at his beck and call. Few local GOP organizations mounted any visible effort on our behalf. There is, I was reminded, a substantial advantage to holding the governor's office during any statewide race.

7. The Wofford campaign conducted a superb effort that presaged the techniques to be used by Carville and Begala in Bill Clinton's 1992 presidential effort. While we failed to define Harris Wofford, they missed few opportunities to define me negatively, and they responded to every riposte in a timely manner.

8. Wofford showed the unexpected ability to fund a campaign that many had initially written off as hopeless. Governor Casey, key union groups and the Democratic Senatorial Campaign Committee all made significant contributions. The committee even borrowed money to provide the maximum funding allowed by law. This was a

surprise to me, as its chairman, Jay Rockefeller, had assured me that it would not be making a serious effort to fund the Pennsylvania campaign.

9. Ginny and I both had to acknowledge that our campaigning skills had grown rusty. After all, I had not run for office since 1982. Moreover, we didn't have nearly the personal energy and stamina that had characterized our earlier campaigns.

10. In retrospect, my heart had not been in the effort. All the uncertainty about running for the Senate in the first place turned out to be well founded. I was an executive, not a legislator. And I was reminded of Richard Nixon's comment after losing the California governor's race in 1962: "A reluctant candidate is always a lousy candidate."

One final blow was yet to fall. I knew that we had run up a campaign debt by election day. This is normal. But it wasn't until early January that I learned (from newspaper accounts) that it amounted to $350,000. In the last weekend of the campaign, our management team had apparently panicked. Though no money was available, they had committed substantial funds, without consulting me, to the paid "get out the vote" effort. Attempts by the Thornburgh for Senate Committee to raise further funds were predictably ineffectual (particularly as my almost immediate appointment to service at the UN expressly prohibited any political fund-raising activity). Two of the principal creditors sued both the committee and me, and after three years of litigation (which established for the first time the legal obligation of a candidate, as distinguished from his or her campaign committee, for unpaid campaign bills), Ginny and I were obliged to cover the shortfall from our own personal funds. A very expensive object lesson for those considering seeking public office in this day and age!

Wofford, of course, was unable to fulfill his extravagant promises of free health care and was soundly defeated by Congressman Rick Santorum when he sought election to a full term in 1994.

ADJUSTING TO AN unexpected defeat was a new experience for Ginny and me. We soon realized, however, that we were more embarrassed than disappointed. And we had little time to wallow in reflection, as we were off to Rome to participate in a Vatican-sponsored conference on drug and alcohol abuse. It was attended by experts from around the world, and Ginny was able to start developing the agenda for the November 1992 disability conference.

Subsequently Sam Skinner, who had by now replaced John Sununu as the president's chief of staff, asked if I were interested in serving as ambassador in any one of a dozen or so posts. I was not. Early in December, I had returned to Kirkpatrick & Lockhart, visiting both the Washington and Pittsburgh offices in an attempt to carve out a professional niche that would benefit the firm.

Little did I suspect that yet another unusual challenge was just over the horizon.

19

A Sojourn at the
United Nations

THE CALL FROM President Bush came about 9:30 on Monday morning, February 3, 1992.

"Dick," the familiar voice began, "I'm not sure if this is something you would be interested in, but we need some help at the United Nations." He went on to explain that he and Secretary of State Jim Baker were concerned about the management problems that the organization faced in meeting its post–Cold War responsibilities. Would I consider a one-year appointment to the UN's top management position: undersecretary-general for administration and management? As a longtime supporter of the UN, I knew immediately that this was yet another "offer I couldn't refuse."

What a challenge my new assignment was to be! The United Nations was formed at the end of World War II as a mechanism to pursue collective security and a better standard of living for a world exhausted by global conflict. The fifty founding members provided for institutions to cope with a wide variety of problems. The General Assembly was to be a representative body giving each country one vote on policy matters. However, the five major end-of-the-war powers—the United States, the Soviet Union, the United Kingdom, France and China—were given reigning status as permanent members of the more powerful Security Council, with the ability to veto any proposed collective security action. A raft of alphabet agencies, such as the United Nations International Children's Emergency Fund (UNICEF), the UN Development Programme (UNDP), the UN Educational, Social and Cultural Organization (UNESCO), the World Health Organization (WHO), the Food and Agricultural Organization (FAO), the World Food Program (WFP) and the International Labor Organization (ILO), were also created.

During the Cold War, vetoes stymied much meaningful action in the Security Council, while the General Assembly was given over to ritual attacks upon the West by the Soviet Union and its satellites and fellow travelers. A "nonaligned bloc" of developing nations exerted considerable obstructive influence but was increasingly frustrated by its lack of clout on major issues. Peacekeeping forces were dispatched to a number of trouble spots in Africa and the Middle East. But aside from the action on the Korean peninsula in the 1950s (made possible only by a temporary Soviet boycott of Security Council sessions), major issues remained the exclusive province of the two superpowers.

With the end of the Cold War in the 1990s came an opportunity to rejuvenate the organization—by now grown to 166 members—and return to its first principles. The breakup of the Soviet Union removed a roadblock to effective Security Council action, and the developing worldwide consensus in support of the rule of law, democratic principles, market economics and human rights offered opportunities for a new beginning.

Moreover, the UN was becoming what I would frequently term a "worldwide 911 emergency number." Whereas thirteen peacekeeping efforts had been mounted from 1948 through 1987, an additional thirteen had been implemented since then. On the agenda as 1992 began were a dozen or so ongoing peacekeeping operations as well as major institution-building exercises in formerly war-torn Angola and Cambodia. Demands were escalating for UN efforts in the former Yugoslavia and in Somalia. In addition, peacekeeping was evolving from the traditional separation of former combatants to institution building, provision of humanitarian aid to areas and populations torn by strife, and even interventions "where there is no peace to keep." This last posed particularly vexatious challenges. President Bush, a former ambassador to the UN, was a strong supporter of its aims and had masterfully fashioned the Desert Storm coalition under the mantle of the Security Council.

However, the prognosis for the organization was not very optimistic as newly elected secretary-general Boutros Boutros-Ghali, a veteran career diplomat from Egypt and the first UN chief from the African continent, came to office. *Time* accurately summarized, "The U.N. is over-staffed, underfunded and mismanaged. Its activities are often badly conceived, wasteful and hobbled by petty politics." I was warned that self-interest governed day-to-day activity within the organization and that there was widespread cynicism about reform and change.

In response to these problems, the secretary-general pledged to "examine every proposal for streamlining our operations, eliminating what is wasteful or obsolete." My assignment was to further this agenda and to monitor the UN's management and administration on behalf of the United States, its principal financial supporter. I was the highest-ranking American in the organization, and I would have the opportunity to participate in its significant revamping—if the commitment to reform proved sincere. At my first meeting with the secretary-general, I got the distinct impression that my appointment had been foisted upon him, but he was most cordial and seemed resigned to my position.

Such media reaction as there was to my appointment was generally favorable, though some observers seemed unable to understand that public service could mean anything more than self-aggrandizement. The *Washington Times*, for example, called my appointment a "consolation prize" for losing the Senate race and having had my putative presidential hopes dashed. The *Washington Post*, however, called it "a shift in emphasis by the United States" to a concern over "profligate mismanagement and pork-barrel dispensing of jobs and benefits to Third World countries that dominate the membership. . . . UN sources say that if Thornburgh takes the job, Boutros-Ghali will gain three big advantages. He will have the weight of the world's only remaining superpower directly behind the reform effort; he will be giving the United States a chance to show that its ideas about reform are workable; and he will have a deputy who stands a better chance than anyone else at the United Nations of making the United States pay its arrears."

The last point was significant. The United States was being called upon to pay 25 percent of the UN's $1.2 billion annual budget and over 31 percent of its burgeoning peacekeeping costs. Although we had built up substantial arrears during the 1980s, Presidents Reagan and Bush had committed to a five-year program to pay them down. This effort was, at least implicitly, related to the UN's undertaking of necessary reform measures to reassure American taxpayers of the soundness of their investment.

The unwinding of my arrangement with Kirkpatrick & Lockhart was, I fear, not as well received as on previous occasions, though close friends agreed that the UN opportunity was too promising to pass up. I rented a small apartment in New York near the UN, while Ginny remained in our Washington quarters to pursue her career, as we embarked on a one-year "Metroliner marriage." One or the other of us commuted almost every weekend. Due to Ginny's absence during the week, I begged off most social events, where, I later suspected, a lot of UN business was actually transacted.

I recruited two longtime associates as special assistants. Murray Dickman handled administrative and personnel matters, Cuyler Walker scheduling and liaison matters. We all worked long hours and normally ate at the staff cafeteria, a regimen that mystified both our management counterparts and our subordinates. Most "big shots," real or imagined, went to the sumptuous delegates' dining room for the proverbial two-hour lunch —where, again, substantial business was no doubt transacted.

One early warning sign about the difficulty of even minor reform came shortly after I assumed office. Each morning I observed a platoon of burly security guards raising each of what was to become 184 national flags outside the headquarters building. At nightfall, they would lower the flags. On the weekends, when visitor traffic was the highest, and at night, none of the colorful flags flew at all. Why not, I wondered, simply leave them flying, lighting them at night? The savings in personnel expenditures would more than compensate for the cost of the lighting. This solution was, it turned out, all too simple. I was told that some countries would not permit their flags to be flown at night. "Which?" I asked. "Denmark." "Well, tell the Danes that we will raise and lower *their* flag every day, but the others will stay up." "That would not be proper; they might feel singled out for special treatment." I had an ominous feeling that this proposal was going nowhere. And I was right. I sensed that the inaction stemmed from inertia and concern for job security among the flag handlers rather than from the sensitivities of member states.

Boutros-Ghali moved swiftly to slim down operations, however, reducing the number of high-level posts from thirty to a mere eight. My colleagues at the undersecretary level came from Russia, Sierra Leone, Britain, the Peoples Republic of China, and Sweden; other top managers hailed from Poland and Germany. Boutros-Ghali also wisely imposed a hiring freeze, then directed all department heads to assess their departments' activities, identify existing posts with overlapping or redundant functions and make recommendations for their redeployment. This undertaking was bound to send shock waves through a bureaucracy to which "business as usual" had been a forty-five-year watchword. These were intensified by our acceptance of an extraordinary offer from McKinsey & Co., the international management consulting firm, to provide pro bono services in aid of our restructuring.

As the point person on reform, I felt obliged to set an example of doing more with less. My department made fifty-eight professional positions, approximately 5 percent of our management complement, available for redeployment. Across other departments, we identified a total of seventy-four such positions. This enabled us to beef up peacekeeping operations by adding personnel there and create a pool of some sixty-five additional vacant positions for further redeployment. We pledged to continue our review with an eye to further reductions, not just in New York but also in Geneva, Vienna, Nairobi and the five regional commissions, and we suggested similar rigorous scrutiny of the nonprofessional posts that constituted 60 percent of the organization's staff. The secretary-general approved all our recommendations.

As anticipated, the redeployments produced a fair amount of grumbling among my colleagues and formal protests from the employee unions, which saw a shrinking pool of professional posts available to be filled by promotions. Employee morale was alleged to be at an "all-time low," a familiar union complaint. But we fully expected a higher level of output from a more efficiently deployed professional workforce. And I worked to keep open the lines of communication between my office and the employee union heads, feeling it was crucial to create a working environment that fostered a sense of purpose and mission in our day-to-day activities. As I put it in an interview with the *UN Staff Report*, "We are, after all, engaged in really basic pursuits that are among the most important on the face of the earth: bringing peace to the world, providing opportunities for people to develop socially and economically [and] providing a forum for dealing with differences between nations, groups and peoples."

In June 1992, the secretary-general released an Agenda for Peace, developed in response to a request from a summit meeting of world leaders. I was one of the group asked to generate ideas for this document, which occasioned a good bit of favorable comment. Noting that the "deepest causes of conflict [are] economic despair, social injustice and political oppression," the secretary-general set forth the need for improved capabilities in preventive diplomacy and in making, keeping and building peace. In particular, he called for a permanent, rather than an ad hoc, UN military capability to deter, as well as respond to, potential aggressors. He also suggested that prepositioned or standby stocks of peacekeeping equipment would hasten response times. Regional organizations were encouraged to take a more prominent role in response to regional conflicts.

Boutros-Ghali's next goal was an examination of the development programs. The integration of a number of previously separate programs into a new Department of Economic and Social Development (DESD) marked an important first step in rationalizing the secretariat's approach to these endeavors. But it left untouched the need to rationalize the entire UN effort in economic and social development, most of which was carried out by subsidiary programs such as UNDP and the multitude of specialized agencies. As part of an advisory group convened by the secretary-general, I had our department conduct a six-month study of these structural issues. We discussed them with, among others, colleagues in the secretariat, most of the heads of the development agencies, and representatives of the Nordic Group (Scandinavian countries long concerned with bringing some order to the development area), the reform-minded Geneva Group and the Group of 77, representing the developing countries.

The key recommendation of the resulting concept paper, which I conveyed to the secretary-general in October 1992, was the creation of a central Development Council to establish policy for all UN development programs and the suppression or conversion to expert advisory bodies of the separate governing bodies of UN development entities. This "would obviously have implications for the future of a number of current entities engaged in development activities . . . all of which should be scrutinized . . . in particular, the roles of the present DESD and UNDP would require attention" through either merger or a careful sorting out. The new council "would give Member States the opportunity to reach consensus on a comprehensive set of priorities for development activities and to allocate resources accordingly. . . . Currently, the separate governing body of each entity deals with its own substantive area and has the ability to set its own priorities, which may be inconsistent with the priorities established by the General Assembly or by the governing bodies of other organizations. . . . [E]ven when the policies of the separate governing bodies are fully consistent with the priorities of the General Assembly, priorities may be distorted by the uncoordinated allocation of resources. . . . This skewing of priorities is heightened by the extra-budgetary funding provided to the separate agencies which is allocated without reference to any central coordination or to the expenditures of other programs." About 70 percent of UN development expenditures were "off budget" and not subject to the review process established for the general budget. Without wishing to discourage the flow of voluntary contributions, we suggested that the new council could at least compensate for the distortions.

At the same time, we proposed that the UNDP representatives in each country be given greater authority over the implementation of all UN development programs, acting as "ambassadors" with supervisory authority over a staff of experts from all relevant agencies. We also recommended a broadened role for the five regional commissions. In most cases, these were closer to development problems and thus at least potentially more responsive to differing political, environmental, geographic, economic and cultural circumstances. We recommended that the commissions also offer a forum for dealing with humanitarian, political and peacekeeping issues, quoting the secretary-general's earlier observation that it is "futile, if not counterproductive, to separate out the political and the economic and social missions of the Organization."

Finally, we recommended a dramatic reconfiguration of all UN entities dealing with subjects related to development to "eliminate duplication and overlap." As a possible first cut, we suggested reducing the number of these entities from twenty-three to twelve, with focal points in trade and industry, the environment, population, food and agriculture, humanitarian programs, children's programs, drugs, social affairs, human settlements, health, labor and the existing UNESCO. All missions would be reevaluated in light of the end of the Cold War and the accompanying movement away from authoritarian governments and centrally planned economies toward democratic governments, market-driven economies and increased environmental concerns. In addition, we recommended a second Bretton Woods conference to evaluate the development activities of the World Bank, the International Monetary Fund and GATT so that they, too, could reposition themselves for new challenges.

Our proposals were far-reaching but not out of sync with recommendations made by others inside and outside the organization. Indeed, they were entirely consistent with observations Boutros-Ghali himself had made in an article written for *Foreign Affairs*: "Duplication is widespread; coordination is often nominal; bureaucratic battles aimed at monopolizing a particular subject are rife, and organizational objectives are sometimes in conflict." By the time the advisory group had finished its work, however, President Bush had lost his bid for reelection, and any authority his sponsorship had given me was to erode rapidly. Even so, I was astonished at the course the secretary-general chose. Disregarding our recommendations, he ordered that the newly consolidated DESD be split up anew into three new departments, each headed by an appointee at the undersecretary-general level. One of the appointees was Chinese, one French and one Indian. Clearly, power politics had displaced management instincts, and the restructuring exercise essentially ground to a halt thereafter.

ANOTHER VITAL area that seemed ripe for reform was the UN's budget process, which I was later to call "almost surreal" in its complexity and in the degree to which it entailed the rigorous review and micromanagement of minutiae. Our department was responsible for handling budgetary matters before the General Assembly. This meant initially presenting them to the sixteen-member Advisory Committee on Administrative and Budgetary Questions (ACABQ). The Fifth Committee of the General Assembly then considered the ACABQ's recommendations and was, in fact, the final arbiter, as the larger body seldom altered the committee's determinations.

Speaking to the Fifth Committee on October 13, I expressed my dissatisfaction with the budget process, particularly the great effort expended on the so-called Medium-Term Plan, a rolling assessment of five-year goals that was singularly unrealistic during a time of tumultuous change. I also raised publicly for the first time the need for a system-wide inspector general to deal with allegations of fraud, waste and abuse and suggested a moratorium on worldwide conferences at least through 1995, while an indepth examination of the worth of costly past gatherings was undertaken.

My sense was that the committee was not used to such candor and that not all of my views had been well received by the secretary-general's office. Nonetheless, as I had earlier told the *New York Times*, "The compelling rationale for the United Nations is not the bottom line, but to ignore sound management would be a tragic mistake." We had laid down the gauntlet regarding the need for dramatic change in the organization's modus operandi.

Even with its vastly increased commitments, the UN's combined budgets amounted to less than New York City paid for police and fire protection. Funding shortfalls nonetheless regularly threatened the viability of many of its far-flung operations. As of December 31, 1992, contributions were over a billion dollars in arrears. The Russian Federation, with a shortfall of over $400 million ($110 million in the regular budget and $290 million in peacekeeping), and the United States, at $287 million ($239 million in the regular budget and $48 million in peacekeeping), were the two biggest offenders, accounting for nearly 70 percent of the total. A reluctant U.S. Congress had allowed arrears to build up during the turbulent 1980s, and the bottom had fallen out of the Russian economy in the 1990s. Moreover, the formulae for contributions were dated, failing to take into account the changing world landscape in trade and economic growth.

The secretary-general authorized our department to appoint an outside group of experts to examine this situation. This multinational blue-ribbon panel of eleven business, financial and economic experts, chaired by Paul Volcker and Shijuru Ogata, rendered its report in February 1993, just prior to my departure.

The report dealt separately with the regular and peacekeeping budgets, which are quite differently structured. (In addition, governments made voluntary contributions to a number of UN agencies, mostly for humanitarian or economic development efforts, and to some 136 special-purpose trust funds. This made it difficult to establish and control any overall agenda.)

For regular budget contributions, which finance the operations of the secretariat, the UN's Committee on Contributions draws up and the General Assembly approves a complicated scale of assessments. Member states are billed for these contributions on January 1 of each year. Payments are due within thirty days but are consistently late. In 1993, for example, only eighteen countries, which provided about 16 percent of the budget, met the January 31 deadline. Many countries fail to pay on time because their budget cycles do not correspond to the UN's. The United States is regularly nine months in arrears because our fiscal year begins on October 1 and the decision was made in the 1980s to "slip a year," funding UN contributions retrospectively rather than prospectively. By my stint at the UN, these shortfalls and distortions had created a cash flow crisis, prompting frequent borrowing from peacekeeping funds and other sources to keep operations afloat. The increased drain on the secretariat from mission assignments was beginning to take a toll as well, particularly with the hiring freeze still in effect.

Peacekeeping had its own assessment formula. Member states were divided into four groups: Group A, the five permanent members of the Security Council; Group B, the other more developed nations; Group C, the economically less developed members; and Group D, the least developed states. Groups B, C and D paid percentages of their regular budget shares (100 percent, 20 percent and 10 percent, respectively), and Group A made up the balance. This is why the United States paid only 25 percent of the regular budget but over 30 percent of the peacekeeping costs.

Peacekeeping budgets were also mission-specific and required separate review by the ACABQ, the Fifth Committee and the General Assembly. The secretary-general could allocate $3 million for each operation, plus another $10 million following ACABQ approval, but these amounts were minimal relative to the expanding size and scope of these operations. For example, my first budget request, which was presented to ACABQ and approved in the spring of 1992 and was the largest ever made up to that time, asked for more than $1.7 billion to fund the first year's operation of the UN Transitional Authority in Cambodia (UNTAC). This undertaking grew out of the Paris Conference agreement of the previous October which called for a cease-fire and the conduct of free elections in that long-beleaguered country. The UNTAC effort included such nontraditional peacekeeping activities as rehabilitation and reintegration of returning refugees, establishment of a radio station and clearance of mines, as well as the normal civilian staff, police, military personnel and equipment.

Full assessments for each peacekeeping operation were forwarded following General Assembly action on the budget for that operation. As a result, member states received several of these requests per year at unpredictable times. Only about one-third of peacekeeping dues were being paid within the first three months of a mission, so much interaccount borrowing and fancy financial footwork was required even to provide bare necessities. I was to compare this process later to a financial "bungee jump": missions were undertaken in hope and faith, but with no assurance, that they would eventually be funded. By the fall of 1992, ten peacekeeping operations were under way, with others in the works in Mozambique and South Africa. With contributions in arrears, these operations were woefully underfinanced. Reimbursement for troop contributions was the major victim of the shortfalls. A large payment that fall from the United States provided only temporary financial relief.

The Volcker-Ogata group made twenty recommendations. Among the most significant were the following: A shift to quarterly installments for the payment of regular budget dues; the charging of interest on late payments; an end to borrowing from peacekeeping accounts to cover regular budget expenditures; a revision in the regular budget assessment scale to reflect a three-year rather than a ten-year average of member states' GDP; establishment of a $400 million revolving reserve fund for peacekeeping operations, to be financed by three annual assessments; consideration of a unified peacekeeping budget financed by a single annual assessment; and delegation of authority to the secretary-general to obligate up to 20 percent of the estimated cost of a peacekeeping operation immediately upon Security Council approval of the mission. The group rejected my suggestion for UN authority to undertake short-term borrowing to cover shortfalls during a given year, although most businesses and governments used such mechanisms to smooth out the peaks and valleys of revenue realization, and the authority to do the same would not erode the commendable requirement in the Charter that the organization not run at a deficit. The group emphasized above all the need for member states to meet their obligations in a timely manner, but noted that prospects for improvement in this area would "be dependent upon a perception that funds are economically managed and effectively spent," a condition that clearly had not yet been met.

In November 1992, I flew to Moscow and made a brief pitch for the Russian government to pay its arrears. The talks were cordial but produced only a commitment that "we will do our best." All concerned identified the shortage of hard currency and the lack of a specific line item in the Russian budget as roadblocks. Support was expressed for UN reform initiatives, especially a reduction in the number of permanent (as distinguished from term) contracts in the secretariat.

Before we left, the Russians made what I facetiously characterized as a serious tactical error. Our proud hosts treated us to a tour of the Kremlin museums and their spectacular collection of utilitarian and decorative arts, including the world-renowned diamond exhibit. "Hmmm," I observed. "These would just about pay off your arrears at the UN, I suspect." Our hosts blanched, laughed nervously and hustled us out of the hall before we could fully articulate our intentions for the crown jewels. Some months later, the Russian Federation in fact made some $60 million in payments. This was a positive signal but still left their obligations considerably short of being current. Nevertheless, overall nearly 94 percent of the regular budget was contributed during 1992.

IN THE COURSE of carrying out my responsibilities, I also made trips to Geneva, Vienna, Addis Ababa and Nairobi. Geneva is the home office of the UN High Commissioner for Refugees (UNHCR), the UN Conference on Trade and Development (UNCTAD), WHO and the European Economic Commission, one of the five regional UN commissions charged with localizing responses to development problems. Geneva's reputation as a productive post was not very high. Once, when asked how many people worked in the Geneva office, Boutros-Ghali is reputed to have responded, "About half."

In Vienna were located the UN Industrial Development Organization (UNIDO) and separate offices dealing with Palestinian refugee problems, disability, drugs and crime. Over time, our presence there was to be reduced.

Addis Ababa was home to the Economic Commission for Africa (ECA). When I asked program managers there for a progress report, they responded with an hour's whining about inadequate resources. Not one of them so much as mentioned a single specific project upon which he or she was working or showed a spark of interest in ECA's development mission. Furthermore, ECA was suspected of widespread fraud and abuse. Addis Ababa was also home to one of the true monuments to UN excess—the construction site of a new $100 million conference center. This effort was difficult to justify, particularly since the Organization for African Unity had its own lavish headquarters in the same city, presumably available for any group wishing to meet there. However, the project, like its counterpart in Bangkok, had acquired champions within the General Assembly and was too far along to abandon without more criticism and waste.

Nairobi hosted the UN Environment Programme (UNEP) and the UN Center for Human Settlements (HABITAT). In northeastern Kenya, UNHCR refugee camps accommodated some 150,000 Somalis forced to flee their own country. We visited Hagadara, which housed about 40,000 of these refugees. The facility was remarkable, well laid out in lanes flanked by dwellings. Some of these were tents, some made of fabric stretched over wooden frames; many were quite well engineered. Food distribution was well organized so that each family got its proper daily allocation of salt, sugar, beans, grain and flour from CARE, and private markets sold meat and other provisions. Somali physicians capable of handling routine ills staffed a clean and efficient dispensary. At a nearby camp at Ifo, we met representatives of various private relief organizations. Clearly devoted to relieving the trauma and misery of these thousands of displaced persons, these workers deserve an honored place among history's heroes.

We heard chilling reports on security in Kenya from both UN personnel and the relief organization representatives. In a meeting with President Daniel arap Moi and Minister of Foreign Affairs Wilson Ndolo Ayah, I pointed out that whether the UN expanded or contracted its commitment in Nairobi would depend in large part on resolution of the security matter. I also stressed the importance of President Moi's moves toward creating a multiparty political system, reminding him of how vital this was to Kenya's credibility. Although cordial, he criticized the West for pressuring him to modify Kenya's political system without extending necessary financial aid.

Upon my return to New York, I dispatched a team of security experts to Kenya. Within the year, however, our friend and host during our Nairobi visit, Michael Reitzel-Neilsen, was shot and killed in broad daylight, resisting yet another in a rash of attempted downtown carjackings. This was a dreadful reminder of the hazards that these dedicated international civil servants face on a daily basis.

Early in my UN tenure, Ginny, Cuyler and I traveled to Prague for the Eastern European Conference on Disability. We advocated the relevance of the ADA to the estimated half a billion people with disabilities worldwide, 80 percent of whom live in poverty in developing countries. Although disability issues were not part of my official portfolio, I also pledged that the UN would seek to advance the rights, interests and dignity of persons with disabilities as part of its broadened agenda.

In November 1992, we went to Rome for the Vatican Conference on Religion and Disability in which Ginny had invested so much effort. The conference exceeded its sponsors' most optimistic expectations and was most gratifying to Ginny, in particular. It had as many as 9,000 registered participants. Ginny stole the show with a solid and emotional speech that was interrupted by applause several times and accorded a standing ovation at its end. Meanwhile, activity on the disability front was increasing worldwide in connection with the close of the UN's Decade of the Disabled, observed in the General Assembly in October 1992.

THE DRAMATIC CHANGE in U.S. leadership at the end of 1992 had uncertain implications for the UN. Although the secretary-general's office clearly relished my impending departure, some noted it with regret. The *Diplomatic World Bulletin*, a weekly publication serving the international community in New York, noted that my leaving "could undo much of the good work accomplished since he took office last winter." In an effort to sustain momentum, I undertook to assure a permanent occupant of my position who was committed to reform, as well as to memorialize my experiences and recommendations in a report on insights gained from my experiences.

I wrote to Warren Christopher, head of the Clinton transition team and later secretary of state, urging the importance of choosing another American committed to a reform agenda to hold my position on a permanent basis. I observed: "Pockets of corruption and favoritism, slipshod practices and unnecessary programs and activities which have benefited certain national interests and individuals will be sought to be preserved at all costs and many of the reforms already in place may be undone in the absence of continued attention to these matters." While the letter was somewhat overheated, I knew I had to capture the administration's attention before defenders of the status quo could advance their own candidates for the position. Unfortunately, the Clinton administration displayed no sense of urgency in filling the post, although an American, former ambassador Melissa Wells, was ultimately appointed to it.

I also prepared a detailed report for the secretary-general. Having spent a year identifying what was wrong with the UN, I hoped here to outline some ways to fix the problems. Touching first on restructuring and redeployment in general, I urged an examination of staffing outside headquarters. I also criticized the awarding of costly consulting contracts to high-level officials who left the organization, especially as there were already too many people serving in high-paying permanent posts without specific job assignments. To cut down on waste, I called for a "thorough review of the unnecessarily wide array" of publications (sometimes described as "printed in six languages and read in none") and the vast internal printing operation, and repeated my suggestion for a moratorium on costly worldwide conferences.

Turning to personnel management, I referenced haphazard recruitment, insufficient training, complicated promotion exercises and seemingly interminable dismissal and disciplinary procedures. "The result," I concluded, "is too much 'deadwood' doing too little work and too few good staff members doing too much, over-extending themselves sometimes to the point where they have become counterproductive." Staff had misread the secretary-general's well-intentioned assurance that restructuring would cause no one to lose his or her post as a guarantee of continued employment, even of the unqualified, the incompetent and the nonproductive. I recommended buyouts for those otherwise not terminable; even substantial cash payments would not exceed the cost of keeping nonperformers on the job. I further recommended that permanent contracts become the exception rather than the rule; there should be no "right" to a permanent contract.

The organization had other far-reaching personnel problems. For example, I had previously pointed out that only 30 percent of the posts subject to geographical distribution were occupied by women, most of whom were compressed at the lower levels. In this report, I urged the resolution of two additional issues. The first was "ratings inflation." The evaluation system had reached the point where over 90 percent of the staff were rated positively. This frustrated the ability to reward superior performance and to sanction substandard performance. I noted that "a system where all are *rated* superior is one where none *are* superior." The second problem was featherbedding, employees' and their staff representatives' unwillingness to reduce the workforce by introducing modern technology. In one classic example, translators in our Office of Conference Services would receive a document, dictate a draft translation, have a typist transcribe it, edit the draft and resubmit it for final typing. The use of word processors with their on-screen editing capability was never considered, although many translators in other settings used them regularly. The result was the unnecessary employment of some 500 typists at a cost of $20 million a year.

On budgeting, I proposed reducing General Assembly micromanagement; creating a unified regular budget incorporating the substantial off-budget expenditures; scrapping the Medium-Term Plan; implementing the Volcker-Ogata recommendations; and continuing to implement the Integrated Management Implementation System, a computerized communications network. I also called for "more attention to the particulars [of] financing peacekeeping budgets," including increased use of standard-costing modules for operations with cost elements in common.

My principal recommendation regarding field operations was the funding of a full outside management study. Despite the drastic changes in the number and character of its peacekeeping operations, the UN was still doing "business as usual" in many key areas. McKinsey's preliminary finding was that better management might save as much as $100 million per year. I also recommended establishing a twenty-four-hour communications center in New York to connect high-ranking officials there with field missions.

I repeated my call for a complete overhaul of UN activities in economic and social development. I added a plea for continued progress in treating the needs of persons with disabilities, endorsing a greater role for the regional commissions and a move of the office concerned with disability matters from Vienna to New York (a move that was later to occur).

The final section of the report focused on fraud, waste and abuse. I urged the creation of a new Office of Inspector General. I also summarized my previous suggestions, such as adoption of a common set of accounting standards and principles; amendments to the code of conduct to compel full financial disclosure by senior management and persons in sensitive positions; a requirement that employee evaluations include assessments of staff members' integrity; and expedited treatment of allegations of wrongdoing, in fairness to both the organization and the accused individuals.

My report was delivered to the secretary-general at the close of business on Friday, February 26, my last day on the job, and made available to other interested parties. Although Boutros-Ghali had requested the report, I later heard tales of an order to confiscate or even shred undistributed copies. To this day, copies cannot be obtained from the organization. No objection has ever been made to the report's accuracy or to the soundness of its recommendations. The principal complaint seemed to be that this was an "internal document" that should not have been widely disseminated.

Outside of the UN, the report was generally well received. The *Washington Post*'s front-page story was headlined "'Deadwood' and Inefficiency Hobble U.N., Official Says." UN Ambassador Madeleine Albright was to testify diplomatically before a House subcommittee, "Mr. Thornburgh's report as a whole is a very constructive assessment of the UN that includes recommendations meriting serious examination." Numerous media opportunities were forthcoming for me, reaching a crescendo in 1995, the year of the UN's fiftieth anniversary.

I also testified on the report before several congressional subcommittees and reviewed it with Doug Bennet, then the Clinton administration's assistant secretary of state for international organizations, and with my successor, Melissa Wells. Ms. Wells had a short-lived and rocky tenure at the UN, partly because she also was serious about reform, even speaking well of my report on a *60 Minutes* exposé. (I refused to appear on the show because of my previous shabby treatment on it, turning down even a personal plea from Mike Wallace himself.)

The reform effort continued, needless to say, long after what became known as the Thornburgh Report. And my efforts did not go unnoticed. I was particularly pleased by the *National Journal*'s assessment over two years after my departure from the UN: "The impetus for administrative and fiscal reforms at the United Nations can be credited in large part to intense prodding during the Reagan and Bush administrations. Many of today's cost-cutting stratagems, including the creation of a quasi-inspector general's post to ferret out fraud and waste, stem from a management review conducted by President Bush's Attorney General Dick Thornburgh."

By 1996, however, concern over the lack of progress rose so high in the Republican-controlled Congress that payment of U.S. contributions was once again suspended. Partly, no doubt, to preempt GOP criticism during the presidential campaign, President Clinton let it be known that he intended to veto the reappointment of Boutros-Ghali, whose five-year term as secretary-general was due to expire at the end of 1996. As a result, my friend Kofi Annan of Ghana, who had served in peacekeeping operations during my tenure and later headed that department, took over the post in early 1997, acknowledging the importance of reforming the organization. I was gratified to receive a letter from Annan noting, "[Y]our report has been a continuing and frequent point of reference as we move through the process of reform. Your analysis and thoughtful recommendations have been most helpful to support steps already taken and others in progress." Annan quickly announced a set of cutbacks and reforms (including a recombination of the DESD) intended to send Washington a signal. On the whole, his stewardship of this important international institution has been well received, and he secured a second term in 2001 with little opposition.

Meanwhile, I joined in a number of efforts to encourage the United States to pay its arrears to the UN. Alas, Congress had learned too well that withholding contributions gets results. The "quasi-inspector general" mechanism would never have been adopted had Congress not threatened to withhold a portion of the U.S. contribution. Nevertheless, as committed as I was to UN reform, I felt it was shameful that we, as the sole remaining superpower, should once again default on our treaty obligation to support the organization. Instead, we should pay our arrears, establish a set of goals for reform and press that agenda vigorously in New York. Unfortunately, those in power in Washington chose a different approach. In 1998, for example, appropriations to pay over $1 billion in back dues were withheld as a result of a battle between the White House and Congress over UN efforts relating to the availability of abortions abroad. Both sides dug in their heels, leaving unresolved the greater issue of meeting our treaty obligation to fund the UN. Behaving like a petulant deadbeat posed a real threat to the effectiveness of the United States within the organization contributing, I fear, to the difficulty in getting the Security Council to authorize action against Iraq in 2003.

Naturally, I was disappointed in the failure of the UN Security Council to take effective steps to enforce the 1991 cease-fire agreement that ended the first Gulf War. Throughout the 1990s, Iraqi dictator Saddam Hussein consistently violated or ignored with impunity various resolutions calling upon him to disarm and to give UN inspectors access to weapons sites within his country. Finally, in November 2002, at the insistence of the United States, the Security Council unanimously adopted Resolution 1441, offering Saddam a last chance to comply and threatening "serious consequences" for failure to do so. When noncompliance persisted, Security Council members France and Russia, together with Germany and others, balked at enforcing Resolution 1441. The U.S. and the United Kingdom were thus obligated to fashion a military coalition of their own in 2003, which swiftly and decisively defeated Iraqi forces once again. But considerable damage had been done to the credibility of the Security Council as a force for collective resistance to tyrants like Saddam Hussein. Its future prospects appear uncertain.

20

Return to the Law
and Other Pursuits

A T THE END OF FEBRUARY 1993, I left New York and headed back
to Washington, my twenty-five-year career in public office at an end. I
looked forward to resuming life under one roof with my beloved Ginny.
And after over two decades of the pressure-cooker environment of public
responsibility, I was ready for a transition to the role of "useful citizen."

Ginny had, of course, already more than achieved that status. Her work
as Director of the Religion and Disability Program at NOD had continued
to prosper. Her principal effort was the writing and editing of a handsome
and useful guide for congregations seeking to become more welcoming to
persons with disabilities. Entitled *That All May Worship*, it was a superb
publication, easy to read and liberally illustrated, and received wide praise
and favorable reviews in both the religious and the disability communities.
It was to sell over 60,000 copies. She subsequently launched a series of
"That All May Worship" conferences across the country to address the
challenges of particular communities in opening the doors of their religious institutions to persons with disabilities. Her initial publishing effort
was followed by two other works: *Loving Justice*, a guide to ADA compliance for the religious community, and *From Barriers to Bridges*, a community action guide for those wishing to sponsor a "That All May Worship"
conference. Both were equally well received.

At the turn of the century, the Religion and Disability program sought to obtain the commitment of 2,000 congregations nationwide to become more accessible and welcoming to persons with disabilities. The "2,000 in 2000" campaign met its goal and substantially raised the profile of Ginny's program. Through her service on the board of trustees of the Princeton Theological Seminary, she also sought to increase the level of awareness among faculty and seminarians of the unique gifts and needs of children and adults with disabilities. Her contributions were regularly recognized through awards and publicity around the nation.

Peter increasingly asserted himself during his visits with us. His principal complaint concerned his group home and, in due course, he moved into a nearby supervised apartment, where he enjoyed more independence and less hassle from staff and other clients. In 1995 he changed jobs, accepting a full-time volunteer position at the Central Pennsylvania Food Bank. Under caring management, Peter was introduced to mainstream employment and amazed us all with his accomplishments, for which he was honored as a Volunteer of the Year.

THE SEARCH FIRM handling the quest for a new baseball commissioner contacted me in May 1993, and I journeyed to Chicago to meet with the owners' committee. I was eventually told that I had survived several cuts, but that the owners wanted someone more "media-oriented." However, 1993 ended with the vacancy still open, as did 1994, 1995 and 1996. The position was an ongoing temptation to me, and friends who knew of my absorption with the game kept encouraging my interest. My final contribution on this matter, however, turned out to be an op-ed piece in the *Wall Street Journal* in August 1994, calling for a return to a Judge Landis-type commissioner to help solve the game's problems and for recognition of the special needs of small-market teams like my beloved Pirates. Eventually, the owners turned to one of their own, Bud Selig of the Milwaukee Brewers, to serve as commissioner, but the game's ills continued into the new century.

After considerable scrutiny of the alternatives, I decided to return to Kirkpatrick & Lockhart as counsel in its Washington office. The firm had well over 400 lawyers by the mid-1990s, with over 100 in Washington alone. In my previous stints with the firm, my sense was that I had not justified my generous compensation packages, and that there was a risk of some dissatisfaction among "producing" partners. Furthermore, I wanted time for writing, speaking and travel. Nonetheless, I felt that my insights and contacts could be of considerable use to the firm and its clients. We finally agreed upon terms that permitted me the desired leeway and paid me 60 percent of what I would have made as a partner, leaving me free to supplement my income with outside engagements. This arrangement has turned out to be very satisfactory from my point of view. I have spent over half my time on client work, the rest pursuing the other outside interests I have developed over the years.

THE NEED FOR A commitment to the rule of law in both developing countries and those emerging from Soviet domination commanded my continuing interest. If these nations were to see more democracy, respect for human rights and market-oriented economies, as they usually sought, the rule of law was an absolute sine qua non. Without it, free elections, corruption-free government and due process would be impossible. Moreover, foreign businesses would be wary of making necessary commitments to promote economic growth and jobs where their investments might be summarily expropriated or their contracts proved unenforceable in independent courts. Thus, I became a veritable missionary for the rule of law.

In the summer of 1993, I traveled to Taiwan to discuss its interest in the UN. Taiwan (as the Republic of China, ROC) had been one of the original Security Council members but had been replaced in 1972 by the PRC, both as a UN member and on the Security Council. Now moving swiftly toward multiparty democracy and with a burgeoning economy, the Taiwanese were interested in regaining official recognition in the world community.

In meetings with Taiwanese leaders, I suggested the following arguments in support of an effort to rejoin the UN. The ROC had made great economic and political progress in recent years. It now had the world's thirteenth-largest trading economy, the second-largest foreign exchange reserves and a thriving multiparty political system. The ROC could be a major financial contributor to UN peacekeeping, humanitarian, economic development and social programs. I noted that the two Germanys and the two Koreas had set a precedent (albeit a somewhat tenuous one) for UN membership by both Taiwan and the PRC. This argument came perilously close, however, to advocating an "independent" Taiwan, which was opposed by President Lee Tung-hei and his Kuomintang (KMT) Party, but espoused by the opposition. And less deserving states already had UN membership. Libya, Iran and Sudan had been identified as sponsors of state-supported terrorism, while Iraq and others systematically denied basic rights to their citizens. Size was not a limitation; much smaller states, such as Vanuatu and Andorra, were UN members. Despite minimal formal diplomatic relations with other UN member states, the ROC had de facto relations with most of the principal world powers. The ROC could be a role model for both developing countries and nations in transition, showing how democratic institutions and market economies could be fashioned from more authoritarian regimes and centrally planned and/or largely agricultural economies.

It was, of course, impractical for Taiwan to seek full UN membership due to the PRC's veto power, but I recommended that it continue to seek observer status in as many international and regional organizations as possible, in the expectation that some of these relationships might eventually ripen into full membership and increased recognition and status. With the new century, the impasse between the "two Chinas" persists, although changes in the political leadership of each have raised some hopes for a more permanent solution—and armed hostilities appear to have been averted for the foreseeable future.

THE INTERNATIONAL Republican Institute (IRI) gave me a remarkable opportunity to observe the Russian Federation's first multiparty legislative elections in December 1993 and its first presidential election in June 1996. An arm of the National Endowment for Democracy, the IRI worked to help establish democratic institutions around the world.

Both election-monitoring missions were chaired by the IRI chairman, Senator John McCain (R–Ariz.), and comprised veterans of the American political process, including elected officials, political consultants, academics and a variety of persons from the legislative and executive branches at all levels. In each case, we assembled in Moscow well in advance of election day for briefings from American embassy personnel, officials of the Russian Central Election Commission, representatives of the political parties and various candidates, as well as members of the media and other experts on the political climate in Russia. We were assigned to make random unannounced visits to polling places around the country on election day, monitoring everything from the opening of the polling station to the ballot count. Our responsibility was to verify the integrity of the electoral process and detect any fraud or intimidation. In both cases, we found the elections to be free and fair, though we had suggestions for improvement. On the whole, our experiences were most reassuring as to the process of electoral democracy, if somewhat jarring as to the outcomes.

The fall of 1993 had seen President Boris Yeltsin dissolve the parliament and ultimately take military action against the building housing it. Thus, the prospects for continued democracy were somewhat in doubt as we arrived on December 7. Elections were to be held for both houses of parliament. The Duma had 450 members, of whom half were to be elected directly, the other half by proportional representation from national lists compiled by the parties. The Federation Council had 176 members, two from each of 88 regions. Also to be voted upon was a referendum on a hastily drafted new constitution, which required approval by a 50 percent vote and a turnout of at least 50 percent. Including local elections in some areas, voters might be called upon to cast as many as five ballots. I could not help but reflect on the monumental changes that had taken place since my first visit to the Soviet Union. In 1979, at the height of the Brezhnev era, a multiparty free election of a true legislative body would have been unthinkable.

Election day was Sunday, December 12, and we began our rounds about seven in the morning. We stopped at eleven Moscow polling places and were well received at each. Many of them were well stocked with food (and some with vodka) for sale. We observed a number of peculiar practices (most notably communal voting, including discussions and ballot marking outside the voting booths) but no serious irregularities. The biggest complaint of the voters we spoke with seemed to be the lack of party labels for the candidates. That night we observed one polling place's vote count, a series of very formal procedures, including the driving of a spike through unused ballots, the dumping of the ballots onto a table for separation into piles and the manual counting of the votes. Separately accounted for were the ballots contained within a portable box taken to shut-ins, the aged and others unable to get to their polling places.

The results of the election were a shock to many, although not to some of the reformers. The candidates receiving the most votes were those aligned with Vladimir Zhirinovsky's Liberal Democratic Party (said to be neither liberal nor democratic). The reform effort nominally led by President Yeltsin was so divided that no one element gained an edge. According to some reformers, this was partly because Yeltsin had failed to explain adequately the reform movement, had allowed it to splinter around individual personalities and had refused to put his own prestige on the line for any party or group of candidates.

Following the election, our observers gathered and confirmed that the process had been free and fair. While Senator McCain was our principal spokesman, I offered my own recommendations at our press conference and in an op-ed piece for the *Washington Times*: (1) the addition of party labels to the ballots; (2) a prohibition against government ministers running for the legislature without resigning; (3) a "who gave it, who got it" preelection campaign finance reporting law; and (4), unrelated to elections, refinement of the term "mafia" to distinguish between organized-crime figures and "new capitalists," together with passage of a RICO-type statute and the commitment of sufficient law enforcement resources to combat the real mafia. These suggestions and many more were incorporated into a lengthy and comprehensive IRI report that was conveyed to the Russian government and served as the basis for the significant reform measures that governed subsequent elections.

The drill in 1996 was very similar. We underwent briefings and met with most of the ten presidential candidates or their representatives as well as other experts on Russian politics. Many electoral reforms had been made since 1993, the most significant being the opening up of the governing and observation process. The president had previously appointed the entire Central Election Commission; now the president, the Duma and the Federation Council each appointed one-third of its members. Similarly, local election commissions included party and candidate representatives as observers. Most saw these changes as providing credible deterrents to wide-scale or centrally directed fraud or irregularity. The Russians had not made equivalent progress on campaign financing and reporting, but we felt somewhat constrained in criticizing a facet of the electoral process where our own nation had made little headway.

The electoral process required a 50 percent vote to win a first-round victory or else a second round runoff between the two top vote getters. The race was really one between President Yeltsin and Communist leader Gennady Zyuganov, with some nuisance value added by Vladimir Zhirinovsky and some further interest by former general Alexander Lebed.

A second round of legislative elections in 1995 had produced a Communist Party plurality in the Duma, and Zyuganov clearly hoped to convert this to the presidency. His was the best organized of the campaigns, but it had shortcomings as well. Unlike resurgent former Communists in Eastern Europe, he had resisted creating a broader, less doctrinaire, social democrat-type appeal. Instead, he had clung to the traditional Communist Party base, which, while solid, was not in itself broad enough to provide a margin of victory.

As the year began, however, a Zyuganov victory seemed entirely possible, as Yeltsin's reforms were imposing widespread hardships on Russian citizens. His health was also of considerable concern, and crime, corruption and the war in Chechnya had provoked much discontent. Moreover, despite the 1995 parliamentary election debacle, Yeltsin still had not formed his own party or attempted to coalesce the reform elements. By our arrival, however, he had made a remarkable recovery and taken the lead in most polls. He had run an effective campaign, exhibiting considerable vigor and doling out numerous promises and substantial cash to key constituencies. He also had the advantage of a supine media, not given to fair coverage and rightfully disturbed over the prospects for continued press freedom in the event of a Communist victory. Yeltsin was widely favored to lead the first round of voting, but with less than a majority, and then to capture the runoff.

Some had sought to portray Zhirinovsky as a total madman, but this was not our observation. While eccentric and often hard to follow, he exhibited some shrewd insights and came across as clever, opportunistic and manipulative. He claimed that the election results had been "cooked" and predicted an outcome pretty close to what came to pass.

The true wild card was Lebed, whose law-and-order, anticorruption television message was resonating with more and more voters. While he was not given a chance to win, his possible third-place finish would (and did, as it turned out) give him a superb bargaining position with the one-two finishers.

Former premier and Nobel Laureate Mikhail Gorbachev was also a candidate, despite the almost universal disdain felt for him by the Russian people. Although during our meeting he estimated his chances at "between zero and 1 percent," he felt that his signal contribution was that "they couldn't cancel the election if Gorbachev participates." Many of those we interviewed privately praised Gorbachev for his achievements, some even acknowledging that the elections would not have been possible without his efforts.

During our stay in Moscow, I took a break to meet with my old friend Veniamin Yakovlev, chief judge of the Supreme Court of Arbitration Appeals. He seemed more positive about the commercial court system now and was particularly pleased that he was attracting some new blood into the judiciary. Ten "circuit courts" had been established to hear intermediate appeals and help reduce the caseload of his court to about 800 cases a year. Yakovlev commented favorably on new banking and credit statutes, while lamenting delay on bankruptcy and securities laws and the continued indefinite status of laws on property transfers.

On election day, our delegation again toured polling places in and around Moscow. We confirmed the absence of irregularities and a sense of pride among election officials. Yeltsin received 35 percent of the votes cast, Zyuganov 32 percent and Lebed 15 percent (and Gorbachev, as a sad footnote, only 0.5 percent). On July 1, President Yeltsin won the runoff with 53.8 percent of the vote to Zyuganov's 40.3 percent, the balance being for neither candidate. Predictably, Lebed had thrown his support to Yeltsin and was rewarded with a short-lived position as a key adviser before being dumped. Lebed was later to win a provincial governorship, where he served until his death in 2001.

I was to return to the Russian Federation a number of times after these two seminal electoral events. On three occasions I visited the Moscow School of Political Studies, whose extraordinary leader, Elena Nemirovskaya, brought together younger political leaders, journalists and academics from throughout Russia to examine issues of the day in two- or three-day retreats staffed by "experts" from other countries. I addressed rule-of-law issues, including the need for an independent judiciary and a vigorous anticorruption effort. I also spoke to members of Judge Yakovlev's court in Moscow and various visiting groups in Washington on similar subjects.

The IRI also asked me to chair an observer mission to Ukraine for the November 1999 presidential election. The autocratic incumbent, Leonid Kuchma, was reelected, as expected. Ukraine's history as a crossroads for conquering nations from both East and West and its multiethnic heritage made for some unique insights. Most of all, our hosts reminded us of the barbaric cruelty visited upon its people during both the Nazi and the Soviet occupations.

IN JUNE 1994, I headed an IRI delegation to study the prospects for the rule of law in Hong Kong in view of its impending 1997 reversion to the PRC. Whereas the IRI's mission was usually to help establish new democratic institutions, here it was to help ensure the continuance of established ones. Considerable concern was developing over the future viability of this bustling center of commerce and trade, and over the political rights of its 6.2 million residents, fully half of them refugees from Communist China. During a week of briefings from political, labor and business leaders, journalists and lawyers, we heard a wide variety of views on many issues related to these concerns.

Negotiations between Britain and the PRC had resulted in a 1984 Joint Declaration that contemplated the creation of a Special Administrative Region with a "high degree of autonomy," leaving Hong Kong's social, legal and economic systems substantially unchanged for at least fifty years. A legislature would be elected locally and a chief executive appointed by Beijing. The common law would be retained, and "[r]ights and freedoms, including those of the person, of speech, of the press, of assembly, of association, of travel, of movement, of correspondence, of strike, of choice of occupation, of academic research and of religious belief will be ensured by law." Power of final adjudication in the courts, then vested in the Privy Council in London, would move to a court of final appeal in Hong Kong, not in Beijing. By February 1990, the National People's Congress of the PRC had passed a basic law "fleshing out" the Joint Declaration that created a whole set of new issues. Within the year, the Legislative Council (Legco) of Hong Kong had adopted its own Bill of Rights ordinance.

At the time of our visit, much of Hong Kong's business community espoused a pro–PRC, "don't make waves" attitude. Some business leaders believed that self-interest would require the PRC to recognize the political aspirations of Hong Kong residents in order to maintain the city's economic vitality. They predicted the fifty-year guarantee would be a force for changing the form of governmental and economic endeavor on the mainland and would provide a model for solution of the Taiwan problem. A more cynical observer described the business viewpoint as, "Look at Southern China. . . . No rule of law, they make lots of money." Of course, this stance is easy to sustain in good times, but less so when problems arise in business transactions.

Others expressed concerns for business: the potential desire of party cadres for roles beyond their capabilities, the PRC's culture of corruption as it would interact with the Hong Kong "fast buck" syndrome, the PRC's lax enforcement of industrial safety laws and its "life is cheap" attitude. Several of those we spoke with focused particularly on corruption, noting that the Chinese had a tendency to reward their friends (e.g., by awarding them big public contracts) and to punish their enemies. They did not trust the PRC to provide the level playing field implicit in (and necessary to) Hong Kong's market economy.

Meanwhile, lawyers worried about a potential legal vacuum. The 1,000 lawyers in the office of Attorney General Jeremy F. Matthews saw themselves as the bulwark of the rule of law. They handled all prosecutions and civil proceedings as well as drafting and translating all legislation. Frustrations ranged from the slow pace of translation of the laws into Chinese to the lack of PRC lawyers who understood the common law. Moreover, we were told, PRC legal cadres had difficulty grasping the notion of an independent judiciary. They simply could not envision any mechanism of government not under party control. A diplomat we spoke with added, "When the first son of a high Chinese official is nabbed for corruption in Hong Kong, will a phone call come from Beijing to the judge?" Clauses providing for overseas arbitration of commercial disputes were becoming increasingly popular.

For their part, the somewhat battle-weary pro-democracy and human rights activists clearly felt that the British had not done enough to secure the rights of Hong Kong citizens. The Joint Declaration's guarantees, the Legco, the Bill of Rights ordinance and the common law were all at risk. Some expressed pessimism about the ability to accommodate the common law within a Chinese system based on "clout," and about the future of the judicial system. Problems were also noted with some of the remnants of British rule: the British had made a controversial last-minute attempt to extend the franchise, and some draconian colonial-era laws were still on the books.

Personally, I concluded that Hong Kong could not become, as some suggested, "an economic and not a political city" unless its people chose to forgo all those elements of their quality of life that had made them unique in the Asia-Pacific region. My journal set forth my final assessment of our mission: "[T]he real controversy is not, as would appear on the surface, between Governor [Chris] Patten and the British Government, on the one hand, and the PRC on the other. The real controversy is between those residents of Hong Kong who are committed to human rights and the rule of law and a business community unwilling to press the case for these principles for fear of upsetting their present and potential economic and financial relationships with the PRC." I could not resist adding: "[T]his differs little from the attitude of the U.S. where President Clinton relinquished the coupling of human rights concerns to the MFN [most-favored-nation] renewal because of fear of losing an economic advantage. Such recent history makes it awkward for the United States to now assert human rights arguments in Hong Kong as forcefully as we might otherwise do."

Our pessimistic report, which commanded little attention, found a "steady erosion" of the commitments made in the Joint Declaration. The report focused on several needs: a credible court of final appeal, continuation of the common law, repeal or modification of certain British laws potentially impinging on human and civil rights, and attention to corruption and freedom of the press. We concluded, "No effort should be spared . . . to make sure that commitments made by the current and future governments of Hong Kong regarding the legal, as well as the political and economic systems of Hong Kong, will be kept."

I returned to Hong Kong twice following the July 1, 1997, handover to the PRC. In the spring of 1998, I chaired a fact-finding mission sponsored by the National Democratic Institute, IRI's counterpart, prior to the first legislative elections since the PRC's designated chief executive, Tung Chee-Wa, had assumed office. I visited again with many of those I had met in 1994 as well as other journalists, political leaders and academics. I greatly enjoyed renewing my acquaintance with Martin Lee, leader of the democratic forces, and came to appreciate even more how important he is to the cause of the rule of law in Hong Kong. Following our meetings with Tung (who openly disparaged the election process) and other officials, we issued a report critical of the overly complicated and only partly democratic election procedures and the government's unwillingness to host observer missions.

In January 1999, the Hong Kong government sponsored a further visit largely for the purpose of demonstrating to me the continuity of the rule of law since the handover. I had to give it credit for hosting a sometimes vocal critic of its political culture. My meeting with Tung Chee-Wa again was cordial and touched on electoral procedures and structural reform of the government. I offered the Pennsylvania Constitutional Convention and the Ben Franklin Partnership as possible models for action in Hong Kong. The vitality of the court system was evident; at the opening ceremonies for the beginning of the Law Year, bewigged and richly outfitted judges gathered en masse for a solemn ceremony and speeches. An interesting side trip took me to the boundary between Hong Kong and the PRC, adjacent to the thriving Shenzhen Special Economic Zone, which I had first visited almost twenty years before and which was now a stronghold of something like capitalism. The border nonetheless resembled the Korean DMZ more than it did a state border in America, with checkpoints and sentries in clear evidence.

Hong Kong seems to have survived the turnover with only minimum damage. There is continuing concern, however, about the future of the rule of law (especially the independence of the courts); the outcome will likely depend on the direction of PRC mainland politics. The present Hong Kong government keeps a pretty tight lid on almost everything and has thus far avoided any major confrontation with pro-democracy forces, but the potential is always there.

I VISITED GUATEMALA in the fall of 1994 and again in early 1995 as leader of an IRI effort to deal with governmental corruption in that country. The cosponsor of our program, the nonpartisan Institutio Pro-Democracia y Desarrollo (Institute for Democracy and Development), was described as being pro-U.S., somewhat right of center and devoted to democratic government and free-market economics.

President Jorge Serrano Elias, whose inauguration I had attended, had been deposed and fled the country in June 1993 on the verge of being investigated for alleged misuse of public funds. Serrano had previously used concern about public corruption as a pretext for suspending the constitution and dissolving the National Congress and the Supreme Court. The congress elected Ramiro de Leon Carpio, the former human rights ombudsman, to finish Serrano's term. He immediately called for a referendum to reform the constitution, a new slate of Supreme Court justices and new congressional elections in August 1994. The referendum passed, a new court was installed and the elections took place. They were followed by additional reforms in the legal system, including establishment of a new prosecutor's office to step up the effort to deal with endemic corruption.

That fall, we held a two-day "good governance" conference and also met with government officials, including President Carpio and Guatemala's strongman, General Efrain Rios Montt, Speaker of the National Congress and leader of the dominant Guatemalan Republican Front. The sixty-eight-year-old Rios Montt was clearly scheming as to how he could regain the presidency he had once held.

My keynote speech at the conference emphasized that a strong anticorruption commitment was necessary to create a climate where the rule of law could survive. As I pointed out, corruption had consequences transcending mere concerns about morality: an undermining of the electoral process; cynicism about the justice system; illegal police and military activity; market distortions through kickbacks, payoffs, price fixing and bid rigging; and government waste that upped the bill for all taxpayers. I also dwelt on the need for well-trained and justly compensated police and prosecutors. Finally, I introduced the concept of citizen action and the need for vigilant media.

Our February 1995 program followed a similar format. We also convinced representatives of the six main political parties to sign a Declaration of Ethical Principles in advance of the fall presidential elections. None of us had any illusions that the signing would magically clean up a corrupt and discredited system. I felt the important thing was that these conferences were held at all and captured the attention of the country's political leadership.

Free and fair elections were held in the fall of 1995. Rios Montt was held to be disqualified under constitutional provisions denying the office to those who had previously participated in a coup, and the PAN party's Alvaro Arzu defeated Rios Montt's stand-in. By December 1996, President Arzu, with UN assistance, had engineered an end to the country's thirty-six-year-long civil war and seemed well on the way to restoring some much-needed integrity to the governmental process and some tranquility to this long-suffering society. The past continues to haunt Guatemala, however, and the pattern of progress seems to be "two steps forward, one step back."

IN JUNE 1995, the extraordinary Dr. Young Woo Kang, a blind leader of the disability movement in the United States and the Republic of Korea, invited Ginny and me to visit Korea to discuss issues of religion and disability. In Korean society, disability is viewed with much shame and superstition.

The centerpieces of our weeklong stay were a series of addresses drawing upon Ginny's *That All May Worship* texts, which Young had arranged to have translated and printed in handsome Korean-language editions. These sold like hotcakes at each stop on our tour.

During this visit, we met with many political and governmental leaders. We were most impressed by Dr. Kun Mo Chung, the minister of science and technology. Formerly with the UN International Atomic Energy Agency, he was serving as a trustee of Dr. Kang's foundation and had donated a kidney to his son. We were also impressed by Samsung's $30 million residential, work and recreation facility for about 150 men and women with physical disabilities who worked on telephone production lines.

Our visit left us feeling that Korea had a long way to go in affording dignity to its citizens with disability, but we were heartened that so many people of goodwill, particularly within the religious communities, were trying to meet these challenges. Two years later, in 1997, the World Committee on Disability awarded President Kim Young-Sam the very first Franklin D. Roosevelt Award for having made noteworthy progress in providing support to people with disability in his nation.

We returned to Korea in 1998 to speak at the sixth annual Conference on Rehabilitation of People with Disabilities, sponsored by Dr. Kang's organization and Yonsei University. "Focus on people's ability, not their disability" was the conference slogan. We also met with Chief Justice Yong Joon Kim of the Constitutional Court, who uses a cane due to polio and is the most prominent Korean with a disability. Naturally, one of the highlights of the trip for me was a baseball game between teams sponsored by L.G. Electronics and O.B. Beer at the impressive stadium built for the 1988 Olympic Games.

A 1999 NDI ASSIGNMENT took me to Nigeria's capital city, Abuja, to meet with thirty-six newly elected state governors in a country just emerging from years of military dictatorship. We discussed federalism, federal–state relations, interstate relations and a variety of other governance issues. The most populous black nation in Africa and possessed of vast oil resources, Nigeria has continued to struggle against ethnic and tribal rifts and turmoil created by attempts to enact Islamic law (including death by stoning for certain offenses) in the states. Transparency International ranked Nigeria the second most corrupt nation in the world in 2002, but that year an unusual and effective effort was made to recover over $1 billion stashed in Swiss banks by now-deceased dictator Sani Abacha and his family. President Olusegun Obasanjo, installed shortly after our 1999 visit, has been the subject of three separate unsuccessful impeachment proceedings and faces a problematic future, as does the nation.

Drawing on my experience in law enforcement and at the UN, I took part in a number of efforts to increase transparency and provide advice on how to fight fraud and corruption. In March 1997, I was recruited by the UN to participate in an international conference in Buenos Aires on fighting corruption. Many of the conference's recommendations eventually became part of the UN Treaty on Transnational Crime, signed by 125 nations in Palermo in December 2000. Thereafter, I became a regular participant in the briefings held by Washington's International Law Institute for developing countries and others interested in combating corruption.

In October 1999, World Bank president Jim Wolfensohn asked me to examine that institution's mechanisms to deal with fraud and corruption connected with its lending. The bank annually disburses over $25 billion to aid in the development of nations around the world, and some estimated that as much as 25 percent of this funding was finding its way into the pockets of corrupt public officials or crooked tycoons. The bank's 1999 annual report identified the consequences of this phenomenon: "Corruption and poor governance worsen poverty directly—by diverting resources away from the needy—and indirectly—by harming the climate for private investment, key to growth and poverty reduction." Until the late 1990s, the bank had chosen to identify these ills as "political" and not its concern. With the help of former associates from the Department of Justice and the UN, I set out to learn the culture of the bank and figure out methods to address the problem. Our report was delivered in early 2000, and the new Office of Institutional Integrity that we recommended was up and running within months. We continued to act as consultants to the bank on the implementation of our recommendations.

TWO DOMESTIC INTERESTS of mine, technology transfer and civil justice reform, moved center stage in the early to mid-1990s, and I was able to remain active in both areas. My interest in science and technology as a contributor to economic development dated back, of course, to the Ben Franklin Partnership, which had become a national model for government-industry-university cooperation in technology transfer. My involvement in civil justice reform grew out of the report on that subject prepared by the Department of Justice in 1991 for the President's Council on Competitiveness.

In the 1990s international competition, especially from the Asia–Pacific region, was posing insistent challenges to our industrial strength. During our Taiwan visit, a U.S. banker had noted that country's preference for "making things . . . not deals." Our ability to compete in a much more challenging economic environment would depend upon our ability to "make things," which would, in turn, depend upon our ability to commercialize our science and technology assets through technology transfer.

A rethinking of federal research and development priorities was long overdue. While annual federal R&D expenditures had reached $70 billion (about 40 percent of the U.S. total) by the end of the Cold War, thinking in this area was still focused on traditional national defense and security concerns. The late 1980s had, however, seen the first federal programmatic initiatives on commercialization of R&D results. Meanwhile, separate state programs had been charting their own enviable paths in relating science and technology to economic development. As befitted their traditional role as laboratories of democracy, most states had developed technology transfer programs by the beginning of the 1990s.

In September 1993, former Ohio governor Dick Celeste and I co-chaired a colloquium attended by representatives from all fifty states and relevant federal agencies to try to establish a dialogue on federal-state cooperation in science and technology. We subsequently co-chaired a twenty-member State-Federal Task Force on Science and Technology to make recommendations on structuring and implementing a partnership effort.

The task force's September 1995 report made four recommendations: (1) presidential leadership to create a truly national, not just federal, policy on science and technology; (2) establishment by each state of a science and technology policy and a lead office to interface with federal counterparts; (3) development of an investment strategy to catalyze private-sector initiatives, with particular attention to small businesses; and (4) more support for the Manufacturing Extension Program, which helps manufacturers keep abreast of the state of the art in their sectors. I later chaired a study commissioned by the National Research Council that reached similar conclusions. Many of our recommendations drew, as might be expected, on my experience with the Ben Franklin Partnership.

I traveled across the country to promote the concepts embodied in the task force report among state officials and industry leaders. We also established, with the financial help of the Carnegie Corporation and Battelle Institute, a State Science and Technology Institute. This nonprofit think tank serves, among other things, as a clearinghouse for the exchange of programmatic information. I became its first board chairman and served until the end of 2002.

Following the rude reception given to Vice President Quayle at the 1991 ABA meeting as he presented the report on civil justice reform that the Department of Justice had prepared for the Council on Competitiveness, this issue went into remission. Two widely publicized cases, however, revived public interest in the problems of lawsuit abuse, particularly frivolous lawsuits and excessive damages. The first was the $2.7 million jury verdict (reduced to $480,000 by the judge) awarded against McDonald's for serving dangerously hot coffee to a patron upon whom the coffee spilled in her car while she was trying to open the lid with the cup between her legs. The second was an award by an Alabama jury to a doctor who had purchased a BMW automobile unaware that it had had a touch-up paint job before delivery. The award added $4 million (reduced on appeal to $2 million) in punitive damages to a compensatory award of $4,000.

Knowing of my role in preparing the 1991 report, a number of groups approached me to speak or write on this subject, which had also become a priority item in the 104th Congress's "Contract with America," authored by House Speaker Newt Gingrich and others during the 1994 congressional campaign.

My approach was a common-sense one. I noted that we seemed to seek a risk-free environment where, when anything went wrong, the first question was, "Who do I sue?" This attitude had far-reaching ramifications. It made American companies less competitive in world markets due to higher costs (judgments, legal fees and insurance) as well as diversion of funds from research and development. Reduced competitiveness threatened jobs and the quality of life in our nation. Lawsuit abuse also endangered our health care system by raising the costs of unjustified medical malpractice claims, encouraging the practice of excessive defensive medicine and discouraging innovation and research, thus threatening the bringing to market of new medicines and medical devices. Moreover, our courts were clogged with frivolous litigation that sidetracked and delayed legitimate claims by deserving plaintiffs.

Most of the remedies I proposed came from the 1991 Department of Justice report. The prime one was enactment of a national product liability law to replace the fifty separate state laws. The second was a cap on punitive damages. I believed that compensatory damages, awarded to make a party whole for injuries and/or property loss, were properly a matter for a jury under appropriate judicial instruction and subject to appellate review. Punitive damages, however, were another matter. Juries were given virtually no guidance on the proper parameters of these awards and were increasingly assessing them on a "sky's the limit" basis. Even the criminal law, designed to punish the most serious offenses against society, puts limits on fines for particular offenses. Reformers proposed similar limits for punitive damages. One of the most popular versions was a multiple of the compensatory damages (often a multiple of two or three).

The more technical problem of joint and several liability was already being addressed in many states, but not at the federal level. This legal principle obliges each defendant held liable for *part* of the harm done to a plaintiff to pay *all* of the damages, thus making the defendant with the deepest pockets the most logical target for actual recovery. I suggested limiting each defendant's proportion of the damages to its proportion of the harm inflicted. I also championed revisiting the English rule compelling the loser of a lawsuit to pay the winner's fees; increasing court sanctions for the bringing of frivolous lawsuits; relying on court-appointed expert witnesses rather than swearing contests between highly compensated "experts" on either side; and, one of my perennial favorites, removing the selection of judges from the partisan political process.

Among my appearances on behalf of civil justice reform, of particular interest were my debates with consumer advocate Ralph Nader, who opposed any change in the present system. I chided him, as a longtime and widely admired champion of the "little guy" against the special interests, for becoming a spokesman for one of the biggest special-interest groups of all—the plaintiffs' lawyers whose economic well-being was wrapped up in the litigation status quo. In many of the most punishing class actions, the lawyers profited far more than the allegedly wronged parties. And the efforts of the plaintiffs' bar to defend their interests were monumental. Studies indicated that they gave more to congressional candidates from 1988 through 1993 than the Big Three automakers and the top ten oil and gas companies combined! They strongly supported Bill Clinton's successful 1992 presidential campaign. And, in states where judges were elected, candidates favored by particular elements of the bar always found their coffers amply filled.

Congress finally passed federal product liability legislation in 1996. This bipartisan bill addressed many of the problems and incorporated many of the solutions outlined above. It included caps on punitive damages, an end to joint and several liability and a modified English rule. Predictably, the plaintiffs' bar lobbied furiously for a presidential veto. Although President Clinton had twice supported similar legislation backed by the National Governors Association when he was governor of Arkansas, he vetoed this bill. One of the key sponsors, Democratic senator Jay Rockefeller, noted, "The President needs these lawyers and their money more than he needs good public policy."

All was not lost in 1996, however. *BMW of North America v. Gore*, the $2 million punitive damage award from Alabama, reached the United States Supreme Court, which, for the first time in history, reversed a "grossly excessive" award as an unconstitutional denial of due process to the defendant. A number of states also enacted significant tort reform, including Ohio and California, where I had put forth a major effort for our client, the Civil Justice Reform Group.

DURING THE 1990s, I also embarked upon a new mini-career as a television "personality." Although I had appeared on a variety of news shows during my public life, I did not anticipate the opportunities afforded by the explosion in twenty-four-hour-a-day cable television news. These shows created a huge demand for commentary on the events of the day, and I soon became a regular on many of them.

The first call came on July 6, 1994, from the producer of *Larry King Live*, asking if I would consider a guest appearance that night to discuss some of the legal issues in the O. J. Simpson case. I had been in Hong Kong when the news had come of the brutal killing of Simpson's wife, Nicole, and Ronald Goldman. Like millions of other Americans, I had watched via CNN the low-speed freeway chase of Simpson and his friend Al Cowlings by officers of the Los Angeles Police Department, and I was to become engrossed in "the trial of the century." One television appearance led to others; in total I appeared forty-five times on CNN to examine various aspects of the Simpson case.

Based on Simpson's criminal trial, I would argue for several improvements in our criminal justice system: removal of racist policemen like Mark Fuhrman from police forces across America; closer scrutiny by prosecutors of the background of all witnesses, including police officers, and better trial preparation to prevent fiascoes such as the "glove incident"; more cooperation between police and prosecutors on matters such as search warrants; judicial gag orders on trial lawyers to prevent running commentary at press conferences; a thorough review of crime laboratory operations and the standards by which they are evaluated; judicial appointment of scientific experts to replace highly paid, partisan "hired guns" engaged in scientific swearing contests; more control by judges over jury selection and lawyers' conduct in court; restrictions on the number of lawyers permitted to participate on either side (the highly paid Simpson "dream team" stood in stark contrast with the inadequate representation provided to hundreds of thousands of defendants daily charged with equally serious crimes); prohibitions on contact by agents and publishers with lawyers, witnesses, jurors and others involved in an ongoing criminal trial; and finally, some method of countering "rushes to judgment"—the Simpson jury deliberated a scant four hours, in obvious disregard of the judge's instructions to thoroughly review all the evidence.

On the hotly debated question of television cameras in the courtroom, I found myself in a minority. I had occasion to visit Judge Lance Ito's courtroom during the trial, and I found the environment little different from those of a number of venues in which I had tried cases myself. Barely perceptible cameras unobtrusively recorded the proceedings. All the distractions occurred outside the courtroom as counsel for both sides held daily press conferences to "spin" the day's testimony. This should have been dealt with by a comprehensive gag order such as the one utilized to great advantage in the subsequent civil case against Simpson.

The televising of trials offers three advantages. First, and most important, it breathes life into the constitutional guarantee of a public trial. If the small gaggle of observers able to crowd into a given courtroom is expanded to include millions of television viewers, all the virtues of a public trial are magnified accordingly. Second, televising proceedings raises the level of accountability of judges, lawyers, witnesses (including expert witnesses), police departments and their crime laboratories, and even jurors, all of whom must answer publicly for any shortcomings. Third, a remarkable educational opportunity ensues when fascinated viewers are reminded of the burden of proof, the Fifth Amendment rights of a defendant and the technicalities of the rules of evidence. More knowledge of the intricacies of our criminal justice process surely cannot be a bad thing. My sense is that televised coverage of trials of major interest will be commonplace not far into the twenty-first century. And I believe our system will be the better for it.

During and after the trial, I also acted as a guest host from time to time when Larry took the night off. This brought me into contact with a number of interesting guests and topics. In the spring of 1997, I did a short stint as a weekly commentator on Court-TV's *Prime Time Justice*, a nightly hourlong review of the day's legal news, and I thereafter made periodic appearances on various network shows on legal and political issues. Following the Simpson case, I was regularly asked to comment on legal questions arising out of other high-profile criminal cases, such as the murders of JonBenet Ramsey and Chandra Levy, but the major challenge presented was the saga of President Clinton's misadventures.

The president's sexual relationship with Monica Lewinsky, a White House intern nearly half his age, was to preoccupy the nation for much of the final portion of his presidency. Disgusted with his conduct and the systematic attempt by him and his inner circle to frustrate investigations into these goings-on, I spoke out on this tawdry affair whenever possible.

Independent counsels Bob Fiske and Ken Starr had originally been authorized, successively, by Attorney General Reno and the special court established under the independent counsel statute to investigate some complicated Arkansas financial dealings by the Clintons involving a real estate project called Whitewater. Numerous other inquiries spun out of this. The most prominent one was into the president's alleged obstruction of justice and false testimony concerning a lawsuit by Paula Jones, a one-time Arkansas state employee, who had sued over alleged sexual advances made to her by then-governor Clinton. This melancholy tale was so circuitous and potentially confusing that the networks evolved a cottage industry of legal commentary in response.

I appeared on a wide variety of talk shows and interview programs, particularly CNN's *Late Edition*, hosted by Wolf Blitzer every Sunday at noon. For well over a year, I regularly exchanged views on legal developments in the investigation and ultimately the impeachment of President Clinton, usually appearing opposite Lanny Davis, a former member of the Clinton White House Counsel's staff. In the end, it became clear that however distasteful the president's behavior had been, neither the public nor Congress had an appetite for removing him from office.

Moreover, the Republican leadership in the House of Representatives made three crucial mistakes in handling this matter. At the outset, they created an unnecessarily partisan environment by insisting on the broadest possible impeachment inquiry at the cost of Democratic support for the more limited inquiry, based on the Starr report, that was ultimately pursued. Had unanimous, or at least bipartisan, support for the limited inquiry been expressed from the beginning, the process could not later have been characterized as partisan.

Their second error was simply dumping Starr's exhaustive report into the public domain, rather than using it as a basis for their own impeachment inquiry. Predictably, the salacious account of the president's relationship with the intern diverted attention from the more serious legal offenses of obstruction of justice and false testimony with which he was to be charged.

Finally, when it became apparent that no Democrat in the Senate was disposed to vote for the articles of impeachment adopted by the House, the Republicans erred in not seeking instead a strongly worded expression of condemnation from both houses along the lines suggested by concerned Senate Democrats. The upshot of the Republicans' full-speed-ahead approach was acquittal on all impeachment counts, which gave the president a colorable basis for claiming he had been exonerated of all allegations made against him.

The final chapter in this affair was not written until President Clinton's last day in office, when he in effect entered into a plea agreement with the independent counsel to charges of lying under oath and "conduct prejudicial to the administration of justice" during the Paula Jones civil proceedings and subsequent criminal investigations. He forfeited his license to practice law in Arkansas for five years and paid a $25,000 fine in proceedings brought before that state's supreme court.

By this time, the final scandal of the Clinton administration had captured widespread attention. This was the last-minute pardon given to fugitive financier Marc Rich, who had fled the country in 1983 and renounced his citizenship after being charged in one of the biggest white-collar scams in history. As might be expected, this occasioned further debate between Lanny Davis and me on CNN. While pardons are wholly discretionary and subject to no review, this extraordinary exercise of the president's power was distinguished by the involvement of Rich's ex-wife, who was a substantial donor to Clinton campaigns and causes, and former Clinton White House counsel Jack Quinn, who importuned the White House right up to the last minute on Rich's behalf. Also pardoned were twenty-seven Arkansans (including the president's brother, Roger, previously convicted on drug charges, and persons involved in the Whitewater investigation).

As President Clinton left office, I wrote in the *Wall Street Journal*: "Much about the Clinton presidency was obscured by his seemingly effortless maneuvering around the notion that there are fixed and immutable principles of right and wrong that should govern public and private conduct. The ex-president's farewell performance was entirely in character in this respect. History will not overlook it."

By this time, however, another blockbuster story had emerged and prompted another round of television debate in which I was to join. The 2000 election, one of the closest in our history, was ultimately decided in the United States Supreme Court in favor of George W. Bush, the son of the president I had served. He and his opponent, Clinton vice president Al Gore, fought tooth and nail in the state and federal courts following the election in an entirely unprecedented legal battle for the nation's highest office. Most of the controversy surrounded the vote count in Florida (which introduced the "hanging chad" into America's political lexicon) and the necessity or propriety of various recount requests. Whatever one's sentiments (and mine, of course, were for Bush), the process was not an orderly one, and we can only hope that it is not repeated in years to come.

President Bush's first year in office was hardly half over when he was obliged to respond to the horrific September 11 attacks by al Qaeda aircraft hijackers on the World Trade Towers in New York, on the Pentagon and on a third, unknown target; the third attack was thwarted by passengers over Pennsylvania. When the immediate shock wave passed, entirely new national security and law enforcement questions were on the nation's agenda, and I was called upon to help translate these to the public. The predominant concerns seemed to be how to handle the investigation and prosecution of terrorists posing current threats, and how to prevent such threats in the future. Difficult choices had to be made, with civil liberties often at odds with national security. The administration, for example, revived a World War II mechanism to deal with terrorists in secret military tribunals, and questions arose as to secrecy of deportation proceedings and suspects' right to counsel. The USA Patriot Act, passed quickly by Congress at the administration's request, liberalized wiretapping and surveillance authority, authorized much closer cooperation between intelligence and law enforcement agencies and extended the reach of anti-money-laundering laws as a tool to shut down terrorist cells.

Much of the controversy derives from the quite different roles of intelligence agencies and law enforcement authorities. In simplistic terms, the job of the former is to collect information from any source whatsoever that can provide a basis for taking action, often preventive action, against terrorists. The job of the latter is to collect legally admissible evidence sufficient to prove to a judge and jury beyond a reasonable doubt that identified individuals have committed specific crimes. The distinction is between prevention and prosecution, between action before an event and action after it.

Thus, federal agencies cannot necessarily all gather, share or use the same information. Clearly, even evidence that is improperly obtained under criminal law standards can be used forthwith to prevent a terrorist from acting. But that same terrorist can walk away if insufficient legally admissible evidence exists to charge and convict him in our criminal courts. Moreover, there may be problems with the use of certain admissible evidence. Public testimony by an informant or undercover operative could well jeopardize that person's life, family or well-being. Similarly, presenting evidence obtained by sophisticated electronic surveillance techniques in open court could give future terrorists a road map for avoiding detection.

One constructive by-product of these dreadful attacks has been a top-to-bottom review of law enforcement and intelligence agencies. I chaired one component of this review for the National Academy of Public Administration, which was asked to examine FBI Director Bob Mueller's plan for reorganization of that agency. Our testimony before Congress was generally positive about my old colleague's plans to modernize and update his agency's operations.

Despite the sometimes long hours of preparation required to present accurate and well-informed views during my television appearances, I must acknowledge that the whole process of offering views on matters of concern to the nation via the talk show circuit was most satisfying. It obliged me to keep on top of a variety of developments, and it was quite fulfilling to be asked my opinion on the issues of the day.

ALL THIS TIME, I was increasingly engaged in my assignments as a lawyer in Kirkpatrick & Lockhart's Washington office. In many of these matters I represented corporate clients in their dealings with the Department of Justice and various regulatory agencies on matters in which they faced prosecution or other sanctions. I met with department officials on alleged civil rights, antitrust and money-laundering violations. While often my role was primarily to "open the door," I always tried to add a little extra to our presentations based upon insights gained from my years of experience with the department.

Other representations were less conventional. Among the more interesting were those with an international flavor. We provided background advice to Swiss banks, recommending that they settle the claims of Holocaust victims on an expedited basis. I also acted as a spokesperson for a Puerto Rican foundation espousing self-determination for that island's residents, a cause I had first taken up as attorney general. And we represented the Republic of the Marshall Islands on its claims growing out of the post–World War II atomic tests in that area.

There were also, as might be expected, Pennsylvania matters. One stemmed from the investment management services provided by an investment adviser named John Gardner Black and his Devon Management to a large number of Pennsylvania school districts during the 1990s. When his portfolio went bad and losses in the $150 million range were threatened, I was appointed to act as a trustee in securities fraud proceedings initiated by the SEC in the U.S. District Court in Pittsburgh. Through our vigorous pursuit of the assets of all those involved in the fraud (and a subsequent bankruptcy proceeding), nearly all of the school districts were made whole in near record time.

Also during the 1990s, attacks were mounted against the board of trustees of the Milton Hershey School, established in the early twentieth century by a grant in trust by the founder of what is now Hershey Foods to educate "poor white male orphans." By the end of the century, the value of the school's endowment had grown to nearly $6 billion, larger than that of any other U.S. educational institution save Harvard, MIT and Stanford. The eligibility rules had been broadened, but the trustees still could not spend all the income generated by the trust. A fractious group of alumni charged them with mismanagement and failure to abide by the terms of the trust, primarily because they had modernized its agrarian-oriented educational policies. Our exhaustive review determined that the law had been observed and that the trustees had been faithful to Mr. Hershey's intent. Privately, I expressed to school officials my personal concern over the concentration of Hershey Foods stock in the trust, the interlocking directorates of the school and the trust, and the need to expand the school's services beyond the town of Hershey. The whole matter came to a rather ugly head in 2002 when the board first adopted, then abandoned, plans to sell the entire company so as to diversify the trust portfolio. The matter remains unresolved.

In the spring of 1997, my firm represented NOD in an effort to secure an addition to the Franklin D. Roosevelt Memorial, then under construction, that would celebrate the president's triumph over his disability—his dependence upon crutches or a wheelchair for the last twenty-four years of his life, including his entire presidency, as a result of a 1921 polio attack. NOD had been unable to convince the Memorial Commission to add a statue showing FDR in a wheelchair. We organized a whirlwind round of entreaties to various officials, stating the case for an additional historically accurate statue as an exemplar of how people could become leaders at the very highest level despite disability. President Clinton was finally induced to support legislation authorizing the enhancement of the memorial, and the demonstrations planned for the dedication ceremonies were turned into a celebration. A most worthy endeavor.

FOLLOWING MY 1991 Senate campaign, my involvement in Republican politics dwindled considerably. While I campaigned successfully for several GOP candidates, a younger and more conservative group was coming to the fore. Those of us who had campaigned and governed as fiscal conservatives and social moderates were becoming scarce. The dispirited Bob Dole presidential campaign in 1996 called upon me for little substantive effort. I made my peace with the fact that a different political era was taking shape for both parties, and I determined to wish them both well from the sidelines.

I could not help but ponder, though, how the landscape had changed during the nearly three decades of my political career. The three Republican presidents under whom I had served had had very different influences on the nation and the party. Nixon, of course, left in disgrace following the Watergate scandal, only to be rehabilitated in large part by his persistent and generally well received effort to be heard on international issues. His devastating effect on the party, beginning with the 1974 elections, was overcome rather quickly by the combination of a lackluster Carter presidency and the sheer force of Ronald Reagan's political savvy.

Reagan's eight years were a case study in the power of basic (some said simplistic) principles to engage the American electorate. His winning personality made him an effective salesman for conservative principles such as the need to reduce taxes, return power to the states, reduce regulatory burdens on business and appoint more conservative judges. But it was in the area of foreign policy that he most confounded his critics. His adamant anticommunism, his stridency and his unwillingness to veer from his course yielded major changes in the balance of world power. The Iran-Contra imbroglio muddled his legacy, but, as in the past, Reagan himself emerged relatively unscathed. This may have been partly because of his laissez-faire leadership style: he hired the best people he could find, let them know the overarching philosophy of his administration and then gave them a free hand to implement it. He left behind a true cult of personality, as demonstrated by the persistent and ongoing efforts to rename after him one public site after another.

George Bush's presidency was marked by the best of intentions, but a combination of virulent partisan opposition and his failure to communicate a consistent message to the public eventually brought him down. His major contribution, like Reagan's, was in the international arena: on his watch the Berlin Wall fell and the Soviet Union came to an end, and he fashioned a strong multinational alliance under UN auspices to turn back Saddam Hussein after his invasion of Kuwait. On the home front, perhaps due to diffidence or lack of sound political instincts, the "read my lips" debacle and the seeming tin ear to citizen concern over the dip in the economy set the stage for the slick Clinton effort, which never missed a beat ("It's the economy, stupid!") in 1992. Thus, a good man was prematurely retired from the presidency he had sought so avidly.

Bill Clinton—a talented politician, whatever his other shortcomings— preempted much of the basic Republican agenda and earned credit for balancing the budget, reforming the welfare system, growing the economy and cracking down on violent crime. While the 1994 elections catapulted the GOP into congressional control and provided much of the impetus for these attainments, the Republicans were never able to identify these major breakthroughs with their efforts or with their underlying philosophy.

Considering the low point reached by the Republicans following the 1964 elections, when I first became involved politically, the party's accomplishments over the time I was privileged to be a part of its effort were by no means minimal. But, in the final analysis, the party failed to respond to the challenge I had identified in my 1986 Yale speech to "build upon a [three] term presidency to create a new majority party in America." Of course, implementing what I identified as basic Republican principles during my two terms as governor and as attorney general in the service of two presidents gave me considerable satisfaction. But, like many who have enjoyed the opportunity to serve in public office, I could not help but lament what might have been had the stars been a little more favorably aligned.

Meanwhile, Pennsylvania Republicans had regained the governor's office in 1994. They also held both U.S. Senate seats, control of both houses of the state legislature and all the statewide offices except that of auditor general (a position won in 1996 by Robert P. Casey Jr., the son of the governor who had succeeded me). Once again, my home state could proclaim itself "the most Republican state in the nation."

My own son John entered the political world by running for an at-large Republican State Committee seat in Allegheny County in 1994. He led the ticket comfortably ("There's life in the old name yet, Dad," he graciously told me) and was reelected in 1996, serving until obliged to resign when assuming his Penn's Southwest position. Both John and David served on the transition team for incoming governor Tom Ridge in 1994. Although neither of them has ever mentioned it to me, I would not be surprised to see one or both of them seek elected office one day.

The only for-profit board of directors upon which I served was that of Élan Pharmaceuticals LP, a drug delivery systems manufacturer based in Ireland, which was to undertake some leading-edge research in areas such as Alzheimer's disease, multiple sclerosis and Parkinson's disease, all of which coincided with Ginny's and my interests in disability. When the company had severe financial problems in early 2002, I was among those taking a lead role in replacing top management and seeking to restore its good name. I declined other private board opportunities for reasons ranging from insufficient compensation to insufficient interest.

Throughout this period, I made a constant round of speeches around the country. These often included a plea for involvement in public life. My most comprehensive review of this subject was my Webb Lecture to the National Academy of Public Administration in November 1999. To this group, I summed up "Democracy is not a spectator sport. All of us must exercise the opportunity to contribute to improving and sustaining higher levels of performance in public life. This involves much more than simply being part of a focus group or responding to poll questions. And it is just as important in contests for the local school board as in those for higher office."

Many of my speeches were given on college campuses, always a good antidote to a hardening of the attitudes. Throughout my public career, I have spoken at over 100 different college and university campuses. Graduation addresses were a particular favorite of mine, as they gave me an opportunity to trot out some of my favorite quotations:

An excellent plumber is infinitely more admirable than an incompetent philosopher. The society which scorns excellence in plumbing because plumbing is a humble activity and tolerates shoddiness in philosophy because it is an exalted activity will have neither good plumbing nor good philosophy. Neither its pipes nor its theories will hold water.
(John Gardner)

The skeptic may be distinguished from the cynic by a simple test: when confronted by something that seems too good to be true, the cynic denies that it is really good, the skeptic denies that it is really true.
(Sydney Harris)

All that is necessary for the triumph of evil is that good men do nothing.
(Edmund Burke)

Democracy is the worst system man could possibly devise for governing himself—except for all the rest.
(Winston Churchill)

And one of my own, particularly apt for young people:

Don't worry about making mistakes; you will make mistakes. Experience is a collection of mistakes. Just don't make the same mistake twice.

In the fall of 2002, the U.S. Bankruptcy Court in the Southern District of New York appointed me to serve as examiner in the WorldCom bankruptcy, the largest in American history. This sorry tale of corporate wrongdoing involved playing fast and loose with accounting rules and misreporting nearly $11 billion in revenues and expenditures, all in a failed effort to sustain an appearance of profitability during a dramatic downturn in the telecommunications business. The Dow Jones News Service head-lined its story about my appointment "Thornburgh Says WorldCom Probe Will Follow the Evidence Wherever It Leads." So began yet another chal-lenging adventure, which is ongoing as I write.

Afterword

LIFE HAS PROVIDED ME with a wonderful succession of opportunities, for which I will be eternally grateful. Never would I have dreamed during my schooling or the early years of my career that so many exciting challenges would be forthcoming or that they would lead me to so many fascinating people and places. Thanks to these opportunities, I have been able to heed in some measure the admonition of Justice Oliver Wendell Holmes: "It is required of a man that he should share the passion and action of his time, at peril of being judged not to have lived." I have been privileged to play a role in public management, law enforcement, legal reform, state-federal relations, the empowerment of people with disabilities, economic development, the rule of law and protection of the integrity of the governing process itself. All of these remain important items on humankind's agenda to this day.

The lessons I have learned from my endeavors have been rich and varied:

1. The overriding importance of the rule of law. Upon this principle rest many of the other attributes of a civilized society—equal justice, respect for individual rights and liberties, due process in the protection of our lives and property, independent courts, effective law enforcement and a workable system of civil justice.

2. The necessity of a strong value system—one that promotes individual responsibility and respect for the law, for faith and for the family. Such a value system diminishes the appeal of incivility in our discourse, of violence and abuse in our relationships and of dependence upon drugs and alcohol.

3. The need for bedrock integrity in the conduct of our affairs, public and private, and for a commitment to rooting out corruption wherever it occurs; and for a maximum effort to see that "the good guys are on top" in all our daily endeavors.

4. The need for government to remain close to the people by carrying out needed services at the state and local level, recognizing the worth of a federal *system*, not just a federal *government*.

5. The need for a constant battle against discrimination in all its forms, on the basis of race, religion, gender, national or ethnic origin or disability, so that all citizens can fully participate in the opportunities offered by a free society.

6. The need for government to stay out of our day-to-day economic activities so far as is consistent with creating and maintaining a level playing field. This governmental philosophy includes efforts to minimize the tax and regulatory burden imposed upon our free-enterprise system.

7. A recognition that we all live on the same planet and that the interests of the citizens of each country are bound up in the interests of all others. Americans, in particular, as exemplars for the rest of the world in so many respects, have an obligation to model the principles of democracy, human rights, the rule of law and free enterprise, and to remain engaged in encouraging the pursuit of these principles by others.

I have devoted my professional life to the law, but as important as it is, law is secondary to values. We establish laws to codify certain rules and standards that allow us to live together peacefully as free people. But it is our values that inspire our laws, not our laws that establish our values. Laws tell us what we must do; values summon us to what we should do. The better we maintain our values, the less we need to resort to the law. And it is the values by which we choose to live that define our civilization. My own key values have always been religion, for the soul; education, for the mind; arts, for the spirit; family, for love and nurture; and freedom, because it is God's gift and man's achievement. In the economy, the key values are enterprise, opportunity, risk and reward; in the community, a decent regard for the rights and feelings of others; and in politics, a vigorous debate, then a closing of ranks as we accept the people's verdict and get on with the people's business.

Values are not merely private guides to individual behavior. They are what will settle the great conflicts of our time, for better or for worse. The forces of law will never be enough, for example, to conquer terrorism. Terrorism is a war of values: the terrorist's belief in his cause versus our belief that, whatever the cause, a civilized world must enforce certain decent limits on what can be done to advance it. By sharing our intelligence and training techniques internationally, we can stop many terrorists before they strike and catch others afterward. But to put an end to terrorism itself, we must win the battle of values. We cannot live together in freedom unless we live in mutual respect and with mutual forbearance, with decency and civility and a readiness to see things from the other person's point of view.

As IMPORTANT AS I have found the lessons learned from my public life, the fulfillment I have received from my family has been even greater. The blessings of a loving spouse and caring children are denied to so many in today's society. I marvel at my good fortune in being sustained and supported by their love and concern throughout my life. Especially meaningful to me has been Ginny's constant presence by my side, through thick and thin, always trying to ensure that I was my "best person." We learned early that sustaining a strong marriage required hard work, and the rewards have been more than worth the effort. And our sons have been ever willing to share with us their triumphs and setbacks; to seek and to give advice, where appropriate; and to support us in times of need.

An additional blessing has been our participation in the lives of the next generation in the form of our six grandchildren. It is their future that presents us with the most promising opportunities and most vital challenges. Our role is to keep working to improve the environment within which they and their generation will raise their own families and make their own contributions.

Although I have seldom commented publicly about religious feelings that I consider basically private, my Christian beliefs have permeated my life. Prayer has always been a sustenance in my daily life and a solace in times of stress. Never was an evening meal in our home opened without asking the Lord's blessing on our food and our lives, and regular church attendance has reminded us of the value of scripture as a polestar in our everyday endeavors. Both Ginny and I will be forever grateful for the blessings of our faith and the strength it has imparted to us. I think often of a yellowed newspaper clipping that Ginny pasted on the kitchen wall of our beloved home in Pittsburgh. The author is unknown to us. It asked, "If you were arrested for being a Christian, would there be enough evidence to convict?" My fondest hope is that the evidence presented in these reflections would be at least enough to get to a jury on this question.

INDEX

ABA. *See* American Bar Association (ABA)

Abacha, Sani, 347

Abbell, Rick, 207

abortion viewpoint, 84, 151–52, 204, 269–71

academic institutions investigations, 253–55

ACHIEVA. *See* Allegheny County Chapter of the Pennsylvania Association for Retarded Citizens

ACT-UP, 305

admissible evidence, 356

Advanced Technology Centers, 135–36

Advisory Commission on Intergovernmental Relations (ACIR), 176

Advisory Committee on Administrative and Budgetary Questions (ACABQ), 323, 325

AFL-CIO, 91, 139, 184

Africa, 170–72

African American vote, 96–99, 183–84, 189, 279–80

AFSCME, 91, 184

Agenda for Peace, 320–21

Agnew, Spiro, 66, 220

agriculture, 144–45

Aguilar, Robert, 225

Aid to Families with Dependent Children (AFDC), 147

Ailes, Roger, 304, 312

airline industry investigations, 252–53

Albertson, Kenneth D., 45

Albright, Madeleine, 331

Alexander, Lamar, 156, 202–3, 272

Allegheny County Bar Association, 21

Allegheny County Chapter of the Pennsylvania Association for Retarded Citizens, 34

Allegheny County Regional Planning Council, 38

Allen, Ethel, 102, 172

Allen, Mel, 183

Allison, Graham, 200

Altman, Robert, 213–14

Aluminum Company of America (ALCOA), 12

Alvarez del Castillo, Enrique, 232–33

Alvarez Machain, Humberto, 232–33

American Bar Association (ABA), 292–94

American Civil Liberties Union (ACLU), 33, 39

American Federation of Labor and
Congress of Industrial Organizations
(AFL-CIO). *See* AFL-CIO
American Federation of State, County
and Municipal Employees
(AFSCME). *See* AFSCME
American Institute of Architects (AIA),
253
Americans for Democratic Action, 31
Americans with Disabilities Act (1990),
261–64
Anderson, Jack, 70
Anderson, Marian, 165
Andreotti, Giulio, 229
Annan, Kofi, 332
Anstine, Ann, 304
Anti-Defamation League, 268
antidrug efforts. *See* drug trafficking
antitrust investigations, 252–56
Aquino, Corazon, 275
Armed Career Criminal Act (1986), 245
Aronica, Joe, 223
Arzú, Alvaro, 346
Asher, Bob, 161–62, 180
Ashland Oil Company, 251
assistant attorney general, U.S. Depart-
ment of Justice: appointment, 62–63;
Central Intelligence Agency (CIA)
investigations, 64–65; criminal justice
reforms, 64, 67; Federal Bureau of
Investigation (FBI) investigations, 65;
political corruption investigations, 64–
71; social life, 72–73
attorney general, U.S. Department of
Justice: abortion issues, 269–71;
accomplishments, 302–3; air travel
issues, 288–89; Americans with
Disabilities Act (1990), 261–64;
antitrust investigations, 252–56;
appointment, 199–200, 204–5; civil
rights activities, 261–69; criminal
justice reforms, 244–47, 296–97;

criminal prosecution cases, 240–44;
departmental appointee battles, 277–
84; as domestic policy adviser, 272–76;
drug enforcement efforts, 227–38;
environmental pollution investigations,
248–51; human rights issues, 258–60;
interactions with Capitol Hill, 295–98;
interactions with Ronald Reagan, 206;
interactions with staff, 297–98;
interactions with the media, 213–19,
234, 237–38, 240, 280–89, 298–99, 302;
international criminal investigations,
255–56; judicial selection process, 291–
93; organized crime investigations,
239–40; political corruption investigations, 225–26, 239; pornography
investigations, 247; prison inmate
rehabilitation, 271; resignation, 302–3;
rule of law efforts, 257–59; social life,
298–99; staffing, 205, 207; Supreme
Court appointees, 290–91; technology
transfer, 252; Thornburgh Memorandum, 293–95; victims' rights efforts,
242–44; visit to Soviet Union, 257–58;
volunteer efforts, 272; white-collar
crime investigations, 208–26
Ayah, Wilson Ndolo, 327
Ayer, Donald, 281–83

Babbitt, Bruce, 203
Baily, Doug, 250
Bakatin, Vadim V., 257
Baker, Jim, 180, 260, 316
Bakker, Jim, 225
balanced-budget amendment, 175–76, 198
Baldrige, Malcolm, 168
Baltimore Orioles, 166
Banca Nazionale del Lavoro (BNL), 214–
18, 219
Bank of Credit and Commerce Interna-
tional (BCCI), 212–14, 219, 235
Banks, Ernie, 183

Baraldini, Silvia, 255

Baran, Walter, 102, 129, 142, 172

Barber, Red, 183

Barco, Virgilio, 231

Barlett, Donald, 308

Barr, Alice, 98

Barr, Bill, 207, 216–17, 219, 268, 283, 298, 303

Barr, Henry, 205, 237–38

Barr, Joseph, 22, 96

Barry, John M., 211

Barry, Marion, 237

Bartle, Harvey, III, 103, 173

baseball, 3, 14, 91, 166–67, 256, 335, 347

Batavia, Drew, 263

Battelle Institute, 349

Beasley, Leslie, 159

Beers, Paul, 189

Begala, Paul, 306–7

Begler, Sam, 39

Bell, Griffin, 66, 71–72, 221

Benedict, Al, 162

Ben Franklin Partnership, 134–36, 199, 344, 348–49

Benko, Bob, 108

Bennet, Doug, 331

Bennett, William, 236

Berger, Dan, 33

Biden, Joe, 282, 297

Bienvenue, Dick, 73

Biester, Eddie, 72

Biester, Edward "Pete," 72, 102, 173

Bingler, John, 78

Bittenbender, Bob, 173

Black Caucus, 125

Black, Gorham, 103, 173

Black, John Gardner, 357

Blackwell, Lucien, 187

Blatt, Genevieve, 19

Blaxter, Harold, 23

Blinder, Meyer, 224–25

Blitzer, Wolf, 354

BMW of North America v. Gore, 351

Bodine, James F., 102, 173

Bok, Derek, 254

Booth v. Maryland, 243

Bork, Bob, 63, 198, 278

Boutros-Ghali, Boutros, 317–24, 329, 331–32

Bowen, Joseph "Jo Jo," 158

Boyle, W. A. "Tony," 45–46

Bradford, William, 1

Bradlee, Ben, 205

Brady Bill (1994), 245–46

Brady, Nick, 206, 272, 295

Bravo, Ken, 44

Bray v. Alexandria Women's Health Clinic, 270

Brennan, William, 290

bridge rehabilitation programs, 141

Brinkley, David, 288

Brock, Bill, 86

Broder, David, 184, 263, 288

Brokaw, Tom, 115

Brooks, Jack, 218, 282, 297

Browne, Michael, 173

Brown, Pat, 67

Bruno, Frank, 52–53

Bua, Nicholas, 219

Budzanoski, Michael, 45

Bufalino, Russell, 45

Burns, Ken, 167

Bush, George H. W.: Americans with Disabilities Act (1990), 262–63; analysis of presidency, 359; appointee nominations, 277–79, 290–93; as CIA director, 64; civil rights legislation, 265–67; domestic policy, 272–76; election, 177; interactions with attorney general, 206–7, 250, 295, 303; Mexican government, 232; Operation Just Cause, 233; running mates, 192, 203; support for Senate campaign, 304; United Nations, 316–18

Bush, George W., 198, 264, 355
Bush, Mrs. George H. W., 304
Bush, Neil, 210
Butera, Bob, 77, 80, 82–83
Butler, Charles H., 186

Cable News Network (CNN). *See* CNN
Cahn, Edward N., 302–3
Califano, Joseph, 118
Caligiuri, Dick, 97
Calloway, Howard "Bo," 66
Camarena, Enrique "Kiki," 232
Cammora, 239
campaigns: campaign debt, 314; candidate image, 88–89; controversial events, 86–91, 185–86; election results, 85, 100, 188–89, 312; fourteenth congressional district, 25–30; funding, 27, 75–76, 81–82, 86–87, 97, 100, 104, 304; gubernatorial campaign, 74–100; interactions with the media, 77–79, 83–84, 86–89, 91–99, 180–87; Nelson Rockefeller, 32, 33; organized crime, 93; political debates, 95–98, 182–83, 185–86, 307, 310–11; polling information, 95, 97, 304, 311; reelection as governor, 178–87; strategic plan, 90; U.S. Senate campaign, 300–314
Capizzi, Anthony "Wango," 93
Capozzi, Al, 23, 25
Cardinal Krol, John, 152, 166
Caring Program for Children, 149
Carnegie Corporation, 349
Carnegie High School, 5–6
Carnish, Carl, 45
Carter, Jimmy, 66, 71, 98, 116–17, 119, 177
Carville, James, 191, 305–7, 309
Casey, Robert P. (auditor general/governor), 82, 168, 190–92, 196, 198–99, 300, 306

Casey, Robert P. (schoolteacher), 82, 85, 90, 97, 99
Casey, Robert P., Jr., 360
Casey v. Planned Parenthood, 269
Casolaro, Danny, 219
Cavazos, Lauro, 272
Celeste, Dick, 349
Centralia, Pennsylvania, 164
Central Intelligence Agency (CIA), 64–65
Cerezo, Vinicio, 256
Cerilli, Egidio, 71
Cheney, Dick, 206, 299
Chernobyl, 123
Chicago Board of Trade, 224
Chicago Mercantile Exchange, 224
Chick, James, 48
childhood years, 2–7
Child Protection and Obscenity Enforcement Act (1988), 247
Children's Institute. *See* Home for Crippled Children
Chiles, Lawton, 251
China. *See* People's Republic of China
"China syndrome," 114
Christopher, Charisse, 242–43
Christopher, Lacie Jo, 242–43
Christopher, Nicholas, 242–43
Christopher, Warren, 328–29
Chung, Kun Mo, 346
Cianfrani, Henry "Buddy," 71, 106
Citadel, 269
civil justice reform, 348–51
Civil Liberties Act (1988), 267
Civil Rights Act (1866), 265
Civil Rights Act (1990), 265
civil rights activities, 18, 33, 39, 57, 109, 201, 264–67. *See also* Americans with Disabilities Act (1990)
Civil Rights Division, U.S. Department of Justice, 261–69, 279–80
Clark, Frank, 47

Classified Information Procedures Act
(1980), 221–22
Clean Water Act (1977), 249, 251
Clifford, Clark, 213–14
Clinton, Bill: analysis of presidency, 359;
budget issues, 276; crime legislation,
244; election, 100, 203; product
liability legislation, 351; scandal
coverage, 353–55; welfare reform, 150,
201
CNN, 234, 352, 354–55
Cochran, Jay, 103
Coe, Howard, 47
Coelho, Tony, 280
Cohen, Howard, 103, 160
Cohen, Walter, 150
Cohill, Maurice "Pinky," 23–24, 38
COINTELPRO, 65
Colafella, Nick, 142
Cold War, 317
Cole, Charlie, 250
Collins, Doc, 116
Collins, Robert F., 225
Colombia, 230–32
Community Work Employment Program
(CWEP), 149
compromise, viewpoint on, 201–2
Conference on Rehabilitation of People
with Disabilities, 347
Constitutional Convention, 31–32, 344
constitutional reform, 30–32, 36
Coon, Eugene, 39, 53, 62, 63
corruption, political: Andreotti, Giulio,
229; developing countries, 347–48;
Guatemala, 345–46; investigations
while assistant attorney general, 64–71;
investigations while U.S. attorney, 44–
55; Liquor Control Board (LCB), 167–
68; Nigeria, 347; Pennsylvania
Department of Transportation
(PennDOT), 80, 162; priority while
attorney general, 225–26; Teamsters

Union, 239; testimony before
Congress, 77. *See also* organized crime;
white-collar crime investigations
Cosby, Bill, 165
Council on Competitiveness, 272, 275,
348, 349
counterfeiting cases, 57–58
Cox, Archibald, 220
Cramer, Richard Ben, 285
Crampton, Scott, 63
Crandall, Donald, 47
Crawford, Carol, 207
Criminal Division, U.S. Department of
Justice, 62–73, 281–83
criminal justice reforms, 38–46, 64, 67,
157–63, 244–47, 296–97
Critchlow, Paul, 76, 87, 102, 108, 113, 119,
161, 174
Cronkite, Walter, 117–18
cultural programs, 165–66
Culvahouse, A. B., Jr., 199–200
Cuomo, Mario, 175–76
Curl-Adams, Louise, 105
Curran, Robert E. J., 71, 90

Dallas Task Force, 210
Darman, Dick, 272–73, 276
Davis, Lanny, 354–55
Davis, Michele, 176, 304, 309
Davis, William, 103, 172–73
Deardourff, John, 87, 92
DeBenedictis, Nick, 173
Dees, Morris, 268
Dennis, Ed, 207, 280
Dennis, Shirley, 173
Denton, Harold, 117–21
Department of Economic and Social
Development (DESD), 321, 323
Department of Environmental Resources
(DER), 163
Derwinski, Ed, 272
Desert Storm, 299, 301

Detroit News, 287

Deukmejian, George, 189

Development Council, 321–22

Dewey, Thomas E., 9

Dickman, Murray, 76, 174, 205, 282, 285–86, 304, 319

disabilities, persons with. *See* Americans with Disabilities Act (1990); Thornburgh, Ginny Judson

Dixon, Don R., 211–12

Dole, Bob, 300

Domestic Policy Council (DPC), 272–74

Donaldson, Sam, 288

Dornsife, Bill, 113

Doyle, Robert, 30–31

Drake, Barbara, 205

Drexel Burnham Lambert, 224

Drogoul, Christopher, 214–16

Drug Enforcement Administration (DEA), 55, 235–36

drug trafficking, 55, 212–13, 227–38, 255. *See also* organized crime

Duberstein, Ken, 200

Duff, James, 165

Duggan, Robert W., 23, 33, 37, 48–52

Dukakis, Mike, 203

Dumbauld, Edward, 39

Duncan, Pete, 173

Dunn, Dan, 103

Dunn, James, 37

Dunne, John, 280

du Pont, Pete, 202

Dvorchak, Bob, 99

Dwyer, Budd, 160–62

Eagen, Michael, 103

Eastern European Conference on Disability, 328

Economic Commission for Africa (ECA), 327

economic development strategy: agriculture, 144–45; cost containment, 129–30; Enterprise Zone Program, 131–34; foreign investors, 169–70; infrastructure improvements, 139–43; job training programs, 137–39; quality-of-life improvements, 143–44; small business assistance, 128–31; state planning board, 126; strategic plan, 127–28; taxation, 128–30, 141; technology transfer, 134–37

Economic Policy Council, 272, 275–76

education, 2–11

educational reforms, 153–57

Edwards, Don, 281

Eichel, Larry, 187–88

Eilburg, Joshua, 71

Eisenhower, Dwight D., 9, 290

Eisenhower, Mamie, 94–95

Élan Pharmaceuticals LP, 360

election-monitoring missions, 337–41

employment discrimination, 265–67

endorsements, 26, 84, 95–99, 153, 179, 183–87, 189, 311

England, 169, 170

environmental pollution investigations, 55–57, 248–51

environmental programs, 163–65

Erie Soldiers and Sailors Home, 152

Ertel, Allen, 178–79, 181–83, 185–86, 188–90

Escobar, Pablo, 231

Ethnic Intimidation Act (1982), 267

European Economic Commission, 326

Executive Office for Asset Forfeiture, 236

Exner, Judith Campbell, 70

extradition, 255

Exxon Corporation, 249–51

Exxon Valdez, 249

Ezrine, Ivan, 57

false identification investigations, 67–68

Faulkner, Danny, 211

Federal Bureau of Investigation (FBI), 45,
    65, 162, 235, 240–42, 246, 280, 289,
    356
Federal Insurance Contributions Act
    (FICA), 160
Fenno, Dick, 199
Fernandez, Joseph, 222
Ferraro, Samuel G., 49–52
Ferrick, Tom, Jr., 99, 107
Ferrone, Augustine, 42
Fhimah, Lamen Khalifa, 241
Field, Cyrus West, 15
Field, David Dudley, 15
Field, Stephen, 15
Fields, Barton, 186
Filling, Dick, 87–88
financial aid investigations, 253–55
Financial Crimes Enforcement Network
    (FINCEN), 235
Financial Institution Task Force, 210
Fineman, Herbert, 71, 106
firearms offenses, 157–58, 245. See also
    handgun regulations
Fish, Hamilton, 218
Fiske, Bob, 277–79, 353
Flaherty, Pete, 61, 71, 78–79, 84–98, 100,
    177
Flake, Floyd, 226
Flood, Dan, 98
Florida Everglades, 251
Foley, Tom, 274
Fonda, Jane, 264
Ford, Gerald, 64, 65, 69, 71, 73, 97
Ford, Harold, 226
Ford, Mrs. Gerald, 73
Ford, Pronty, 53
forfeiture program, 235–36, 256
Foxman, Abraham H., 268
Franklin, Benjamin, 258
Franklin D. Roosevelt Memorial, 358
Freeland, Wendell, 23
Fried, Charles, 298

Friendly, Fred, 311
Fromme, Lynette "Squeaky," 69
Fuhrman, Mark, 352
Fuller, John G., 114

Galan, Luis Carlos, 231
gambling operations. See organized crime
Garment, Suzanne, 210
Garth, David, 81, 86–87
Garza, Emilio, 291
Gaubert, Thomas Merrill, 211
Gaviria Trujillo, Cesar, 231
gay rights, 109
Gekas, George, 116
General Assistance (GA) program, 147–49
Germany, 169–70
Germond, Jack, 123, 179
Gerson, Stuart, 207
Gerusky, Tom, 113, 116
Giamatti, Bart, 238
Giancana, Sam, 70
Gibble, Hilda, 194
Gideon v. Wainwright, 18
Gilly, Annette, 45
Gilly, Paul, 45
Gingrich, Newt, 350
Giuliani, Rudy, 224
Glanton, Richard, 108
Gleason, Rob, 173
Glendon, Mary Ann, 270
Goldberger, Paul, 143
Goldwater, Barry, 18
Gonzalez, Henry, 215–17
Gorbachev, Mikhail S., 257–58, 273–74,
    340–41
Gordon, Tucker, 5, 47
Gore, Al, 198, 355
Gorelick, Jamie, 256–57
Gotti, John, 239
Gourley, Wallace, 39–40
governor of Pennsylvania: advocacy for
    persons with disabilities, 150–51;

budget proposals, 109–12, 125–26, 148; campaigns, 74–100; criminal justice reforms, 157–63; cultural programs, 165–66; educational reforms, 153–57; election victory, 100–101; environmental programs, 163–65; federal budget issues, 175–76; governing style, 107–8; inauguration, 103–4, 189–90; infrastructure improvements, 142–43; international travel, 168–72; line-item vetoes, 145–46; media interactions, 107–8, 123, 180–87, 192–93; political appointments, 102–3; political corruption investigations, 160–63, 167–68; political goals, 79, 80–81; primary election, 85; reelection campaign, 178–87; reelection victory, 188–89; social reforms, 147–53; sporting events, 166–67; Three Mile Island (TMI) nuclear power plant crisis, 112–24. *See also* economic development strategy

Governor's Home, 105–6, 165

Governor's Schools, 155

Graham, Katharine, 206

Gramm, Phil, 301

Gramm-Rudman-Hollings Act (1985), 198

Graterford Prison, 158

Gray, Bill, 280–84

Gray, Boyden, 262, 265–66, 282, 290–91

Gray, George, 14

graymail, 221

Grimstad, Chuck, 15

Grode, George, 173

Grosso, Anthony Michael, 29, 44, 49, 50, 52–53, 92–93

Grosso, Sam, 44, 50

Grubb, Dick, 173

Gualtieri, Fred, 45

Guatemala, 345–46

Gurulé, Jimmy, 207

Guthman, Ed, 193

Haabestad, Harold "Bud," 87–88, 177

Hager, Henry, 77, 80, 88, 106, 119

Hallowell, Penrose "Penny," 102, 173

Hamilton, William, 218

Hammer, John, 53

Hampton, Rick, 240

handgun regulations, 58–59, 82–83, 245–46. *See also* firearms offenses

Harrisburg Patriot-News, 78, 168, 189, 311

Hartman, Barry, 205

hate crimes, 267–68

Hays, Wayne, 70

hazardous waste disposal programs, 163–64, 249

Health Care Cost Containment Program, 150

healthcare programs, 149–50, 307–12

Hearst, Patty, 69

Heinman, John, 47

Heinz, H. John, II, 81, 86

Heinz, H. John, III: campaign contributions, 86–87, 97; death, 300; election to U.S. House of Representatives, 61; election to U.S. Senate, 71; interactions with Dick Thornburgh, 23, 26, 77; reelection campaign, 180–81, 189

Heinz, Mrs. Clifford, 86

Helmsley, Leona, 225

Helms, Richard, 64–65

Henderson, Oran, 112

Hendrie, Joseph, 114, 117

Herbert, David, 162

Heritage Affairs Advisory Commission, 165

Hershey, Richard, 14

Hickel, Walter, 250

Hickton, John, 63

highway improvements, 139–42

Hilbert, Paul, 45
Hill, Anita, 291
Hill, Christon, 272
Hillman, Elsie, 22–23, 25, 36–37, 81, 88, 98
Hillman, Henry, 81
Hilton, Frank C., 53–54
Hockenberry, Jim, 50
Hoffa, Jimmy, 70
Hoffman, Frank, 181
Hogan, John, 217
Holland, H. Russell, 250
Home for Crippled Children, 16, 34
Homer, Max, 47
home rule, 36
Hong Kong, 341–45
Honors Incentive Program, 155
Hooton, Virginia Kendall. *See* Thornburgh, Virginia Kendall Hooton
Huddleston, Silous, 45
Hughes, Harry, 166
Humphrey, Gordon, 204
Humphrey, Hubert H., 34
Hussein, Saddam, 273–74, 333
Hutzler, Robert, 57

Iannelli, Robert "Bobby I," 43
Immigration and Naturalization Service (INS), 259–60
Ince, Jane Hooton, 73
independent counsel process, 66, 204–5, 216–17, 219, 220–23, 281, 353–55
insider trading investigations, 224–25
Institute for Law and Social Research (INSLAW), 218–19
Institute of Politics (IOP), Harvard University, John F. Kennedy School of Government, 196–200
Institutio Pro-Democracia y Desarrollo (Institute for Democracy and Development), 345
Internal Revenue Service (IRS), 48–53

International Criminal Investigative Assistance Program (ICITAP), 234
International Drug Enforcement Conference, 228
International Law Institute, 347
International Longshoremen's Association, 239
International Republican Institute (IRI), 337, 341, 345
international terrorism, 240–41, 255, 355–56
Iran-Contra case, 220–22
Iraqgate, 215–17
Irish Republican Army, 230
Irvis, K. Leroy, 32, 96, 106–7
Ito, Lance, 352
Ivory, Robert, 40

Jabril, Ahmed, 241
Jackson, Rev. Jesse, 99, 186, 264, 265–66
Jackson, Thomas Penfield, 237
Jacobs, Alma, 173
Jacobson, Alvin Joseph, 82, 180
Janis, Byron, 165
Japan, 169, 253, 256
Japanese-American internment compensation, 267
Jeffes, Glen, 173
Job Training Partnership Act (1982), 138
John Paul II, 165–66, 264
Johnson, Lyndon, 18, 32, 67
Johnson, Tom, 166
Johnson, Wally, 63
Joint Declaration (1984), 341–43
joint ventures. *See* technology transfer
Jones & Laughlin Steel Corporation, 56
Jones, Cliff, 102, 173
Jones, Edith, 290
Jones, Paula, 354
Joseph, Myron, 103, 173
judicial reform, 17, 30–31
Judson, Cyrus Field, Jr., 15

Judson, Ginny. *See* Thornburgh, Ginny Judson

Juster, Kenneth L., 217

Kang, Young Woo, 346
Kauper, Tom, 63
Kearns, Henry, 66
Keating, Charles, Jr., 211
Kelley, Clarence, 63, 65–66
Kelly, Patrick, 270
Kelso, Frank, 299
Kemp, Jack, 272, 274
Kennedy, Edward, 98, 204, 266, 309
Kennedy, John F., 18, 70
Kennedy, Robert, 32, 33, 303
Kennedy, Victoria, 309
Kerrey, Bob, 203
Kerry, John, 213
Keystone State Bank, 53–54
KGB, 257
Khashoggi, Adnan, 309
Kilpatrick, James J., 144, 218
Kim, Yong Joon, 347
Kim, Young Sam, 346–47
King, Gwen, 174
King, Larry, 352
King, Martin Luther, Jr., 32
King, Rodney, 268
Kirkpatrick & Lockhart law firm, 12, 17, 35, 197, 309, 315, 318, 335–36, 357
Kissinger, Henry, 183
Kleindienst, Richard, 50
Kline, Ernest, 55
Knapp, Charles, 211
Knepper, Jim, 173, 199
Kopp, Elizabeth, 235
Koppel, Ted, 288
Korea, 346–47
Kratz, Sharon. *See* Thornburgh, Sharon Kratz
Kryuchkov, Vladimir, 257, 259
Kuchma, Leonid, 341

Kuhn, Bowie, 166
Ku Klux Klan Act (1871), 270
Kutler, Michael, 57

labor organizations, 91, 98–99, 184
Lacalle, Luis Alberto, 256
Lacey, Frederick, 216
Laffey, Cyril, 103
Lance, Bert, 215
Landauer, Jerry, 210–11
Lara Bonilla, Rodrigo, 230
La Rocca, Sebastian John, 41, 45
LaRouche, Lyndon, Jr., 225
Larsen, Rolf, 163
Larson, Thomas, 102, 140, 142, 172
Lautenberg amendment (1990), 259
Lawn, Jack, 207, 228
Lawrence, David L., 29
lawsuit abuse, 349–51
Lebanese Connection, 55
Lebed, Alexander, 339–41
Lee, Martin, 344
Lee, Rex, 63
Lee Tung-hei, 336
legal career, 12, 17, 35, 335–36, 357–58
Lehrer, Jim, 288
Lehtinen, Dexter, 251
Lemons, Woody, 211
León Carpio, Ramiro de, 345
Lesko, John, 159
Levi, Edward, 62–63, 65, 204
Lewinsky, Monica, 353
Lewis, Craig, 170
library funding, 157
Liddy, G. Gordon, 61
Lieberth, Charlie, 173
line-item vetoes, 145–46, 175–76
Liquor Control Board (LCB), 167–68
Little League Hall of Fame, 183
Li Xiannian, 169
Lloyd, Jim, 178
Lockheed Aircraft Corporation, 68–69

Lomonosov, Mikhail, 258
lottery, 153, 160
Lucas, Bill, 279, 287
Lujan, Manuel, 272
Lukens, Alan, 170, 171
Lukyanov, Anatoly I., 257–58
Luttig, Mike, 218

MacLeod, Gordon, 103, 118–19, 173, 186
MacNeil, Robert, 288
Madigan, Ed, 272
Mafia, 229–30, 239–40
Magrann, Thomas J., 98
Mahesh Yogi, Maharishi, 191
Major, John, 274
Maloney, Paul, 213
Mandel, Marvin, 66–67
Manderino, Jim, 107
Marcos, Ferdinand, 287
Marcus, Ruth, 205, 298
Marshall, Thurgood, 244, 291
Marsh, Rabe F., 55
Marston, David, 71, 82
Martin, Aubran "Buddy," 45
Martinez, Bob, 236
Martinez Romero, Eduardo, 231
Martin v. Wilks, 265–66
Matthews, Jeremy F., 342
Matz, John, 47
Mauro Hoya, Carlos, 230
May, Cordelia Scaife, 51–52
Mazzei, Frank, 54–55, 106
McBirney, Ed, 211
McCain, John, 337–38
McCarthy, Colman, 237
McCarthy, Eugene, 32
McCarthy, Joseph, 9
McCloskey, Bill, 59–60
McDade, Joseph, 304
McEnteer, Ben, 102, 172, 209–10
McGrory, Mary, 218, 219
McKay, James, 221

McKevitt, Mike, 63
McKillip, Rebecca. *See* Thornburgh, Rebecca McKillip
McKinzie, Janet Faye, 211
McNary, Gene, 207
McShane, Larry, 240
McWilliams, Sallie, 2
Mecham, Evan, 177
media interactions: Banca Nazionale del Lavoro (BNL), 215–18, 219; Bank of Credit and Commerce International (BCCI), 213–14, 219; criminal justice reforms, 244–45; drug enforcement efforts, 237–38; election for governor, 77–79, 83–84, 86–89, 91–99; Institute for Law and Social Research (INSLAW), 218–19; journals, 17–18, 58, 140, 142–43, 149, 254, 278, 328; leaks, 59, 280–83, 285, 289; Manuel Noriega, 234; negative sources, 286–88; news magazines, 77, 184, 216, 287–88, 294–95, 302, 318; newspapers, 84, 98, 181, 187, 283, 286–87; organized crime investigations, 240; during reelection campaign, 180–87; Robert Wayne O'Ferrell, 241; during Senate campaign, 308–11; television, 216–17; Three Mile Island (TMI) nuclear power plant crisis, 123; during United Nations appointment, 318; while attorney general, 213–19, 234, 237–38, 240, 280–89, 298–99, 302; while governor, 107–8, 123, 180–87, 192–93; while U.S. attorney, 59–60. *See also specific news magazines; specific newspapers*
Meehan, Billy, 31–32, 187
Meese, Edwin, 196, 199–200, 204, 221, 228, 236, 247, 287
Megrahi, Abdel Bassett Ali, 241
Mercersburg Academy, 6–7
Metzenbaum, Howard, 252

Mexico, 232–33
Michel, Bob, 281
Michener, James, 165
Middle East, 172
military procurement investigations, 223–24
Milken, Michael, 224
Miller, Harold, 108, 307–8
Milton Hershey School, 357–58
Mitchell, Clarence, 96
Mitchell, George, 274
Mitchell, John, 43, 60–61
Mitterrand, François, 274
Moi, Daniel arap, 327–28
Molloy, Kevin, 116
Mondale, Walter, 184
money laundering, 212, 224–25, 228, 231, 233–36, 255–56, 356
Moody, Susan, 242
Moody, Walter Leroy, Jr., 241–42
Moore, Arch A., Jr., 67, 225, 237
Moore, Jonathan, 196
Moore, Mike, 207
Moore, Sara Jane, 69
Moorhead, William S., Jr., 25, 28–30
Morgenthau, Robert, 213
Morrison, David, 182
Mosbacher, Bob, 252, 272
Mothers Against Drunk Driving (MADD), 159
Mowod, George, 71
Mudd, Daniel, 72
Mudd, Roger, 72
Mueller, Bob, 356
Mugabe, Robert, 171
Mullen, Martin, 53
Muller, Arnold, 173
Murray, Martin, 106
Murtaugh, Mrs. Danny, 166
Musmanno, Michael, 19
Mutual Legal Assistance Treaties (MLATs), 69

NAACP, 185–86
Nader, Ralph, 252, 309, 351
Naqvi, Swaleh, 214
Nard, Jack, 63
National Academy of Public Administration, 361
National Cooperative Production Amendments (1993), 252
National Drug Policy Board (NDPB), 236
National Governors Association (NGA), 168–69, 175–76
National Journal, 286, 301, 331–32
National Organization on Disability (NOD), 195, 264, 334–35, 358
National Security Council (NSC), 272, 275
N'Drangheta, 239
Neal, Steve, 78
Needham, Virginia Walton, 15
Nee, Thomas, 47
Negroponte, John, 233
Nelligan, Jim, 174
Nemirovskaya, Elena, 341
Neustadt, Dick, 199
Newman, Michael, 46–47
New York Times, 100, 143, 200, 215, 217, 240, 247, 323
Nicholas, Henry, 99
Nigeria, 347
Nixon, David, 55–57
Nixon, Richard M., 19–20, 33–34, 61, 359
Noriega, Manuel, 204, 230, 233–34
North, Oliver, 221–22
nuclear power plants. See Three Mile Island (TMI) nuclear power plant
Nuclear Regulatory Commission (NRC), 114–17

O'Bannon, Helen, 102, 148, 150
Obasanjo, Olusegun, 347
O'Ferrell, Robert Wayne, 241–42
Office of Institutional Integrity, 348

Office of International Affairs, 259
Office of Legal Counsel, 295
Office of National Drug Control Policy, 236
Office of Professional Responsibility, 65, 280–84
Ogata, Shijuru, 324
O'Hara, John, 203
Olen, Maurice, 57
Olmstead v. L.C. and E.W., 264
Omnibus Crime Control and Safe Streets Act (1968), 38, 41
O'Neill, Eugene T., 46–47
O'Neill, Mrs. Eugene T., 47
Operation Crossroads Africa, 15–16, 73
Operation Desert Shield, 274
Operation DIG, 33
Operation Hedgeclipper, 224
Operation Ill Wind, 208, 223–24
Operation Just Cause, 233
Operation Polar Cap, 235–36
Operation PUSH, 99, 265–66
Operation Rescue, 269–71, 303
Operation Sourmash, 224
Operation Weed and Seed, 246–47
Oppenheim, David, 53–54
organized crime: gambling operations, 42–44, 48–49; international criminal investigations, 255–57; legal professionals code of ethics, 294; Manuel Noriega, 234; political involvement, 39, 83, 93; prosecutions, 40–51, 239–40; racketeering, 40–42, 45, 213, 224–25. *See also* corruption, political; white-collar crime investigations
Organized Crime Control Act (1970), 42, 43, 48–49
Osborne, David, 127, 134, 145
overlap, 253–54

PACE. *See* Pharmaceutical Assistance Contract for Elderly (PACE)

Packel, Israel, 45
Paisley, Melvyn R., 223–24
Panama, 233–34
Pan American flight 103, 240–41
Parejo, Enrique, 230
Parker, Sheldon, 23
Park, Tongsun, 69
Pass, Albert E., 46
Patriarca, Raymond, 239
patronage jobs, 101, 140
Patten, Chris, 343
Patterson v. McLean Credit Union, 265–66
Paul, David, 211
Payne, Pervis Tyrone, 242–43
Payne v. Tennessee, 242–43
Paz Zamora, Jaime, 230
Pecora, Tom, 45
Peirce, Neal, 123, 146
Pennhurst, 150–52
PennPRIDE, 145–46
Pennsylvania Capital Loan Fund, 131
Pennsylvania Council on the Arts, 165
Pennsylvania Crime Commission, 38, 40, 44–45
Pennsylvania Department of Transportation (PennDOT), 80, 83, 140–42, 162, 163
Pennsylvania Economic Revitalization Fund (PERF), 146
Pennsylvania Federation of Teachers (PFT), 153–54, 184
Pennsylvania General Assembly, 106–7, 119
Pennsylvania Industrial Chemical Company (PICCO), 56
Pennsylvania Industrial Development Authority (PIDA), 131
Pennsylvania political climate, 74–75
Pennsylvania Science and Engineering Foundation. *See* Ben Franklin Partnership

Pennsylvania State Education Association (PSEA), 91, 153–54, 182, 184

People's Republic of China, 168–69, 341–44

Perry, Nick, 160

Peterson, Shirley, 207

Petrignani, Renaldo, 215

Pharmaceutical Assistance Contract for Elderly (PACE), 153

Philadelphia Daily News, 84, 97, 158, 184, 186–88

Philadelphia Inquirer: Critchlow, Paul, 76; gubernatorial campaign, 78, 88–89, 99; negative sources, 286; prison hostage incident, 158; Senate campaign, 308, 309, 311; support for Dick Thornburgh, 181–82, 187–88, 193, 199; welfare reform, 149

Philadelphia Tribune, 96–97, 98, 187

Pickard, Jim, 173

Pinchot, Gifford, 163, 165

Pittsburgh Post-Gazette: abortion viewpoint, 270; congressional campaign, 26; corruption investigations, 49; endorsements, 97, 187; judicial reform, 31; media interactions, 59; organized crime, 41; Pennsylvania governor's campaign, 84, 93; political philosophy editorial, 19; reelection campaign, 181, 184, 185; Senate campaign, 311; Three Mile Island (TMI) nuclear power plant crisis, 122

Pittsburgh Press, 26, 62, 81, 140, 180, 187, 236

Pizza Connection, 229

Places Rated Almanac, 144

Plevel, Edward, 160

Plosila, Walt, 108, 126

Poindexter, John, 222

police brutality, 57, 268

political action committees (PACs), 68

political debates, 95–98, 182–83, 185–86, 307, 310–11

political interests and involvement, 4–5, 9, 18–19, 22–24, 38–39, 358–61

political philosophy, 18–21, 27, 200–201

"politico-racket complex," 48

Pomeroy, Tom, 38

Pommerening, Glenn, 63

Popular Front for the Liberation of Palestine—General Command, 241

pornography, 247

Porter, Roger, 272–73, 275

potassium iodide, 118

Pott, George, 23

Pottinger, J. Stanley, 63

Powell, Colin, 299

Powell, Jody, 119

Prater, William, 46

presidential aspirations, 202–3

price-fixing investigations, 253–55

Principi, Tony, 272

prison inmate rehabilitation, 271

product liability legislation, 349–51

Profit, Mr. and Mrs., 14

Project Triggerlock, 245

Proposition 13 (California), 88

Proxmire, William, 66

PSEA. *See* Pennsylvania State Education Association (PSEA)

Public Integrity Section, Criminal Division, U.S. Department of Justice, 64, 66, 225–26

public service career, 17–18

al Qaeda, 355–56

quality-of-life improvements, 143–44

Quayle, Dan, 203, 275, 304, 349

Quinlan, Mike, 271

Quinn, Jack, 355

quotations, favorite, 361

Raab, Selwyn, 240

Racketeer-Influenced and Corrupt Organizations (RICO) Act (1970), 42

racketeering. *See* organized crime

radioactive contamination. *See* Three Mile Island (TMI) nuclear power plant

Rafeedie, Edward, 233

Raith, Tom, 26

Raiz, Karmella, 259

Raiz, Vladimir, 259

Rape and Domestic Violence Fund, 160

Rashid, Mohammed Said, 255

Rawls, Lee, 207

Ray, Elizabeth, 70

Reagan, Nancy, 206

Reagan, Ronald: analysis of presidency, 359; attorney general appointment, 199–200; campaigns, 77–78; drug enforcement efforts, 236; elections, 20, 33; fund-raising appearance, 180–81; interactions with attorney general, 206; line-item vetoes, 146; Reaganomics, 185, 188; tax reform, 176–77

redistricting process, 268–69

Refuse Act (1899), 56, 251

refuseniks, 168, 259

Reggie, Edmund M., 309

Reich, Samuel, 49

Reihl, Michael, 48

Reilly, Bill, 248, 272, 295

Reitzel-Neilsen, Michael, 328

Religion and Disability Program, 264, 334–35

Renaissance Communities program, 133

Reno, Janet, 217, 219, 224, 249, 263, 353

Reno Memorandum. *See* Thornburgh Memorandum

Republican Governors Association (RGA), 176–77

Republic of China (ROC), 336–37

Resolution 1441, 333

Reynolds, Brad, 287

Richardson, Elliot, 218, 220

Rich, Marc, 355

Richmond v. Croson, 265–66

Ridge, Tom, 156, 173, 174, 302, 360

Rill, Jim, 207, 254

Rinaldi, Arthur, 48

Rios Montt, Efrain, 345–46

Rivers and Harbors Act (1899). *See* Refuse Act (1899)

Rizzo, Frank, 71, 90, 94, 98, 165–66

Robinson, Robert E., 241

Rockefeller Commission, 64

Rockefeller, Jay, 225, 314, 351

Rockefeller, Nelson, 32, 33

Rocky Flats, 249

Roe v. Wade, 269

Rooney, Art, 166

Rose, Evans, Jr., 75–76, 81

Rose, Pete, 225

Rosslyn Farms, Pennsylvania, 1

Ross, Robin, 108, 205, 259, 281–83, 285–86

Rovitto, Vince, 23

Rowan, Carl, 237

Rudenstine, Neil, 254

Rudman, Warren, 290

rule of law efforts, 257–59, 336, 341–44, 363

Runkel, Dave, 161, 207, 281–83, 286

Russia, 337–41. *See also* Soviet Union

Ryan, Matt, 106

Safire, William, 215–17, 237–38, 286

Salinas de Gortari, Carlos, 232–33

Sandinista government, 221

Santorum, Rick, 314

Sassou-Nguesso, Denis, 170–72

savings and loan scandal, 209–12

Scaife, Dick, 81

Scalera, Ralph, 52

Scales, John, 90

Scalia, Antonin, 63

Scanlon, Robert, 102, 154

Scarfo, Nicodemo "Little Nicky," 239

Scheiner, Jim, 160

Schmoke, Kurt, 237

Schoeninger, Martha Bell, 180

Schumer, Charles, 281

Schwarzkopf, Norman, 299

Schweiker, Richard, 30, 79, 97, 177

Scott, Dick, 102, 172

Scott, Hugh, 19, 29, 71

Scotzin, John, 78–79

Scranton, William W., 17, 95, 101

Scranton, William W., III, 82, 85, 97, 112–13, 116, 119, 177–78, 190–92

securities fraud investigations, 224–25

Seelye, Kit, 310

Seidel, George, 108, 174

Seif, Jim, 42, 56–57, 63, 76, 102, 108–9, 174

Selig, Bud, 335

Seltzer, H. Jack, 88, 106

Sematech, 252

Senate Judiciary Committee appearances, 63, 198, 204

senior citizen programs, 153

Seper, Jerry, 238

Serrano Elias, Jorge, 256, 345

Sessions, Bill, 207, 280, 289–90

Shafer, Ray, 29, 30, 32, 38

Shaheen, Michael, 282–83

Shapp, Milton, 53–54, 61–62, 70–71, 89, 109, 153, 155, 159

Shea, Bill, 183

Shoob, Marvin, 216–17

Shultz, George, 196

Simpson-Mazzoli Act (1986), 260

Simpson, O. J., 352–53

Skinner, Sam, 253, 272, 300, 315

Small Business Advisory Center, 130

Smith, Bill, 161–62

Smith, John, 14

Smith, Nate "Available," 33, 99

Smith, Peg, 173

Smith, Tom, 58

Smith, William French, 239

Snyder, Bill, 205

Souter, David, 290–91

South Carolina v. Gathers, 243

Soviet Jewish emigration, 259

Soviet Union, 168, 257–58. *See also* Russia

Specter, Arlen, 29, 71, 77, 80, 83, 177, 190, 270, 301

Sprigle, Ray, 41

Stafford, Rick, 76, 90, 96, 101–2, 108, 113, 125, 174

Stahl, Leslie, 288

Star Car, 28

Starr, Ken, 207, 275, 282–83, 353–54

State Capitol addition, 142–43

State Correctional Institution, 158

State-Federal Task Force on Science and Technology, 349

State Science and Technology Institute, 349

Stauffer, Jack, 106

Steele, James, 308

steel industry, 132–33

Stengel, Sandy, 173

Stern, Barry, 173, 205

Stevens, Greg, 312

Stevens, John Paul, 244

Stevenson, Adlai, 9

Stevenson, Adlai, III, 189

Stewart, Dick, 207

Stewart, Jimmy, 165, 210

Stewart, Potter, 285

Stokes, John, 216

Stone, Chuck, 98, 158, 186–87

Stout, Earl, 99

Strategy 21 program, 133, 143

Strohmayer, John, 132

Subchapter S, 128

Sukharev, Aleksandr Y., 257

Sullivan, Leon, 98, 186

Sullivan, Louis, 272–73

Sununu, John, 262, 265–66, 272–74, 276, 278, 289, 301

Superfund programs, 164, 249

Supreme Court decisions, 243–44, 264–66, 269–71, 351

Susce, Andrew, 41

Sweeney, Leonard, 47

Swindall, Patrick, 225

Switzerland, 234–36

Symbionese Liberation Army, 69

Tabor, John, 17, 38

Taft, Robert A., 9

Taiwan. *See* Republic of China (ROC)

Talmadge, Alex, 99

Tamilia, Pat, 23

Taylor, Paul, 89

Taylor, Stuart, Jr., 217, 288, 298

Teamsters Union, 239

technology transfer, 134–37, 252, 348–49

Teeter, Bob, 88, 304

television commentary, 352–57

Terrorism, Radicalism, Extremism, Violence International (TREVI), 229

Teslovich, Greg, 142

Testing for Essential Learning and Literacy Skills (TELLS), 155

Thatcher, Margaret, 274

Thomas, Clarence, 290–91

Thompson, Jim, 189

Thornburgh, Alice McKillip, 193

Thornburgh, Alice Sanborn, 1–2, 26

"Thornburgh amendment," 92

Thornburgh, Ann, 2

Thornburgh, Blair Elizabeth, 193, 305

Thornburgh, Bradford Scott, 193

Thornburgh, Charles, 2

Thornburgh, Charles Garland, 2, 8

Thornburgh, David Bradford: childhood years, 12–14, 16, 60; education, 72,

105; family, 193; political involvement, 83, 161, 301, 360

Thornburgh, Devon Virginia, 193

Thornburgh, Ginny Judson: advocacy for persons with disabilities, 34–35, 60, 150–51, 171, 195, 314–15, 328, 346–47; advocacy for persons with disabilities at Harvard, 199, 206; air travel issues, 161, 288; Americans with Disabilities Act (1990), 262–64; career during United Nations appointment, 319; Director of the Religion and Disability Program, 264, 334–35; family life, 16, 72–73, 365–66; first meeting with Dick Thornburgh, 15; Governor's Home, 105–6; inauguration events, 104, 189–90; international travel, 168–72; marriage, 16; political campaigns, 23–35, 76, 83, 85, 90–91, 96–101, 190, 311–12, 314; President's Committee on Mental Retardation, 195; reelection campaign, 188; social life, 298–99; sporting events, 166–67; stock holdings in oil companies, 250; support for husband, 63–64; visit to Korea, 346–47; youth advocacy activities, 58

Thornburgh, John Kendall: appointment to State System of Higher Education, 156; career, 193; childhood years, 12–14, 16, 33; education, 72, 105; family, 193; political involvement, 59–60, 76, 83, 100, 360; reelection campaign, 185; Senate race support, 301

Thornburgh, Kendall Leigh, 193

Thornburgh Memorandum, 293–95

Thornburgh, Peter Lewis, 12–16, 34–35, 60, 72–73, 105–6, 193–95, 264, 299, 335

Thornburgh, Rebecca McKillip, 193, 305

Thornburgh, Richard Lewis, II, 193

Thornburgh, Sharon Kratz, 193

Thornburgh, Thomas, 2

Thornburgh, Virginia, 2

Thornburgh, Virginia Kendall Hooton, 7,
10, 11–12, 13–14

Thornburgh, William Field, 30, 60, 72,
105–6, 161, 194–95, 299, 301

"Thornfare," 148–50, 184, 187

Three Mile Island (TMI) nuclear power
plant, 112–24

Torquato, John, Jr., 160–62

Torquato, Robert and Constance, 39–40

Totenberg, Nina, 288

Tower, John, 221

Toxic Waste Investigation and Prosecution
Unit, 164

Transparency International, 347

Travaglia, Michael, 159

travel and tourism industry, 144

TREVI. *See* Terrorism, Radicalism,
Extremism, Violence International
(TREVI)

Trinsey, Jack, 302

Trotto, Henry, 45

Truman, Harry S., 9

Tullio, Louis, 185, 189

Tung Chee-Wa, 344

Turnblazer, William J., 46

Tyler, Harold "Ace," 63

Uehlein, Julius, 185

Uhl, Sherley, 62, 81, 180

Ukraine, 341

Ullmann, Owen, 286–87

UN Center for Human Settlements
(HABITAT), 327

UN Conference on Trade and Development (UNCTAD), 326

UN Development Programme (UNDP),
317, 321–22

UN Environment Programme (UNEPP),
327

UN High Commissioner for Refugees
(UNHCR), 326

UN Industrial Development Organization
(UNIDO), 327

United Mine Workers (UMW), 45–46,
184

United Nations: Addis Ababa office, 327;
Agenda for Peace, 320–21; appointment as undersecretary-general for
administration and management, 316–
26; budget reform proposals, 323–26,
330; Department of Economic and
Social Development (DESD), 321,
323; Development Council, 321–22;
Economic Commission for Africa
(ECA), 327; European Economic
Commission, 326; financial contributions, 323–24, 332; Geneva office, 326–
27; historical background, 316–18;
Nairobi office, 327–28; peacekeeping
budget, 324–26; personnel issues, 329–
30; Republic of China (ROC)
membership, 336–37; Resolution 1441,
333; restructuring proposals, 321–23,
329–31; Vienna office, 327; World
Health Organization (WHO), 326

United Nations Drug Convention, 228–29

United States attorney: appointment, 37–
38; criminal justice reforms, 38–46;
drug trafficking cases, 55; environmental pollution cases, 55–57; as federal
prosecutor, 39–58; handgun regulations, 58–59; political corruption
investigations, 44–55; political
involvement, 38–39; youth advocacy
activities, 58

United States Steel Corporation, 56

University of Pittsburgh School of Law,
10–12

UN Transitional Authority in Cambodia
(UNTAC), 325

UN Treaty on Transnational Crime, 347

Updike, John, 165

Ursomarso, Frank, 95, 97

USA Patriot Act (2001), 356

Usiadek, Tom, 174

values, importance of, 363–66

Vance, Robert, 240, 241–42

Vatican Conference on Disability, 264, 328

Vealey, Claude, 45

Verity, Bill, 251–52

Veterans' Outreach and Assistance Centers (VOACs), 152

veterans' programs, 152–53

victims' rights, 242–44

Victim's Bill of Rights, 160

Virginia Military Institute (VMI), 269

Volcker, Paul, 324

Voting Rights Act (1965), 226

Waldheim, Kurt, 286

Waldman, Jay: as assistant attorney general's staff member, 63; departure, 174, 205; as governor's staff member, 102, 108, 177–78, 182; gubernatorial campaign, 76, 79, 90–91, 94; Senate race support, 301; Three Mile Island (TMI) nuclear power plant, 113; as U.S. attorney's staff member, 42; voter registration, 188

Walker, Cuyler, 205, 259, 319, 328

Wallace, George, 34

Wallace, Mike, 217, 331

Wall Street Journal: baseball, 335; editorials, 234–35, 251–52, 263, 275, 283, 355; gambling investigation, 29; Manuel Noriega, 204; scandal coverage, 210–11; support for governor, 184–85

Walsh, Lawrence J., 221–23

Wanniski, Jude, 313

Ward's Cove Packing Co. v. Antonio, 265–66

Warren, Earl, 290

Washington Post: editorials, 122, 184, 217–19, 222–23, 237; Katharine Graham, 206; media leaks, 272, 282; name usage, 205; political cartoon, 214; Ruth Marcus, 298; United Nations appointment, 318; United Nations reform, 331

Washington Times, 238, 318, 338–39

Water Pollution Control Act (1972), 56

Watkins, Jim, 272, 295

Watson, Andrew, 82

Watson, Nancy, 90

Watson, Will, 9

Watts, Mike, 57

Weatherbee, Dick, 205

Weber, Gerald, 54

Webster v. Reproductive Health Services, 269

Wednesday Group, 198

Weinberger, Caspar, 222

Weld, Bill, 199

welfare reform, 147–50

Wells, Melissa, 329, 331

Westinghouse Electric Corporation, 137, 253

Wetherington, Ron, 49

Whalley, Irving, 47

Wheeling-Pittsburgh Steel Corporation, 56

white-collar crime investigations: agenda as attorney general, 208–9; Banca Nazionale del Lavoro (BNL), 214–18, 219; Bank of Credit and Commerce International (BCCI), 212–14, 219, 235; Clinton administration, 212; during governorship, 160–62; Institute for Law and Social Research (INSLAW), 218–19; Iran-Contra case,

220–22; legal professionals code of
ethics, 294; media coverage, 209–12;
Operation Ill Wind, 208, 223–24;
political corruption investigations,
225–26; savings and loan scandal, 209–
12; securities fraud investigations,
224–25. *See also* corruption, political;
environmental pollution investigations;
organized crime
white supremacy groups, 267–68
Whittlesey, Faith Ryan, 82
Wilburn, Bob, 102, 108–9, 113, 131, 142,
154–55, 173, 174
Wilke, Harold, 262
Wilkinson, Tom, 205
Will, George, 288
Williams, Bill, 78
Williams, Frank, 52–53
Williams, Jacob (Jakie), 52–53
wiretapping, 41, 43, 47, 223, 257, 356
Witcover, Jules, 123, 179
Wofford, Harris, 199, 300, 304–14
Wolfensohn, Jim, 347
Wolfgang, Marvin, 158
Wolf, Mark, 204
women's educational rights, 269
Woods, Jarrett E., Jr., 211

World Bank, 347–48
WorldCom bankruptcy, 361–62
World Health Organization (WHO), 326
Wright, Jim, 280
Wyeth, Andrew, 165

Yablonski, Charlotte, 45
Yablonski, Joseph "Jock," 45–46
Yablonski, Margaret, 45
Yakovlev, Veniamin F., 257–58, 340–41
Yale University, 7–11
Yeltsin, Boris, 258, 337–41
Yeutter, Clayton, 272
youth advocacy activities, 58
Youth Conservation Corps, 163

Zavodni, John, 55–57
Zelnick, Robert, 218
Zemprelli, Edward, 106, 170
Zettlemoyer, Keith, 159
Zhao Ziyang, 169
Zhirinovsky, Vladimir, 338–40
Zimmerman, Roy, 190
Zuckerman, Mortimer B., 216, 287–88
Zweiman, Robert M., 182
Zyuganov, Gennady, 339, 341